SPECIAL EDUCATION FOR TODAY

SPECIAL EDUCATION FOR TODAY

Rebecca Dailey Kneedler

with Daniel P. Hallahan and James M. Kauffman

all of The University of Virginia

Prentice-Hall, Inc., Englewood Cliffs, New Jersey 07632

Library of Congress Cataloging in Publication Data

Kneedler, Rebecca Dailey.
  Special education for today.

  Includes bibliographies and index.
  1. Exceptional children—Education—United States.
I. Hallahan, Daniel P.   II. Kauffman,
James M.   III. Title.
LC3981.K57   1984   371.9′0973   83–16137
ISBN 0–13–826453–8

Chapter Opening Photo Credits

 1 Ken Karp.
 2 Bruce Roberts, Photo Researchers, Inc.
 3 Marion Bernstein.
 4 Dan Grogan, University of Virginia Children's Rehabilitation Center.
 5 Dan Grogan, University of Virginia Children's Rehabilitation Center.
 6 Michael Philip Manheim, Photo Researchers, Inc.
 7 Mitchell Payne, 1972, Jeroboam, Inc.
 8 Dan Grogan, University of Virginia Children's Rehabilitation Center.
 9 Ken Karp.
10 Bruce Roberts, Photo Researchers, Inc.

Editorial/production supervision: Joyce Turner
Interior design: Suzanne Behnke
Cover design: Suzanne Behnke
Manufacturing buyer: Ron Chapman
Cover photo by Daniel P. Hallahan
Photo researcher: Christine A. Pullo

Special Education for Today
Rebecca Dailey Kneedler with Daniel P. Hallahan and James M. Kauffman

Printed in the United States of America
10 9 8 7 6 5 4 3 2 1

ISBN 0-13-826453-8

Prentice-Hall International, Inc., *London*
Prentice-Hall of Australia Pty. Limited, *Sydney*
Editora Prentice-Hall do Brasil, Ltda., *Rio de Janeiro*
Prentice-Hall Canada Inc., *Toronto*
Prentice-Hall of India Private Limited, *New Delhi*
Prentice-Hall of Japan, Inc., *Tokyo*
Prentice-Hall of Southeast Asia Pte. Ltd., *Singapore*
Whitehall Books Limited, *Wellington, New Zealand*

CONTENTS

2 MENTAL RETARDATION 35

3 LEARNING DISABILITIES 74

6 HEARING IMPAIRMENT 176

9 GIFTEDNESS   270

10 PARENTS AND FAMILIES   308

PREFACE

OVERVIEW

This book is an introduction to what is known today about the characteristics and educational approaches for exceptional children. It has been our intent to write a highly readable text that presents clear, comprehensible, and practical information that is also well-grounded in research and theory. The text is designed for students preparing to be regular or special education teachers who want an introduction to the full spectrum of special education.

The first chapter provides important issues and controversies pertaining to all of special education. Chapters 2 through 9 present the latest information on today's commonly used categories of special education. Although there is a great deal of overlap in both the characteristics and approaches among categories, we feel a categorical treatment is the most practical and comprehensible way to organize such a vast amount of information. Each categorical chapter includes information on characteristics, definitions, prevalence, causes, and assessment. For each chapter, educational methods are provided at the preschool, elementary, and secondary levels, as well as the important but often neglected postsecondary level. These methods represent today's most common and effective approaches in special education. Finally, reflecting today's newest educational developments, each categorical chapter concludes with a brief section on technological advances for that particular handicap.

Chapter 10 focuses on parents and families of exceptional children. We believe that in order for professionals to have the greatest impact on these exceptional children, they will need a thorough understanding of the family perspective and influence.

SPECIAL FEATURES

We have written, we hope, a book that you, the reader, will not only consider thorough but will also find interesting. In keeping with our desire to present the field of special education in as interesting a way as possible, we have included a number of special features. We have, for example, included an extensive glossary at the end of the book with definitions of all boldface words appearing throughout the text.

As another special learning aid for the reader, each chapter begins with some of the most frequently asked questions pertaining to the content of that chapter. No doubt you've encountered some of these questions even if you've had little previous exposure to the field of special education. Although we've provided our own answers to these questions at the end of each of the chapters, you should, from reading the chapter, be able to formulate your own answers. We believe this question and answer feature will help you to be alert to some of the main concepts presented in each chapter.

Another special feature we've included are the FOCUS boxes. These include such things as practical teaching suggestions, human interest stories, and excerpts from a variety of unusual sources. We have chosen material for the FOCUS sections that we thought you would find especially interesting. Throughout the book—especially with the opening dialogues of Chapters 2 through 9 and with much of Chapter 10—we have tried to present information in ways which help you to understand the feelings and the perspective of exceptional individuals and their families. We feel such empathy and sensitivity is an essential quality for today's educators.

ACKNOWLEDGMENTS

We would like to thank a number of individuals for their help in the preparation of this book. Three students here at Virginia—Kathleen Marshall, Donna Murphy, and Regina Sapona—provided invaluable assistance, without which we could never have successfully made the deadlines we did. We also appreciate the review efforts of Drs. Carolyn Callahan, University of Virginia; C. Julius Meisel, University of Delaware; Cecil D. Mercer, University of Florida; Douglas C. Smith, University of Illinois at Chicago Circle; Keith Stearns, Illinois State University; and James Van Tassel, Ball State University. At Prentice-Hall, we are grateful to Susan Katz, Joyce Turner, Shirley Chlopak, and Jeannine Ciliotta for their help in the various stages of production. And for their typing efforts, we thank Ms. Karen Dwier and Ms. Sharron Hall.

Rebecca Dailey Kneedler
Daniel P. Hallahan
James M. Kauffman

SPECIAL EDUCATION FOR TODAY

SPECIAL EDUCATION IN TODAY'S SCHOOLS

1

Each chapter begins with some frequently asked questions about the topic under discussion. We hope the questions will help you to focus on important concepts as you read. You will find the answers we would give to them at the end of the chapter. Most can be answered in a straightforward manner. But in a few cases involving issues that are controversial, you may find that the best answer is that there are different points of view. We recommend that in addition to reading the chapter for answers to the questions, you pose your own questions before you read and look for answers to them as well.

1. When I told my parents I was taking a course in special education, they asked me why I was interested in retarded children. I tried to explain that special education includes other kinds of kids, but I wasn't really sure I could tell them all the kinds that are included. Who does special education include?

2. How many children in the United States need special education?

3. When did special education get started in the public schools?

4. I've heard a lot about mainstreaming. Some of the things I've read lead me to believe it means closing down institutions for the mentally retarded and putting those people in schools or at jobs along with everyone else. What exactly does mainstreaming mean?

5. Does the federal special education law (Public Law 94-142) require mainstreaming of all handicapped children?

6. I've made the decision that I want to be a special education teacher, and I want to join at least one professional association that will help me keep up with the field. What associations should I consider?

7. Some of the people I've talked to seem to believe that schools are required by law to provide anything and everything in the way of special services for handicapped children. Is it true there is no limit to what a school system must provide?

8. I hear that technological advances are making it possible for handicapped people to do things nobody ever thought they could. And I get the impression that if I go into special education, I'll need a lot of technical knowledge. What will I actually need to know?

Children vary greatly in their ability to learn. Most children have around average ability. Some children learn much more rapidly than most; others learn much more slowly than the average. And some children need special teaching procedures or materials if they are to learn very much of what schools are supposed to teach. The idea of variability in learning rates is nothing new: It was recognized by the first special educators in America, who taught handicapped children in the early 1800s. It was stated in the first general special education textbook published in the United States (Horn, 1924). Yet this old and seemingly simple concept—that children differ in their ability to learn—is the basis for much of the progress and controversy in special education today.

The recent progress in special education can be attributed in part to the decision by the United States Congress that no child can legally be considered too different from the norm (too severely **handicapped**) to be educated. Public Law 94-142, the Education of All Handicapped Children Act of 1975, mandates education for all handicapped children regardless of their special needs. But the concept of variability also underlies the newest and potentially most divisive controversy in special education: How different must children be from the average before they need special education? When PL 94-142 was passed, Congress and the special education profession stated that there were over 8 million handicapped children in the United States. Now, only a few years later, some government officials and some members of the profession are saying there are only about 4 million. One reason they are saying this is that today only about 4 to 4.5 million children are receiving special education services. The difference between the estimated number of handicapped children (over 8 million) and the number actually identified and currently receiving services (about 4 to 4.5 million) has created the controversy. Is it that nearly half of all handicapped children have not yet been identified? Or that not all those identified are receiving services? Or does it mean the estimates were wrong?

Today we know a great deal more about teaching exceptional children than we did even a few years ago. Research and technological advances have helped us a great deal. So this is an exciting time for special educators. We have many new tools, and there is much change and many issues that need to be discussed and resolved.

To introduce you to some of the conflicting ideas about what is new and old, right and wrong, accurate and inaccurate about special education today, we have made up a conversation between two special educators. Imagine, if you will, that you are sitting in a lounge of a large hotel. The hotel is the conference headquarters for the annual convention of CEC (the Council for Exceptional Children, the major professional organization for special educators). You are overhearing a conversation between Henry Whitney, an 84-year-old retiree who has spent over fifty years working as a special education teacher and administrator, and Phyllis Johnston, a senior majoring in special education at State University. Whitney and Johnston have just been introduced by Dr. Eugene Marks, Ms. Johnston's advisor at SU and a long-time friend of Mr. Whitney.

Whitney: Is this your first CEC conference, Miss Johnston?

Johnston: It's my first national convention. But I've gone to a couple of our state CEC conventions.

Whitney: I don't know if Dr. Marks told you, but I've been to every national convention of CEC since the first one in Cleveland in 1923.

Johnston: I'll bet you've seen a lot of changes in special ed since 1923. Everything must be really different now.

Whitney: Well, in some ways things are a lot different, but you might be surprised how much the same they are, too. After all, special education wasn't invented just yesterday, you know. I hear a lot of people these days talking about appropriate education for *all* the handicapped as if it were some fantastic new idea that no one thought of before PL 94-142. We called for exactly that in our very first convention of this organization back in 1923.

Johnston: I had no idea. But I haven't read much about the history of special education.

Whitney: You read up on it, and you'll find out that a lot of ideas you thought were new have been around for a long time.

Johnston: Can you give me some more examples?

Whitney: Oh, sure. At that first meeting in Cleveland, we said there are many more exceptional children than the public realizes, and many more types of exceptionality than most people suppose.

Johnston: Did you have categories then, like emotionally disturbed and learning disabled?

Whitney: Of course we had categories! Some of the terms we used were a little different: We might have talked about incorrigibles or truants instead of emotionally disturbed kids, and we didn't have anything called learning disability. But we sure had LD kids. We just called them retarded or slow learners or problem children. Learning disability is a term dreamed up by Sam Kirk in the early 1960s, you know. Now it's a popular label with a lot of people.

Johnston: Why do you think that's so?

Whitney: Because people don't think it's so negative or demeaning a term as "retarded" or "disturbed" or something else.

Johnston: Do you think it will always be that way?

Whitney: Absolutely not! Remember, Miss Johnston, LD is only a few years older than you are. In time, LD will be an old, damning label just like all the others. Before my time, terms like "idiotic" and "moron" and "imbecile" were perfectly acceptable. Can you imagine someone giving a paper at this convention about testing or teaching idiots? Why, they'd be hooted out of the hotel!

Johnston: But were you concerned about labeling kids in 1923?

Whitney: You bet we were! We said in our meeting that we should be more concerned about educating exceptional children than about labeling them. We knew then that what you call a kid can change the way he feels about himself, and we were very sensitive to the problem of trying to avoid stigma.

Johnston: Why do we always have to use some kind of label, anyway? I think we ought to do away with them all.

Whitney: Unfortunately, Miss Johnston, my personal opinion is that we can't. I know a lot of people—good people, too—who disagree with me. But I don't think doing away with labels will work, because whenever you do something special or notice something unusual, you have to have a name for it. The alternative to having labels for what we do and the kinds of kids we serve is to deny there's anything remarkable about them at all. If we did that, we'd be taking the specialness right out of special education. I do agree with the people who say that labels can be stigmatizing. I just hope that someday someone comes along and finds a better way of talking about exceptional kids without resorting to labels that are stigmatizing.

Johnston: Wouldn't it be nice if labels like mentally retarded or deaf *didn't* automatically stand for something negative in people's minds? I suppose I'm too idealistic, but I haven't given up hope that our society will change its way of looking at differences. I hope someday we can simply treat people as people. Am I hoping for too much?

Whitney: No—and don't ever give up hope. All *good* special education teachers are, by definition, idealists. If I'm honest with you, I have to admit that you young people have actually made a lot of changes in society's attitudes toward the handicapped. The number of TV movies and specials and newspaper and magazine articles on the handicapped is a good indication of how far society's moved toward accepting exceptional individuals. Hell, they've even got retarded actors on that TV show for preschoolers, that . . . what's it called?

Johnston: *Sesame Street?*

Whitney: Yes, that's it. *Sesame Street.* Why, I don't think I saw more than half a dozen retarded people myself until I was out of high school. Now they're everywhere! I don't think there are more retarded people, mind you. It's just that they aren't hidden away any more. And this is a very good thing for everyone. Things have got to be better today for the 4-year-old who sees the retarded kid on *Sesame Street*—he's bound to have a better understanding of what mental retardation is as he grows up. And as far as the retarded kid on the show is concerned, he's learning about how he's *like* other kids, not how he's different.

Johnston: Let me ask you about something else. Teacher training in your day: was it good?

Whitney: Nowhere near as good as it is today. We were concerned about it in 1923 and said so at that conference. You'll know a lot more about teaching before you graduate than most of us did.

Johnston: How about the people who went into special education then. About the same as today?

Whitney: Some were good, some not so good, the same as now. But I think, generally speaking, students today are brighter and better all around than they were then. *Everybody* concerned with special education is a lot better off now than they were fifty years ago.

Johnston: What's gotten so much better?

Whitney: I've already mentioned better teachers. Parents have the law behind them now when they ask for a decent program for their kids. They might still have to beg, but PL 94-142 has made a lot of school boards and administrators aware of what handicapped children ought to have, believe me. There seems to be more interest in gifted kids these days, and I think that's a very positive thing. And the equipment and materials you have to work with—just look at the things on display in the exhibit area. Then there's all the research going on today, and the advances in technology. Sometimes it makes me wish I could start all over again as a new teacher like you.

TODAY'S DEFINITION
OF EXCEPTIONAL CHILDREN

Exceptional children are those whose characteristics are so different from most children's that the usual educational programs of the public schools are not appropriate for them. These children are extremely unlikely to achieve their full human potential without a special program designed to capitalize on their abilities and/or help them overcome their disabilities. Although the categories of exceptionality may be labeled differently in different states and have changed over the years in federal laws and regulations, the following groups typically are included:

Mentally retarded
Learning disabled
Emotionally disturbed
Physically handicapped
Hearing impaired
Visually impaired
Speech and language disordered
Gifted and talented

Kids on the Block, Inc. produces the handicapped puppets like those shown below along with scripts designed to entertain young elementary school children as well as to inform them about different types of handicaps. Kids on the Block.

We will define each of these categories in later chapters. You should note, however, that the definition of exceptional children and the definitions of various categories of exceptionality are frequently revised by professional groups and government agencies. For example, the definition of mental retardation has gone through several changes over the years, and the definitions of learning disability and emotional disturbance are always being questioned. In addition, although the category of gifted and talented has traditionally been included in definitions of exceptional children and special education, it is not defined or included in any way in the nation's major special education law, PL 94-142.

Do not be fooled into thinking that exceptionality for educational purposes is defined very objectively. Exceptional children are defined by differences that can be observed. But the particular differences observed, their measurement, and the degree of difference that is considered exceptional are determined by cultural tradition, money, and politics. The point is that exceptionality can be defined in many different ways. One definition is not more *correct* than another, but some definitions may be more socially acceptable or useful than others.

TODAY'S DEFINITION OF SPECIAL EDUCATION

Special education is specially designed instruction intended to meet the particular needs of exceptional children. It may require special teaching procedures, materials, equipment, and/or facilities. Manual communication for the deaf, Braille for the blind, behavior modification for the emotionally disturbed, classrooms in hospitals for the physically disabled, advanced classes for the gifted, and communication devices for those who have severe language or speech disabilities are examples of special provisions that may be needed by exceptional children.

Exceptional children may need not only special education, but related services as well. In fact, PL 94-142 requires special education *and* related services for all handicapped children. **Related services** are services necessary in order for a handicapped child to benefit from special education. For example, transportation, physical and occupational therapy, psychological and counseling services, recreation, and diagnostic medical services are called related services.

Education for exceptional children may be provided through a variety of administrative arrangements. The alternatives range from the least to the most restrictive or intensive level (see Table 1-1). At the least intensive level, a regular teacher makes special provisions for the exceptional child's needs in the regular classroom. This alternative is not special education. At the least intensive level of special education, the regular teacher receives help from a **consultant teacher** who gives advice on special methods, equipment, materials, and so on. A slightly more intensive service is provided when an **itinerant teacher,** who visits children and teachers in different schools, gives special instruction to the child and advice to the regular teacher. A **resource teacher** may provide instruction in specific subjects from a half-hour each week to several hours each day in a special resource room.

Sometimes children are taken to diagnostic–prescriptive centers. There their abilities and disabilities are carefully assessed, and instruction is given on a trial basis. The idea is to send the child to another setting, along with a recommended instructional

Transportation to and from school is a related service to which every handicapped child is entitled by law.
Ken Karp.

plan. Special **self-contained classes** are more intensive or restrictive because an exceptional child spends most or all of every school day with a small group of other exceptional children and a specially trained teacher. Special day schools are an even more segregated alternative, since the entire student body of the school is classified as exceptional. Some children who are confined to their homes or hospitals due to illness, physical injury, or other problem are given **homebound** or **hospital instruction** by an itinerant or visiting teacher. The most intensive or restrictive alternative is a residential school in which

---

TABLE 1–1

Placement Alternatives for Exceptional Children

Regular class, regular teacher (no special education).
Regular class, regular teacher; consultation from special education teacher.
Regular class, regular teacher; visits from itinerant teacher.
Regular class, regular teacher most of the time; some time spent in a resource room with a resource
   teacher.
Diagnostic-prescriptive center for assessment and trial instruction.
Special self-contained class, with special teacher most or all of the school day.
Special day school.
Homebound or hospital instruction.
Residential school.

    Note: Variations and combinations of these types of placement are common and make the actual number of alternatives much larger than this list.

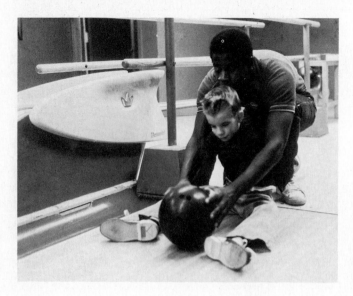

All handicapped children are entitled by law to physical education and recreation that are adapted to their abilities and needs. United Nations/Photo by S. Dimartini.

the child lives and is instructed with other children who have similar exceptionalities.

During the past decade, there has been great controversy over the definition of special education and related services and the choice of arrangements for educating exceptional children. Just where does special education's responsibility for a child end? How many hours per day of care and services should be provided? What services to exceptional children, if any, should not be defined as related services under the law and paid for by the public schools? How does one decide which administrative alternative is least restrictive but appropriate for a given child? These questions are not easily answered. Furthermore, the laws and regulations that govern special education are likely to change over the years as educators, parents, and voters decide what is most desirable, what our society can tolerate, and what it can afford.

TODAY'S ESTIMATES OF PREVALENCE

For about twenty-five years, the federal government published estimates of the **prevalence** of various handicaps in children of school age. These estimates were based on surveys of school officials and the opinions of professionals who worked with the handicapped. The general conclusion was that about 10 to 15 percent of American school children should be considered exceptional for special education purposes. Today, some politicians, bureaucrats, and critics of special education suggest that considerably less than 10 percent of American children should receive special education. Their suggestion that exceptionality has been overestimated is based to some extent on a report published in 1981 by the United States General Accounting Office (GAO, 1981). In that report, the proportion of children served under federal special education laws was compared to a range of prevalence estimates for each category. The findings reported by the GAO are shown in Table 1–2.

As you can see from the table, for most categories the proportion served is larger

TABLE 1–2

Percentage of Children Ages 3–21 Served During the 1980–81 School
Year and Estimated Prevalence of Handicapping Conditions

HANDICAPPING CONDITION	PERCENTAGE OF CHILDREN SERVED	RANGE OF PREVALENCE ESTIMATES	
		LOW	HIGH
Mentally retarded	1.74%	1.3%	2.3%
Hard of hearing	0.08	0.3	0.5
Deaf	0.08	0.075	0.19
Speech impaired	2.40	2.4	4.0
Visually handicapped	0.06	0.05	0.16
Emotionally disturbed	0.72	1.2	2.0
Orthopedically impaired	0.13	0.1	0.75
Other health impaired	0.21	0.1	0.75
Specific learning disabled	2.93	1.0	3.0
Total	8.35	6.525	13.65

Source: *Disparities still exist in who gets special education. Report to the Chairman, Subcommittee on Select Education, Committee on Education and Labor, House of Representatives of the United States.* September 30, 1981. Gaithersburg, Md.: U.S. General Accounting Office, p. 54.

than the low prevalence estimate, but in no case is it as large as the high estimate. Only the specific learning disabled category comes very close to the high estimate. And for some categories (emotionally disturbed, hard of hearing, and deaf) the percentage served is below the lowest prevalence estimates in the range. Both the table and the text of the GAO report indicate that during the 1980–81 school year, a substantial number of children who needed special education were not receiving it. Although progress has undoubtedly been made since then, it is quite safe to assume that some exceptional children, perhaps a very large number, still are not receiving the services they need and to which they are entitled under the law.

The prevalence estimates published by the federal government before the GAO report were approximately the same as the high figures in the range of estimated rates shown in Table 1–2. So the difference between the number of children receiving special education and the number needing such services is very large when the traditional estimates are used. The prevalence estimates on which PL 94-142 was based led Congress to state in the law that there are over 8 million handicapped children in the United States. Thus, if PL 94-142 is working the way it should, we would suppose that about 8 million children are receiving special education. But this is not the case. The GAO report indicated that in 1981 only a little more than 4.3 million children were receiving special education, and the secretary of education referred in 1982 to "the nation's 4 million handicapped children" (Omang, 1982).

Are there closer to 4 million or to 8 million children who need special education? One point of view is that the 8 million estimate was far too high and that nearly all the children who need special education are getting it today. Another point of view is that the estimate was about right and that nearly half the handicapped children in the United States are being denied an appropriate education.

Those who favor the lower estimate, many of whom are not special educators, argue that PL 94-142 is working very well. They claim that for many years we overestimated the number of children who are handicapped and that many of those who formerly were said by special educators to be mildly handicapped are merely children who are slightly below average in ability or achievement, or both. These slow learners or remedial education cases can be dealt with adequately by regular teachers. Those who favor the higher estimate argue that many handicapped children are not being identified by school personnel. The people who take this point of view tend to be special educators or advocates for exceptional children.

Ironically, some handicapped children may go unidentified because of the high cost of special education and the requirements of PL 94-142. The law makes such great financial demands that school systems simply cannot afford to identify all handicapped children. Definitions are vague and subjective enough that teachers and administrators can conceivably get away with ignoring the needs of many mildly handicapped children. The public schools may not be identifying all handicapped children because if they did so, they would be risking financial disaster or prosecution for failure to provide special services to all identified children, as the law requires (Kauffman, 1982; Magliocca and Stephens, 1980).

Regardless of how you interpret the prevalence estimates and figures showing the number of children receiving special education, you can find convincing evidence that not all exceptional children are getting the special education to which they are entitled (Children's Defense Fund, 1982; GAO, 1981; Polloway and Smith, in press). Exceptionality may be defined in a variety of ways, and political and economic factors influence the definition. Today there is the danger that handicapping conditions will be redefined to match current economic and political realities. If this happens, we are likely to see government estimates shrink to match the number of children receiving special services, rather than a substantial increase in the number of children being served. Politicians could then justify lack of support for increased allocations of money for special education and say that there is no problem of noncompliance with the law. Exceptionality would have been neatly redefined in terms of what the public believes can be afforded, and the percentage of children served would match the estimates.

TODAY'S ATTITUDES TOWARD THE FEDERAL LAWS

You had probably heard about PL 94-142 before you began reading this book. We referred to the law in the opening of this chapter as the Education of All Handicapped Children Act, although it is most commonly referred to simply by its number. PL 94-142 is important because it is a *federal* law requiring that exceptional children be educated and because it attempts to guarantee the right of every handicapped child in the United States to a free, appropriate education.

It is the broadest and most complex law related to education ever passed by the federal government. The regulations that govern how the law is carried out are detailed and in many cases difficult to interpret. Not surprisingly, then, an enormous amount of energy has gone into in-service education for educators, attempts to define what compliance with the law means for public school officials and teachers, and lawsuits related to what the regulations demand (Bateman, 1982; Bateman & Herr, 1981).

BASIC PROVISIONS OF FEDERAL SPECIAL EDUCATION LAWS

Public Law 94-142: The Education of All Handicapped Children Act

PL 94-142 requires that each state and local school system have a plan including:

1. *Child Find.* Systematic procedures must be followed to screen and identify all handicapped children.

2. *Full Service at No Cost.* An appropriate education at no cost to the parents or guardians must be assured for every handicapped child.

3. *Due Process.* Each child's and parent's rights to information and informed consent must be assured before the child is evaluated, labeled, or placed in special education; parents have a right to an impartial due process hearing if they disagree with the school's decisions.

4. *Parent Consultation and Parent Surrogates.* The child's parent or guardian must be consulted about the child's evaluation and placement and about the school's educational plan for the child; a surrogate parent must be appointed to represent the child's interests if the parents or guardians are unknown or unavailable.

5. *Individual Education Plan* (*IEP*). Each handicapped child must have a written individualized education plan stating present levels of functioning, long-term and short-term goals, services to be provided, and a schedule for initiating and evaluating the services.

6. *Least Restrictive Environment* (*LRE*). Every handicapped child must be educated in the least restrictive environment that is consistent with his or her educational needs and, to the extent possible, with nonhandicapped children.

7. *Nondiscriminatory Evaluation.* A child must be evaluated in all areas of suspected disability and in a way that is not biased by language or cultural characteristics or handicaps; the evaluation must be done by a multidisciplinary team, and placement and planning must not be based on any single evaluation criterion.

8. *Confidentiality.* Information related to evaluation and placement must be kept confidential, and parents or guardians may have access to records regarding their child.

9. *Personnel Development and In-Service Training.* Training must be provided for special teachers and other professionals, including in-service training for regular teachers.

Section 504 of the Rehabilitation Act of 1973

No otherwise qualified handicapped individual . . . shall, solely by reason of his/her handicap, be excluded from participation in, be denied the benefits of, or be subject to discrimination under any program or activity receiving federal financial assistance.

Almost no one questions the good intentions of PL 94-142 or the fact that the law has benefited many handicapped children. It was designed to bring about significant changes in the education of the handicapped and to make sure that every handicapped child and youth in America is given a reasonable chance to learn. And there can be no question that the law has dramatically increased public awareness of the needs and rights of handicapped children and resulted in education for many children who otherwise would not have had a decent opportunity. The basic provisions of PL 94-142, outlined in the above Focus Box, seem to most people to be only reasonable and fair.

Besides PL 94-142, another federal law, Section 504 of the Rehabilitation Act of 1973, is important in educating the handicapped. Section 504 is a civil rights statement, and it makes illegal any discrimination against the handicapped. If education is provided for nonhandicapped children in any state, it must be provided for handicapped children on terms that ensure equal opportunity.

Perhaps you think that these laws can hardly be controversial, since they seem to assure the handicapped basic opportunities and fair treatment. But consider these facts: Complying with the laws can be very expensive in the case of some children; the regulations are complicated and may not always produce the intended result of more appropriate education; and many children thought to be in need of special education are not being served under the law. In addition, remember that education has traditionally been considered a responsibility of the states, so federal activity goes against tradition and the recent emphasis on decentralization of government. Finally, keep in mind that the federal government pays very little of the cost of special education; most of it is paid for from local and state taxes.

Some teachers have complained that although the intent of the law is good, they are required to spend too much time testing and filling out forms. The law interferes with teaching because so much time must be spent meeting detailed technical requirements (Katzen, 1980). But although the law and the accompanying regulations have critics, changes are not easy. When revisions of the regulations were proposed in 1982, special educators, parents of the handicapped, advocacy groups, and the handicapped themselves protested at public hearings. The secretary of education was forced by public opinion to withdraw the revisions (Omang, 1982). The regulations, and perhaps even PL 94–142 itself, will undoubtedly be changed someday, but any proposed changes will need to be thought through very carefully to make certain that the rights of handicapped children are not lost. The handicapped and those who work for and with them are not about to give up the progress federal laws have brought.

TODAY AND YESTERDAY: SPECIAL EDUCATION'S HISTORY

The more you know about the history of the treatment of handicapped people, the easier it is to understand why the handicapped and advocates for them are reluctant to take any chances when it comes to losing what has been gained through federal legislation. PL 94-142 was passed in 1975 and went into effect in 1978. Most states now have passed legislation that supports the federal law. But prior to 1975, most special education laws were permissive rather than mandatory. That is, local school systems had the option of providing special education and receiving financial assistance from the state for the additional cost; they were not required to make special education available. Many local school systems decided not to provide special education or to provide services that were clearly inappropriate, and parents or other advocates had no legal basis for appeal. Little wonder, then, that PL 94-142 and Section 504 are looked upon as revolutionary.

The past few decades have been revolutionary years in special education not only because of federal legislation, but also because of court action. Many lawsuits were filed by and for handicapped citizens whose rights and educational needs were neglected. Some of these suits were filed because severely handicapped individuals were *not* receiving education; others were filed on behalf of minority children who were placed in special

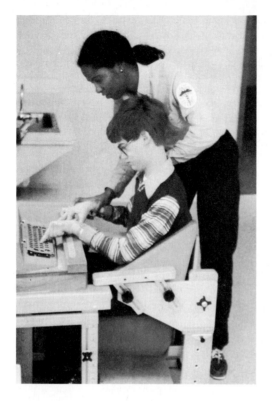

Historically, persons with disabilities have been denied equal access to education and preparation for work. Today, laws give the disabled rights to training that will allow them to function in school and society. American Occupational Therapy Association Calendar, March 1983.

education on the basis of questionable procedures or criteria. The litigation as well as the legislation has served to clarify who is entitled to special education and what protections must be extended to children who are, or are thought to be, handicapped.

Today it is difficult to imagine the neglect and degradation to which the handicapped have been subjected throughout most of history. In ancient times, the handicapped were often killed or cruelly treated. Systematic efforts to teach them were uncommon until the early nineteenth century, when Europeans and Americans began to establish special schools and asylums for the deaf, blind, and retarded (Lane, 1976). When mandatory public education became common in America in the late nineteenth century, special classes for children who did not conform to the norm were started in large cities. Immigrant children who had difficulty because they knew little English, truants, and mildly retarded children were placed in these classes (Hoffman, 1975; Sarason and Doris, 1979). Gradually, special education grew to include more categories of exceptional children and to become a regular part of the public education system. Special services for the handicapped did not show much growth until after World War II, when they expanded rapidly. But the recognition that handicapped children are entitled to a full range of services appropriate to their needs was not highlighted until the late 1960s and early 1970s. The Focus on pages 16–17 shows landmarks in the history of special education.

PL 94-142 and other federal and state action on behalf of the handicapped was prompted in part by exposés revealing how handicapped children have been treated *recently* in American public schools. Here are some examples of the careless or abusive treatment that prompted legislation and litigation:

Misidentification. Children were sometimes identified as handicapped when in fact they were not. Often the identification was based on a single test or other criterion, or on a test administered by an unqualified examiner or in a language they did not fully understand.

Misplacement. Children were sometimes needlessly placed in institutions or in special schools or classes when they clearly could have been taught in a more integrated environment. They were denied the opportunity to lead as normal a life as possible, to interact as much as possible with nonhandicapped people, and to achieve maximum independence.

Denial of service. Some handicapped children were denied special education services simply because the local school system or institution did not have the trained personnel or facilities and did not feel they could be afforded. The parents of these children were then forced to choose between no educational program for their child or paying for education in a private school.

Nonrecognition of parental interests. In some cases, children were tested for placement or even placed in special classes without parental consent or even notification of the parents. Schools often felt justified in making decisions without the benefit of the parents' knowledge of their child's characteristics, their cooperation, or their informed agreement that the decisions were in their child's best interest.

Lack of planning. Children were sometimes placed without any plan for their education other than to segregate them from nonhandicapped children. School personnel often could not state what the educational goals were for the child or what special procedures were being provided.

Failure to reassess. When children were placed in special education, they were sometimes placed there for the rest of their school years. No attempt was made to determine whether a different placement was appropriate. Some children languished in special classes, schools, or institutions for years when they could have been successfully placed in regular classes or the community.

1920s. The Council for Exceptional Children is founded by a group of special education teachers. Its first president, Elizabeth Farrell, calls for suitable educational programs for all exceptional children. Teacher training programs for special educators grow. Sterilization of the mentally retarded becomes a common practice.

1930s. Several states establish certification requirements for special education teachers. The first attempts are made to integrate handicapped and nonhandicapped children in a private school. The U.S. Office of Education establishes a section on exceptional children. The Great Depression slows the growth of special services.

1940s. World War II results in recognition of the value of handicapped workers in industry and of the needs of the disabled. European scholars who have come to the United States begin research and demonstration programs with handicapped children.

1950s. The first institute for research on exceptional children is established. The National Association for Retarded Citizens ("Children" at that time) and other associations of parents of exceptional children are founded. The U.S. Office of Education begins providing funds for research on education of the mentally retarded and for training teachers of the retarded.

1960s. The term "learning disability" is coined. The Bureau of Education for the Handicapped is established in the U.S. Office of Education, and funding is provided for training teachers and leadership personnel in all areas of exceptionality. Deinstitutionalization becomes a movement. Special education becomes identified with the civil rights movement, and segregated special classes and schools for the handicapped are questioned.

1970s. Federal laws establish the right of every handicapped child to a free, appropriate education. State and federal court decisions uphold the rights of the disabled to therapy, education, and nondiscriminatory treatment. All states have laws supporting educational programs for exceptional children.

1980s. In the U.S. Department of Education, the Office of Special Education and Rehabilitative Services (OSERS), and Special Education Programs (SEP) are established. The U.S. General Accounting Office publishes reports showing a continuing need for expansion of special services to handicapped children.

Today we recognize such practices as inappropriate and illegal. But every profession can find aspects of its history of which it is not proud. Special education does have a history of good intentions, and its leading professionals have for the most part done their best in terms of available knowledge. The challenge of our history is to practice special education within the spirit of today's legal framework—to work toward fulfillment of its promise of appropriate public education for every exceptional child.

TODAY'S PROFESSIONAL ORGANIZATIONS

One way special educators work toward fulfillment of the promise of PL 94-142 and other legislation is through professional organizations. When they work together as a large group, they can accomplish much more than they can as individuals. They can band together to influence the political process and offer one another support for research and better professional practices.

Since its founding in 1922, the Council for Exceptional Children (CEC) has been the primary organization of special educators. Today it has many thousands of professional and student members. It is a national organization with state and local

ALPHABET SOUP: ORGANIZATIONS SERVING THE HANDICAPPED

Many organizations are known by the initials that represent their full names. So many organizations serve handicapped children that a conversation about them can be gobbledygook to someone new to the field of special education. Here are some of the most common organizational names (and initials) you are likely to see in print or hear discussed.

AABT—Association for Advancement of Behavior Therapy
AAMD—American Association on Mental Deficiency
ACLD—Association for Children and Adults with Learning Disabilities
AOA—American Orthopsychiatric Association
ASET—Association for Special Education Technology
ASHA—American Speech-Language-Hearing Association
*CASE—Council of Administrators of Special Education
*CCBD—Council for Children with Behavioral Disorders
CEC—Council for Exceptional Children
*CEC–MR—Council for Exceptional Children–Mental Retardation
*CEDS—Council for Educational Diagnostic Services
CLD—Council for Learning Disabilities (formerly DCLD, Division for Children with Learning Disabilities, a division of CEC)
*DCCD—Division for Children with Communication Disorders
*DCD—Division for Career Development
*DEC—Division for Early Childhood
*DLD—Division for Learning Disabilities
*DOPHHH—Division on the Physically Handicapped, Homebound, and Hospitalized
*DVH—Division for the Visually Handicapped
NAGC—National Association for Gifted Children
NARC—National Association for Retarded Citizens
NSAC—National Society for Autistic Children
OSERS—Office of Special Education and Rehabilitative Services (U.S. Department of Education)
SEP—Special Education Programs (in OSERS; formerly known as BEH, Bureau of Education for the Handicapped)
SRCD—Society for Research in Child Development
*TAG—The Association for the Gifted
TASH—The Association for Severely Handicapped
*TED—Teacher Education Division

* Division of CEC.

federations. Divisions of CEC offer membership to qualifying CEC members who are interested in particular categories of exceptionality. For example, TAG (The Association for the Gifted) is open to CEC members whose special interest is the gifted and talented, and CCBD (Council for Children with Behavioral Disorders) serves those who work with emotionally disturbed children. Other CEC divisions include groups that specialize in other categories of exceptionality and in special education administration, teacher education, diagnostic services, and career development.

Besides CEC and its divisions, numerous other professional organizations are involved in special education (see Focus on page 18 for a partial listing). The American Association on Mental Deficiency (AAMD) is one of the oldest organizations concerned with education of the mentally retarded. The American Orthopsychiatric Association (AOA) includes members who are educators, and it focuses on the problems of emotionally disturbed children. Many professional organizations, typically associations of psychologists and medical professionals, are concerned with special education and offer full or associate membership to special educators.

Strictly *professional* organizations are not the only ones serving the interests of exceptional children. Parents of the handicapped and the gifted have banded together to work for more appropriate education for their children. For example, the National Association for Retarded Citizens (NARC), the National Association for Gifted Children (NAGC), the National Society for Autistic Children (NSAC), and the Association for Children and Adults with Learning Disabilities (ACLD) are organizations founded primarily by concerned parents. Although professionals are welcome as members of many parent-initiated organizations, the parents themselves must be credited with a major role in bringing about progress in special education. Parents have become such an important factor in many aspects of special education today that we have devoted the last chapter of this book to their concerns.

TODAY'S ISSUES

The controversy about prevalence, which we have already mentioned, undoubtedly will continue until the problems of defining certain handicapping conditions are resolved. Other controversies have arisen about exactly what the law demands for children who have been identified as handicapped. We will discuss just two in this chapter:

1. What is appropriate education?
2. What is the least restrictive environment?

The controversies arose primarily because of the wording of PL 94-142. The law does not state merely that handicapped children must be educated, nor does it state that an "adequate" or "special" or "equal" education will do. It says that a handicapped child must be provided an "appropriate" education. But it does not define what "appropriate" means. The law also requires that handicapped children be educated in the "least restrictive environment" consistent with their educational needs. It does not require that every handicapped child be placed in a regular public school classroom; it does require that, to the extent possible, handicapped children be educated with nonhandicapped children.

Differences of opinion about what constitutes appropriate education and least restrictive environment are found not only among special educators, but among lawyers and judges as well. Special educators may have their own opinions, but they must abide by legal interpretations. Clarification of the meaning of the law ultimately must come from court decisions or additional legislation.

Public Law 94–142 requires that children be educated in the least restrictive environment. Here, a hearing impaired child is receiving instruction along with his normally hearing peers. Freda Leinwand, Monkmeyer.

APPROPRIATE EDUCATION

Try, for a few minutes, to make up your own definition of appropriate education for handicapped children. Remember that PL 94-142 does not include any detailed definition of the term, although it does state what procedures must be followed in designing appropriate education. Appropriate education must not cost the child's parents or guardians anything, must meet state standards, and must be designed to meet the unique needs of the child in accordance with an individual education plan (IEP). You might find it somewhat easier to decide what appropriate education is when you consider the needs of a particular child than when you try to define it in an abstract way that applies to all handicapped children. But in considering what appropriate education means for handicapped children in general, it is very likely that you have thought of one of these four standards, which have been suggested by judges and lawyers:

1. *Self-sufficiency.* An appropriate education will enable a handicapped child to attain self-sufficiency as an adult. Public education is intended to prepare children to become independent, productive citizens, and education is appropriate for a handicapped child to the extent that it is able to meet this goal.
2. *Accessibility.* If the education for a handicapped child makes the public education system accessible, then it is appropriate. This standard means that appropriate education is being provided if the public schools have a special program for the handicapped child that is individually designed and can be reasonably considered to benefit the child.
3. *Equal opportunity.* A handicapped child must have an opportunity to learn equal to the opportunity of nonhandicapped children. The test of appropriateness is whether or not the child achieves at the same level as a child who does not have the handicap. Special education should, in effect, allow the child to overcome any disability so that he or she is not at a disadvantage in school.
4. *Highest potential.* Appropriate education ensures that the handicapped child achieves maximum potential. Every effort must be made and every service must be provided to improve

the child's ability to learn. This standard means that the best possible education must be provided regardless of the cost or the standards of education for the nonhandicapped.

These four standards and variations of them have been argued by attorneys in various court cases and have been debated by special educators. Each standard has different implications for carrying out PL 94-142, and each has advocates and critics. Courts have adopted different standards in different cases. So far there is no consensus regarding the meaning of "appropriate" for all handicapped children.

In 1982, the United States Supreme Court made its first interpretation of PL 94-142 in the case of *Board of Education of the Hendrick Hudson Central School District, Westchester County, et al.* v. *Rowley, by Her Parents, Rowley et ux.*, better known as the Rowley case. The Supreme Court was not unanimous in its opinion of what constituted appropriate education for Amy Rowley, a deaf child. But the majority opinion was that the law calls for access to an individualized educational program that benefits the child, not for the best possible education that will allow the child to realize his or her maximum potential. The Court was careful to restrict its ruling to the case of Amy Rowley, so other cases may be argued differently and have different outcomes. In this case, however, the Court found that Amy was getting an appropriate education because she had an individualized program with special services designed to help her achieve in school. And Amy was, in fact, achieving at or above the average level of her classmates in a regular public school class. In the Court's opinion, the fact that she might have been able to learn more if she had been provided with a sign language interpreter, as her parents had contended, did not mean that her education was inappropriate under PL 94-142.

Other court cases undoubtedly will lead to different interpretations of what appropriate education is for other handicapped children. But the Rowley case can be seen as a great victory for the handicapped. After all, as Martin (1982) points out, the Supreme Court did affirm handicapped children's right to education and related services under the law. Furthermore, the court's decision in this case points to seven essential features of "appropriate" education for any handicapped child:

1. Instruction specifically designed to meet the individual child's unique needs.
2. Related services, if they are necessary.
3. A program based on adequate evaluation of the individual child's needs.
4. Services in accordance with an individual education plan (IEP).
5. An IEP jointly formulated by the education agency and the child's parents.
6. Services reasonably calculated to enable the child to meet reasonable goals.
7. Review of the child's progress at least annually.

LEAST RESTRICTIVE ENVIRONMENT

Many people have been confused by the terms "least restrictive environment," "mainstreaming," and "normalization" (Cruickshank, 1977; Dybwad, 1980). These terms can be defined as follows:

Normalization. Making the handicapped child's life, including his or her education, as much like that of the nonhandicapped as possible.

Mainstreaming. Placing handicapped and nonhandicapped children together for education.

APPROPRIATE AND LEAST RESTRICTIVE: AN ANALYSIS

Barbara Bateman is a professor of special education at the University of Oregon. She is also an attorney who specializes in special education law. In November, 1982, she gave a lecture at the University of Virginia Law School in which she discussed the relationship between the legal concepts of appropriate education and least restrictive environment, two key concepts in PL 94-142. This is a summary of several of the points she made in her lecture.

PL 94-142 says that every handicapped child must have a free, appropriate public education. Interestingly, there is no definition in the law of what appropriate means. So one of the big legal issues has been, "Just what is appropriate?" One of the major reasons the law has become so controversial and so many lawsuits have been filed is that special educators have tended to say that what is appropriate is whatever kind of program the schools already have. But the law says you must have a truly individualized program, even if it is not something the schools already offer. Not only must an appropriate program be individualized, but it must be one that benefits the child. In a recent Supreme Court case, this criterion of benefit to the child was clearly upheld.

The issue of appropriateness is often tangled with the issue of restrictiveness. School systems have argued in court that the most appropriate education is always the one in the least restrictive setting. Moreover, the schools have said that a public school regular classroom is obviously the least restrictive, and therefore the most appropriate. You can see how this line of argument, if successful, would save the schools a lot of money. Placing a child in a regular classroom is a lot cheaper than placing him or her in a special self-contained class, special school, or institution.

A court in Virginia analyzed the problem correctly. This court said, "You can't resolve the issue of least restrictive environment until you first resolve the issue of appropriateness. That is, you must first be able to describe at least two programs that are appropriate without considering the issue of restrictiveness. Only then can you consider the issue of which of the programs is least restrictive."

You should be aware of the origins of the least restrictive environment requirement of PL 94-142. It came from two concerns. First of all, Congress had the impression when it passed the law that placement in a special class was something very, very negative, maybe close to ruining a child for life. Second, the deinstitutionalization or normalization movement also influenced the thinking of Congress. This movement involved moving severely handicapped adults out of institutions and into community placements. But it didn't make much sense when it was applied to the problem of restrictiveness of placement of a mildly handicapped third-grader.

One interesting aspect of the issue of least restrictive environment is what parents say they want for their children—what they ask for in the lawsuits based on PL 94-142. Very clearly, most parents do not want the least restrictive environment for their handicapped children, as least restrictive has usually been defined. Seven-to-one in the lawsuits, parents have been seeking the so-called *more* restrictive placement. They want the residential placement, the special education class, the special school. If you don't consider the cases involving deaf children in the analysis, then the figures are even more lopsided: 50 to 1, parents want the more restrictive, more specialized placement.

Least restrictive environment. Placing the handicapped child in as normal an environment as is consistent with an appropriate education.

As you can see, the least restrictive environment for a particular child cannot be determined until appropriate education has been described for that child (see above Focus).

Unfortunately, "least restrictive" has sometimes been interpreted to mean "mainstream" in all cases, and "normalization" has been interpreted to mean that every child should be mainstreamed. Cruickshank (1977) pointed out that least restrictive does not necessarily mean most like normal or mainstreamed. Restrictiveness must be interpreted in terms of what a placement means for the child's emotional and academic development. He stated:

> A child placed in a so-called least-restrictive situation who is unable to achieve, who lacks an understanding teacher, who does not have appropriate learning materials, who is faced with tasks he cannot manage, whose failure results in negative comments by his classmates, and whose parents reflect frustration to him when he is at home, is indeed being restricted on all sides. (p. 194)

Clearly, PL 94-142 does not call for mainstreaming all handicapped children. What it does require is that children not be needlessly segregated. The law was a response to too many handicapped being placed in special classes, schools, and institutions where they had little or no chance to interact with others or to learn academic skills, daily living skills that would allow them to become independent and self-sufficient adults, or social skills that would make their acceptance by society more likely.

The trouble over the definition of least restrictive environment has arisen partly because of the reaction to past abuses. Beginning in the 1960s, special segregated classes were criticized as violating the rights of the handicapped (Dunn, 1968). Institutions were exposed as abusive environments that dehumanized both residents and staff (Blatt and Kaplan, 1966). Much of the criticism was justified, and it led to public outrage and legal action. Mainstreaming became a major concern in education. **Deinstitutionalization**—moving the handicapped from large institutions to smaller community homes— became a major movement in the mental health field. In the 1970s, many special educators and mental health experts began to recognize that while segregated placements can be damaging to the handicapped, they are not necessarily so and are not always inappropriate (Bassuk and Gerson, 1978; Cruickshank, 1977). The contrasting statements in the next two Focus Boxes should help you understand both sides of the controversy.

Determining the least restrictive environment for a handicapped child is not simple. Consideration of the needs of the child and the parents, as well as the range of placements available in a community, is required. Today, most special educators support the idea that a wide variety of placement options should be available. Research has shown that most mildly handicapped children can be taught effectively in several types of settings,

One purpose of requiring education in the least restrictive environment is to allow the handicapped child to interact with nonhandicapped children. Ken Karp.

FOCUS

INSTITUTIONALIZATION: RIGHT OR WRONG?

Institution Is Not a Dirty Word

Our child Zachariah has not lived at home for almost four years. I knew when we placed him, sorry as I was, that this was the right decision, for his care precluded any semblance of normal family life for the rest of us. I do not think that we "gave him up," although he is cared for daily by nurses, caseworkers, teachers and therapists, rather than by his mother and father. When we come to visit him at his "residential facility," a place housing 50 severely physically and mentally handicapped youngsters, we usually see him being held and rocked by a foster grandma who has spent the better part of the afternoon singing him nursery rhymes.

The media still relish those institution horror stories: a page-one photo of a retarded girl who was repeatedly molested by the janitor on night duty . . . But there are other scenes from the institution as well. I've seen a young caseworker talk lovingly as she changed the diapers of a teen-age boy. I've watched as an aide put red ribbons into the ponytail of a cerebral-palsied woman, wipe away the drool and kiss her on the cheek. When we bring Zach back to his facility after a visit home, the workers welcome him with hugs and notice if we gave him a haircut or a new shirt.

Most retarded people do not belong in institutions any more than most people over 65 belong in nursing homes. What we need are options and alternatives for a heterogeneous population. We need group homes and halfway houses and government subsidies to families who choose to care for dependent members at home. We need accessible housing for independent handicapped people; we need to pay enough to foster-care families to show that a good home is worth paying for. We need institutions. And it shouldn't have to be a dirty word.

Source: Kupfer, F. "Institution Is Not a Dirty Word," *Newsweek,* December 13, 1982, p. 17.

FOCUS

"MAN'S INHUMANITY TO MAN . . ."

Many dormitories for the severely and moderately retarded ambulatory residents have solitary confinement cells or, what is officially referred to as "therapeutic isolation." "Therapeutic isolation" means solitary confinement—in its most punitive and inhumane form. These cells are . . . generally tiny rooms, approximately seven feet by seven feet, shielded from the outside with a very heavy metal door having either a fine strong screen or metal bars for observation of the "prisoner." Some cells have mattresses, others blankets, still others bare floors. None that we had seen (and we found these cells in each institution visited) had either a bed, a washstand, or a toilet. What we did find in one cell was a thirteen or fourteen year old boy, nude, in a corner of a starkly bare room, lying on his own urine and feces. The boy had been in solitary confinement for several days for committing a minor institutional infraction . . .

In some of the children's dormitories we observed "nursery programs." What surprised us most was their scarcity and the primitiveness of those in operation. Therefore, we were not unprepared to see several children with severe head lacerations. We were told these were "head bangers." Head banging is another condition that some people think is inevitable when confronted with young severely mentally retarded children. We challenge this. We have reason to believe that head banging can be drastically reduced in an environment where children have other things to do.

The "Special Education" we observed in the dormitories for young children was certainly not education. But, it was special. It was among the most especially frightening and depressing encounters with human beings we have ever experienced.

Source: Blatt, B., and Kaplan, F. *Christmas in Purgatory: A photographic essay on mental retardation.* Boston: Allyn & Bacon, 1966, pp. 10 & 34.

including special self-contained classes and regular classes with help from a resource teacher. When it is possible for a child to be taught effectively in any one of several types of placements, strong cases can be made for choosing the least restrictive or most normal setting (Leinhardt and Pallay, 1982).

TECHNOLOGICAL ADVANCES

Special education has changed because of laws and court decisions, but it has also changed because of advances in technology. This technology involves advances in prevention of handicapping conditions, early detection of disabilities, new teaching procedures, and a variety of equipment and materials designed to allow handicapped people to function more normally. Technology now plays such an important part in the practice of special education that an entire professional journal, the *Journal of Special Education Technology*, is devoted to the topic. Each chapter in this book contains a section on technological advances that are changing special education for the particular exceptionality being discussed. Here we will give you an overview of how technology affects special education and illustrate some of our points with examples intended to get you thinking about what the future might hold.

Many technological developments in our society are linked to the types of handicapping conditions children are born with or acquire after birth, and also to the types of handicapping conditions that can be prevented. But we must caution you that although technological advances hold great promise for the relief of suffering, they also hold the danger of causing them accidentally. Technology of almost any kind has its price. Only if the "advancement" is managed carefully do the benefits outweigh the costs. Moreover, the true costs and benefits of many developments are not known when they occur. So being cautious is sometimes the wisest course.

When people think of technology, they often think of sophisticated electrical equipment or machines. But technology is much more than that: It is the application of knowledge to the solution of practical problems. Medical technology includes drugs and vaccines, diagnostic tests, and surgical procedures, as well as life-sustaining equipment. Technology in the fields of psychology and education includes the application of knowledge about how children learn to the problem of remediating learning deficits.

Your understanding of what we have to say about technology does not require any detailed knowledge of electrical circuits or biochemistry. We will explain in simple terms why technological advances have been important to the handicapped and the people who teach them. Some people are frightened by technology. However, even if you become a user of technology as a teacher of exceptional children, you are not likely to be required to master the inner workings of the technology itself, except the technology of instruction. Most of today's technology is becoming increasingly "user friendly": The user need not have a sophisticated knowledge of its components and their workings to use it skillfully.

PREVENTING DISABILITY

One example of how special education has been affected by technological development in medicine is the case of polio (the neurological disease known by the medical term poliomyelitis). During the late 1940s and early 1950s, many of the physically handicapped

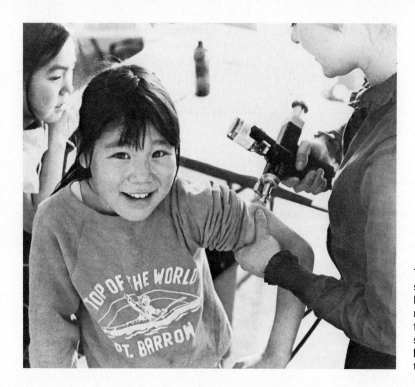

Today's technology makes possible the prevention of many handicapping conditions. Vaccinations prevent diseases that formerly left many children with serious physical or mental disabilities. Centers for Disease Control, Atlanta.

children in special education classes had become paralyzed by this disease. During the 1950s, polio was nearly wiped out by the development of an effective vaccine. So it is rare today to encounter someone under the age of 30 who has been disabled by polio.

A more complicated example, in which a technological advance resulted in many infants acquiring a handicapping condition that was later preventable by other technological developments, is retrolental fibroplasia, or RLF. RLF is a condition that causes blindness in infants. Beginning in the early 1940s, physicians noted an alarming increase in the incidence of this condition but were baffled about its cause. In 1953 the cause was pinpointed—the administration of high concentrations of oxygen to premature infants. The oxygen saved many babies from death, but left them with serious handicaps (many of the RLF babies had other disabilities besides blindness). When the cause of the condition was found, the level of oxygen administered in incubators was controlled to save infants' lives but avoid blinding them in most cases.

Today, advances in medical technology are allowing physicians to prevent or correct many conditions that formerly resulted in early death or serious disability. At the same time, medical technology is contributing to an increase in the number of people who have severe or profound disabilities. Today physicians can sustain lives that would have been lost a few years ago, and the result is the survival of individuals who have extreme limitations. Obviously, some medical advances may appear to be mixed blessings, and the new possibilities for prolonging human life can create painful moral and ethical dilemmas.

In the future we will undoubtedly see technological developments that will lead to the prevention or cure of many more diseases and handicapping conditions and to the ability to sustain increasingly fragile life. You might give some consideration to questions such as these:

Under what conditions, if any, should life not be artificially prolonged?
What handicapping conditions should we be most concerned about reducing or eliminating?
What technological developments will be necessary to solve the social problems that result in the handicapping of many children (child abuse, teenage pregnancy, and drunk driving, for example)?

EARLY DETECTION

Some technological developments are aimed at identifying handicapping conditions. Early identification may make early correction possible or prevent a condition that is relatively minor from getting worse.

Any developments in early detection may seem at first to have only good results. But unless the detection procedure is highly reliable and a therapeutic or remedial program is available for children who are identified, the outcome may be more damaging than helpful. Consider the frustration and anxiety of parents and children when a child

Screening young children to determine whether or not they have a disability is an important part of comprehensive special education services. Centers for Disease Control, Atlanta.

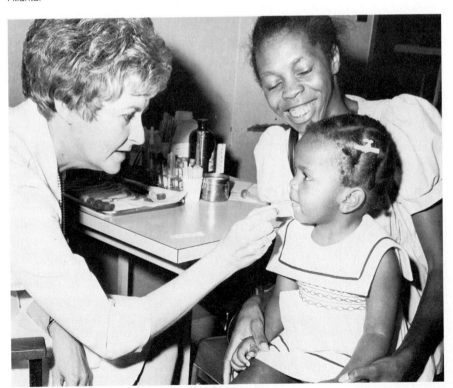

RESEARCH TO AID SCHOOLS IN IDENTIFYING EPILEPSY

University of Virginia researchers have developed new techniques to identify epilepsy or seizure disorders in children and are now preparing to make the information available to schools all over the country.

"By identifying and treating the neurological condition early, we prevent the problem of seizures, the secondary psychological effects of uncontrolled seizures and may prevent the disease from becoming intractable," said Dr. Fritz Dreifuss, the head of the project.

At the heart of the project is a seizure screening questionnaire. It was administered last year among third graders in the Charlottesville and Albemarle County schools, and will soon be given in other areas of the state before becoming available to school systems throughout the country, Dreifuss said.

Initially, parents are asked to complete a questionnaire identifying possible symptoms of epilepsy in their children, such as fainting spells, inattentiveness, black-out periods or a history of convulsions in other family members.

If problems exist, the child is brought to UVa's neurology outpatient unit for tests, including a neurological exam and an electroencephalogram, or EEG, a test that measures the brain's electrical activity.

The National Commission for the Control of Epilepsy and Its Consequences reports 75 percent of all individuals with epilepsy develop the condition before age 18.

Dreifuss said there are many kinds of epilepsy, but the kind affecting children is often hereditary and caused by chemical imbalances in the brain. The disorder affects more than 1 percent of those under 18, the doctor added.

Source: The Daily Progress, January 10, 1983, p. B–1.

is misidentified or when the parents can find no help in overcoming the disability. Think too of the possibilities of identifying handicapping conditions before birth and the moral and ethical problems this presents. Already, some handicapping conditions, such as Down's syndrome (a chromosomal abnormality associated with mental retardation), can be detected long before birth through a procedure called amniocentesis.

If a seriously handicapping condition can be detected early enough, is an abortion justified? Today, as a result of progress in medical genetics, we can predict the chances that children of certain individuals will be born with seriously handicapping conditions. Are people justified in having children when they are extremely likely to bring a seriously handicapped child into the world? Perhaps future developments will allow people to select many of the characteristics of their children or to correct defects detected in the fetus. But if it is possible to select characteristics before children are born, should the government set limits on what prospective parents may select?

TEACHING METHODS

Some educators argue that teaching is an art; some say it is a science. Regardless of your bias, teaching is undeniably a technology as well, an application of scientific knowledge to the practical matter of helping people learn. This technology is the most important part of special education. Recent research on effective schools and the new technology of instruction have given teachers a great deal of guidance in how to teach children,

ONE TECHNOLOGY EVERY SPECIAL EDUCATION TEACHER MUST MASTER

The technology of instruction involves designing teaching routines that are logically flawless. If flawless routines are presented appropriately to a child who has the capacity to respond to the logic of the presentation, then the child will learn the concept represented by the routine. Being a good teacher requires knowing how to set up routines at which children who have the capacity to learn a concept or skill will be successful. Here we will give you just one example of a routine for teaching one type of cognitive problem-solving.

This routine can be used for teaching someone to solve problems of the class $5 - 3 = [\ ]$. Notice that what the teacher shows, says, and requires of the student is carefully and logically sequenced. Keep in mind, too, that this example is isolated from other routines that would make learning to solve problems of the class $5 - 3 = [\ ]$ meaningful in the child's life. In addition, the child must have learned certain skills before being presented with this routine (reading such problems, making and counting slash marks, writing numerals that correspond to the number of marks).

TEACHER	LEARNER
$5 - 3 = \square$	
1. Read it.	Five minus three equals how many?
2. (Touches under 5.) What does this tell us?	Start with five.
3. Do it.	(Learner makes 5 lines: $5 - 3 = \square$)
	/////
4. (Points to −3.) What does this tell us?	Minus three.
5. Do it.	(Learner crosses out 3 lines: $5 - 3 = \square$)
	////////
6. (Points to equal sign.) What does this tell us?	We must have the same number on both sides.
7. What number is that?	Two.
8. Make the sides equal.	(Learner makes lines and writes answer:)
	$5 - 3 = 2$
	////// //
9. Read the problem and the answer.	Five minus three equals two.

Source: S. Engelmann and D. Carnine. *Theory of instruction: Principles and applications.* New York: Irvington, 1982. Figure 3.3, p. 23.

especially those who have difficulty learning (Engelmann and Carnine, 1982; Rieth, Polsgrove, and Semmel, 1981). For example, an effective teacher must allocate a high percentage of time to instruction, keep children engaged in academic tasks, and provide tasks at which children can usually be successful. And a teacher must specify objectives, select and sequence examples of concepts to be taught, provide corrective feedback and reinforcement, and monitor student progress. Today, as the above Focus shows, a technology of direct instruction that can be applied to the problem of teaching nearly any handicapped student is available (Engelmann and Carnine, 1982). Furthermore, today's instructional technology is demonstrating that under some conditions, handicapped children can be taught to direct and monitor their own learning (Hallahan, Lloyd, Kauffman, and Loper, 1983; Kneedler and Hallahan, 1981).

The development of a sound technology of instruction may challenge some dearly held notions about teaching. The more we know about effective teaching, the more the mystique of teaching may seem to disappear. But there is always a need for human warmth and feeling regardless of how precisely a teacher instructs a child. In the future, teachers will need to consider such questions as these:

Is a teacher ever justified in ignoring or failing to use technological information about instruction?

Given that any number of concepts or skills can be taught to a handicapped child, which ones should be taught first?

What skills and concepts will be most important to the child's future life?

What types of effective feedback and reinforcement are in the child's best interest?

EQUIPMENT AND MATERIALS

The most visible and dramatic technological developments related to special education involve equipment and materials not even dreamed of only a few years ago. Developments in this area are so numerous that we cannot mention them all. The most important influence in special education technology now is the microcomputer. Indeed, microcomputers are changing the way all of us live, handicapped and nonhandicapped alike (Boraiko, 1982; Myers, 1982). Here are only a few of the applications that are being made to problems of the handicapped:

Tests that are given and scored by computer.

Instructional programs in which the student is tutored by a computer.

Artificial limbs controlled by computers that read motions and electrical signals from the skin and translate these into limb movements.

A "bio-ear," a tiny computer implanted behind the ear that may help some profoundly deaf persons hear some sounds.

Computers programmed to send sequences of electrical signals to the muscles of paralyzed persons, enabling them to ride a bicycle, walk, or do other tasks.

A computer that reads print and translates it into spoken language for the blind.

Talking computer terminals and calculators for the blind.

Computerized wheelchair controls that allow a paralyzed person to control motion by very slight movements and to set the chair on "automatic pilot."

Computer programs that instruct deaf persons in finger spelling, lip reading, and vocalization.

 A variety of programs that facilitate the communication of people who cannot speak because of a physical disability—systems that will print or sound out words and sentences in response to relatively simple movements, such as moving a "joy stick," raising and lowering an eyebrow, thrusting the tongue, extending the neck, or even moving the eyes to look at a particular object or image on a TV screen.

All these developments in the use of microcomputers are impressive and exciting. But the ones most relevant to what a special educator does are those that involve communication, for communication is the basis of the technology of teaching (Engelmann and Carnine, 1982). Advances in communication technology, microcomputer-assisted or not, can help us prevent the tragedy of the child who must live without an effective means of expressing feelings and ideas articulately. Think of the things the woman described in the following story would like to have been able to say during her childhood.

HOW CAN A PERSON WHO IS DEAF AND BLIND COMMUNICATE WITH OTHERS?

Communication with the deaf-blind began about one hundred years ago, when Anne Sullivan began her work with Helen Keller. Since that time, the deaf-blind have relied primarily on placing their hand on a speaking person's mouth and cheek or feeling the hand of someone who is finger spelling (using a manual alphabet to spell out words) to understand what is being told them. The following is a report on technological developments that will make communication with and among deaf-blind people simpler.

The approaches used for the blind or deaf won't work for the deaf-blind. What is used is the manual alphabet—finger positions produced by the speaker in the deaf-blind person's palm. The handicapped person then replies on a normal typewriter.

Obviously, manual fingerspelling is slow, but perhaps worse is the shortage of people to do it. If it could be done by machine at a reasonable cost, this group of double-handicapped could receive much more information over more hours each day. A mechanical hand was designed in 1963 with this hope in mind.

Now Winalee E. Beeson of the University of Oklahoma has interfaced a new version of this hand to a microcomputer. The hand is manipulated by pneumatic "muscles" which, in turn, are activated by small electronic air valves. As each letter is supplied to the microcomputer, it triggers an algorithm which causes the hand, starting in a neutral position, to produce the corresponding sign and then return to neutral. At present the prototype system is slower than a human manual signer, but Beeson has ideas for speeding it up.

With a network of these systems, Beeson points out, a group could carry on a "discussion," with each member "listening" through an artificial hand and "talking" by typing on his computer terminal which would drive other members' artificial hands.

Source: Myers, W. Personal computers aid the handicapped. *IEEE Micro,* 1982, 2(1), p. 35.

The experience of Howard F. Batie of Herndon, Virginia, gives us a glimpse of how important the mere act of communication can be to a handicapped person. After Batie demonstrated the use of his communication system to his first user, a nonvocal 50-year-old cerebral palsy victim named Lois, she sent Batie her first verbal message to another human being:

"THANKS, THANKS, THANKS, THANKS."

According to Batie, Lois' first connected sentence in 50 years was addressed to her mother:

"Dear Mother: Thank you for all the patient love I have received all my life." (Myers, 1982, p. 39)

Great imagination is required to forecast the future. You and the other students in the class might find it enjoyable to brainstorm the advances that might occur in your lifetimes. Perhaps trying to predict the developments that may occur in the next twenty years would be difficult enough. But keep in mind that many of the technological solutions to problems that we have described so far and that you will read about in the other chapters are very costly and not available to most handicapped individuals today. You might want to think about these questions, too:

How can technological developments be made more available to handicapped children and adults?

How can our society afford to make the newest technology available to every person who can benefit from it?

How can it afford not to?

1. Special education is not just for the mentally retarded. It includes special services for the learning disabled, emotionally disturbed, physically handicapped, hearing impaired, visually impaired, speech and language disordered, and gifted and talented.

2. Answering the question of how many children in the United States need special education depends on the person you ask. When Public Law 94-142 was passed, it was assumed that over 8 million children were handicapped for educational purposes. Many special educators and advocates for the handicapped still believe that is a reasonable estimate, but some government officials now argue that the figure is closer to 4 million. Studies published by the U.S. General Accounting Office in 1981 showed that about 4.3 million children were receiving special education services, but the same studies indicated that many handicapped children still were not receiving any special education or were receiving inadequate services.

3. The first special education services in the United States were provided in the early part of the nineteenth century. At first special education was something provided in public and private institutions and special schools. After compulsory education laws became common in the late 1800s, special classes in public schools were begun in large cities. The first special classes served truants, delinquents, mildly retarded children, and immigrant children whose language and cultural differences made it difficult for them to be assimilated into the regular public school classes.

4. Mainstreaming means placing handicapped and nonhandicapped children together for education. To some extent, you have confused mainstreaming with deinstitutionalization. In some cases children who were in institutions may be placed in public schools, usually in special classes. But a more common mainstreaming practice is moving handicapped children from full-time placement in segregated special classes into regular classes for part or all of the school day.

5. The federal special education law (PL 94–142) states that handicapped children must be educated with nonhandicapped children to the greatest possible extent consistent with appropriate education. For some children this will mean mainstreaming, for others it will not. The notion that all handicapped children must be mainstreamed is a gross misinterpretation of the letter and the intent of the law.

6. You could join a variety of professional organizations that might contribute to your professional development. We suggest that you first give consideration to joining the Council for Exceptional Children, the major professional organization for special educators. CEC has a number of divisions you can join for a small additional membership fee. The divisions serve special educators with interest in particular categories of exceptionality or types of service. We'd like to point out that CEC has state and local chapters (of which you are automatically a member when you join the national organization) and that student membership rates are available.

7. It is not literally true that appropriate education for a handicapped child means there is no limit to what a school system must provide. Appropriate education is not defined in PL 94-142, and exactly what services must be provided for a handicapped child is an issue still being debated in the courts. A variety of interpretations have been suggested. However, in a recent decision involving a deaf child (the Rowley case), the U.S. Supreme Court held that a school system did not need to provide every service that might improve the child's ability to achieve. You should remember that the Court was very careful, though, to restrict its judgment to this single case; future cases may yield a different outcome. Furthermore, the Supreme Court did affirm the right of handicapped children to a specialized, individualized education reasonably calculated to benefit the child.

8. The most important technology for you to master is the technology of instruction. You will need to know a lot about the conditions under which children learn, how to state objectives, to choose examples, to sequence tasks, to analyze errors, to provide feedback and reinforcement, and to monitor progress. You will probably need to know something about the other technologies that may be applied to the children you teach, but you probably will not need an in-depth understanding of those technologies. New technologies tend to be "user friendly." You will be able to leave a lot of technical expertise in the hands of other specialists. But don't lose sight of the fact that you must become a specialist in helping children learn. You *will* need to be an expert in the technology of teaching.

SUMMARY

The concept of variability—the fact that children differ markedly in the rate at which they learn—is the foundation for the field of special education. It is also the cause of some of the current controversies in the field.

Special educators work with exceptional children—children who are so different from most others that the usual educational programs are not appropriate. These children may be mentally retarded, learning disabled, emotionally disturbed, physically handicapped, hearing impaired, visually impaired, speech and language disordered, or gifted and talented. How exceptionality is defined is often the subject of debate, since the definitions are often determined by cultural tradition, money, and politics rather than scientific research. Today special education is defined as specially designed instruction intended to meet the needs of exceptional children. It encompasses teaching procedures, materials, equipment, and/or facilities.

Education for exceptional children is provided through a variety of arrangements from regular classrooms to residential schools.

Estimates of the prevalence of various handicaps among American children of school age range from 4.5 million to 8 million. But regardless of which figure is correct, it is clear that today not all exceptional children are receiving special education services.

One of the most important events in recent years in opening doors for the handicapped and in bringing the plight of exceptional children to public attention was a federal law, PL 94-142, the Education of All Handicapped Children Act, passed by Congress in 1975. It requires free and appropriate education for all exceptional children, in the least restrictive environment possible. This law and Section 504 of the Rehabilitation Act of 1973, which prohibits discrimination on the basis of handicap, have also been controversial because compliance can be expensive in some cases, and because the accompanying regulations are complicated and subject to varying interpretation.

Systematic efforts to teach the handicapped were uncommon until the early nineteenth century. By late in the century, when free public education became the norm in America, special classes began to be established in the public schools in major cities. But the recognition that handicapped children are entitled to a full range of educational services did not become widespread until the late 1960s, when activists began to publicize abuses such as misidentification, misplacement, denial of service, nonrecognition of parental rights, lack of planning, and dumping of children into special classes or schools on the basis of only one or a cursory evaluation.

To combat abuses and to improve their efforts, special educators work through a variety of professional organizations. The Council for Exceptional Children is the primary organization for special educators, but they also work with and belong to associations of psychologists and medical professionals, as well as parent associations that work for more appropriate education for their children.

Current issues in special education today revolve around accurate estimates of the prevalence of handicapping conditions among American children, around defining the scope and limits of what constitutes an appropriate education, and around defining criteria for the "least restrictive environment" required by federal law. The question of the limits of appropriateness is currently being interpreted and decided in the courts. The definition of least restrictive environment has led to reexamination and redefinition of concepts such as normalization and mainstreaming, and to support for the idea of a wide variety of placement options for exceptional children.

In addition to new legal tools, special education is also being revolutionized by technological advances that are making it possible for the handicapped to live more independently and more fully in society. Some advances are aimed at prevention of handicapping conditions and at early detection; others are providing new teaching methods, as well as new equipment and materials. But technology can only provide tools, not solutions to problems. And it has costs as well as benefits, for it sometimes solves one problem and creates others. Special educators today work on an exciting frontier, one where rapid change is likely to continue.

REFERENCES

BASSUK, E.L., & GERSON, S. Deinstitutionalization and mental health services. *Scientific American*, 1978, *238*, 46–53.

BATEMAN, B. Legal and ethical dilemmas of special educators. *Exceptional Education Quarterly*, 1982, *2* (4), 57–67.

BATEMAN, B., & HERR, C. Law and special education. In J.M. Kauffman & D.P. Hallahan (Eds.), *Handbook of special education*. Englewood Cliffs, N.J.: Prentice-Hall, 1981.

BLATT, B., & KAPLAN, F. *Christmas in Purgatory: A photographic essay on mental retardation*. Boston: Allyn and Bacon, 1966.

BORAIKO, A.A. The chip: Electronic mini-marvel that is changing your life. *National Geographic*, 1982, *162*(4), 420–456.

CHILDREN'S DEFENSE FUND. *Unclaimed children: The failure of public responsibility to children and adolescents in need of mental health services*. Washington, D.C.: Author, 1982.

CRUICKSHANK, W.M. Least-restrictive placement: Administrative wishful thinking. *Journal of Learning Disabilities*, 1977, *10*, 193–194.

DUNN, L.M. Special education for the mildly retarded: Is much of it justifiable? *Exceptional Children*, 1968, *35*, 5–22.

DYBWAD, G. Avoiding misconceptions of mainstreaming, the least restrictive environment, and normalization. *Exceptional Children*, 1980, *47*, 85–88.

ENGELMANN, S., & CARNINE, D. *Theory of instruction: Principles and applications*. New York: Irvington, 1982.

GENERAL ACCOUNTING OFFICE. *Disparities still exist in who gets special education*. Gaithersburg, Md.: Author, 1981.

HALLAHAN, D.P., LLOYD, J.W., KAUFFMAN, J.M., & LOPER, A.B. Academic problems. In R. Morris & T. Kratochwill (Eds.), *Practice of child therapy: A textbook of methods*. New York: Pergamon, 1983.

HOFFMAN, E. The American public school and the deviant child: The origins of their involvement. *Journal of Special Education*, 1975, *9*, 415–423.

HORN, J.L. *The education of exceptional children: A consideration of public school problems and policies in the field of differentiated education*. New York: Century, 1924.

KATZEN, K. An open letter to CEC. *Exceptional Children*, 1980, *48*, 582.

KAUFFMAN, J.M. Social policy issues in special education and related services for emotionally disturbed children and youth. In M.M. Noel & N.G. Haring (Eds.), *Progress or change: Issues in educating the emotionally disturbed.* Vol. 1. *Identification and program planning.* Seattle, Wash.: Program Development Assistance System, 1982.

KNEEDLER, R.D., & HALLAHAN, D.P. Self-monitoring of on-task behavior with learning-disabled children: Current studies and directions. *Exceptional Education Quarterly,* 1981, *2*(3), 73–82.

LANE, H. *The wild boy of Aveyron.* Cambridge, Mass.: Harvard University Press, 1976.

LEINHARDT, G., & PALLAY, A. Restrictive educational settings: Exile or haven? *Review of Educational Research,* 1982, *52,* 557–578.

MAGLIOCCA, L., & STEPHENS, T.M. Child identification or child inventory? A critique of the federal design of child-identification systems implemented under PL 94-142. *Journal of Special Education,* 1980, *14,* 23–36.

MARTIN, R. Report on recent Supreme Court decision. *Association for Children with Learning Disabilities Newsletter,* 1982, No. 146, 20–24.

MYERS, W. Personal computers aid the handicapped. *IEEE Micro,* 1982, *2*(1), 26–40.

OMANG, J. Bell withdraws 6 proposals for educating handicapped. *The Washington Post,* September 30, 1982, Sec. A.

POLLOWAY, E.A., & SMITH, J.D. Changes in mild mental retardation: Population, programs, and perspectives. *Exceptional Children,* in press.

RIETH, H.J., POLSGROVE, L., & SEMMEL, M.I. Instructional variables that make a difference: Attention to task and beyond. *Exceptional Education Quarterly,* 1981, *2*(3), 61–71.

SARASON, S.B., & DORIS, J. *Educational handicap, public policy, and social history.* New York: Free Press, 1979.

MENTAL RETARDATION

2

1. Tim, my 7-year-old son, is in the second grade. He has just been diagnosed as educable mentally retarded. I know he does not do well in school and is behind his classmates, but he doesn't seem to have any difficulty at home. Everything seemed all right until he started school last year. Wouldn't we have noticed earlier if Tim really is mentally retarded?

2. My husband has a sister who has been severely mentally retarded since birth. My husband and I both want to have children, but we're afraid. Is there a chance that my sister-in-law's retardation was caused by an inherited condition? Do my husband and I have a greater chance of having a severely retarded child?

3. Although I teach in a self-contained class for educable mentally retarded children, some of my children have IQs that are considered to be in the trainable range. I'm not sure what to do when developing programs for these children. Should I attempt to teach these children some academic skills, or would that only frustrate them?

4. Bill, our son, is 18 years old and has been in special education classes for the educable mentally retarded since he was 9. Next year he will be graduating from high school, and we are concerned about his future. He can read, although not very well, and he has received training in some job-related skills. He is responsible and wants to get out on his own. We are afraid it will be difficult for him to find a job, especially if he discloses the fact that he is mentally retarded. How should we deal with this situation?

5. Our neighbors have a baby with Down's syndrome. They plan on raising the little girl by themselves. I know they can take care of her while she is an infant, but isn't it true that the child will eventually have to be placed in an institution? Wouldn't it be easier on them and on her to institutionalize her now?

6. As a resource teacher for EMR children in an elementary school, I am required to use the same basal readers and arithmetic texts used by the school system. I had been taught that mentally retarded children learn at a slower rate and require a lot of repetition. I have adapted the presentation of the available material. Yet many of my students are not grasping the concepts, even with the extra practice sessions. Am I using the wrong approach, or should I assume the material is just too difficult?

7. Our friends' son John is mentally retarded and at the age of 3 has not yet begun to speak and cannot walk unassisted. They have requested that we bring over our child, who is about the same age, to play with John. Our son is very verbal and active, and we are afraid that he may be slowed down by playing with John. Will it harm our child developmentally to play regularly with John?

8. Two mentally retarded children are mainstreamed into my fifth grade class. Ann and Carl are in the resource class for academic subjects, but they are in my class during physical education, lunch, music, art, assemblies, and so on. The problem is that none of the other children in my class will approach these children. To make matters worse, Ann and Carl do not even associate with each other. I hate to see these children so isolated, but what can I do to help?

The field of mental retardation has undergone a number of changes, ranging from whom we now call mentally retarded to how we now go about educating them. Today's special educator must be attuned to ideas from a variety of fields—medicine, sociology, psychology, physical therapy, and regular education, to name but a few of the more obvious ones. And more than ever, professionals from these other fields are finding it necessary to keep current on developments in the education of mentally retarded individuals. Let's listen in on the following hypothetical cocktail party conversation between Tim Bowen, a pediatrician, and Elaine Walker, an elementary school principal. Both professionals have been in the field for years, and both have found that rapid changes in how we deal with the mentally retarded have meant that they too must be willing to keep up to date.

One of the things that should be immediately apparent from the conversation is just how much changes in how special educators deal with the mentally retarded has also changed others' attitudes and behaviors toward the retarded. Although it is far from accurate to say that all physicians and school principals are as enlightened as Tim and Elaine, we are much more likely today to find professionals taking the time to learn more about the special children who enter their lives.

Bowen: I did want to ask you some questions about your school the next chance I got. What I'm most interested in is how this mainstreaming idea is working out at your school. Living right down the block from the school, I can't help but notice how different some of the children are. Some of the kids I see bused in there in the mornings are really severely involved—the kind of kids I and my colleagues used to recommend should be institutionalized.

Walker: I'll be the first to admit that I've been surprised by how well it's going. I'd been a principal for almost ten years when they told me they wanted to put a class of severely and profoundly retarded kids in my building. Well, we'd had a class for educable kids and a class for trainable kids for a number of years, but I was really skeptical about putting kids with IQs in the 20s and 30s in the same building with regular education kids.

Bowen: I would have been too.

Walker: Well, it's working beautifully. The teacher is great. She really works on the basic self-help skills—feeding, toileting, dressing themselves, things like that. As you know, many kids functioning at that low a level intellectually also have a lot of physical handicaps. So the teacher works with the physical therapist and occupational therapist in helping the children to learn independent living skills.

Bowen: But how about the mainstreaming aspect? How's that working?

Walker: There's no really good way to measure it, of course. But I can't help but think that their being in the same building with regular-ed kids is good for them, as well as their families and the other regular-ed children. I think it's a lot healthier for all concerned to let these kids mingle with others so everyone feels they don't need to be hidden away. We try to integrate them as much as possible. They eat in the cafeteria at the same time as everyone else and go to assemblies with everyone else. In addition, we just started a program where some of the regular-ed seventh- and eighth-graders volunteer to work with some of the kids on a supervised basis.

Bowen: You mentioned a few minutes ago the classes for educable and trainable students. What are some of the major changes in educational programming for those kids?

Walker: Well, the biggest change is in the prevocational focus, especially for the trainable class. It used to be that vocational programming didn't start until high school. Now, much of the curriculum emphasis for trainable-level students is on preparing them to benefit from vocational programming.

Bowen: What, specifically, is different?

Walker: There's a lot more emphasis on what's called "functional academics"—academics with a purpose, I like to call it. For example, they're teaching them how to read in order to read instructions for recipes, how to use telephone directories, how to read the newspaper.

Bowen: I see. You and I were taught academics for their own sake or in order to learn more academics, but they're being taught them to learn how to live independently.

Walker: Right. At least, there's much more emphasis on that. The way Jack Harper, the trainable class teacher. . . .

Bowen: You mean Bill Harper's boy?

Walker: Right. He's been with us for three years. Anyway, Jack says that since these kids are not the quickest learners in the world, it makes sense to work on making sure they are able to have truly functional academic skills. Independent living skills are crucial for their adjustment prospects, as well as for how we define them. It used to be that a child merely had to score low on an IQ test to be labeled retarded. Many special educators pointed out that it didn't make sense to call someone retarded just because he had a low IQ if he also held a job and raised a family. So now a student needs to be low in IQ as well as in what's called "adaptive behavior" in order to be diagnosed as retarded.

Bowen: How do you measure adaptive behavior?

Walker: That's the hard part. There are some scales available that give a pretty fair indication of adaptive behavior skills—things like ability to go shopping alone, to dress themselves, to get along with others. But Tim, tell me, what's new in the world of pediatric medicine that we educators should know about?

Bowen: I have to confess that one of the reasons I was asking about mainstreaming was that until a couple of years ago, I used to encourage parents to institutionalize their kids if they were severely and profoundly retarded. From what I'd been reading in the papers about deinstitutionalization and some of the miscellaneous reading I was doing in professional journals, I decided to back off quite a bit. I was hoping that you were favorably impressed with the classes for the retarded in your school. Not that institutionalization isn't appropriate in some cases, but I think it shouldn't automatically be the only alternative.

Walker: How about other medical advances? How about causes of mental retardation, for example?

Bowen: Unfortunately, we're not much closer to figuring out the causes of the milder cases. We are finding out, however, that a lot of things in our environment in excessive concentrations can affect the unborn child. High lead levels and excessive radiation are real dangers.

Walker: How about genetics? Any new discoveries?

Bowen: Yes, but these breakthroughs apply to rare types of severe and profound retardation.

Walker: How about that procedure where the doctor draws out fluid from around the unborn child? What's that called? Amniocentesis?

Bowen: Right. Well, it works, if that's what you mean. Unfortunately, most cases of retardation can't be determined that way. A few can, however. Down's syndrome is the most common one. Since the chances of Down's syndrome increase dramatically in babies of mothers in their late thirties and early forties, many doctors encourage older pregnant women to undergo this test.

Walker: Doesn't it have to do with chromosomes?

Bowen: Right. Down's syndrome results from chromosomal abnormality. In amniocentesis, the doctor draws out some of the fluid around the fetus and that fluid is tested to see if the chromosomes are normal. Listen. I hate to break off this conversation, but I think I see Ruth trying to get my attention.

Walker: It's been good chatting with you, Tim. Stop by the school, and I'll give you a tour of the building, including our special classes.

TODAY'S DEFINITION OF MENTAL RETARDATION

At one time, mental retardation was viewed as a permanent condition. At one time, a low score on an intelligence test was enough to label a person. Today, however, we take a much more flexible view. We allow for the possibility that sometimes a person can be retarded at one point in time, but not at another. We allow for the possibility that sometimes an individual can score low on an intelligence test, but still be able to function adequately in society. Read on and you will see that IQ is only half the picture when it comes to declaring a person mentally retarded. Something called "adaptive behavior" is equally important.

The AAMD (American Association on Mental Deficiency), the primary professional organization in mental retardation, has adopted the following definition in its *Manual on Terminology and Classification in Mental Retardation*:

> **Mental retardation** refers to significantly subaverage general intellectual functioning resulting in or associated with impairments in adaptive behavior and manifested during the developmental period. (Grossman, in press)

WHAT IS "SIGNIFICANTLY SUBAVERAGE GENERAL INTELLECTUAL FUNCTIONING"? General intellectual functioning is measured by means of an individually administered intelligence test (we will have more to say about IQ tests later). The AAMD manual uses as a guideline the position that a person should not be considered retarded unless he or she scores 70 or below on an IQ test. The manual does state, however, that the cutoff point could go as high as 75, especially in school settings. This higher cutoff score reflects the fact that schools have traditionally used a score of 75 as the criterion for placement in classes for the mentally retarded.

WHAT IS "ADAPTIVE BEHAVIOR"? **Adaptive behavior** refers to how well a person is able to adapt to environmental demands. Today's special educator recognizes that some people may score low on an IQ test but still be able to hold a job, get along with friends, and in a variety of other ways "fit in" with peers. What is meant by adaptive behavior is different from one *age* to another and from one *situation* to another. If you are a preschooler, you will need sensory-motor, communication, self-help, and socialization skills to adapt to your environment. If you are an adult, you will also need job-related skills. If you are an inner-city black teenager, you may need "street-smarts." If you're a "country boy," you may need to know how to chew tobacco. Admittedly difficult to define and measure, adaptive behavior is still crucial to today's definition of mental retardation. Whereas it was formerly not only possible, but actually the rule, to identify individuals as retarded based on the results of an IQ test, today they must also show signs of poor adaptive behavior before they are so classified.

WHAT IS "DEVELOPMENTAL PERIOD"? The AAMD manual specifies that the mental retardation should occur sometime between conception and the eighteenth birthday.

CLASSIFICATION

In addition to deciding whether a person is retarded, special educators are also concerned with just how retarded the person is. Two systems are typically used to classify retarded individuals according to severity of retardation—that of the AAMD, and that primarily used by school systems. In practice, both systems are based on how high or low a person scores on an IQ test (see Table 2–1).

CLASSIFICATION BY SCHOOL PERSONNEL

Traditionally, school officials have divided retarded pupils into classes for the educable and for the trainable. The original idea behind this separation was the belief that educable students, being closer in IQ to normal pupils (IQs between 75 and 50), could be *educated*, although at a lower level, in academic subject matter. Trainable individuals (IQs between 50 and 25), on the other hand, would need to be *trained* in lower-level skills necessary

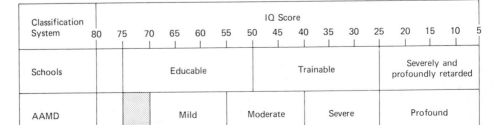

TABLE 2–1

The Two Most Common Classification Systems

Classification System	IQ Score
	80 75 70 65 60 55 50 45 40 35 30 25 20 15 10 5
Schools	Educable (70–50) Trainable (50–25) Severely and profoundly retarded
AAMD	Mild Moderate Severe Profound

for independent living. These labels have sometimes made us think in narrow terms regarding retarded people's abilities. While it is true that, in general, educable children will benefit more from academic materials than trainable students, this distinction will not always hold up for individual pupils. Today's special educator realizes that the line drawn between the two should not be taken too literally, but should be viewed merely as a guideline to instruction. Another recent development depicted in Table 2–1 is the classification of "severely and profoundly retarded" for students with IQs below the trainable level. It is only in recent years that the public schools have established classes for these children. In the past, they were often called "custodial," reflecting the attitude that they automatically belonged in a residential institution.

CLASSIFICATION BY THE AAMD

The AAMD classification system is an attempt to avoid the problems of stereotyping that have sometimes resulted from the use of the labels "educable" and "trainable." The terms "mild," "moderate," "severe," and "profound" are more neutral in tone. This is probably due to the fact that they can mean a variety of things other than retardation. It is not stretching the point too far to state that one could, for example, be mildly, moderately, severely, or profoundly heavy, good-looking, or even smart. The shaded area between IQ 70 and 75 in Table 2–1 reflects the AAMD's position that scores obtained on IQ tests should not be viewed as infallible. According to the AAMD, an IQ of 70 can be used in most cases as a cutoff for mild retardation, but children whose IQs are between 70 and 75 should not be denied special education services if they truly need them.

PREVALENCE

Taking a strictly statistical view of how many people *should* test in the retarded range on a standardized IQ test, we arrive at a figure of 2.27 percent of the population. This is based on the assumption that measured intelligence is normally distributed. A **normal distribution** is a continuum of scores that vary from the average score by predictable amounts. Fewer scores fall away from the average score at the lower and higher ends of the continuum and more scores fall near the average score in the middle. Figure 2–1 shows the normal curve for intelligence based on scores on the most popular individual intelligence test, the Wechsler Intelligence Scale for Children–Revised (WISC-R), which has an average score of 100. You'll note from the shape of the curve that most people are "bunched up" in the middle ranges—for example, between scores of 85 to 115—while many fewer individuals score in the lower or higher ranges—for example, below 70 or above 130. According to Figure 2–1, we see that a total of 2.27 percent of the population should score below 70, the usual cutoff score for mental retardation.

When actual surveys are conducted, however, they rarely show a prevalence figure of exactly 2.27 percent. In fact, estimates vary considerably, with some figures nearly twice as high as others. A 1981 federal government report, for instance, stated that prevalence estimates for mental retardation range from 1.3 to 2.3 percent of the popula-

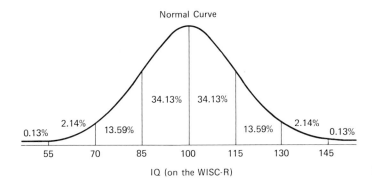

FIGURE 2-1
Normal Curve of IQ Scores

tion. One of the reasons for this variation is the trend toward considering adaptive behavior as important as IQ in identifying mental retardation. Using the AAMD definition, which states that a student must have poor adaptive behavior as well as lowered intelligence in order to be considered mentally retarded, results in lower prevalence than if we use lower intelligence alone (MacMillan, 1982).

ASSESSMENT OF MENTAL RETARDATION

Two broad areas are assessed to determine whether a person is retarded—intelligence and adaptive behavior. Although related to a certain degree, there are enough cases of individuals scoring in the retarded range in intelligence and still displaying adequate adaptive behavior that we need to consider the two separately.

IQ TESTS

There are two different categories of intelligence tests—those that can be administered to groups of individuals and those that must be administered individually. Individual IQ tests should always be used instead of group tests when a child is being tested for possible special education placement. Because of their complexity, individual IQ tests should only be administered and interpreted by qualified psychologists. The extra time and effort required for an individual IQ test is well worth it in terms of its superior accuracy.

Two of the most common IQ tests are the Stanford-Binet and the WISC–R (Wechsler Intelligence Scale for Children—Revised). The WISC–R is the most popular. One reason is that it is divided into a verbal and performance scale. The psychologist can thus obtain a verbal IQ, a performance IQ, and a full-scale IQ (a composite of the verbal and performance scale) for each child tested. Some psychologists find differentiating between verbal and performance IQ helpful in interpreting a person's strengths and weaknesses.

IQ tests such as the WISC–R are constructed by administering test items to large groups of individuals at several different age levels. In this way, it can be determined, for example, how many items the *average* 10-year-old should get right. Roughly speaking,

IQ TESTS: MYTHS AND FACTS

There are a number of myths surrounding IQ tests. While certainly not held by everyone, we've listed some of the more common ones below.

Myth: IQ is inherited.
Myth: IQ is not inherited.
Fact: Both are myths. Virtually all authorities now agree that how well a person will score on an IQ test is determined by an interaction between genetic and environmental factors (see Focus on p. 47).

Myth: IQ tests are not predictors of school success.
Fact: A score on an IQ test is the single best index, even though not perfect, of how well a child will do in school.

Myth: IQ scores are a completely accurate predictor of how successful and happy a person's life will be.
Fact: They may be the best predictor of school achievement, but IQ tests are not the ''be-all and end-all'' when it comes to assessing ability to function in society. A high IQ does not automatically guarantee success or happiness. Creativity, artistic ability, and motivation are just a few of the other areas that are also important in success and happiness.

Myth: Because of cultural bias, IQ tests are useless with minority groups.
Fact: All tests, including IQ tests, that have been standardized on the dominant white culture are culturally biased to some degree. Because they are biased, however, does not mean they are useless. Even for minority children they are still the best predictor of academic success in our schools today. They are much less useful, however, as an indicator of a minority child's inherent ability.

Myth: IQ tests alone determine eligibility for special class placement.
Fact: IQ tests are only one of a number of measures in the decision-making process. Other components may include such things as measures of current academic performance, teacher reports, information from parent interviews, and medical histories.

Myth: IQ scores do not change.
Fact: Environmental factors can have a positive or negative impact on IQ scores. In addition, the earlier in the life of a child that the IQ test is administered, the more likely it is that the score obtained will not be representative of that child's intelligence. Infant and preschool IQ tests in particular are not very accurate, except for cases of severe retardation.

if you are 10 years old (this is your **chronological age**) but only get right as many items as the average 8-year-old (this is called **mental age**), you will have an IQ of 80. This is determined by dividing your mental age (8) by your chronological age (10) and multiplying by 100 to eliminate the decimal point: $(8/10) \times 100 = 80$.

Two other intelligence tests that are newer and not as widely used as the Stanford-Binet and WISC-R are the SOMPA (System of Multicultural Pluralistic Assessment) (Mercer and Lewis, 1978), and the K-ABC (Kaufman Assessment Battery for Children) (Kaufman and Kaufman, 1983). Both tests attempt to minimize cultural bias by including methods for scoring that compare a child's score with that of his or her own cultural group. In addition, the K-ABC is more oriented toward viewing intelligence as problem-solving ability rather than acquired knowledge. Both the SOMPA and K-ABC are too new to determine just how useful they will be to educators.

ADAPTIVE BEHAVIOR

There is much folklore surrounding IQ tests (see Focus on p. 44). When done by competent professionals, IQ tests can be useful tools. But they do not measure completely accurately a person's ability to cope with everyday living. A superior IQ does not automatically translate into a successful life. Nor does a low IQ doom a person to misery. Today, special educators and psychologists are more aware than ever that other factors are also important in deciding how well an individual will function in society. The importance

---

TABLE 2–2

Major Areas Assessed by AAMD Adaptive Behavior Scale—School Edition

PART ONE: EVERYDAY LIVING SKILLS	PART TWO: PERSONALITY AND BEHAVIOR
DOMAIN 1 Independent Functioning *Subdomains:* Eating Toilet use Cleanliness Appearance Care of clothing Dressing and undressing Travel Other independent functioning	DOMAIN 10 Aggressiveness
	DOMAIN 11 Antisocial versus Social Behavior
	DOMAIN 12 Rebelliousness
	DOMAIN 13 Trustworthiness
	DOMAIN 14 Withdrawal versus Involvement
	DOMAIN 15 Mannerisms
	DOMAIN 16 Interpersonal Manners
DOMAIN 2 Physical Development *Subdomains:* Sensory development Motor development	DOMAIN 17 Acceptability of Vocal Habits
	DOMAIN 18 Acceptability of Habits
	DOMAIN 19 Activity Level
DOMAIN 3 Economic Activity *Subdomains:* Money handling and budgeting Shopping skills	DOMAIN 20 Symptomatic Behavior
	DOMAIN 21 Use of Medications
DOMAIN 4 Language Development *Subdomains:* Expression Comprehension Social language development	
DOMAIN 5 Numbers and Time	
DOMAIN 6 Prevocational Activity	
DOMAIN 7 Self-Direction *Subdomains:* Initiative Perseverance Leisure time	
DOMAIN 8 Responsibility	
DOMAIN 9 Socialization	

Travel Subdomain

Item 14	Sense of direction (circle only one)
Goes a few blocks from school grounds without getting lost	3
Goes around school grounds without getting lost	2
Goes around school room alone	1
Gets lost whenever outside school room	0

Item 15	Public transportation (circle all that apply)
Rides on train, long-distance bus, or plane independently	1
Rides in taxi independently	1
Rides subway or city bus for unfamiliar journeys independently	1
Rides subway or city bus for familiar journeys independently	1
Does none of the above	0

of everyday living skills has resulted in the development of adaptive behavior measures. Two of the most commonly used are the AAMD Adaptive Behavior Scale—School Edition (Lambert and Windmiller, 1981) and the Adaptive Behavior Inventory for Children (ABIC) (Mercer and Lewis, 1977).

THE AAMD ADAPTIVE BEHAVIOR SCALE—SCHOOL EDITION. The AAMD scale is divided into two sections. One is designed for use in assessing daily living skills, and the other for personality and behavior. Table 2–2 lists the domains and subdomains included in the parts of the scale. Table 2–3 contains two items from the AAMD scale that are used to assess the travel subdomain of the independent functioning domain.

THE ADAPTIVE BEHAVIOR INVENTORY FOR CHILDREN (ABIC). ABIC assesses adaptive behavior in six areas—family, community, peer relations, nonacademic school roles, earner/consumer, and self-maintenance. Like the AAMD scale, the ABIC measures a variety of things that common sense tells you are necessary for a productive and happy life.

CAUSES

There are many different ways to group the various causes of mental retardation. We will discuss the causes for mild versus more severe cases of retardation separately. For more severe retardation, we will look at causes related to genetic factors and those related to physical damage to the brain.

In very few cases (estimates range between 6 and 15 percent) can we specify the cause of an individual's retardation. If you wonder why we cannot be more certain, it helps if you think of the mentally retarded population as being composed of two subgroups—the mildly retarded (those with IQs roughly between 50 and 70) and those whose retardation is in the moderate range or lower (those with IQs below 50). As MacMillan (1982) has noted, these two subgroups, while overlapping to some degree, are distinct in many ways, especially with regard to causes of the retardation.

MILD RETARDATION

The vast majority of the retarded are mildly retarded. Their retardation is relatively subtle. They usually differ very little from others in physical appearance and are typically not identified as retarded until they enter school and fail to keep up with their peers. They are often from economically deprived backgrounds. The term **cultural-familial retardation** is frequently applied to persons in the mild range of retardation. Originally, the term was restricted to persons in the mildly retarded range who had no evidence of brain pathology, and who had at least one retarded parent and one or more retarded brothers or sisters (Heber, 1959). The assumption was that the retardation was due to genetic or social-environmental factors.

In recent years, popular use of the term has focused more on the social-environmental rather than the genetic factors. Today when you hear someone say that a particular child is "culturally-familially retarded," it usually means that the child is mildly retarded, with no evidence of brain pathology, and comes from an economically disadvantaged background. The assumption is that the poor social environment in some way leads to the child's retardation. The "in some way" of the previous sentence is the key to why so few cases of mild retardation can be specified. We know that a whole host of factors often associated with belonging to the lower socioeconomic segments of society—poor parenting, nutrition, schools, for example—could place children at risk for mental retardation. It is almost always impossible, however, to document the links in individual cases. We may *guess* that William, with an IQ of 65, who lives with his maternal grandmother because his father has abandoned the family and his mother is an alcoholic, who has always attended the poorest schools, and who has never been encouraged to achieve academically, is mildly retarded because of social-environmental circumstances. But we cannot prove it. And one of the reasons we cannot is because for every William who does score in the mildly retarded range, there are a number of Jonathans who also come from deprived backgrounds but who do not end up being retarded (see the next Focus).

 ## NATURE VERSUS NURTURE

One of the oldest controversies in the fields of special education and psychology concerns how much intelligence is determined by heredity (nature) versus environment (nurture). In fact, the debate has not been confined to the pages of scientific journals; it has also received widespread coverage in the popular media (Herrnstein, 1982). Nearly everyone believes intelligence to be an important thing to have as much of as possible. So when you start talking about how it is that some people have more of it than others, you immediately enter the arena of sociology and politics. Once this happens, unfortunately, scientific arguments for and against nature or nurture tend to get lost.

At one time, scientists spent their careers attempting to prove that either nature or nurture was the all-important factor. Today, most authorities agree that it is not really a case of "either-or." We recognize that there is some interaction between hereditary and environmental factors. What still remains a topic for debate, however, is exactly how much of a person's intelligence can be explained by hereditary versus environmental factors.

Unfortunately, there is no simple answer. The data we have available are simply not clear enough to provide us with the definitive answer. The proponents of nurture point to a number of experiments with animals and a more modest number done with humans in which intelligent behavior was raised through environmental enrichment and educational intervention. The proponents of nature point to a large number of studies (some of which

FOCUS

have been questioned on methodological grounds) comparing the relationship between IQ scores of pairs of individuals with varying degrees of environmental and genetic similarity (for example, twins reared apart versus separately, children and their natural parents versus children and parents who adopted them).

Even though we don't have a precise answer to the question, "How much is our intelligence due to heredity and how much is it due to environment?," we do know enough from careful reviews (Bouchard and Mcgue, 1981; Scarr-Salapatek, 1975) to make the following statements:

1. Genetic factors are at least as important as environmental factors in determining intelligence.
2. An individual's IQ score can change dramatically based on environmental conditions. Even the most steadfast proponent of the genetic position would argue that (except for the severely retarded or extremely gifted) a person's IQ could be changed by about 25 points due to environmental factors (Scarr-Salapatek, 1975).
3. Attempts to boost IQ scores through educational intervention have met with mixed success. We now know that to do it is not impossible, but we also know that it is a more challenging task than we had at first thought.

MORE SEVERE RETARDATION

Causes of retardation are more easily determined for those scoring in the moderate range or below. Unlike the mildly retarded, the more severely retarded often differ from others in physical appearance. Their retardation is more apparent overall and is frequently diagnosed before entrance into school, sometimes shortly after birth. MacMillan (1982) divides the known causes into two broad categories—those due to genetic factors and those due to physical damage to the brain.

GENETIC FACTORS. The study of genetics has led to some important discoveries regarding the causes of some types of mental retardation. Three such conditions are Down's syndrome, PKU (phenylketonuria), and Tay-Sachs disease.

Down's syndrome accounts for approximately 10 percent of moderate and severe cases of mental retardation (MacMillan, 1982). In the past, most individuals with Down's syndrome were moderately or severely retarded. This picture is changing, however, with more and more scoring in the mildly retarded range. The more optimistic outlook is no doubt due to a number of factors, including the success of early intervention programs (Rynders, Spiker, & Horrobin, 1978).

Down's syndrome is probably the type of retardation most people think of when they think of retardation. People with Down's syndrome are relatively easy to identify because they have a distinctive set of physical characteristics. The thick folds of skin in the corners of their eyes, which make their eyes appear to slant upward, unfortunately led to the once popular term *mongoloid* ("mongoloid" being another term for "oriental"). You may have read or heard that Down's syndrome children are always friendly and good-natured. There is, however, very little research evidence to support this claim (Belmont, 1971).

Actually, there are different types of Down's syndrome. All of them, however, are due to some type of chromosomal abnormality in the fetus. Everyone's body, both before and after birth, contains cells. Within each cell is a nucleus. Within each nucleus are chromosomes which contain genes from each of our parents. In the normal individual there are 23 pairs of chromosomes, each pair containing a chromosome from the father and a chromosome from the mother. In the most common type of Down's syndrome, trisomy 21, there is an extra chromosome on the 21st set of chromosomes. In this case, the 21st set is a triplet rather than a pair.

The chances of having a Down's syndrome child increase dramatically with the age of the parents, particularly the mother. Hansen (1978), for example, reports that, if you are a woman between the ages of 20 and 30, your chance of having a Down's syndrome baby is about 1 in 1300; if you are between the ages of 30 and 34, your chance is about 1 in 600; if you are between 35 and 39, your chance is about 1 in 300; and if you are between 40 and 44, your chance is about 1 in 80.

Today, more and more pregnant women, especially those over 35 years of age, are having amniocentesis to verify the chromosomal status of their unborn babies. **Amniocentesis** is a medical procedure; the physician inserts a needle into the amniotic sac of the pregnant woman to draw out a small amount of amniotic fluid surrounding the fetus. This fluid can then be checked for a number of abnormal conditions, Down's syndrome being the most common one.

At one time it was thought that the age of the mother was the only variable of concern in preventing Down's syndrome. Today, however, researchers are discovering that there may be links between Down's syndrome and the age of the father, the amount of the mother's exposure to radiation, and certain viruses (MacMillan, 1982).

PKU (phenylketonuria) is an inherited condition involving the inability of the body to convert phenylalanine (a common food substance found in such things as milk) into tyrosine. The buildup of phenylalanine results in abnormal brain development. PKU can be detected in the first few days after birth through a routine blood test that is now mandatory in many states. If the child has PKU, it can be treated with a special diet. If the condition is diagnosed and treated early enough, the chances of becoming retarded due to the PKU are virtually none. The longer the baby goes without treatment, however, the greater the chances of brain damage. In addition to treating PKU once it has been transmitted to the child, more and more emphasis is being put today on the genetic screening of parents to determine if they are possible carriers of the gene for PKU. Although the chances are very slim (about 1 in 3600) of two carriers marrying, if this does occur, it is generally recommended that the couple seek genetic counseling to determine their chances of producing offspring with PKU.

Tay-Sachs disease, like PKU, is an inherited condition that can appear when both mother and father are carriers. Tay-Sachs disease results in brain damage and eventual death. It occurs almost exclusively in a particular subgroup of Jews—Ashkenazi Jews—whose origins are a specific area in Europe. Massive genetic screening programs have been conducted to identify carriers. In addition, amniocentesis is available as a way of determining if the fetus has Tay-Sachs disease.

PHYSICAL DAMAGE TO THE BRAIN. Damage to the brain can result from a variety of factors we can place under two general headings—infections and environmental hazards.

INFECTIONS. The most common infections that can lead to mental retardation are meningitis and encephalitis and the maternal infections of rubella, syphilis, and herpes simplex. All these infections can result in a number of abnormalities (blindness, deafness, speech defects) in addition to mental retardation. **Meningitis** is an infection of the covering of the brain; **encephalitis** is an infection of the brain itself. **Rubella** (German measles) is most dangerous to the unborn child if the mother has it during the first three months of pregnancy. Because women can now be immunized against rubella, the number of cases is on the decline. Not on the decline, however, are cases of mental retardation due to pregnant women with the venereal diseases of syphilis and, particularly, herpes simplex. Both conditions result from sexual contact. Herpes simplex is on the rise, and unfortunately no cures have yet been found for it.

Two conditions that can result from infections, as well as for other reasons, are microcephalus and hydrocephalus. **Microcephalus** is characterized by a small head with a sloping forehead. **Hydrocephalus** results from an excess of fluid inside or outside the brain. It can be treated by surgically placing a tube in a vein behind the ear or in the neck to drain the fluid.

ENVIRONMENTAL HAZARDS. Today, we are more aware than ever of a variety of environmental hazards that can adversely affect young children or even unborn children. More and more doctors are recommending that pregnant women limit their intake of subtle "poisons" such as tobacco, caffeine, food additives, and alcohol. **Fetal alcohol syndrome** is a term used to describe the condition of impaired offspring of mothers who drink heavily during pregnancy. Mental retardation and a variety of physical problems accompany the fetal alcohol syndrome (Delaney and Hayden, 1977). Radiation is another environmental hazard pregnant women need to be concerned about. The Three-Mile Island incident of 1979 has made us all more aware of the potential power and hazards of atomic radiation. Less dramatic than the hazards of radiation from improperly supervised nuclear plants, but still potentially devastating, is radiation contained in X

More and more doctors are recommending that pregnant women limit their intake of subtle "poisons" such as tobacco, caffeine, food additives, and especially alcohol. Stan Goldblatt, Photo Researchers, Inc.

rays. Physicians should not expose expectant mothers to X rays unless absolutely necessary.

In addition, environmentalists have pointed out that we need to be careful about certain pesticides and metals, such as mercury and lead. Lead used to be a problem when it was used in paint. Although lead-based paint is now outlawed, environmentalists point to high levels of lead in automobile exhaust as a potential hazard. Other environmental factors that sometimes result in mental retardation are anoxia (loss of oxygen to the brain), a blow to the head, malnutrition (of the expectant mother or the young child), and prematurity. Prematurity is sometimes defined as too short a pregnancy or too low a birth weight. In either case, problems such as mental retardation are often the result.

CHARACTERISTICS

INTELLECTUAL CHARACTERISTICS

Through research and experience working with the mentally retarded, we have known for many years that such individuals can have difficulties in virtually all aspects of intellectual functioning—concept learning, memory, attention, and language. These areas of functioning are what we mean when we think of intelligent behavior. Intelligent people typically grasp concepts quickly, remember things easily, are able to attend to the task at hand, and are articulate speakers. The opposite of this profile generally characterizes the mentally retarded. Retarded individuals learn concepts slowly if at all, have difficulty remembering things, exhibit attentional problems, and have speech and language deficiencies.

Knowing that a retarded person is likely to have problems in concept learning, memory, attention, and language, however, doesn't help us much in terms of correcting these difficulties. Today, special educators and psychologists are focusing on discovering why these problems exist and how to go about improving them. Much of their attention is devoted to looking for more general problems that influence such things as concept learning, memory, attention, and language.

At one time, most special educators viewed mental retardation as resulting primarily in structural or physiological defects. They believed that a vast percentage of retarded individuals' poor performance in such things as concept learning, memory, attention, and language could be explained by the idea that they were physiologically defective. The implication of this viewpoint was that therefore not much could be done to improve performance. The reasoning went something like this: "If they suffer physiological defects that result in poor performance, we'll have a hard time helping them because we can't cure their basic physiological deficiencies." Today's orientation is a more optimistic one. Special educators and psychologists are studying what are called executive control processes (Baumeister and Brooks, 1981; Campione and Brown, 1977).

Executive control processes are strategies the individual can use to help himself or herself do better on a variety of tasks involving concept learning, memory, attention, and language. In the area of memory, for example, two such strategies are rehearsal and organization. If you were given a list of ten words—tulip, dog, cat, milk, fox, bread, rose, daffodil, pie, and bird—to memorize, you would probably organize them into three groups: animals (dog, cat, fox, and bird), flowers (tulip, rose, and daffodil), and foods (milk, bread, and pie). You would then rehearse the groups. The retarded individual is unlikely to use executive control processes. What is important, however, is that the retarded individual can be taught to use these strategies. Performance difficulties due to control processes can be helped by educational intervention.

PERSONALITY CHARACTERISTICS

There is much evidence that mentally retarded individuals often have social and emotional problems. This shouldn't be surprising. It is logical that a person's well-being would be influenced by intellectual abilities and limitations. If we experienced more than our share of failure experiences, we too would be likely candidates for developing poor self-concepts. If our intellectual capabilities were limited, we would have a reduced capacity to cope with the complexities of interpersonal relationships.

Many authorities believe that the bulk of the personality problems experienced by the retarded center around their reduced motivation to succeed (Harter, 1978; Harter and Zigler, 1974; Turnure and Zigler, 1964). Harter's (1978) views on the problem of motivation in the retarded are well accepted. She has studied normal versus retarded children's motivation to master tasks. Along with others, she believes that normal children take pleasure in manipulating and mastering their environments. As an adult, you know how good it can feel to accomplish a challenging task. It's no different for children and even infants. The more we succeed, the more we want to try new and more challenging tasks. In other words, success itself is motivating.

Unfortunately, because retarded children have a longer history of failure than do normal children, they are less likely to have this motivation to succeed. In addition, because of their failure experiences, they are candidates to develop what has been referred to as an external rather than an internal locus of control. Individuals with an external locus of control are less apt to believe they are in control of their own destinies. They are dependent on others and believe they are controlled by external forces (such as chance or luck) rather than by their own internal or inner capabilities.

Research has shown that a reduced motivation to succeed and an external locus of control are not characteristic of all retarded individuals. Whether a person develops these motivational problems depends on a wide variety of environmental conditions. For example, mentally retarded individuals who live in institutions are more likely to develop motivational problems than those who do not. This makes sense: Given the regimented life some institutionalized people lead, it is not surprising that they have motivational problems.

TODAY'S EDUCATIONAL METHODS FOR THE MENTALLY RETARDED

The most common placements for mentally retarded children are regular classes, resource rooms, special self-contained classes, special day schools, and residential institutions. The related movements of deinstitutionalization and mainstreaming have had their greatest impact in the area of mental retardation.

Mildly retarded children are more likely than ever to be placed for part of the day in the regular classroom and for the rest of the day in a resource room where they can receive special help. Mildly retarded children who receive most or all of their education in a special self-contained class rather than in a regular classroom with resource room help are more likely than before to be at the lower end of the mildly retarded range. Moderately and severely and profoundly retarded individuals are much less likely to be placed in residential institutions. Moderately retarded children are now usually placed in special self-contained classes, and even severely and profoundly retarded children are beginning to take part in special classes in the public schools. The face of the residential facility is changing, too. The once-popular large residential institution is giving way to large numbers of smaller, **community residential facilities (CRFs)**. A CRF, sometimes called a group home, is a place in an urban or residential neighborhood where from about three to ten retarded adults live under the supervision of houseparents. Before 1960, there were 222 CRFs in the United States; from 1960 to 1970, 1092

OLD REPULSIONS ARE FADING

"I'm going to do the best I can when we get to that church, because if I don't that building will go away." That's a strange perception, but that's the way eleven-year-old Marie Voccaro saw it in 1958, when she and fourteen other residents from an institution traveled to an experimental Saturday special-education program in a mid-western community church. Ever since Marie had been committed to the institution five years earlier by a judge who "found her to be mentally retarded," in her spunky way she had been trying all sorts of methods to shield herself from the full force of that wounding repulsion. And somehow, in this vivacious young girl's mind, it was less painful for her to believe that buildings—and people—literally were moving away from her, than to think that any entity, human or not, would totally eject her from the community where she had started to grow up.

Even so, Marie never knew about the awkward discussions with the church board and how the church janitor became angry because a classroom "would be used by those kids when everything needs to be kept spotless for Sunday." Also, none of the fifteen special education students-for-a-day knew that when the board finally approved the use of a classroom, they issued a stern admonition to those of us who had volunteered as faculty. "Since children like this are known to be unkempt, you are being held responsible to see that the classroom is left exactly as you found it." The way it was said did sting a bit. Nevertheless, we agreed to comply. It was the last request, however, that hurt most. "We want you to bring your students into the church by the alley entrance."

In that situation, we the faculty—who were seen as upstarts for bringing people back into a community that had sent them away—had to answer softly every attempt to repulse our boys and girls. But really, since it was 1958, that church board was to be commended for even listening to us. After all, we had tried to get the same previous fifteen youngsters into the YMCA swimming program that same year and had received a flat no, because the YMCA administrator was convinced beyond a doubt that the children would urinate in the pool.

These happenings were only minute slices of the massive mountain of repulsions that persons with developmental disabilities were accustomed to receiving from almost every corner of the community. . . .

In those days, you and I were *conditioned* to feel uncomfortable around such people. Somehow, our parents and our teachers, by what they said (or didn't say), very subtly *programmed* us to believe that if we got too close to people like that, whatever evil they had would rub off on us.

This terrible prejudice came about because persons with developmental disabilities offended our society at the point where it was most vulnerable: *We worshiped the idea that we were becoming better and better!* And everyone was expected ultimately to develop

a pure heart
a brilliant mind
a beautiful body
a successful marriage
a high status job—or a beautiful home
and live in a perfect society.

Then along came this tiny number of defenseless persons with obvious physical and mental handicaps. Their presence challenged our fondest dreams—and they had to go. . . .

Since *nonpersons* were not expected to be capable of hurt, humor, or love, it was easier to send them out of the community to live in institutions. When that happened, the repulsion was complete, and we could get on with our business of making a perfect world. . . .

Today it is interesting to note that we no longer worship the idea that our civilization is continuously progressing toward perfection. Such a belief first fell apart when our minds tried to comprehend Buchenwald, Auschwitz, Hiroshima, and Nagasaki. At this point in history, we do not know whether the world is getting better and better—we only know it has gotten more complex. And yet, it is an astonishing fact that the general public's healthy interest in persons with developmental disabilities began to mushroom after the Holocaust and the Atom Bomb. One cannot help wondering if there is a connection.

new facilities were opened; and from 1971 to 1976, 2659 new CRFs were opened (Bruininks, Hauber, and Kudla, 1980).

Mainstreaming and deinstitutionalization have thus led to new arrangements for retarded children and adults. In order for both movements to be successful, however, society's attitudes must change even more. Old prejudices about the handicapped die hard. In the Focus "Old Repulsions Are Fading," Robert Perske sounds a hopeful note for the mainstreaming and deinstitutionalization movements.

METHODS FOR THE MILDLY RETARDED

Most school systems divide educational programs for the mildly retarded into preschool classes, elementary primary classes, elementary intermediate classes, and secondary classes. In addition, more and more schools are offering infant stimulation classes and postschool programs.

INFANT STIMULATION AND PRESCHOOL CLASSES. Technically, you will not find infant or preschool classes for the mildly mentally retarded. Instead, you will find programs for children who have been labeled "at risk" to develop mental retardation. Because mild mental retardation is usually not diagnosed until a child is of school age, professionals are hesitant to label infants and preschoolers. We do know, however, that some children are at risk to be diagnosed as retarded after they enter school. Infant and preschool classes have been established in an attempt to prevent mental retardation from developing in these children.

One of the best-known infant stimulation programs is the Abecedarian Project (Ramey and Campbell, 1979; Ramey and Smith, 1977). Infants as young as 1½ months have been enrolled in a program that provides them with experiences designed to promote perceptual, intellectual, language, and social development. In addition to the educational features of the project, the infants and their parents are given a variety of other social and medical services, such as nutritional supplements. The results of this project are encouraging, because they suggest that IQ deficits can be prevented with a program that begins in early infancy.

Educational programs are also available for the older preschool child. Some of these programs too have prevented children from later being identified as mentally retarded. For example, an 11-year follow-up of at-risk preschoolers in the Perry Preschool Project found them to have higher achievement scores, fewer years of special education placement, and less evidence of delinquency (Schweinhart and Weikart, 1980).

ELEMENTARY PRIMARY CLASSES. The major emphasis in elementary primary classes is on providing mildly retarded children between the ages of about 6 to 10 years with readiness skills. It is at this level that we teach beginning skills necessary for the learning of reading, math, and handwriting. In many ways, the goals of elementary primary instruction for the mildly retarded are similar to those of preschool instruction for nonhandicapped children—learning to hold a pencil correctly; to identify the alphabet; to sort on the basis of colors, shapes, sizes; to pay attention to the teacher while he or she is talking.

ELEMENTARY INTERMEDIATE CLASSES. For mildly retarded children between the ages of about 9 to 13 years, elementary intermediate classes provide instruction in academic skills such as reading, math, and handwriting. Although some readiness training may continue, the emphasis is on academics. But the academics are slightly different than those taught in regular classrooms. For the nonretarded child, academics such as reading are taught almost exclusively in order for the child to learn other academic material at a later stage. For the retarded child, the emphasis is on teaching academics with the eventual goal of enabling the student to function independently. This is called **functional academics.** The student is taught to use academics in order to do such things as read the newspaper, read street signs, read labels on products in stores, use telephone directories, make change, and fill out job application forms.

SECONDARY CLASSES. A functional academic approach is even more pronounced in secondary classes. At the secondary level and beyond, today's focus is on a life career model (Rose and Logan, 1982). One career education model is Brolin's (1982) model, which consists of three major curriculum areas—daily living skills, personal-social skills, and occupational guidance and preparation. These three areas are further subdivided into 22 competencies (see Table 2–4).

Work-study programs are a popular feature of secondary programming for mildly retarded students. The basic philosophy of the work-study concept is that a person can be better prepared to find and hold a job if he or she is given real-life work experience while still in school. The assumption is that John, who actually works three half-days

---

TABLE 2–4

Brolin's Career Education Model

Daily Living Skills
1. Managing family finances
2. Caring for home furnishings and equipment
3. Caring for personal needs
4. Raising children, family living
5. Buying and preparing food
6. Buying and making clothing
7. Engaging in civic activities
8. Using recreation and leisure
9. Getting around the community

Personal-Social Skills
10. Achieving self-awareness
11. Acquiring self-confidence
12. Achieving socially responsive behavior
13. Maintaining good interpersonal skills
14. Achieving independence
15. Making good decisions, problem-solving
16. Communicating adequately with others

Occupational Guidance and Preparation
17. Knowing and exploring occupational possibilities
18. Making appropriate occupational decisions
19. Exhibiting appropriate work behaviors
20. Exhibiting sufficient physical and manual skills
21. Acquiring a specific salable job skill
22. Seeking, securing, and maintaining satisfactory employment

The basic philosophy of the work-study concept is that a person can be better prepared to find and hold down a job if he or she is given real-life work experience while still in school. New York State Office for Mental Retardation.

SESAME STREET BOY HELPS THE DISABLED

When the county observes the International Year of Disabled Persons on Wednesday, awards will be given to several organizations that have helped the handicapped, but only one individual award is scheduled.

The recipient, Jason Kingsley of Chappaqua, is 7 years old.

Jason, a winsome lad with brown eyes and an English schoolboy haircut, is familiar today to millions of preschoolers who have seen him on "Sesame Street" reciting the alphabet with his Muppet friend, Ernie, or learning to play soccer with the other children on the block. But when he was born, his future was uncertain.

Jason was born with Down's syndrome. . . . When the Kingsleys decided to take their son home, against the advice of doctors, they were warned that the burden would wreck their marriage and be a lifelong heartache.

This was ironic for Emily Kingsley, "Sesame Street" writer who had written many scripts for the show that incorporated children with mental and physical disabilities.

"We were completely broken up when he was born and just did not know what to expect," Mrs. Kingsley recalled recently, "My first inkling of hope came when I took Jason to the Mental Retardation Institute in Valhalla, for a therapy program. I was actually crying as I sat in the waiting room holding my infant. Another mother of a 5-year-old came up to me and said, 'I wish I could tell you how wasted those tears are. That child will be the joy of your life.' "

Despite the disability, Jason is enrolled in a regular school in Chappaqua. He reads on the third-grade level and can count in four languages. And despite the common notion that children with Down's syndrome are not capable of creativity or imagination, Jason enjoys miming and role-playing.

Mrs. Kingsley gives much of the credit for Jason's progress to a program called InfantStim, which she entered at the Mental Retardation Institute.

"The idea is to begin as early as possible with a super-enriched environment for these infants," she said. "They are born with low muscle tone, and left on their own may just lie limply. They need to strengthen their muscles and have their senses awakened. That means doing the same kinds of things all parents do—but more of them. . . ."

At the institute, Jason was given physical therapy to help him control his muscles and body movements. One exercise helped him get ready to crawl. He was placed on a beach ball and gently rolled forward until reflex made him put his arms out to protect himself. Then the ball was rolled just a bit further to give him the feeling of putting his body weight on his arms.

Jason was sitting at eight months and walking at 18 months, within the normal range of infant development, but at the low end of the scale, according to his mother. . . . By age 4 he was reading, and had been placed in a Montessori nursery school.

The Kingsleys had to fight with local school authorities to have their son placed in a regular school class for children with learning disabilities. Down's syndrome children . . . had traditionally been sent off to separate schools. The Kingsleys won the battle, partly because of the "mainstreaming" laws passed by Congress in 1975 which mandated access to public schools for disabled children.

It was the new mainstreaming, and the introduction it brought for young children to peers with physical and mental disabilities, that caused "Sesame Street" to attempt to ease the transition by including disabled youngsters in the regular activities on the show.

"These children are incredibly grateful for this kind of normalization, for being shown doing the same kinds of things all kids are doing," said Mrs. Kingsley, who still writes for the television series. "It is so important for them to be accepted by other kids."

Jason, who began appearing on the show when he was 3, finds that he is something of a celebrity with his schoolmates because he knows Big Bird. . . .

It is for these appearances that Jason is being honored. "In your young life you have changed attitudes and opened new doors to understanding for all disabled people through your willingness to share your personal achievements with others," County Executive Alfred B. DelBello wrote to Jason, inviting him to be present Wednesday to receive a New Horizons Award from the county.

"Much of the problem in the past was that everyone gave up on these children," Mrs. Kingsley said. "Jason's speech is not as clear as other children his age, and he is less sophisticated. But he has wonderful qualities. He is always trying, he soaks up learning and he has a wonderful personality and sense of humor. He's always doing the very best he possibly can. There are special rewards for parents of a child like this. Each new accomplishment is doubly satisfying.

"It's not the dream you had as an expectant parent, not what you had planned. But the joys, too, are beyond anything you expected."

a week at a local bakery and learns functional academics related to measuring, reading recipes, and the like while in school, will be better off then Tim, who spends all his time in school and does not have the opportunity to try his hand at an actual job. Work-study programs involve more than simply placing the student in any available job. The teacher needs to help the student choose which of many jobs is (are) most suitable. In addition, there must be close coordination between the work and school aspects of the program (Smith, Coleman, and Payne, 1981).

METHODS FOR THE MODERATELY RETARDED

INFANT STIMULATION AND PRESCHOOL CLASSES. Preschool programs for the mildly retarded are primarily aimed at children who are at risk to develop mental retardation. Because moderate retardation (IQs between 55 and 40) is easier to diagnose, other infant and preschool programs have been established for children who have already been identified as mentally retarded. Many of these programs also include a parent intervention component in which parents are taught to work with their children on a variety of skills. Whereas the goal for preschool programs for at-risk children is to prevent retardation, the goal for programs for the moderately retarded is "to improve their ultimate level of achievement" (MacMillan, 1982, p. 489). In reviewing preschool programs for the moderately retarded, MacMillan (1982) has made the following observations:

> Programs like the ones we have described have been successful in preparing established risk children to enter public school programs. Their goal has been not so much to make the children "normal," but to optimize their development through early stimulation. . . . The preliminary finding—that these children are capable of higher levels of functioning than was formerly thought—indicates that early intervention holds some promise for established risk children. (p. 512)

ELEMENTARY AND SECONDARY SCHOOL CLASSES. The goal for both elementary and secondary educational programming for the moderately retarded is to enable them to achieve as much independence as possible. For many moderately retarded individuals, the goal of economic and personal independence is not out of the question. In order to achieve a level of independence where they can live on their own, however, they must be taught a variety of daily living and job-related skills. Prevocational training at the elementary level and vocational training at the secondary levels are even more important than they are for the mildly retarded. Today's special educator recognizes that functional academics is a must for the moderately retarded.

PROGRAMMING FOR THE MODERATELY RETARDED ADULT. Today, we can be much more optimistic in our attitude toward the status of moderately retarded adults. At one time, many moderately retarded people could look forward only to institutionalization during their adult years, especially once their parents died. Now, with appropriate educational experiences during their childhood and teenage years, and with the various support services that are now available in adulthood, a relatively high degree of independent living is within the reach of many of the moderately retarded. Most will not be able to achieve the degree of independent living the rest of us enjoy, but they can live in supervised settings with a small number of other retarded housemates (in a group home). And many can, with appropriate training, hold down jobs in a variety of situations (see Focus on p. 60).

SHELTERED WORKSHOPS. A common means of providing the moderately retarded individual with work training and actual employment is by placing him or her in a **sheltered workshop,** a structured work setting where handicapped people are taught skills necessary to perform various jobs. Although some will hold relatively permanent jobs, for many of the moderately retarded the workshop can be used as a training site, with the ultimate goal employment in the community at large. Since training is a primary function of good sheltered workshops, most workshops are not economically self-sufficient.

THE McDONALD'S EXPERIMENT

One of the biggest headaches for the fast food industry is employee turnover. In addition to contributing to disruption of a smoothly run operation, employee turnover is costly, with estimates ranging between $300 and $2000 per person (Poplai, 1978). When a vacancy occurs, money needs to be spent on such things as advertising, physical exams, and training.

The king of the fast food market, McDonald's, decided in 1978 to try to solve its particular problem by hiring a number of unusually qualified workers. The company agreed to hire 17 mentally retarded individuals for 15 of its restaurants. The retarded workers, ranging in age from 21 to 52 years and in IQ from 37 to 70, were trained to work in a variety of nonmanagerial positions. Counter positions were ruled out because they require money handling, writing, and social skills.

This experiment in hiring the retarded, conducted by Brickey and Campbell (1981), was a resounding success for employees and employer alike. Turnover rate for the 17 workers was 41 percent in the first year of the project and 0 percent in the second year. This compares very favorably with a total employee turnover rate of 175 percent for McDonald's in 1979.

We can only hope that other employers in private industry will eventually be convinced to explore the possibilities of hiring the mentally retarded. More efforts such as the McDonald's experiment are undoubtedly needed before other companies will take a more creative and open position on hiring the retarded. The important thing to remember is that through careful and thorough planning, it can be done.

In fact, Smith, Coleman, and Payne (1981) cite economic sufficiency and the difficulty of providing a wide array of occupational tasks to match the range of skills of the retarded as being the two major obstacles to the success of sheltered workshops.

THE IMPORTANCE OF WORK HABITS AND INTERPERSONAL SKILLS. It is not always job competencies that pose the most difficulty for retarded workers. Research has consistently shown that work habits and interpersonal skills are more likely to cause the retarded worker problems on the job (Cunningham and Presnall, 1978; Gold, 1973; Malgady, Barcher, Touner, and Davis, 1979). These problems are not necessarily unique to the retarded. We all know individuals who had the necessary abilities to do well on the job but who were ineffective because they were unable to do such things as get to work on time, line up the necessary transportation to get to and from work, know when they needed to work fast and when they could take it easy and relax, and get along with their co-workers. Unless measures are taken to eliminate these problems, however, the retarded are prime candidates to display these behaviors.

METHODS FOR THE SEVERELY AND PROFOUNDLY RETARDED

At one time relegated to the back wards of institutions, the severely and profoundly retarded of the 1980s are riding the crest of PL 94–142, which stipulates that all handicapped children must be provided an education by the public schools. Rather than paying for expensive institutional care, many school systems are opening their doors and classrooms to the severely and profoundly retarded. Although many people are still placed in institutions, it is now much more likely than ever before that these placements will be made only *after* other alternatives have been carefully ruled out.

TWELVE CHARACTERISTICS OF APPROPRIATE EDUCATIONAL PROGRAMMING. Bates, Renzaglia and Wehman (1981) list twelve characteristics that should be included in an appropriate program for the severely and profoundly handicapped: age-appropriate curriculum and materials, specific objectives, functional activities, consistent cue hierarchy, regular data collection, periodic IEP revision, detailed classroom schedule, instruction outside the classroom, integrated therapy, small group instruction, interaction with the nonhandicapped, and family involvement.

AGE-APPROPRIATE CURRICULUM AND MATERIALS. Because even the older severely and profoundly retarded student scores similarly to a very young nonhandicapped child on an IQ test, there has been a tendency to treat him or her as a young child. We now recognize that "babying" the severely or profoundly retarded adolescent or adult is not only demeaning, it can also hinder the individual's attempts to lead as independent an adult life as possible. As Bates et al. (1981) state:

> Although "Mickey Mouse" and "Peter Rabbit" may be at home in preschool or primary classrooms, they should not adorn the walls or bulletin boards of secondary classrooms regardless of the student's level of functioning. Both classroom decor and educational activities in a secondary classroom should reflect an emphasis on preparation for adult living in the least restrictive environment possible. (p. 143)

SPECIFIC OBJECTIVES. Vague teaching objectives are of limited value when working with the severely and profoundly retarded. Adelle is much more likely to learn to dress herself if you specify that she is to learn such things as buttoning her blouse and making sure that it is tucked in than if you simply state that she's to learn how to dress herself (see Focus on p. 62).

CONSISTENT CUE HIERARCHY. What is meant by a consistent cue hierarchy is the use of consistent cues or prompts (such as pointing) to aid the individual in making correct discriminations:

> For example, when instructing a child to "pick up the cup," a teacher may accompany the instructions with a gesture towards the cup. This gestural cue is an extra stimulus or prompt which facilitates the student's correct response. (Bates et al., 1981, p. 145)

REGULAR DATA COLLECTION. It is important that the teacher maintain close tabs on the progress of each student. If at all possible, it is recommended that a daily record be kept of each child's performance on every task assigned.

FUNCTIONAL ACTIVITIES. Whenever possible, teaching activities should be made as practical as possible. For example, if the goal is to teach a child to tie his or her shoes, you should have him or her practice on real shoes rather than on a lacing board shoe.

"CLOTHES MAKE THE MAN AND WOMAN MORE NORMAL"

The ancient Latin proverb "Vestis virum facit" (clothes make the man) is at least as true today as it was in ancient Rome. It is probably even truer today that "Clothes make the woman." Our society's emphasis on fashionable dress has made it almost the norm to be well dressed. It may not be true that a fashionably dressed woman will always stand out in a crowd, but an unfashionably dressed one certainly will.

We can debate about how healthy it is for our society to be so fashion conscious, but the fact remains that, in order for individuals to fit in with the rest of the community, they will need to dress so as not to draw attention to themselves. Unfortunately, the mentally retarded, especially the severely and profoundly retarded, are notoriously poor dressers. Although lack of sufficient money is definitely a factor to be considered, that's not always the major problem. Think about how often your attention has been drawn to a mentally retarded person by the glaring contrast of his or her blue and green checked pants and grey and white striped shirt. Although it has probably been so subtle that you are not aware of it, such bizarre color and pattern combinations have probably become cues to you that the wearer is different in some way, possibly retarded or disturbed.

Recognizing that integration with society at large requires the mentally retarded to be able to dress in a relatively popular fashion, Nutter and Reid (1978) conducted an ingenious training program for severely and profoundly retarded women (IQs ranging from 22 to 29). Prior to training, Nutter and Reid sent observers out into a shopping center in the community where the women would live if deinstitutionalized. Sticking to just solid colors (they felt patterns would be too difficult to train, and solid colors were the most common), the observers tallied the various color combinations (top versus bottom garments) they saw on 649 women. With this information, the trainers composed a list of "popular" and "unpopular" combinations and took to training the women to discriminate between the two. The women were trained via modeling, instructions, practice, feedback, and praise to clothe a wooden Barbie-Doll puzzle with pieces of fabric.

After training, the women were not only better able to pick out popular color combinations for the Barbie-Doll, they were also better at choosing popular color combinations using real clothes.

PERIODIC IEP REVISION. Because the learning rates of many severely and profoundly retarded students are highly variable, their individualized educational plans may need to be modified frequently.

DETAILED CLASSROOM SCHEDULE. A daily schedule of activities should be posted at the beginning of each day. This schedule helps promote structure in the students. The schedule should include a minute-by-minute record of activities for all students and the teacher.

INSTRUCTION OUTSIDE THE CLASSROOM. Today, authorities in the education of the severely and profoundly retarded all agree that instruction needs to take place in other than just the classroom setting (Brown, Branston, Hamre-Nietupski, Pumpian, Certo, and Gruenwald, 1979; Snell, 1982). It is not enough to teach students to go grocery shopping at a make-believe store, with make-believe items, using make-believe money. The student needs to try his or her skills out in a real grocery store.

INTEGRATED THERAPY. Many severely and profoundly retarded students need help from one or more of the following professionals—speech therapists, physical therapists,

It will not be enough to teach
this student about cars by using models. He will also need
experience with the real thing.
New York State Office for Mental
Retardation.

and occupational therapists. The roles of these individuals often overlap with one another
as well as with that of the teacher. As an integrated team, the classroom teacher and
the therapists work on a variety of problems, such as feeding, head control, sitting,
walking, and finger dexterity.

SMALL GROUP INSTRUCTION. Traditionally the tendency has been to use a lot of
one-to-one instruction with the severely and profoundly retarded. To promote one
student's learning from another, Bates et al. recommend that some time should be
devoted to small group instruction.

INTERACTION WITH NONHANDICAPPED. A few short years ago it would have been
practically impossible to find a classroom for the severely and profoundly retarded in a
regular public school. Today, however, more and more such classrooms are opening.
Bringing the severely and profoundly retarded within the regular schools also brings
opportunities for interaction between them and nonhandicapped students.

FAMILY INVOLVEMENT. A truly successful program for the severely and profoundly
retarded must include the students' families in some way. After all, as Bates et al.
point out, most of the daily living skills being taught the students in school are primarily
used at home.

DEALING WITH BIZARRE BEHAVIOR. Severely and profoundly retarded individuals are more likely to exhibit maladaptive behavior than are those whose retardation is
less severe (Snell, 1982). In addition, the maladaptive behavior often takes bizarre forms.
Two of the most common types of behavior problems are stereotypic behavior

and self-injurious behavior (Snell, 1982). **Stereotypic behaviors** are any of a variety of behaviors (eye rubbing and hand flapping, for example) that are engaged in repetitively— that is, over and over again in a short period of time. They are also sometimes found in the severely disturbed and the blind. In fact, they used to be called "blindisms" until authorities pointed out they were also found in the severely retarded and disturbed. Self-injurious behavior also comes in a variety of forms. Some examples are eye gouging, hair pulling, and head banging. As yet, we are not sure what causes some severely retarded, severely disturbed, and blind individuals to display these peculiar behaviors while others do not. Some experts believe that extreme environmental and social isolation may be at the root of stereotypic and self-injurious behavior. In other words, these individuals might be creating their own stimulation in order to make up for the lack of stimulation in their environment.

The primary method of treatment for stereotypic and self-injurious behavior is behavior modification. **Behavior modification** is the use of reinforcement and/or punishment to increase or decrease behaviors. Behavior modification is used with virtually every type of exceptional child. *Although its use is often debated in other areas of special education, today's special educator recognizes that behavior modification is the treatment of choice with the severely and profoundly retarded, especially for reducing stereotypic and self-injurious behavior.*

A variety of forms of behavior modification have been used to treat stereotypic and self-injurious behavior. One type that has been used is differential reinforcement of other behaviors (DRO). If you were working with Martha, who engages in the stereotypic behavior of hand flapping and the self-injurious behavior of eye gouging, you might decide to use DRO by purposely reinforcing (with candy and/or social praise) other behaviors incompatible with the bizarre behaviors. You might decide, for example, to reinforce Martha for using her hands in a more functional manner, such as folding them in her lap when she is sitting down. If Martha sits with her hands folded, she will be unable to flap her hands or gouge her eyes.

TECHNOLOGICAL ADVANCES

Technological advances have just begun to result in the development of devices designed specifically for the mentally retarded. Fortunately, many mentally retarded individuals have been benefiting from the use of materials created for people with sensory or motor disabilities. An electronic communication board is an example of a device that can be used by individuals with language disabilities, hearing impairments, severe physical handicaps, and/or mental retardation. Many of the more technologically advanced communication systems, however, are based on prior spelling and reading knowledge and assume that the child has near-average learning capabilities. These prerequisites unfortunately limit the number of mentally retarded individuals who can gain access to, and benefit from, the most efficient communication technology.

Nevertheless, progress is now being made to meet the needs of the mentally retarded in the areas of cognitive development (via instructional technology) and independent functioning (through the creation of aids for self-help skills and environmental control).

COMPUTER-ASSISTED INSTRUCTION

The new instructional technology for mildy retarded children primarily involves micro-computers and innovative software. The mildly retarded person can easily work with the standard computer keyboard, so few equipment modifications are necessary. Examples of programs for Computer-Assisted Instruction (CAI) are drill and practice or tutorial formats, educational games or simulations, and problem-solving formats such as the LOGO program, which enables children to generate problems and solutions (Budoff and Hutton, 1982). Because many CAI programs include immediate performance feed-back, positive reinforcement, and motivating graphics displayed on the TV screen, they can be an effective means of varying lesson presentation and maintaining interest and attention. Certain tutorial programs will branch into review problems when a child makes performance errors, thereby actually assisting in the teaching of academic material.

The following are examples of software programs designed for the instruction of mildly retarded individuals.

1. *Dots and Draw* (Seagrave and Seagrave, 1982). The child uses a game paddle, or joy stick, to draw pictures and write letters or words by connecting dots. Some programs include cartoon characters and additional words to increase motivation and interest in this readiness level activity.
2. *Edufun* (Terpenning, 1982). This program includes arithmetic, spelling, and reading compo-nents. Addition, subtraction, and multiplication problems are available at three levels of difficulty. A star is printed on the screen for every four math problems answered correctly. The individual can also use this program for spelling drills. The reading component is designed as an aid for increasing reading speed by allowing adjustable rates of story display.
3. *Say It* (Geigner, 1982). This talking program is a communication aid designed for use by visually impaired, physically handicapped, and mentally retarded children. It contains a series of incomplete sentences and vocabulary words that can be adjusted for each learner. The computer scans and vocalizes the sentences, including the designated blanks, at a rate determined by student or teacher. By closing a switch, the student can stop the scan at the desired sentence. After the sentence has been chosen, the list of vocabulary words is vocally scanned until the child again closes the switch to designate the appropriate word.
4. Two software programs that can provide valuable knowledge and skills for mildly retarded adolescents are *Money Management Assessment* (Taber, 1981) and *Job Readiness Assess-ment and Development* (Taber and Argue, 1981).

The addition of **videodisc technology** to microcomputer-based instruction has resulted in additional methods of using the computer to supplement educational program-ming (Bennet, 1982). Videodisc images can be displayed on any TV set. A system designed to provide optimum interaction with the mentally retarded is the *Intelligent Videodisc for Special Education Technology* (Thorkildson, Bickel, and Williams, 1979). It provides instruction in readiness and beginning reading and arithmetic skills. Pictures and printed words are presented simultaneously on a television monitor, while the child hears vocal commands. The child responds to questions or commands by touching the appropriate part of the television screen. The program reads the touched response, branches to instruction and review if errors are made, and stores performance data for each child.

If you are involved with teenagers in any way, you're no doubt aware of the attraction of video games, particularly those that can be found in amusement arcades. Some professionals have suggested that programs for the retarded should be designed in the same way in order to maintain motivation and attention. The ARC-ED curriculum presents educationally relevant tasks through a video game format to provide mentally retarded children with exciting and positive academic experiences (Chaffin, Maxwell, and Thompson, 1982).

TECHNOLOGY FOR LOWER-FUNCTIONING RETARDED INDIVIDUALS

THE CONTINGENCY INTERVENTION PROJECT. Microcomputers have begun to play an active role in the cognitive training of mentally retarded infants. In one exciting project (The Contingency Intervention Project), Brinker and Lewis (1982a; 1982b) have applied microcomputer technology to improve the cognitive performance of mentally retarded infants. Their system is designed to help the infant become aware that his or her actions can have some control over the environment. Jenny, a normal infant, learned early on that she could control certain aspects of her environment by her own behavior. For example, when she was hungry, if she cried, her mother would come to feed her. If she made eye contact with her mother and smiled, her mother would respond by talking to her and cuddling her. Lindsey, on the other hand, who is a Down's syndrome infant, will have a more difficult time learning that her behavior can give her control over aspects of her environment.

Brinker and Lewis's project is designed to help infants like Lindsey learn to control their environment. They have hooked up retarded infants as young as 3 months of age to microcomputers so that if they make a certain response, a leg movement for example, they are rewarded with a reinforcer—a recording of music or their mother's voice. If they lose interest in the particular reinforcer being used, the computer automatically switches to a different one. Brinker and Lewis's project holds promise for teaching retarded infants that their world is controllable. But how much this early intervention will pay off in terms of long-term cognitive improvement is still unknown.

EXPRESSIVE AND RECEPTIVE COMMUNICATION. Most severely retarded persons experience deficits in expressive communication. Technology has played a major role in the development of language devices, including machines that produce synthesized speech, and electronic, microcomputer-based, symbolic communication boards. Most of this equipment was designed for the physically handicapped and language impaired. Some of the systems can be used with mentally retarded individuals, depending on the required entry-level skills and the abilities of the individual child (Van Etten, Arkell, and Van Etten, 1980).

Advanced communication systems have the potential to give handicapped individuals the opportunity to receive and transmit information in their homes. Videotex, a new communication medium, provides access to a central computer. Through keyboard transmission and television reception, an individual can use the computer to receive computer-assisted instruction, send purchase orders, and obtain employment listings in his or her home. Modifications that would enable physically, sensory, and cognitively impaired individuals to use the system are on the drawing board (Staisey, Tombaugh, and Dillon, 1982).

THE ARC BIOENGINEERING PROJECT. The Association for Retarded Citizens (ARC) has formed a committee to study the possible applications of computer technology

MENTAL RETARDATION IN THE YEAR 2000

A decision made by the President's Committee on Mental Retardation to look at the impact of future events on the life of mentally retarded individuals culminated in the book *The year 2000 and mental retardation* (Plog and Santamour, 1980). The book is composed of papers written by each committee member that examine the potential effects of economic, social, and technological trends on the mentally retarded populations by the year 2000. An interesting aspect of this committee is that many of its members specialize in predicting the future, rather than in mental retardation. It will be interesting to see just how accurate they were when the year 2000 rolls around. The following statements summarize their projections of changes in the lives of mentally retarded individuals by the year 2000.

- Direct sensory prostheses will increase sensory input, stimulus ranges, and enhance memory performance of mentally retarded persons.
- Neuron regeneration in the brain and direct repairs for some types of damage to the brain may provide a cure for some mentally retarded individuals.
- Drugs will be used to raise intelligence artificially.
- Computer-assisted instruction specifically designed for the mentally retarded will be available in the home. Instruction will be provided for both academic and vocational areas.
- Extensive reliance on technological advances may result in the isolation of mentally retarded persons. That is, devices that allow the retarded to stay at home could actually work against their integration.
- The appearance of some mentally retarded persons will be altered through the elimination of distinguishing facial characteristics, thereby increasing possibilities for social acceptance.
- Interactive televisions in the home will allow the retarded individual to receive on-the-job training, physical therapy, instructions, and medical and legal consultation.
- Miniature communication devices will enable mentally retarded persons to remain in constant contact with a specific person or location. The devices will include emergency numbers and signals to aid in personal navigation.
- Computers will have become so "simplified" in terms of their operation that the mentally retarded will be able to carry out complex intellectual tasks without having the usual necessary background knowledge.

to the education and training of severely and profoundly retarded individuals. Thus far, the committee has listed a number of devices it believes could be created for the severely and profoundly retarded (Progress Report, ARC Bioengineering Project, 1982). Let's look briefly at a few of these suggestions.

One device would monitor and train attention to information presented in a learning situation (attention monitor and trainer). The design includes a set of sensors that could be attached to the individual's clothing or mounted in a learning booth. The sensors would monitor physiological signs of attention and transmit signals to a processor, which would activate a stimulus, such as a small light, a television set, or recorded music. The stimulus would provide feedback that could serve as a reminder to return to attention, or as positive reinforcement for attending behavior.

The committee has also recommended the development of automated memory devices that would help remind individuals via instructions or signals to do certain things. Prerecorded instructional sequences could be available in bathrooms or play areas. A child taught to activate the system on entering the room could receive the information necessary for appropriate performance. A suggested variation of the automated memory is a watchlike device that could provide periodic prompts to the child for going to the bathroom, checking in with a teacher, or changing activities.

SELF-HELP SKILLS. Many of the ARC recommendations are for helping profoundly retarded persons to become more independent through learning self-help skills. One proposed design is the Bladder/Bowel Sensation Exaggerator, which would consist of a device worn by the child that would read bladder or bowel volume. The device would exaggerate bladder or bowel sensations, providing an advance signal for the child to go to the bathroom.

A proposed automated feeding device is the Self-Feeding Tray. The design calls for a rectangular, three-section tray with spoonlike projections leading out of each section. The tray would be adjusted to the person's mouth level, and food would automatically be pushed into the spoons when placed in the back of the tray. This would be particularly helpful for those with multiple disabilities.

The difficulties and dangers encountered by severely retarded individuals in bathing situations have been addressed by the creation of the Parker Bath for disabled and elderly individuals. The bath is mounted on a pedestal that allows it to change from an upright to a reclining position. The individual steps in and takes a seat while the bath is in an upright position and closes a watertight door. The water fills to a predetermined depth and drains before the bath returns to an upright position. The Standing Bathtub/Bodywash Stall proposed by the ARC is a similar device, except that the bath would remain in a permanent vertical position. Proposed extensions of the same concept of enclosed, watertight areas for cleaning with the aid of automation are the Drying Stall, Hand Shower, and Shampooer.

The potential contributions of technology to an improved quality of life for mentally retarded individuals are unlimited. Because much of this potential has not yet been realized, many of the technological aids designed to provide services for the mentally retarded population are still in the planning stages. The future holds the promise of increased acceptance of mentally retarded individuals as productive and important members of society. Many believe that this promise cannot be completely fulfilled until technology is used to meet the specific needs of the mentally retarded for communication and information delivery systems, computer-assisted instruction, and aids for self-help skills and environmental control.

ANSWERS TO FREQUENTLY ASKED QUESTIONS
MENTAL RETARDATION

1. The majority of children identified as mentally retarded through the public school system experience mild retardation. Often, mild mental retardation is not evident until the child is faced with academic tasks in a school situation. Because most mildly retarded children do not have distinguishing physical characteristics and do not often experience severe delays in physical development, the retardation may not be evident even to parents during the child's preschool years.

2. Severe mental retardation is often the result of brain damage or chromosomal abnormalities that are inherited. Down's syndrome is an example of a chromosomal abnormality that is not inherited. If your sister-in-law has Down's syndrome or has brain damage as the result of an infection such as meningitis or encephalitis, you can be sure that your chances of having a severely retarded child are no greater than anyone else's. In some instances, mental retardation can occur due to an inherited condition. Phenylketonuria (PKU) and Tay-Sachs disease are two examples. If you're unsure of the type of retardation your sister-in-law has, you should probably seek genetic counseling. Even in some inherited conditions, both parents—that is, you and your husband—must be carriers of the defective gene before it would even be possible to produce a retarded child.

3. Although the categories of mental retardation are designed to provide general estimates of learning potential, you should develop educational programs based on the needs and abilities of each child. Children whose scores on intelligence tests place them within the moderate or trainable range of mental retardation form a continuum of ability levels. You should not assume that a child with an IQ that falls a few points below the cutoff score for moderate retardation is less capable of learning academic skills than a child with an IQ that is just high enough to fall in the mildly retarded range. Constant assessment and careful instruction will enable you to help each child fulfill his or her potential without causing undue frustration. It is important to assess each child's needs and empha-size those skills most in need of immediate remediation. Instruction in basic self-help or vocational skills is likely to make up most of your educational program for the moderately retarded child. But the program should include at least functional, and possibly more advanced, academic instruction.

4. Most mildly retarded individuals are definitely able to maintain jobs and successfully adapt in society. Your son's desire to be on his own and his reported responsibility will certainly help him adjust. You, your son, his guidance counselor, and his teachers should review the specific skills Bill will need to seek and maintain employment and to live independently. Ask Bill to indicate the areas in which he feels the need for help or about which he feels insecure, and incorporate these areas into goals for next year's individualized educational plan. If Bill is interested in a job that does not require a high school diploma, his school classification of mental retardation may not surface in his interview or on his application. It is important that Bill be honest with future employers about his skill levels in areas that may be related to his job (reading and mathematical ability, for example). Vocational and academic training geared to the requirements of a specific job(s) in which Bill is particularly interested will help to ensure his success, as will any opportunity to begin work before graduation, while he can still draw on the information and guidance of a support system.

5. Children with Down's syndrome have intellectual levels ranging from mild to profound retardation. The majority of Down's syndrome children are moderately retarded. There is a good possibility that your neighbors' child will not have to be institutionalized. Most individuals with Down's syndrome are good candidates for some type of job training, and may live in lightly supervised settings, such as a group home, as adults. Parental attention, care, and appropriate schooling will certainly help your neighbors' child realize her full potential.

6. You are correct in slowing down your presentation of basal materials and providing many opportunities for your mentally retarded students to practice skills. However, further examination of your students' abilities and the tasks are necessary before you can conclude that the material is too difficult. Analyze each task into components and make sure your students possess the necessary preskills. By teaching components of the task in small, sequential steps, you will increase your students' chances of learning the overall task. Research has indicated that mentally retarded children may not know how to approach a learning task—for example, finding the main idea in a paragraph or memorizing spelling words. You may find that by directly teaching the steps of such learning strategies, you will help your students to improve. In addition, the students may not be highly motivated, particularly because of the necessary repetitions. Motivation may be increased by slight variations in the presentation of content, or through behavior modification techniques.

7. Because research has indicated the importance of role models in skill and social development, the hypothesis has been generated that handicapped children will imitate the behavior of nonhandi-capped peers in mainstreamed settings. Parents of nonhandicapped children have expressed the fear that the reverse will occur, and their children will imitate the less desirable behaviors of the handicapped children. This fear has not been supported by research. Not only are your son's verbal and motor skills intrinsically reinforcing, but he is receiving attention from you and his other friends for each new skill he acquires. John's parents will also be attending to and reinforcing John's attempts at speaking and walking. Your son may temporarily adjust his speech or level of activity to communicate more effectively and play with John, but this too is an important social skill. The opportunity exists for a situation that may be beneficial to both children.

8. Ann and Carl may be isolated in your regular classroom not only because they have been identified as mentally retarded, but also because they spend so little time in the regular class. The other children may not perceive them as true class members. You can do several things to promote interaction between the mainstreamed students and the rest of your class. First, examine your own attitudes and behavior toward Ann and Carl. Research indicates that the teacher's behavior toward mainstreamed children serves as a cue for the behavior of other class members. You should demonstrate acceptance of Ann and Carl by initiating social interactions and granting them classroom responsibilities. You could also try to promote opportunities for interaction with the other students by introducing paired activities during the time Ann and Carl are in your room. Pairing children as lunchmates, or for clean-up tasks, and forming teams for the creation of art projects are simple ways to encourage communication between mainstreamed and nonhandicapped children.

SUMMARY

Mental retardation is no longer regarded as a permanent condition, nor is IQ the only measure on which a person is classified as retarded. Today, mental retardation involves significantly subaverage intellectual functioning along with impairment in the person's ability to function in his or her environment. The retarded are not one category; they are also classified by severity of condition. Two systems are used. The schools classify as educable, trainable, and severely and profoundly retarded. The AAMD system uses the categories of mild, moderate, severe, and profound.

Estimates of the prevalence of retardation today vary from 1.3 to 2.3 percent of the population, depending on whether or not adaptive behavior is considered in making the assessment. People may score in the retarded range in intelligence and still display adequate adaptive behavior.

For special education placement, intelligence is assessed by individually administered IQ tests. The Stanford-Binet and the WISC-R are two tests often used to determine IQ—the fit between a person's chronological and mental ages. Adaptive behavior is measured on several scales. The AAMD Behavior Scale measures daily living skills as well as personality and behavior; the Adaptive Behavior Inventory for Children assesses six skill areas that help people lead a happy and productive life.

Mental retardation can be caused by a number of events, although in very few cases can we specify the cause for a particular individual. The vast majority of the retarded are mildly retarded, and their condition is often called cultural-familial retardation. More severe retardation, which is more easily identified as to cause, can be due to genetic factors and to physical damage to the brain. Down's syndrome, PKU, and Tay-Sachs disease, which are genetic conditions, can all cause retardation. Physical damage to the brain can result from infectious diseases such as meningitis and encephalitis, and from environmental hazards and accidents.

Educational methods for the mentally retarded today are varied and range from mainstreaming to placement in residential institutions. The mainstreaming and deinstitutionalization movements have had great impact on special education for the retarded. Programs for the retarded begin in infancy and the preschool years. Elementary and secondary programs often focus on functional academics—academics taught in order to prepare the person to function independently in everyday life. Programs for the moderately retarded also now focus on preparing children to lead as independent a life as possible. Training in work habits and interpersonal skills is important to maximize the chances that the person will be able to work and to live in a supervised group home rather than an institution.

Technological advances in materials created for people with sensory or motor disabilities have also benefited the mentally retarded, who need help in the areas of cognitive development and independent functioning. The new instructional technology has been made possible by the microcomputer and new, innovative software. Self-help devices are multiplying as the microchip and advances in electronics make possible the mass production of devices that are easy for an individual to operate. The prospects today for a mentally retarded person to live a full and independent life in society are good and getting better.

REFERENCES

BATES, P., RENZAGLIA, A., & WEHMAN P. Characteristics of an appropriate education for severely and profoundly handicapped students. *Education and Training of the Mentally Retarded,* 1981, *16,* 142–149.

BAUMEISTER, A.A., & BROOKS, P.H. Cognitive deficits in mental retardation. In J.M. Kauffman & D.P. Hallahan (Eds.), *Handbook of special education.* Englewood Cliffs, N.J.: Prentice-Hall, 1981.

BELMONT, J.M. Medical-behavioral research in retardation. In N.R. Ellis (Ed.), *International review of research in mental retardation,* Vol. 5. New York: Academic Press, 1971.

BENNET, R.E. Applications of microcomputer technology to special education. *Exceptional Children,* 1982, *49,* 106–113.

BOUCHARD, T.J., & McGUE, M. Familial studies of intelligence. A review. *Science,* 1981, *212,* 1055–1059.

BRICKEY, M., & CAMPBELL, K. Fast food employment for moderately and mildly retarded adults: The McDonald's Project. *Mental retardation,* 1981, *19,* 113–116.

BRINKER, R.P., & LEWIS, M. Discovering the competent handicapped infant: A process approach to assessment and intervention. *Topics in Early Childhood Special Education,* 1982, *2,* 1–16. (a)

BRINKER, R.P., & LEWIS, M. Making the world work with microcomputers: A learning prosthesis for handicapped infants. *Exceptional Children,* 1982, 49, 163–170. (b)

BROLIN, D.E. *Vocational preparation of persons with handicaps* (2nd ed.). Columbus, Ohio: Charles E. Merrill, 1982.

BROWN, L., BRANSTON, M.B., HAMRE-NIETUPSKI, S., PUMPIAN, I., CERTO, N., & GRUENEWALD, L. A strategy for developing chronological-age-appropriate and functional curricular content for severely handicapped adolescents and young adults. *Journal of Special Education,* 1979, *13,* 81–90.

BRUININKS, R., HAUBER, F.A., & KUDLA, M.J. National survey of community residential facilities: A profile of facilities and residents in 1977. *American Journal of Mental Deficiency,* 1980, *84,* 470–478.

BUDOFF, M., & HUTTON, L.R. Microcomputers in special education: Promises and pitfalls. *Exceptional Children,* 1982, *49,* 123–128.

CAMPIONE, J.C., & BROWN, A.L. Memory and meta-memory development in educable retarded children. In R.V. Kail & J.W. Hagen (Eds.), *Perspectives on the development of memory and cognition.* Hillsdale, N.J.: Lawrence Erlbaum Associates, 1977.

CHAFFIN, J.D., MAXWELL, B., & THOMPSON, B. ARC-ED curriculum: The application of video game formats to educational software. *Exceptional Children,* 1982, *49,* 173–178.

CUNNINGHAM, T., & PRESNALL, D. Relationship between dimensions of adaptive behavior and sheltered workshop productivity. *American Journal of Mental Deficiency*, 1978, *82*, 386–393.

DELANEY, S., & HAYDEN, A. Fetal alcohol syndrome: A review. *American Association for the Education of the Severely and Profoundly Handicapped*, 1977, *2*, 164–168.

GEIGNER, C. *Say it* (1982). In G.C. Vanderheiden & L.M. Walstead (Eds.), *Trace Center international software/hardware registry*. Trace Research and Development Center for the Severely Communicatively Handicapped, University of Wisconsin—Madison, 1982.

GOLD, M.W. Research on the vocational habilitation of the retarded: The present, the future. In N.R. Ellis (Ed.), *International review of research in mental retardation*, Vol. 6. New York: Academic Press, 1973.

GROSSMAN, H.J. (Ed.) *Manual on terminology and classification in mental retardation*. Washington, D.C.: American Association on Mental Deficiency, in press.

HANSEN, H. Decline of Down's syndrome after abortion reform in New York State. *American Journal of Mental Deficiency*, 1978, *83*, 185–188.

HARTER, S. Effective motivation reconsidered: Toward a developmental model. *Human Development*, 1978, *21*, 34–64.

HARTER, S., & ZIGLER, E. The assessment of effectance motivation in normal and retarded children. *Developmental Psychology*, 1974, *10*, 169–180.

HEBER, R.F. A manual on terminology and classification in mental retardation. *American Journal of Mental Deficiency Monograph*, 1959.

HERRNSTEIN, R.J. IQ testing and the media. *The Atlantic Monthly*, August, 1982, 68–74.

KAUFMAN, A.S. & KAUFMAN, N.L. *The Kaufman Assessment Battery for Children*. Circle Pines, Minn.: American Guidance Service, 1983.

LAMBERT, N., & WINDMILLER, M. *AAMD Adaptive Behavior Scale—School Edition*. Washington, D.C.: American Association of Mental Deficiency, 1981.

MACMILLAN, D.L. Mental retardation in school and society (2nd ed.). Boston: Little, Brown, 1982.

MALGADY, R.G., BARCHER, P.R., TOUNER, G., & DAVIS, J. Language factors in vocational evaluation of mentally retarded workers. *American Journal of Mental Deficiency*, 1979, *83*, 432–438.

MERCER, J.R., & LEWIS, J.F. *Adaptive behavior inventory for children, parent interview manual: System of multicultural pluralistic assessment*. New York: The Psychological Corporation, 1977.

MERCER, J.R. & LEWIS, J.F. *System of multicultural pluralistic assessment*. New York: The Psychological Corporation, 1978.

NUTTER, D., & REID, D.H. Teaching retarded women a clothing selection skill using community norms. *Journal of Applied Behavior Analysis*, 1978, *11*, 475–487.

PERSKE, R., & PERSKE, M. *New life in the neighborhood*. Nashville: Parthenon Press, 1980.

PLOG, S.C., & SANTAMOUR, M.B. (Eds.). *The year 2000 and mental retardation*. New York: Plenum Press, 1980.

POPLAI, B. Six steps to better hiring. *Restaurant Business*, 1978, *77*, 134, 136, 138.

PROGRESS REPORT: Association for Retarded Citizens Bioengineering Project, National Research and Development Institute. Arlington, Texas: August, 1982.

RAMEY, C.T., & CAMPBELL, F.A. Early childhood education for psychosocially disadvantaged children: Effects on psychological processes. *American Journal of Mental Deficiency*, 1979, *83*, 645–648.

RAMEY, C.T., & SMITH, B. Assessing the intellectual consequences of early intervention with high-risk infants. *American Journal of Mental Deficiency*, 1977, *81*, 318–324.

ROSE, E., & LOGAN, D.R. Educational and life/career programs for the mildly retarded. In P.T. Cegelka & H.J. Prehm (Eds.), *Mental retardation: From categories to people*. Columbus, Ohio: Charles E. Merrill, 1982.

RYNDERS, J.E., SPIKER, D., & HORROBIN, M. Underestimating the educability of Down's syndrome children: Examination of methodological problems in recent literature. *American Journal of Mental Deficiency*, 1978, *82*, 440–448.

SCARR-SALAPATEK, S. Genetics and the development of intelligence. In F.D. Horowitz (Ed.), *Review of child development research*, Vol. 4. Chicago: University of Chicago Press, 1975.

SCHWEINHART, L.J., & WEIKART, D.P. *Young children grow up: The effects of the Perry Preschool Program on youths through age 15*. Monograph No. 7. High Scope Educational Research Foundation. Ypsilanti, Michigan, 1980.

SEAGRAVE, J.R., & SEAGRAVE, G. *Dots and Draw* (1982). In G.C. Vanderheiden & L.M. Walstead (Eds.), *Trace Center international software/hardware registry*. Trace Research and Development Center for the Severely Communicatively Handicapped, University of Wisconsin—Madison, 1982.

SMITH, J.E., COLEMAN, L.J., & PAYNE, J.S. Career and vocational planning. In J.S. Payne & J.R. Patton (Eds.), *Mental retardation*. Columbus, Ohio: Charles E. Merrill, 1981.

SNELL, M. Education and habilitation of the profoundly retarded. In P.T. Cegelka & H.J. Prehm (Eds.), *Mental retardation: From categories to people*. Columbus, Ohio: Charles E. Merrill, 1982.

STAISEY, N.L., TOMBAUGH, J.W., & DILLON, R.F. Videotex and the disabled. *International Journal of Man-Machine Studies*, 1982, *17*, 35–50.

TABER, F.M. *Money management assessment* (1981). In G.C. Vanderheiden & L.M. Walstead (Eds.), *Trace Center international software/hardware registry*. Trace Research and Development Center for the Severely Communication Handicapped, University of Wisconsin—Madison, 1982.

TABER, F.M., & ARGUE, H. *Job readiness assessment and development* (1981). In G.C. Vanderheiden & L.M. Walstead (Eds.), *Trace Center international software/hardware registry*. Trace Research and Development Center for the Severely Communicatively Handicapped, University of Wisconsin—Madison, 1982.

TERPENNING, J.L. *Edufun* (1982), In G.C. Vanderheiden & L.M. Walstead (Eds.), *Trace Center international software/hardware registry*. Trace Research and Development Center for the Severely Communicatively Handicapped, University of Wisconsin—Madison, 1982.

THORKILDSEN, R., BICKEL, W., & WILLIAMS, J. A microcomputer/videodisc CAI system for the moderately mentally retarded. *Journal of Special Education Technology*, 1979, *2*, 45–51.

TURNURE, J., & ZIGLER, E. Outer-directedness in the problem solving of normal and retarded children. *Journal of Abnormal and Social Psychology*, 1964, *69*, 427–436.

VAN ETTEN, G., ARKELL, C., & VAN ETTEN, C. *The severely and profoundly handicapped*. St. Louis: C.V. Mosby, 1980.

LEARNING
DISABILITIES
3

1. The boy next door, Andy, has just been diagnosed as hyperactive and has been placed on medication. I know this might sound silly, but I'm concerned that my son Tom will develop the attitude that it's ok to take drugs. He's a good friend of Andy's and they're both at an age, 13, when some of their classmates are beginning to experiment with drugs. I'd hate to stop Tom from associating with Andy. What should I do?

2. Our 8-year-old son Tim has just been diagnosed as learning disabled. He will be receiving resource room help three days a week for one hour each day. My husband and I are both college educated and high achievers and are having trouble adjusting to the fact that Tim will probably not be going on to college. Should we begin now to orient him toward occupations not requiring a college degree, or should we wait until he's older?

3. Two children in my fifth-grade class have been identified as learning disabled. Each of them spends approximately one hour each day with a resource teacher and the rest of the time with me. The resource teacher has never talked with me about what she is doing with these children or what she thinks I should be doing with them. Should I set up a meeting with her?

4. Our 5-year-old son is just beginning to learn how to read. Although he seems to be progressing well in his reading, he does have a tendency to reverse letters and words, such as ''b'' for ''d,'' ''was'' for ''saw.'' Should we be concerned?

5. I have a learning-disabled girl in my fifth-grade classroom who started taking medication for hyperactivity last month. She is now able to concentrate for longer periods of time. However, she hasn't shown any improvements in her area of deficiency—reading. Should I contact her parents and let them know the drug isn't working?

6. Our 10-year-old daughter Linda has been receiving resource room services for the learning disabled for the past six months. My husband and I are generally pleased with her progress, but we're concerned because she has not received any perceptual-motor training. When we lived in a different state, our oldest son, who is now 16, was diagnosed as learning disabled when he was 7 and given extensive perceptual-motor training as part of his educational program. Is Linda beyond a critical age when perceptual-motor training would be helpful?

7. Our 8-year-old daughter has just been diagnosed as hyperactive and learning disabled. She has had problems in school ever since she started, but they have become more severe since she started third grade. In the past six months or so, she has been eating a lot of junk food. I've read in the newspapers about hyperactivity and the Feingold diet. Should I give it a try?

8. A few weeks ago our next door neighbors' son John was diagnosed as learning disabled. What concerns us is that this diagnosis was made without any evaluation by a neurologist. A few years ago our nephew was diagnosed as learning disabled and as having minimal brain dysfunction. Isn't it true that minimal brain dysfunction goes along with learning disabilities? If so, isn't it potentially dangerous for John not to be seen by a neurologist? Wouldn't it help the teacher to know if brain dysfunction was causing John's learning problems?

Learning disabilities is the newest area of special education. It was not until the mid-1960s that classes for the learning disabled began to be established formally. In addition, learning disabilities is the fastest-growing area of special education. A mere 20 or so years ago, there were no formal classes for the learning disabled. Today, it would be difficult to find an individual school, no matter how small, that does not have services. You may be wondering how such a relatively well established profession as special education could have gone for so many years without recognizing such a large group of children. Were "learning disabled" children there all along, but served under different labels, such as emotional disturbance or mental retardation? Or were we ignoring these children because their problems are relatively subtle compared to those of children in other areas of special education?

There is no single answer. To a certain extent, these children had been served under other labels, and to a certain extent, their needs had been ignored. Before the term **learning disabilities** was introduced when the Association for Children with Learning Disabilities (ACLD) (the major parent organization for the learning disabled and now called the Association for Children and Adults with Learning Disabilities) was founded in 1963, many of these children had been called such things as "minimally brain injured," "dyslexic," and "perceptually disabled." These terms were confusing to both parents and special educators. Learning disabilities was a term to which hardly anyone objected.

The development of the ACLD and the focus on the label "learning disabilities" allowed a large number and variety of parents and professionals to rally for educational services for these children. Although rules had often been bent in the past to place these children in classes for the retarded or disturbed because these were the only special services available, parents and special educators alike were uneasy about these placements. Because these children's intelligence was within the normal range, many professionals and parents believed they should not be placed with the retarded. Similarly, because not all of them displayed severe emotional problems, placement with the emotionally disturbed was also unsatisfactory. The one thing parents and special educators could agree upon was that these children did have disabilities in learning that showed up as academic problems.

It is well to keep in mind the rapid growth of the field of learning disabilities when considering the many issues that surround it. As you read this chapter, you will notice the many examples of growing pains in the field. The issues connected with the field of learning disabilities are what make it both unsettling and exciting.

Even though learning disabilities is the newest area of special education, a number of changes have already occurred in how we think about learning disabled individuals, and especially in how we go about educating them. Let's listen in on a hypothetical conversation between Rick Rogers, a 27-year-old manager for a videogame parlor, and one of his steady customers, Kevin, a 12-year-old arcade addict. Both individuals have one other thing in common besides their interest in Donkey Kong—they have learning disabilities. You'll note that, even though only 15 years separate them, they have had quite different school experiences.

Rick: How's school going, Kevin?
Kevin: Not bad, Rick. How about for you?

Rick: Really well. I'm really glad I decided to go back and give college a second try. I think I can make it this time, what with all the new services the college is offering for the learning disabled.

Kevin: Is that program as good as I've heard?

Rick: I think it is. When I went to college the first time, there was no special programming for kids like me with real reading and language problems. Now, I've got a special advisor who's been trained in learning disabilities. And the tutors have been a real help, especially for my French class.

Kevin: That's great. Weren't you telling me that when you were in high school, there were no special programs for you?

Rick: Right. You're a lot better off than I was, Kevin. There's supposed to be a very good learning disabilities specialist over at Central High now. How's the mainstreaming working out, anyhow?

Kevin: I guess I like it pretty much.

Rick: Being mainstreamed and spending part of the day with a resource teacher and part of the day in a regular classroom probably seems natural to you. But when I was your age, the only services for kids like you and me were in self-contained settings. I hardly knew what a regular class looked like until I went to high school.

Kevin: Maybe today you'd be in a self-contained class, too, rather than in a resource room. They still have self-contained settings for some kids with more severe problems. I mean maybe your problems were more serious than mine. After all, weren't you actually in a class for the brain injured rather than the learning disabled?

Rick: Hey! If I were really that bad off, would I be standing here today, the manager of one of the most successful videogame parlors? I *was* in a class for the brain injured, but that's only because when I started elementary school, there were no services for the learning disabled. The focus was more on the brain. It was pretty much standard thinking that kids like you and me couldn't learn because we were brain damaged in some way.

Kevin: But weren't you brain damaged?

Rick: That's an interesting question. For many years, the term "minimal brain damage" was popular because kids like us had subtle symptoms that suggested we might have suffered minor brain injury.

Kevin: I don't think I've heard those terms.

Rick: You probably haven't because they're not used as much today. Special educators decided it made more sense to use a term descriptive of the behavior problem, rather than a vague cause. Listen, you didn't come here to listen to me lecture about the history of learning disabilities. You came here to throw away your hard-earned quarters on Donkey Kong and Space Invaders. That visual-motor training you're getting must be really paying off. You can really handle those joy sticks!

Kevin: But I don't get visual-motor exercises. Only a few of the kids in the learning disabilities program do.

Rick: That's right. I almost forgot. We all used to get it, no matter what. It makes a whole lot more sense to give it to just those few who really need it. Well listen, I'd better get back to work. Do you need any change?

Kevin: Nope.

Rick: See you later. Good luck.

Kevin: Thanks.

TODAY'S DEFINITION OF LEARNING DISABILITIES

As you would expect, some of the most heated debates have surrounded the definition of learning disabilities. The most commonly accepted definition is that of the federal government. It states:

> "Specific learning disability" means a disorder in one or more of the basic psychological processes involved in understanding or in using language, spoken or written, which may manifest itself in an imperfect ability to listen, think, speak, read, write, spell, or to do mathematical calculations. The term includes such conditions as perceptual handicaps, brain injury, minimal brain dysfunction, dyslexia, and developmental aphasia. The term does not include children who have learning problems which are primarily the result of visual, hearing, or motor handicaps, of mental retardation, of emotional disturbance, or of environmental, cultural, or economic disadvantage. (*Federal Register*, December 29, 1977, p. 65083)

Furthermore, the federal definition goes on to state that, before a child can be diagnosed as learning disabled, there must be

> . . . a severe discrepancy between achievement and intellectual ability in one or more of the following areas: oral expression, listening comprehension; basic reading skill; reading comprehension; mathematics calculation; or mathematics reasoning. (*Federal Register*, December 29, 1977, p. 65083)

Each aspect of this definition has advocates and opponents (see Focus).

After reading the positions, you probably have an uneasy feeling that you're still not quite sure what is and what is not a learning disability. Don't worry. This is the

---

FOCUS

TO BE OR NOT TO BE LEARNING DISABLED: SOME ISSUES OF DEFINITION

Every sentence contained in the 1977 federal definition of learning disabilities has its critics. The use of the phrase "basic psychological processes" is confusing. Very few can agree on what a psychological process is. In the past, attempts at training in psychological processes, such as visual or auditory memory or visual or auditory perception, have failed to result in gains in achievement (Hammill, Leigh, McNutt, and Larsen, 1981). The term "perceptual handicap" is confusing, since attempts to correct perceptual handicaps have failed to affect academic achievement. The terms "brain injury" and "minimal brain dysfunction" are unwarranted, since attempts to establish brain injury as a cause of learning disabilities in individual children often fail. It is also very difficult to determine when a learning problem is "primarily" the result of a learning disability instead of some other condition. In addition, the behavioral characteristics of and educational programs for learning-disabled children are often very similar to those for the mildly retarded and disturbed.

reaction you should have. Almost any knowledgeable professional in learning disabilities is troubled to a certain extent by the controversies surrounding the definition. To help clear up some of the fuzziness, it will help to keep two points in mind:

1. The least debatable point, the one on which virtually all authorities agree, is that a learning disability is a discrepancy between an individual's actual academic achievement and what he or she should be achieving based on intellectual ability.
2. Even though the 1977 federal definition is continually debated, no other definitions have come along to take its place. This is all the more noteworthy since this 1977 definition is virtually identical to a federal definition adopted in 1969. What this means is that the field has operated under essentially the same definition since 1969. It might just be that, with all its problems, the current definition is the one with which the most people can live.

PREVALENCE

Given the controversies about definition, it should not surprise you that prevalence estimates of learning disabilities vary dramatically. Depending on what sources you read, for example, you may come across estimates as high as 10, 20, or even 30 percent of school-age children. Most estimates, however, are much lower. The federal government figures we reported in Chapter 1, for example, estimate a range between 1 and 3 percent of individuals between 3 and 21 years of age. This estimate could go higher in the future. Many authorities are concerned about the growth in the number of children who are being identified as learning disabled.

ASSESSMENT

There is a variety of assessment instruments in the field of learning disabilities. If you've ever seen a typical learning-disabled child's folder, you've no doubt been amazed at all the tests that have been administered. No other area of special education equals that of learning disabilities with regard to the multitude of tests that are available. To try to keep them all straight is a heavy burden even for the learning disabilities specialist. It will help if you think of assessment in learning disabilities as falling into three general categories: (1) tests used primarily for diagnosing, or determining whether a learning disability exists; (2) tests used for making educational decisions; and (3) tests used for both purposes.

DIAGNOSIS TESTS

A **norm-referenced test** is one that has been administered to a large group of people so that any one individual's score can be compared to the average, or norm. A good example of norm-referenced testing is IQ testing. On an IQ test, a child's score is compared with those of other children of the same age. If, for example, Jeremy, who is 9 years and 3 months old, gets as many items correct as the average 9-year, 3-month-old child, then he will be assigned an IQ score of 100, which is the average IQ score.

Most achievement tests are also norm-referenced. If Jeremy takes a norm-referenced math achievement test, the number of items he answers correctly will be compared with the scores for other children at his grade or age level, and he will be assigned a score reflecting at what grade or age level he is achieving in math. If the number of items he gets right is equal to that for the average child who is 6.8 years old, his math achievement score will be 6.8 years.

Since in the field of learning disabilities we're concerned with identifying children who are not achieving up to their potential, the use of norm-referenced tests is important. In the case of Jeremy, for example, we can assume that, because he has the intelligence of an average 9-year, 3-month-old child, he should be achieving at approximately that level. The fact that his math achievement on a norm-referenced test is only at the level of an average 6.8-year-old alerts us to the distinct possibility that he has a learning disability in math.

EDUCATIONAL DECISION TESTS

CRITERION-REFERENCED TESTS. A **criterion-referenced test** is one that measures whether or not an individual scores above or below a preset criterion. The purpose of using a criterion-referenced test is to see how closely the child is able to achieve goals that have been set by the teacher. For example, you may decide that Jeremy should be able to compute 15 out of 20 math problems of a certain type within 10 minutes. If on his first try Jeremy does all 20 problems but only gets 12 correct, you would look at what kinds of errors he made and adjust your instruction accordingly before readministering the test to him. You would continue this process until Jeremy achieved the criterion of 15 out of 20.

There are some commercial criterion-referenced tests. For the most part, however, these tests are designed by the teacher to fit the specific needs of the individual child.

INFORMAL READING INVENTORIES. Another assessment tool that is usually teacher-designed is the **informal reading inventory (IRI).** To construct a typical IRI, you would put together a series of progressively more difficult paragraphs. You would ask a child such as Jeremy to read them aloud, starting with the easier ones. In this way, you could arrive at an *informal* estimate of Jeremy's reading level. In addition, by noting if he made any particular kinds of reading errors, you could make decisions regarding what areas of reading Jeremy needed work in.

BEHAVIORAL ASSESSMENT. **Behavioral assessment** is the observation and recording of specific behaviors on a continuous (usually daily) basis. If, for example, you were interested in Jeremy's ability to compute long division problems, you would give him some of these problems to work every day. By keeping a daily chart of such things as his rate of problem solution and his percentage correct, you could get an idea of Jeremy's progress in this skill.

DUAL-PURPOSE TESTS

Some tests have been designed both for the purpose of determining whether a learning disability exists and also for the purpose of providing information useful in remediation. The most popular of these tests are called process tests.

A **process test** attempts to measure underlying processes of learning, such as visual and auditory perception, visual and auditory memory, and eye-hand coordination. Two of the most frequently used process tests are the Illinois Test of Psycholinguistic Abilities and the Marianne Frostig Developmental Test of Visual Perception. These tests are made up of subtests that attempt to measure specific processing skills.

In terms of diagnosis, some professionals have used performance on these tests to determine whether a learning disability exists. Using process tests, you might decide that Jeremy had a learning disability if he scored low in visual perception. Visual perception is not the same as visual acuity. Visual acuity is what we mean when we consider whether or not a person needs glasses. **Visual perception problems** refer to such things as reading "b" for "d" (reversals) and having difficulty seeing one object among many (figure-ground problems). In terms of educational decision-making, some professionals have prescribed training activities based on results of process tests (Frostig and Horne,

1964; Kirk and Kirk, 1971; Minskoff, Wiseman, and Minskoff, 1974). To use a process approach with Jeremy, for instance, you might provide him with a number of activities designed to help his visual perception.

Process testing has created a great deal of debate within the field of learning disabilities. Today's special educator is much more cautious about the use of such tests. Some, in fact, believe them to be inappropriate. Their accuracy in measuring skills that are directly related to academic achievement has been seriously questioned (Coles, 1978; Salvia and Ysseldyke, 1981).

CAUSES

One of the most frustrating aspects of working in the area of learning disabilities is the fact that so little is known about the causes of these learning problems. There are many theories, but unfortunately none of them has proved adequate as an explanation of how children end up with learning disabilities. The result is that in very few cases can we be sure of the cause of a learning disability.

The many theories concerning the causes of learning disabilities can be grouped into four broad categories—brain dysfunction, biochemical disturbances, genetic factors, and environmental factors.

BRAIN DYSFUNCTION

Many experts believe learning disabilities are the result of subtle brain injury. Because of the slightness of the brain damage, many call it "minimal brain damage." Still others prefer to use the label **minimal brain dysfunction.** They point out that "dysfunction" simply means a brain that isn't working right, whereas "injury" or "damage" implies that the brain has suffered tissue damage. In virtually all cases of learning disabilities, it is impossible to prove that actual damage has occurred (Sandoval and Haapmanen, 1981).

Some professionals, however, are willing to say that there is minimal brain dysfunction based on a variety of behavioral signs displayed by the child (Gaddes, 1981). These behavioral signs are called "soft" signs because, unlike the "hard" signs of classical neurology, they are only borderline indicators that brain dysfunction is present. Some examples of soft signs are an awkward gait, clumsiness, and mixed dominance. **Mixed dominance** refers to an inconsistent preference for the left or right sides of the body. If you are right-handed but left-footed and left-eyed, you would be said to be mixed-dominant. Another frequent method of diagnosing brain dysfunction is through an **electroencephalogram** (EEG). An EEG measures the electrical activity of the brain through electrodes attached to the skull.

The major drawback to using soft signs or an EEG to diagnose brain dysfunction is that these methods are not very accurate (Coles, 1978; Winkler, Dixon, and Parker, 1970). Some people who really have suffered brain damage due to illness or an accident do not show abnormal soft signs. Large proportions of apparently healthy people do exhibit abnormal soft signs. It would not, for example, be all that unusual for you, even though you are not learning disabled and have never had any indication that you have brain damage, to have an abnormal EEG or some soft signs of brain dysfunction.

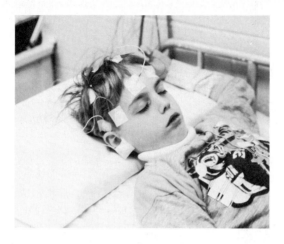

This child is having an EEG, a way of measuring electrical activity of the brain. Epilepsy Foundation of America.

BIOCHEMICAL DISTURBANCES

Some experts believe learning-disabled children may suffer from physiological problems, or biochemical disturbances. Two of the most commonly mentioned sources of these disturbances are vitamin deficiencies (Brenner, 1982) and allergies to certain foods or substances in food, such as food dyes (Mayron, 1979; Weiss, 1982). In the case of the food allergy theory, children have been described as exhibiting what has been called an **allergic tension fatigue syndrome**. This condition is characterized by two stages, with the tension state usually coming before the fatigue stage:

> *Tension Stage.* (1) *motor overactivity*: hyperactive, talkative, restless, inattentive, tremor, stuttering, "restless legs," clumsy, poor coordination, sometimes described as wild and unrestrained; (2) *sensory overactivity*: irritable, nervous, high-strung, whiny, excitable, hot-tempered, hard-to-please, oversensitive, jumpy, moody, fearful, anxious, temperamental, and sometimes markedly timid, especially seen in young children; they may also have insomnia, . . . and be especially sensitive to pain, noise, heat, and cold; the skin is particularly sensitive and the child does not like to be touched.

> *Fatigue Stage.* (1) *motor fatigue*: complaints of weakness, fatigue, achiness, sluggishness; (2) *sensory fatigue*: sleepy, weary, listless, exhausted, dullness of the brain, mental depression, and inability to concentrate. The child may also demonstrate pallor, infraorbital edema (circles or bags around or below the eyes), nasal stuffiness, increased salivation, increased sweating, abdominal pain, headache, and bed-wetting. (Mayron, 1979, p. 38)

Treatments have been designed for children with these suspected disorders. For vitamin deficiencies, some have advocated the use of large doses of vitamins (Cott, 1971). For food allergies, special diets have been recommended (Feingold, 1975). Feingold, for instance, believes that approximately 50 percent of hyperactive children can be helped by a diet that eliminates artificial food colorings and foods such as apples, oranges, tomatoes, and strawberries that naturally contain a substance called salicylate.

There is very little solid evidence to support the theory of vitamin deficiency as a cause of learning disabilities. Support for the food allergy theory is stronger, but most reviews indicate that claims for the importance of food allergies in causing learning disabilities are exaggerated (Henker and Whalen, 1980; Spring and Sandoval, 1976). At best, there may be a small subgroup of learning-disabled children who may respond favorably to the Feingold diet.

GENETIC FACTORS

There is some limited evidence that learning disabilities are inherited. We do know, for example, that if you are learning disabled there is a greater chance that your children will be learning disabled than if you are not (Owen, Adams, Forrest, Stolz, and Fisher, 1971). What we're not sure of is whether this is due to similar genetic or similar environmental backgrounds. The genetic contribution to learning disabilities is still unclear.

ENVIRONMENTAL FACTORS

In Chapter 2 you discovered just how difficult it is to prove that the environment is a cause of mental retardation. It is even more difficult to pinpoint the environment, especially the home environment, as a cause of learning disabilities. The vast majority of learning-disabled children do not come from impoverished homes. In the field of learning disabilities, however, some people argue that poor teaching is a type of poor environment (Engelmann, 1977). Although there is no solid proof that poor teaching accounts for even a small proportion of the cases of learning disabilities, today's special educator must be aware of this as a possibility. If you've been around schools for very long, you've no doubt observed teachers who were unable to provide adequate instruction for some of their pupils.

CHARACTERISTICS

Literally dozens of characteristics have been attributed to the learning disabled. In fact, a national task force (Clements, 1966) identified 99 separate ones. The 10 most frequently found symptoms were these:

1. Hyperactivity
2. Perceptual-motor impairments
3. Emotional lability (frequent shifts in mood)
4. General coordination deficits
5. Disorders of attention
6. Impulsivity
7. Disorders of memory and thinking
8. Specific academic problems (reading, arithmetic, writing, spelling)
9. Disorders of speech and hearing
10. Equivocal neurological signs and EEG irregularities

A COMMON THREAD: METACOGNITIVE DEFICITS

The "top ten" list covers a wide range of behaviors, and very few learning-disabled children exhibit all these characteristics. What this means is that learning-disabled children are a heterogeneous group. Today, most special educators agree that the learning disabled are the most heterogeneous group of children within special education. Each learning-disabled child has his or her own set of behavioral characteristics.

But even given this heterogeneity, researchers are discovering evidence for a common thread among a fairly large proportion of learning-disabled children. In other words, even though "no two are exactly alike," there may be some degree of similarity among many learning-disabled children. This common thread is what is called a **metacognitive deficit.**

A growing body of research suggests that many of the learning disabled exhibit metacognitive deficits (Baker, 1982; Bos and Filip, 1982; Loper, Hallahan, and Ianna, 1982; Wong, 1982). **Metacognition** is the ability to use study skills. It involves two components: "(1) an awareness of what skills, strategies, and resources are needed to perform a task effectively and (2) the ability to use self-regulatory mechanisms to ensure the successful completion of the task, such as planning one's moves, evaluating the effectiveness of one's ongoing activities, checking the outcomes of one's efforts, and remediating whatever difficulties arise" (Baker and Brown, in press) (Baker, 1982, pp. 27–28).

A variety of intellectual tasks can be more easily accomplished if you use metacognitive skills. For example, in reading comprehension, an area that frequently poses problems for the learning-disabled child, authorities have pointed to a number of helpful metacognitive strategies (Anderson, 1980; Baker and Anderson, 1981; Baker and Brown, 1980; Bos and Filip, 1982; Brown, 1980; Wong, 1982). Here are some of the strategies these authorities note as being used by efficient readers:

The efficient reader alters his reading style somewhat depending on the purpose and content of the reading material. This boy can casually skim his "light" reading material for recreational purposes. Nancy Hays, Monkmeyer.

1. *Clarifying the purposes of reading.* Before you read certain materials, it helps if you keep in mind what it is you want to get out of your reading. How you go about reading will vary, depending on whether you are reading a spicy novel or a spicy textbook like this one.

2. *Focusing attention on important parts of passages.* If you are able to pick out the main idea of a paragraph as you read and concentrate on understanding it rather than less important ideas, your overall comprehension will improve.

3. *Monitoring one's level of comprehension.* How often have you caught yourself midway down a page not comprehending what it is you've been reading? As long as you don't have to do this too often, this is actually the sign of a good reader. Knowing when you're understanding something versus when you're not understanding it is an important skill.

4. *Backtracking and scanning ahead.* When you do notice that you're not understanding what you're reading, some options are to stop and reread portions of the passage and/or to scan ahead for information that will help you comprehend the section with which you're having difficulty.

Each of these metacognitive skills contributes to reading comprehension in its own way, but there is also an underlying similarity among them. It helps if you think of them as indicators of a person's reading flexibility. If you are an efficient reader, you are able to adjust your reading behaviors to fit the particular material you're reading. The Focus illustrates how good readers, in comparison with poor readers, are much better able to alter their reading style to match the difficulty level of the reading material.

This child is reading a different type of material for the purpose of writing a school book report. Thus, he must concentrate on major points in the material.
Sybil Shackman, Monkmeyer.

IS IT EASIER TO REMEMBER THAT A TALL BOY PLAYED BASKETBALL OR THAT THE HUNGRY BOY PLAYED BASKETBALL?

Good readers know when and where to concentrate their efforts. As efficient readers, we know it takes less effort to read *People* magazine than to read a textbook. Unfortunately, poor readers are not as adept at making this kind of distinction. They do not adjust their reading style to fit the level of the reading material. An interesting study by Owings, Peterson, Bransford, Morris, and Stein (1980) demonstrates this strategy deficiency nicely. Although they didn't compare *People* magazine with *Special Education for Today*, the results are still instructive. What they did was to compare the most and the least successful fifth-grade readers' reading behavior on an easy versus a difficult reading passage. The difficult passage is reprinted below:

TALKING AT RECESS

All the boys got together during recess and talked about what they had done the day before. The sleepy boy had eaten a hamburger. The hungry boy had played basketball. The thirsty boy had taken a nap. The sick boy had played a trick on his brother. The tall boy had done his homework. The strong boy had drunk some Kool-Aid. The smart boy had helped his father cut wood. The funny boy had gone to the doctor. When the bell rang, all the boys ran to the door and lined up to go indoors. (p. 252)

The easier passages contained identical words, but the subject-predicate pairings were logical: ''The tall boy played basketball''; ''The hungry boy ate a hamburger.'' After reading one of the passages, children were asked questions, such as ''What did the hungry boy do?''

As you would expect, the less successful readers were less able to answer the comprehension questions. In addition, the results clearly point out that the poor readers were less able to adjust their reading style to match the level of the passage. The poor readers spent an equal amount of time studying both paragraphs, whereas the good readers spent more time on the difficult passage. The poor readers were unable to explain why the difficult passages were in fact harder to learn. Furthermore, Owings et al. believe that the less successful did not even notice the difference in difficulty between the two passages until they were asked to tell which paragraph made sense and which one was mixed up.

PERSONALITY CHARACTERISTICS

If we go along with the idea of metacognitive deficits, the picture we get is of a child who does not actively involve himself or herself in the learning situation (Hallahan and Bryan, 1981). Torgesen (1977, 1982), in fact, has referred to learning-disabled children as *inactive, passive* learners. They lack strategies for attacking academic problems (Lloyd, 1980). Many authorities believe there is a link between the metacognitive deficits and the learning-disabled child's tendency to view himself or herself as controlled by external rather than internal forces. Like the mentally retarded children we discussed in Chapter 2, they have personalities characterized by an **external** rather than an **internal locus of control.** They are less likely than their nondisabled peers to attribute the few successes they have to ability and also less likely to blame their failures on lack of effort (Pearl and Bryan, 1982). In other words, learning-disabled children are quick to

SOME LD CHILDREN MAY GET LOST IN THEIR "SEARCH FOR TOMORROW"

A wide array of studies have shown that learning-disabled students are prime candidates for social rejection. They have difficulties in making and keeping friends. For years researchers have been relatively content to point out that such social adjustment problems exist. Today's researcher, however, is interested in discovering the specific behaviors that bring about this lack of peer acceptance. One notion that is receiving considerable support is the idea that learning-disabled children often lack social comprehension (Bachara, 1976; Bryan, 1977; Horowitz, 1981; Wong and Wong, 1980). They have problems in reading social cues from others and are not able to interpret the feelings and emotions of others.

One clever study that highlights their social comprehension failures compared learning-disabled and nondisabled children on ability to judge the feelings of soap opera characters (Pearl and Cosden, 1982). After showing them segments depicting a male and female discussing emotional topics, the researchers asked the children multiple-choice questions requiring them to make inferences about the feelings and interactions of the actors. The results clearly indicated that the "LD group was consistently less accurate than the NLD group in their understanding of the social interactions they viewed" (p. 372).

place themselves in a "Damned if you do, damned if you don't" box. If they succeed, they do not end up feeling good about it because they believe factors other than their own ability, such as luck or task difficulty, were responsible. If they fail, they are not able to rationalize that it was because they did not try hard enough.

Learning-disabled children are also frequently socially rejected by their peers (Bryan, 1976). It's no wonder that teachers so often point out that the social and personality problems of the learning disabled are at least as disabling as the academic problems themselves. It makes us aware that in educating the learning-disabled child we need to be prepared to work on social adjustment problems as well as academic deficiencies (see Focus).

TODAY'S EDUCATIONAL METHODS FOR THE LEARNING DISABLED

Nowhere is today's emphasis on mainstreaming more apparent than in the area of learning disabilities. Although you will run across an occasional residential school specializing in services for the learning disabled and special self-contained classes are not at all uncommon, you are most apt today to find learning-disabled children in a regular classroom–resource room combination.

The proportion of time learning-disabled children spend in the resource room varies greatly from child to child. Harry, a fourth-grader whose only problem is that he's one grade level behind in math, may spend as little as two one-hour sessions each week with the resource teacher. Another fourth-grader, Jason, who's also one grade level behind in math but is also two years below grade level in reading and spelling, may spend as much as two hours every day with the resource teacher.

How successful a resource program is depends to a great extent on the working relationship between the resource teacher and the regular class teacher. Communication is the key here. Today's successful resource teacher is sure to coordinate his or her efforts with those of the regular class teacher. Both teachers need to be aware of what the other is doing so they can complement each other's educational programming.

The ultimate goal for all learning disabled children is to return them to the regular classroom for almost all, if not all, of the school day. Even children whose problems are severe enough to require special self-contained class placement should, with today's educational techniques, have a good chance of returning to the regular class. Often, the LD child who's about to be moved from a self-contained setting to a regular class will gradually spend more and more time in the regular class. In this way, the self-contained class functions as a resource room. Once it has been determined that the child can spend a relatively good proportion of time in the regular classroom—say two or three hours—he or she may be assigned to a regular classroom–resource room combination.

PRESCHOOL PROGRAMMING

Special educators are hesitant to jump in and begin identifying preschool children as learning disabled. There is a very good reason for this reluctance. When we talk about a learning-disabled child, we're usually referring to a child who has problems in academic subjects such as reading and math. A child is not usually faced with academic subjects until first grade. So preschool diagnosis really becomes more a matter of prediction than of identification. And prediction is always less accurate than identification.

Special educators are thus cautious about setting up formal classes for preschool learning-disabled children. They don't want to run the risk of needlessly labeling children as handicapped. Special educators are also reluctant to establish preschool classes for the mildly retarded for the same reasons. What sometimes happens is that school officials will establish preschool services for children who appear to be "at risk" to develop learning disabilities or mental retardation. The children are placed in these classes without being officially labeled as learning disabled or mentally retarded.

ELEMENTARY PROGRAMMING

The major effort in the development of educational approaches and services for learning-disabled populations has been focused on children in the elementary school years. The methods generally fall into two categories: those designed for dealing with attentional problems and hyperactivity, and those designed for dealing with academic problems.

DEALING WITH ATTENTIONAL PROBLEMS AND HYPERACTIVITY. If you ask teachers of the learning disabled what characteristics children most often display that interfere with ability to learn, they will almost invariably mention attentional problems and hyperactivity. It's not at all surprising that they believe these maladaptive behaviors prevent the child from benefitting from instruction. If Billy can't sit still and concentrate on his work, then it follows that he will be difficult to teach. So professionals have devoted much energy to developing procedures for controlling hyperactive and inattentive behavior.

The different approaches to the hyperactive and inattentive child can be grouped into four categories: structure and stimulus reduction, drugs, behavior modification, and cognitive behavior modification. In reading about these methods, keep in mind that they may not always be enough for the learning-disabled child. For Billy, they may get him back on task. But if Billy also has other problems that inhibit him from learning, his teacher will need to attack those directly as well. For Charlotte, on the other hand, one of these approaches might be just right because her only problem is an inability to sit still and concentrate. In the case of Billy, the attentional problems are in addition to his academic deficiencies. In the case of Charlotte, the attentional problems are the cause of her academic difficulties.

STRUCTURE AND STIMULUS REDUCTION. One of the earliest methods for dealing with hyperactive and inattentive children was the structure and stimulus reduction approach. Originally developed for use with the mentally retarded (Strauss and Lehtinen, 1947), a structured program with stimulus reduction was first recommended for children who fit the category of learning disabled by William Cruickshank and his colleagues (Cruickshank, Bentzen, Ratzeburg, and Tannhauser, 1961). In proposing a **structured method,** Cruickshank was advocating a program that is heavily teacher-directed. As much as possible, the teacher plans every minute of every day for each child. The day's schedule is organized in such a way that there is very little wasted or unproductive time. **Stimulus reduction** refers to an attempt to keep the hyperactive and distractible child away from irrelevant stimulation or events that interfere with learning. The rationale here is that if Billy and Charlotte are distracted by things in their environment, such as car noises outside the window, a conversation between the teacher and Timmy in the back of the room, or bright pictures on the bulletin board, they should be shielded from these things so that they can concentrate on their work. Cruickshank recommended a number of environmental modifications for children like Billy and Charlotte, such as

Cubicles and three-sided work areas
Opaque windows
Carpeting
Limited use of bulletin boards
Soundproofing materials

There has been considerable controversy over the value of stimulus-reduction techniques. The conclusion you can draw from research on the subject is that the techniques do lead to enhanced attention, but as you'd expect from the discussion above, they do not automatically lead to increased academic achievement (Hallahan and Kauffman, 1976).

DRUGS. Debate has raged for some time over the use of drugs to control hyperactivity and inattentive behavior. At one time there was disagreement over whether or not drugs were effective in controlling such behaviors, but that is no longer the major issue. Research has demonstrated that medication, especially the stimulant drug Ritalin, is often effective in decreasing hyperactivity and inattentiveness (Gadow, 1981; Henker and Whalen, 1980). What is at issue now is whether the benefits are worth the risk drugs may bring with some children in terms of physiological and/or psychological side effects.

Possible physiological side effects are decrease in appetite and increase in sleeplessness. With regard to psychological side effects, some authorities have expressed fears that using drugs with children might lead to undesirable motivational changes on the part of both the child and the adults who deal with that child. The concern here is that both the child and the adult may become psychologically dependent on the medication. Billy might learn to rely too much on his pills rather than learning to develop his own set of self-control mechanisms. Billy's parents and teachers might feel that once he is on drugs, they can cut back on their efforts to help him. Based on these considerations, today's special educator:

1. Takes a cautious view of the use of medication.
2. Views drugs as a treatment to turn to only when other approaches have failed.
3. Recognizes that medication alone is never enough; it always needs to be used in combination with other educational approaches.

BEHAVIOR MODIFICATION. **Behavior modification** is the use of reinforcement or punishment in order to increase or decrease certain behaviors. We have all used behavior modification at one time or another. For example, every time you thank someone for something he or she has done, you are using behavior modification. You are rewarding that person with praise for doing something nice. Because of that "thanks," the person is more likely to repeat the behavior in the future. Likewise, when you've been confronted by a behavior you didn't particularly like, you've sometimes used a form of behavior modification to attempt to decrease that behavior. Most of us have had the unpleasant experience of having to ignore someone who was being obnoxious in the hope that he or she would go away. The difference between our casual use of behavior modification in everyday situations and our use of it to control hyperactivity and attention is that in the latter case we apply it in a much more systematic, orderly, and purposeful fashion.

There is a wealth of evidence that the use of behavior modification can result in increases in attention and decreases in hyperactivity (Hallahan and Kauffman, 1976). Teachers have successfully used methods such as praise for attentive behavior and ignoring for inattentive and hyperactive behavior. In more difficult cases, they have used concrete reinforcers such as candies, trinkets, or tokens that can be exchanged for prizes.

COGNITIVE BEHAVIOR MODIFICATION (CBM). Whereas in behavior modification you are attempting to modify observable behaviors such as Wanda's getting out of her seat, in **cognitive behavior modification** (**CBM**) you are trying to modify unobservable thought processes, such as getting Wanda to think through what it is she must do to stay seated and concentrate on her work. In contrast to behavior modification, CBM stresses teaching the child self-initiative.

Right from the beginning, the child is alerted to the problem, informed of the CBM procedures, and shown the desirable outcome. The emphasis is on the child's full awareness and independent participation in the intervention. In fact, it is this emphasis on independence and self-control that has made the CBM approach so appealing to some professionals. Today's special educator is concerned about the inactive, passive learning style of many learning-disabled children. To combat this passivity, many authorities are turning to CBM techniques because they are designed to involve the child as an active agent in the learning process.

CBM for attentional problems and/or hyperactivity can take many forms. One method that has been particularly successful is self-monitoring (Hallahan, Lloyd, Kauff-

Today's special educator must be concerned about the inactive, passive learning style of many learning disabled children. Ken Karp.

man, and Loper, 1983; Kneedler and Hallahan, in press). In **self-monitoring**, the individual evaluates his or her own behavior and then keeps a record of that evaluation. Hallahan and colleagues have designed a procedure in which children ask themselves the question "Was I paying attention?" every time they hear a tone on an audiocassette tape recorder. (The tones have been prerecorded by the teacher so that they occur at random intervals, with the average interval being about 45 seconds.) If the child can answer "yes," then he or she makes a check in the Yes column on a sheet of paper; if the answer is "no," then he or she makes a check in the No column. Gradually, the children are weaned from reliance on the tones and the recording sheets. Below is a sample set of instructions for the self-monitoring procedure; the Focus gives an example of the approach in action.

"Johnny, you know how paying attention to your work has been a problem for you. You've heard teachers tell you, 'Pay attention,' 'Get to work,' 'What are you supposed to be doing?' and things like that. Well, today we're going to start something that will help you help yourself pay attention better. First we need to make sure that you know what paying attention means. This is what I mean by paying attention." (Teacher models immediate and sustained attention to task.) "And this is what I mean by not paying attention." (Teacher models attentive and inattentive behaviors and requires the student to categorize them.) "Okay, now let me show you what we're going to do. While you're working, this tape recorder will be turned on. Every once in awhile, you'll hear a little sound like this:" (Teacher plays tone on tape). "And when you hear that sound, quietly ask yourself, 'Was I paying attention?' If you answer 'yes,' put a check in this box. If you answer 'no,' put a

SELF-MONITORING OF ATTENTION:
A PLAY WITH ONE ACTOR

The following scene shows how the self-monitoring procedure might be implemented.

Scene   A classroom of students engaged in various activities. One teacher is walking about the room, preparing for her next activity. Some students are sitting in a semi-circle facing another teacher and answering questions. Other students are sitting at their desks and writing on papers or in workbooks. Edwin is working at his own desk. The teacher picks up some pages that have green strips of paper attached at the top.

Teacher   (*Walking up to Edwin's desk*): Edwin, here are your seatwork pages for today. I'm going to start the tape and I want you to self-record like you have been doing. What are you going to ask yourself when you hear the beep?

Edwin   (*Taking papers*): Was I paying attention?

Teacher   Okay, that's it. (*Turning away.*) Bobby, Jackie, and Anne; it's time for spelling group. (*Starts a tape recorder and walks toward front of room where three students are gathering.*)

Edwin   (*Begins working on his assignments; is continuing to work when a tone comes from the tape recorder. Edwin's lips barely move as he almost inaudibly whispers*): Was I paying attention? Yes. (*He marks on the green strip of paper and returns to work. Later, another tone comes from the tape recorder. Edwin whispers.*) Was I paying attention? Yes. (*He marks on the green strip of paper and returns to work. Later, as the students in one group laugh, Edwin looks up and watches them. While he is looking up, a tone occurs.*) Was I paying attention? No. (*He marks the strip of paper and begins working again. He continues working, questioning himself when the tone occurs, and recording his answers.*)

Source: D. P. Hallahan, J. W. Lloyd, and L. Stoller, *Improving attention with self-monitoring: A manual for teachers.* University of Virginia Learning Disabilities Research Institute, Charlottesville, 1982.

check in this box. Then go right back to work. When you hear the sound again, ask the question, answer it, mark your answer, and go back to work. Now, let me show you how it works." (Teacher models entire procedure.) "Now, Johnny, I bet you can do this. Tell me what you're going to do every time you hear a tone. Let's try it. I'll start the tape and you work on these papers." (Teacher observes student's implementation of the entire procedure, praises its correct use, and gradually withdraws.) (Hallahan, Lloyd, and Stoller, 1982)

DEALING WITH ACADEMIC PROBLEMS. Although attentional difficulties and hyperactivity are widespread problems among the learning disabled, they are not evident in all youngsters. Academic problems, on the other hand, are present in all learning-disabled children. If these academic difficulties are not due solely to problems of inattention and hyperactivity, then the teacher will need to use methods designed specifically for improving achievement in such areas as reading, math, and spelling. Methods for working with academic deficiencies generally fall into four categories: process training, multisensory approaches, behavioral approaches, and cognitive behavior modification.

PROCESS TRAINING. **Process training** involves an attempt to train psychological processes (such as visual and auditory perception) that supposedly underlie the ability to achieve in such things as reading and math. In other words, with a process training approach, we assume that poor reading skills are due to faulty perceptual abilities. (Keep in mind that, as we noted when we discussed process testing earlier, deficient perceptual abilities do not mean that the person has the same problems as someone who is blind or deaf. For the visually or hearing impaired, the problem is one of receiving information. For those with perceptual difficulties, the problem is organizing and interpreting information correctly.)

Rather than working directly on reading, then, the teacher would provide the child with exercises designed to train perceptual abilities. If, for example, your problems were visual in nature, the teacher might have you doing such things as drawing lines on a sheet of paper from one object to another through a narrow "tunnel" without touching the sides. Or you might be asked to pick out "hidden" objects on a sheet of paper containing a variety of different figures.

There are a number of different process training materials available (Barsch, 1965; Frostig and Horne, 1964; Getman, Kane, and McKee, 1968; Kephart, 1971; Kirk and Kirk, 1971; Minskoff, Wiseman, and Minskoff, 1974). At one time, process training was the most popular treatment approach for learning disabilities. Although it is still used, today it no longer enjoys such widespread acceptance. Today's special educator is often skeptical about the worth of process training. Many authorities have pointed out that most of the research on the subject has shown process training to have limited

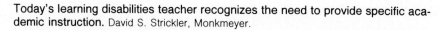

Today's learning disabilities teacher recognizes the need to provide specific academic instruction. David S. Strickler, Monkmeyer.

value for academic gains (Cook and Welch, 1980; Hallahan and Cruickshank, 1973; Hammill and Larsen, 1974; Myers and Hammill, 1982).

MULTISENSORY APPROACHES. **Multisensory programs** use some of the same training activities as those used in process training, although these approaches often focus directly on academic materials (Fernald, 1943; Gillingham and Stillman, 1956). The philosophy behind multisensory methods is that instruction involving a multitude of senses will be more effective. In Fernald's VAKT method (V = visual, A = auditory, K = kinesthetic sensation received from movement, T = tactual), for instance, four different senses are a part of the lessons. If you were taught to read words by the VAKT method, you would first be shown the word to look at (visual). After the teacher would say the word, you would too (auditory). Then you would trace the word (kinesthetic and tactual).

BEHAVIORAL APPROACHES. Behavioral approaches for academic problems, in contrast to process training and multisensory approaches, rarely consider sensory or perceptual processes. Behavioral methods focus on the specific skills involved in performing academic tasks. They are frequently characterized by:

1. **Task analysis** to break down more complex activities, such as reading, into component skills so that these skills can be fostered.
2. Drill to give the child practice in learning these skills.
3. Frequent use of corrective feedback and reinforcement.
4. Frequent, usually daily, measurement of how well the child is progressing.

A good example of a task analysis that has broken down an academic task into its component parts is shown in Table 3–1. Note the specificity.

Siegfried Engelmann (1977) and his colleagues have developed a number of commercially available programs that follow the behavioral model. (Some of these programs are in the DISTAR [Direct Instruction System for Teaching Arithmetic and Reading], series and some are in the Corrective Reading Program and Corrective Mathematics Program.) They are characterized by being (a) fast-paced instruction, (b) directed by the teacher, and (c) on academic materials carefully sequenced into small steps.

COGNITIVE BEHAVIOR MODIFICATION (CBM). As with CBM for inattention and hyperactivity, CBM for academic problems emphasizes getting individuals to think before they act. Many of today's learning disabilities specialists are experimenting with CBM techniques because they believe they help learning-disabled children become less passive in learning style. The goal is to make students self-sufficient learners by providing them with strategies they can use on their own.

Table 3–2 from Grimes (1981) highlights the differences between teaching approaches such as CBM that attempt to foster independence and self-control and those that do not.

CBM approaches to academic instruction are springing up in many different parts of the United States (for example in Virginia [Lloyd and deBettencourt, 1982] and in Kansas [Schumaker, Deshler, Alley, Warner, and Denton, 1982]) and Canada (Wong and Jones, 1982). The Wong and Jones method of teaching learning-disabled students

```
┌──────────────────────────────────────────────────────────────────────────┐
│                              TABLE 3-1                                     │
│                        Strategy for Long Division                          │
│                     (Using 18048 ÷ 48 as an example)                       │
└──────────────────────────────────────────────────────────────────────────┘
```

STEPS IN STRATEGY	EXAMPLE
1. DIVIDE divisor into current dividend.	48 goes into 180
2. Write quotient from step 1 in answer space—last digit in current dividend.	3 times
3. MULTIPLY last digit of divisor by last digit of quotient.	3 times 48 equals
4. Write product beneath current dividend.	144
5. COMPARE current product (from step 4) with current dividend:	144 is less than 180, so . . .
IF product is greater than dividend, return to step 2, substitute (quotient − 1) for last quotient, and continue through steps 3–5 in order.	
IF product is equal to or less than dividend, continue.	
6. SUBTRACT current product from current dividend.	180 minus 144 equals 36
7. COMPARE difference with divisor:	36 is less than 48, so . . .
IF difference is greater than or equal to divisor, return to step 2, substitute (quotient + 1) for last quotient, and continue through steps 3–7 in order.	
IF difference is less than divisor, continue.	
8. BRING DOWN next digit from original quotient and go to step 1; IF there are no more digits to bring down, stop and check answer for accuracy.	Bring down the 4 and go back to step 2 using 364 as the current quotient . . .

Source: J. W. Lloyd and L. J. deBettencourt, *Academic strategy training: A manual for teachers.* University of Virginia Learning Disabilities Research Institute, Charlottesville, 1982.

to use self-questioning strategies while reading in order to improve comprehension is a good example of a CBM approach. They taught students to engage in the following strategies while reading:

1. Ask themselves, "What am I studying the passage for?"
2. Find the main ideas and underline them.
3. Think of a question about the main idea and write it.
4. Look back at questions and answers to see how they provided more information.

SECONDARY AND POSTSECONDARY PROGRAMMING

For many years there were almost no formal educational services for learning-disabled students beyond the elementary school years. In the late 1970s, however, programs for this older population mushroomed. With the passage of PL 94–142, of course, school systems are now held responsible for providing services for the secondary student. In addition, today it is not at all uncommon to find special services being made available for college students with learning disabilities. Some colleges, in fact, have highlighted these services as a way of recruiting learning-disabled students.

    The reason for this sudden rush is the realization that learning-disabled students

TABLE 3–2
Teacher Techniques and Student Outcome

PROCEDURES WHICH APPEAR TO FOSTER STUDENT DEPENDENCY AND FAILURE	PROCEDURES WHICH APPEAR TO FOSTER STUDENT MOTIVATION AND SELF-CONTROL
Norm-referenced evaluation and grading based on peer comparisons.	Criterion-referenced evaluation and grading.
Teacher use of labels such as *distractible, poor memory, impulsive,* to rationalize child's learning problem.	Realistic teacher expectation of child performance considering child's prerequisite skills and level and amount of information to be learned.
Teacher attitude that child's lack of learning is due to deficits within the child.	Child's lack of learning attributed to use of inappropriate instructional strategies.
Low teacher expectation for child performance.	Teaching of self-instructional strategies of inner speech, memory rehearsal, mnemonics, drill, etc. to enable child to direct own learning.
Achievement testing conducted at end of year to evaluate child's learning.	Direct measurement of skills conducted frequently to measure effectiveness of teaching method and child's learning.
Large-group instruction geared to middle ability group.	Small group instruction based on child's level and needs.
Instructional content presented in large units of knowledge.	Instructional content presented by the task analysis method with information broken down to manageable steps of learning.
Evaluative feedback very general. Lack of information given in feedback on how to improve performance.	Evaluative feedback specific with demonstration of how to complete problem correctly.
Teacher as sole director of learning experiences.	Child as collaborator in choosing learning experiences, setting goals, charting skills that have been mastered.
Teacher always places the child in the "being helped" role, thus emphasizing his dependent position.	Role reversal where the child as a peer tutor helps another child with the same problem.

Source: L. Grimes, Learned helplessness and attribution theory: Redefining children's learning problems. *Learning Disability Quarterly,* 1981, *4,* 91–100.

do *not* suddenly outgrow their disabilities. Much research has documented the fact that academic and social adjustment problems often remain into the teenage years and beyond (Gottesman, 1979; Spreen, 1980; Wiederholt, 1978). In addition, vocational success and happiness is especially difficult for learning-disabled adults (Cronin and Gerber, 1982; Fafard and Haubrich, 1981; Patton and Polloway, 1982; White, Alley, Deshler, Schumaker, Warner, and Clark, 1982).

SECONDARY PROGRAMMING. Today's secondary teacher of the learning disabled needs to be ready to offer a variety of educational options for students. It is not enough to provide only more of what has been available at the elementary level. In addition to formal academic instruction, secondary programming needs to prepare some students for the job market. One of the most critical decisions the secondary learning-disabilities specialist makes is whether or not particular children are college-bound. If not, vocational training must be available. The more severe cases of learning disabilities will need some exposure to **functional academics.** With functional academics, the focus is on teaching students to use academics in order to do such things as balance a checkbook, make change, and fill out a job application form. Regular academics emphasize using academic learning, such as math or reading, to achieve more academic learning, such as science or history.

POSTSECONDARY PROGRAMMING. Even though more and more colleges and universities are establishing special services for the learning disabled, there is no agreement on the best type of program. We do know, from what little research has been done, that some of the most common problems experienced by learning-disabled college students are in reading, effective study habits, and written language skills (Vogel, 1982).

Some students with severe reading problems make use of Recordings for the Blind (a service that provides recordings of college texts as well as other materials). Many of these students have great difficulty taking notes during lectures (see Focus). Some colleges provide note-takers for learning-disabled students. Another common procedure is for the students to record their lectures. Written language skills are particularly difficult to deal with because they are so pervasive and so serious. You've no doubt heard complaints among college and university faculty that even their so-called nondisabled students are often poor writers. Many colleges and universities now offer writing clinics for students, whether they have been specifically identified as learning disabled or not.

In many ways, we are still in the experimental stages of educational services for the learning-disabled adolescent and adult. Some of the major future efforts at developing educational programs for the learning disabled will no doubt be aimed at this older population.

One of the most common problems encountered by learning disabled college students is the ability to take notes during lectures. George Zimbel, Monkmeyer.

NOTE-TAKING: AN UNDERESTIMATED SKILL

The ability to take good notes during lectures is probably one of the most underrated skills a college student can possess. The next time you attend the lecture for the course you are taking on exceptional children, note how many high-level skills are involved in taking notes. Vogel (1982) summarizes the problems encountered by some learning-disabled students when taking notes:

> For many LD adults, the task of taking notes in lectures is overwhelming, nor is it any wonder. Note-taking requires simultaneous listening, comprehending, and synthesizing and/or extracting main ideas while retaining them long enough to formulate a synopsis and write it down. The writing act, in turn, requires automaticity and speed in letter formation and sufficient legibility and spelling ability to decipher what has been written at a later time. It is not surprising that LD college students' notes are often sparse, incomplete, and frequently inaccurate. The student may have written down an overabundance of details, obscuring the main ideas, misperceived unfamiliar words or proper nouns, or misunderstood the major concepts. (p. 523)

TECHNOLOGICAL ADVANCES

Technology in the form of microcomputers is beginning to provide new alternatives for educating the learning disabled. Two basic types of microcomputer programs have been developed:

1. Those designed to provide supplemental drill and practice in academic skills.
2. Those designed to attempt to alter learning styles.

Both types of materials are too new to evaluate their effectiveness. There is little doubt, however, that it will be wise for tomorrow's, if not today's, learning disabilities teachers to be familiar with some of these programs.

PROGRAMS FOR DRILL AND PRACTICE

The need to individualize instruction for each child in a learning disabilities class is a challenge faced by special education teachers. Some of the available programs are geared toward minimizing teacher effort and maximizing the variety of instructional material suitable for individual children.

Many commercial programs include features that will place the student at the appropriate skill level and evaluate performance, as well as provide sequential skill review and practice. These programs produce workbooklike displays and use the motivational aspects of computer interaction and display to maintain student interest and attention. Here are a few examples.

LESSONS IN SYNTAX (McCarr, 1982). This is an example of a language arts program. When used with the corresponding workbook, it is a language program for eight syntactic structures including negation, participles, and passive voice. The program allows children to manipulate words and form sentences during the self-instructional lessons.

K–8 MATH WITH STUDENT MANAGEMENT PROGRAM. Developed by Radio Shack, this program provides supplemental math drill and practice for grades 1 through 8 (Paras, 1982). It includes features that automatically place the student at the correct instructional level, provide sequential skill practice, test specific skill acquisition, and allow the student to manage the program with little teacher involvement. The K–8 Math with Student Management Program provides positive feedback in the form of a smiling face, includes the option of a marker above problems in which regrouping is necessary, and emits a prompting message if the student does not respond in 15 seconds. A textbook cross-reference guide accompanies this program. The guide indicates the pages of six popular basal arithmetic texts that correspond to lessons in the math program.

PRIMER 81 (Land and Farmer, 1981). This is a reading package designed to teach letter and word recognition to learning-disabled adults and children. The package requires no specific level of literacy, and the first program, TALKWRITER, uses synthesized speech and visual displays to teach keyboard use. The three major programs are LETTER-FLASH, WORDFLASH, and SENTENCEFLASH, which drill letters, words, and simple sentences. An additional program, TROUBLESHOOT, will statistically test the consistency of errors and identify probable error sources.

COMPUTERIZED SPELLING REMEDIATION PROGRAM (Hasselbring, 1982). This program has been developed to reflect research findings on effective methods of teaching learning-disabled children. Its development was influenced by research indicating that children learn more spelling words when imitation of incorrect spellings precedes modeling of the correct response. This spelling program presents a word by saying it in isolation, using the word in a sentence, and then repeating the word in isolation.

PROGRAMS FOR ALTERING LEARNING STYLES

Some individuals have suggested that the relatively large number of programs designed to provide academic instruction and skill practice fall short of maximizing the instructional potential of microcomputers for learning-disabled children (Kidd and Holmes, 1982; Schiffman, Tobin, and Cassidy-Bronson, 1982). The microcomputer has been proposed as a vehicle for teaching children new approaches for problem-solving, and as a method of overcoming some of the deficits traditionally used to characterize learning-disabled children, such as a short attention span and poor motor coordination. A child usually interacts with a computer through a keyboard or a paddle. The suggestion by Budoff and Hutton (1982) that interaction with microcomputers can improve fine-motor coordination is one example of an indirect way of correcting nonacademic deficits with computers.

Learning-disabled children have been described as passive learners who do not take an active part in the learning process. Computer interaction demands a degree of learner participation, and some programs encourage the development of active learning styles and problem-solving strategies. These programs involve "discovery" learning approaches as opposed to drill or rote instruction (McCann, 1981). Weir, Russell, and Valente (1982) and Geoffrion (1981) propose that the LOGO program, which enables children to program their own learning activities, may be helpful in teaching problem-solving strategies in addition to requiring extensive learner activity.

Crowther (1981) has developed programs that emphasize features that maintain the attention of learning-disabled children and provide constant concept repetition and reinforcement. His program for teaching beginning numerical concepts includes the extensive use of colorful graphics and both auditory and visual reinforcement. The presentation of the number 5, for example, begins with a large visual display of the numeral five, followed by five beeps. A hand with five fingers is then drawn on the screen, the five beeps are repeated, each finger is individually numbered, and a small numeral five appears on the screen. The same presentation appears three times, with each sequence containing different examples and graphics. Review and test procedures also incorporate graphic images. Crowther proposes that the frequent use of constantly changing graphics will overcome the situational attention difficulties experienced by learning-disabled children and maintain their interest throughout an entire lesson.

Microcomputers can be used in a variety of ways for drill, practice, or discovery learning. Microcomputers enable teachers to provide individualized instruction efficiently, regardless of the different subject-specific skill levels of the children in their classes (Maroun, 1980). However, the short- and long-range value of microcomputer technology for improving the education of learning-disabled individuals has yet to be established. The content as well as the format of instructional programs must be carefully developed to meet the needs of specific children (Morsink and Morsink, 1980). But when used in response to students' needs, research-based computer programs may provide an exciting and effective means of teaching learning-disabled children.

ANSWERS TO FREQUENTLY ASKED QUESTIONS
LEARNING DISABILITIES

1. Your fears are not at all unreasonable, but there is no research to indicate that hyperactive children or their friends will develop a desire for, or physiological dependency on, drugs. Nevertheless, until more research is done you cannot rule out the possibility of physiological or psychological dependency, so it would be wise for you to talk this over with your son. Explain to him that there is a difference between using drugs prescriptively, as in the case of Andy, and misusing drugs, as many of his peers at school do. Make sure he understands that Andy is using medication because his doctor believes it will help him. Also make sure he understands that Andy is not getting any "high" from his medication; rather, it is an attempt to help him concentrate better and be less hyperactive.

2. It is much too early to rule out the possibility that your son will be able to attend college. Since he is receiving a limited amount of resource help rather than being placed in a self-contained class, it sounds as though his problems are not severe. Many children formerly identified as learning disabled have received college and even postgraduate degrees. In addition, some colleges are now making adjustments in terms of graduation requirements and tutorial services to accommodate the special needs of learning-disabled students. Learning disabilities is still a relatively new field. As special educators learn more about how to remediate learning disabilities, your son's chances to fulfill his potential should increase even more.

3. Yes, set up a meeting with her as soon as possible. For the child's welfare, it is important that you and the resource teacher decide on who should be doing what. In defense of the resource teacher, it is quite possible that she has experienced a great deal of resistance and even hostility from regular classroom teachers. If you express a desire to work with her, you may be pleasantly surprised to find her extremely receptive to the idea.

4. Not at all. It is quite common for children to exhibit reversals when they first begin to read. If the reversals persist so that he is still having a problem when he is 8 or 9 years of age, you might want to seek help. The fact that he is beginning to read at a relatively early age is also a good indication that he is not going to have reading problems.

5. No. Actually, it sounds as if the drug is working. Drugs for hyperactivity are just that—for hyperactivity. Drugs can reduce a child's hyperactivity and even let him or her perform better on relatively simple tasks. More complex tasks, such as reading, will not be helped automatically by drugs. In other words, drugs can "ready" the student for academic instruction, but we're afraid the burden for teaching the student still falls on your shoulders. From what you say, it sounds as if no one has been in contact with you about the student's progress since she started drug therapy. That is inexcusable. Someone (probably the school psychologist) should have talked with you about how well the drug is working. Such monitoring of the girl's behavior is necessary to ensure that she is on the proper dosage.

6. No. It's more likely that Linda's teacher does not believe such training would be helpful for her. In recent years, fewer and fewer teachers are using perceptual-motor training. Research indicates that, unless a child is exhibiting perceptual motor problems (some learning-disabled children do and some don't), training in this area may not be useful. And even if the child is showing signs of perceptual motor problems, although training may help some of the perceptual problems, there is no guarantee that it will help the academic learning problems.

7. Although there probably would be no harm in trying out the diet as long as you did so under the supervision of a physician, do not expect miracles. Most research on Feingold's diet indicates that many of the claims reported in the popular press have been exaggerated. Before trying out the diet, you might want to give other educational methods, such as behavior modification or cognitive behavior modification, a try first.

8. A few years ago it was a popular practice to diagnose children as having minimal brain dysfunction (MBD). Although some children are still identified as having MBD, it is not as common as it once was because we now know that such a diagnosis does not tell a teacher how to go about teaching the child. Most authorities agree that it is the behavior and not the cause of the behavior that is most important. It is also important for you to know that MBD is a classification based on a loose collection of *behavioral* signs rather than indisputable evidence of brain damage. MBD is therefore not a life-threatening disease, but a term used to describe a set of behaviors (hyperactivity, clumsiness, perceptual problems) that are presumed but not proved to be caused by brain dysfunction. To be on the safe side, of course, the parents might wish to have John seen by a neurologist, especially if he is exhibiting more serious signs of brain damage (headaches, blackouts, dizziness).

SUMMARY

Learning disabilities, the newest area of special education, is also one that still suffers from confusion in definition and classification. The federal definition, which is commonly accepted today, focuses on disorders in one or more basic psychological processes involved in understanding or using language. But this definition has critics as well as advocates.

Because of the controversy over definition, prevalence estimates vary widely, from 1 to 3 percent of school-age children to 10, 20, and 30 percent. In fact, one issue in this field is whether or not too many children are being given the learning disabilities label.

The problems that are called learning disabilities can be assessed with a variety of techniques. Norm-referenced tests are used primarily for diagnosis. Criterion-referenced tests, informal reading inventories, and behavioral assessment are used primarily to make educational decisions. Process tests are used for both diagnosis and educational planning, although today many special educators are skeptical about their value.

Very little is known about the causes of learning disabilities, although there are many theories. The theories can be grouped into four categories: brain dysfunction, biochemical disturbance, genetic factors, and environmental factors. Brain dysfunction refers to behavioral signs such as awkward gait, clumsiness, and mixed dominance. Biochemical disturbances or physiological problems are believed by some to be caused by vitamin deficiencies and food allergies and to be manifested in a condition called allergic tension fatigue syndrome. The influence of genetic and environmental factors has not been pinpointed, and the value of these approaches to causation remains unclear.

LD children display a wide range of characteristics, of which ten have been isolated as the most frequent. These include hyperactivity, perceptual-motor problems, frequent shifts in mood, poor coordination, and attention disorders. One common thread is metacognitive deficits, difficulties in the ability to use study skills. LD children are also often inactive, passive learners who are socially rejected by their peers and suffer disabling social and personality problems.

Educational methods for LD children are changing today, and the emphasis in this area is on mainstreaming—returning such children to the regular classroom for most or all of the school day.

Preschool programming is not widespread to avoid premature and unnecessary labeling. The major effort so far has been focused on the elementary school years. Educational methods usually have one of two basic goals: control of hyperactivity and attention problems, or improvement in academic problems.

Approaches to attention and hyperactivity problems can be grouped into four categories: structure and stimulus reduction, drugs, behavior modification, and cognitive behavior modification. Academic problems are attacked through process training, multisensory instructional methods, behavioral techniques, and cognitive behavior modification.

One major change in educational programming today is the growth of secondary and postsecondary services, because research has shown that learning-disabled children do not suddenly outgrow their problems. Secondary programs include a focus on functional academics; postsecondary and college programs focus on reading problems, study habits, and written language skills.

Educational services for the LD adolescent and adult are still in the experimental stages, but one technological advance, microcomputers, promises new alternatives for the learning disabled of any age. There are now computer programs for drill and practice in academic subjects, as well as programs for altering learning styles, and more are becoming available every day as the software industry develops.

REFERENCES

ANDERSON, T.H. Study strategies and adjunct aids. In R.J. Spiro, B.C. Bruce, & W.F. Brewer (Eds.), *Theoretical issues in reading comprehension: Perspectives from cognitive psychology, artificial intelligence, linguistics, and education*. Hillsdale, N.J.: Erlbaum Associates, 1980.

BACHARA, G. Empathy in learning disabled children. *Perceptual and Motor Skills*, 1976, *43*, 541–542.

BAKER, L. An evaluation of the role of metacognitive deficits in learning disabilities. *Topics in Learning and Learning Disabilities*, 1982, *2*, 27–35.

BAKER, L., & ANDERSON, R. *Effects of inconsistent information on text processing: Evidence for comprehension monitoring.* Technical Report No. 203. Champaign: University of Illinois Center for the Study of Reading, May 1981.

BAKER, L., & BROWN, A.L. *Metacognitive skills and reading.* Technical Report No. 188. Champaign: University of Illinois Center for the Study of Reading, November 1980.

BAKER, L., & BROWN, A.L. Cognitive monitoring in reading. In J. Flood (Ed.), *Understanding reading comprehension.* Newark, Del.: International Reading Association, in press.

BARSCH, R.H. *A movigenic curriculum.* Madison, Wis.: Department of Public Instruction, Bureau for the Handicapped, 1965.

BOS, C.S., & FILIP, D. Comprehension monitoring skills in learning disabled and average students. *Topics in Learning and Learning Disabilities*, 1982, *2*, 79–85.

BRENNER, A. The effects of megadoses of selected B complex vitamins on children with hyperkinesis: Controlled studies with long-term follow-up. *Journal of Learning Disabilities*, 1982, *15*, 258–264.

BROWN, A.L. Metacognitive development and reading. In R.J. Spiro, B.C. Bruce, & W.F. Brewer (Eds.), *Theoretical issues in reading comprehension.* Hillsdale, N.J.: Erlbaum, 1980.

BRYAN, T.H. Peer popularity of learning disabled children: A replication. *Journal of Learning Disabilities*, 1976, *9*, 307–311.

BRYAN, T.H. Learning disabled children's comprehension of nonverbal communication. *Journal of Learning Disabilities*, 1977, *10*, 501–506.

BUDOFF, M., & HUTTON, L.R. Microcomputers in special education: Promises and pitfalls. *Exceptional Children*, 1982, *49*, 123–128.

CLEMENTS, S.D. *Minimal brain dysfunction in children: Terminology and identification.* NINDB Monograph, No. 3. Washington, D.C.: U.S. Department of Health, Education and Welfare, 1966.

COLES, G.S. The learning disabilities test battery: Empirical and social issues. *Harvard Educational Review*, 1978, *48*, 313–340.

COOK, J.M., & WELCH, M.W. Reading as a function of visual and auditory process training. *Learning Disability Quarterly*, 1980, *3*, 76–87.

COTT, A. Orthomolecular approach to the treatment of learning disabilities. *Schizophrenia*, 1971, *3*, 95–105.

CRONIN, M.E., & GERBER, P.J. Preparing the learning disabled adolescent for adulthood. *Topics in Learning and Learning Disabilities*, 1982, *2*(3), 55–68.

CROWTHER, D.K. Microcomputers in special education. *Proceedings of the Johns Hopkins first national search for applications of personal computing to aid the handicapped.* New York: IEEE Computer Society Press, October 31, 1981.

CRUICKSHANK, W.M., BENTZEN, F.A., RATZEBURG, F.H., & TANNHAUSER, M.T. *A teaching method for brain-injured and hyperactive children.* Syracuse: Syracuse University Press, 1961.

ENGELMANN, S.E. Sequencing cognitive and academic tasks. In R.D. Kneedler & S.G. Tarver (Eds.), *Changing perspectives in special education.* Columbus, Ohio: Charles E. Merrill, 1977.

FAFARD, M., & HAUBRICH, P.A. Vocational and social adjustment of learning disabled young adults: A followup study. *Learning Disability Quarterly*, 1981, *4*, 122–130.

FEDERAL REGISTER. Procedures for evaluating specific learning disabilities. Washington, D.C.: Department of Health, Education and Welfare, December, 29, 1977.

FEINGOLD, B.F. *Why your child is hyperactive.* New York: Random House, 1975.

FERNALD, G.M. *Remedial techniques in basic school subjects.* New York: McGraw-Hill, 1943.

FROSTIG, M., & HORNE, D. *The Frostig program for the development of visual perception: Teacher's guide.* Chicago: Follett, 1964.

GADDES, W.H. Neuropsychology, fact or mythology, educational help or hindrance? *School Psychology Review*, 1981, *10*, 322–330.

GADOW, K.D. Effects of stimulant drugs on attention and cognitive deficits. *Exceptional Education Quarterly*, 1981, *2*(3), 83–93.

GEOFFRION, L.D. Computer-based exploratory learning systems for handicapped children. *Journal of Educational Technology Systems*, 1981, *10*, 125–132.

GETMAN, G.N., KANE, E.R., & McKEE, G.W. *Developing learning readiness programs*. Manchester, Mo.: McGraw-Hill, 1968.

GILLINGHAM, A., & STILLMAN, B. *Remedial training for children with specific disability in reading, spelling, and penmanship*. Cambridge, Mass.: Educators Publishing Service, 1956.

GOTTESMAN, R.L. Follow-up of learning disabled children. *Learning Disability Quarterly*, 1979, *2*, 60–69.

GRIMES, L. Learned helplessness and attribution theory: Refining children's learning problems. *Learning Disability Quarterly*, 1981, *4*, 91–100.

HALLAHAN, D.P., & BRYAN, T.H. Learning disabilities. In J.M. Kauffman & D.P. Hallahan (Eds.). *Handbook of special education*. Englewood Cliffs, N.J.: Prentice-Hall, 1981.

HALLAHAN, D.P., & CRUICKSHANK, W.M. *Psychoeducational foundations of learning disabilities*. Englewood Cliffs, N.J.: Prentice-Hall, 1973.

HALLAHAN, D.P., & KAUFFMAN, J.M. *Introduction to learning disabilities: A psychobehavioral approach*. Englewood Cliffs, N.J.: Prentice-Hall, 1976.

HALLAHAN, D.P., KNEEDLER, R.D., & LLOYD, J.W. Cognitive behavior modification techniques for learning disabled children: Self-instruction and self-monitoring. In J.D. McKinney & L. Feagans (Eds.), *Current topics in learning disabilities* (Vol. 1). New York: Ablex Publishing, in press.

HALLAHAN, D.P., LLOYD, J.W., KAUFFMAN, J.M., & LOPER, A.B. Behavior therapy methods for academic problems. In R.J. Morris & T.R. Kratochwill (Eds.), *Practice of child therapy: A textbook of methods*. New York: Pergamon Press, 1983.

HALLAHAN, D.P., LLOYD, J.W., & STOLLER, L. *Improving attention with self-monitoring: A manual for teachers*. Charlottesville: University of Virginia Learning Disabilities Research Institute, 1982.

HAMMILL, D.D., & LARSEN, S. The effectiveness of psycholinguistic training. *Exceptional Children*, 1974, *41*, 5–15.

HAMMILL, D.D., LEIGH, J.E., McNUTT, G., & LARSEN, S.C. A new definition of learning disabilities. *Learning Disability Quarterly*, 1981, *4*, 336–342.

HASSELBRING, T.S. Remediating spelling problems of learning handicapped students through the use of microcomputers. *Educational Technology*, 1982, *22*(4), 31–32.

HENKER, B., & WHALEN, B. The changing faces of hyperactivity: Retrospect and prospect. In C.K. Whalen & B. Henker (Eds.), *Hyperactive children: The social ecology of identification and treatment*. New York: Academic Press, 1980.

HOROWITZ, E.C. Popularity, decentering ability and role-taking skills in learning disabled and normal children. *Learning Disability Quarterly*, 1981, *4*, 23–30.

KEPHART, N.C. *The slow learner in the classroom* (2nd ed.). Columbus, Ohio: Charles E. Merrill, 1971.

KIDD, M.E., & HOLMES, G. Strategies for change: The computer and language remediation. *Programmed Learning and Educational Technology*, 1982, *19*, 234–239.

KIRK, S.A., & KIRK, W.D. *Psycholinguistic learning disabilities: Diagnosis and remediation*. Urbana: University of Illinois Press, 1971.

KNEEDLER, R.D., & HALLAHAN, D.P. Self-monitoring as an attentional strategy for academic tasks with learning disabled children. In B. Gholson & T. Rosenthal (Eds.), *Applications of cognitive development theory*. New York: Academic Press, in press.

LAND, B.R., & FARMER, D.M. PRIMER 81: Computer-assisted training in reading skills. *Proceedings of the Johns Hopkins first national search for applications of personal computing to aid the handicapped*. New York: IEEE Computer Society Press, October 31, 1981.

LLOYD, J.W. Academic instruction and cognitive behavior modification: The need for attack strategy training. *Exceptional Education Quarterly*, 1980, 1(1), 53–63.

LLOYD, J.W., & deBETTENCOURT, L.J. *Academic strategy training: A manual for teachers.* Charlottesville: University of Virginia Learning Disabilities Research Institute, 1982.

LOPER, A.B., HALLAHAN, D.P., & IANNA, S.O. Meta-attention in LD and normal children. *Learning Disability Quarterly*, 1982, *5*, 29–36.

McCANN, P.H. Learning strategies and computer-based instruction. *Computers and Education*, 1981, *5*, 133–140.

McCARR, J.E. *Lessons in syntax.* Beaverton, Ore.: Dormac, Inc., 1982.

MAROUN, R.A. Videodisc for individualization. *International Journal of Instructional Media*, 1980, 7(2), 177–184.

MAYRON, L.W. Allergy, learning, and behavior problems. *Journal of Learning Disabilities*, 1979, *12*, 41–49.

MINSKOFF, E.H., WISEMAN, D.E., & MINSKOFF, J.G. *The MWM Program for Developing Language Abilities.* Ridgefield, N.J.: Educational Performance Associates, 1974.

MORSINK, C.V., & MORSINK, R.C. A model for development and evaluation of special instructional materials. *Journal of Education Technology Systems*, 1980, *8*, 317–328.

MYERS, P.I., & HAMMILL, D.D. *Learning disabilities: Basic concepts, assessment practices, and instructional strategies.* Austin, Tex.: Pro-Ed, 1982.

OWEN, F.W., ADAMS, P.A., FORREST, T., STOLZ, L.M., & FISHER, S. Learning disorders in children: Sibling studies. *Monographs of the Society for Research in Child Development*, 1971, *36*(4, Ser. No. 144).

OWINGS, R.A., PETERSON, G.A., BRANSFORD, J.D., MORRIS, C.D., & STEIN, B.S. Spontaneous monitoring and regulation of learning: A comparison of successful and less successful fifth graders. *Journal of Educational Psychology*, 1980, *72*, 250–256.

PARAS, G. Courseware review: K–8 math with student management program. *Journal of Learning Disabilities*, 1982, *15*, 560–561.

PATTON, J.R., & POLLOWAY, E.A. The learning disabled: The adult years. *Topics in Learning and Learning Disabilities*, 1982, *2*(3), 49–88.

PEARL, R., & COSDEN, M. Sizing up a situation: LD children's understanding of social interactions. *Learning Disability Quarterly*, 1982, *5*, 371–373.

SALVIA, J., & YSSELDYKE, J.E. *Assessment in special education* (2nd ed.). Boston: Houghton-Mifflin, 1981.

SANDOVAL, J., & HAAPMANEN, R.M. A critical commentary on neuropsychology in the schools: Are we ready? *School Psychology Review*, 1981, *10*, 381–388.

SCHIFFMAN, G., TOBIN, D., & CASSIDY-BRONSON, S. Personal computers for the learning disabled. *Journal of Learning Disabilities*, 1982, *15*, 422–425.

SCHUMAKER, J.B., DESHLER, D.D., ALLEY, G.R., WARNER, M.M., & DENTON, P.H. Multipass: A learning strategy for improving reading comprehension. *Learning Disability Quarterly*, 1982, *5*, 295–304.

SPREEN, O. Learning disabled children growing up. Research Monograph No. 36. Department of Psychology, University of Victoria, British Columbia, Canada, 1980.

SPRING, C., & SANDOVAL, J. Food additives and hyperkinesis: A critical evaluation of the evidence. *Journal of Learning Disabilities*, 1976, *9*, 560–569.

STRAUSS, A.A., & LEHTINEN, L.E. *Psychopathology and education of the brain-injured child.* New York: Grune & Stratton, 1947.

TORGESEN, J.K. The role of nonspecific factors in the task performance of learning disabled children: A theoretical assessment. *Journal of Learning Disabilities*, 1977, *10*, 27–34.

TORGESEN, J.K. The learning disabled child as an inactive learner: Educational implications. *Topics in Learning and Learning Disabilities*, 1982, *2*, 45–52.

U.S. GENERAL ACCOUNTING OFFICE. *Disparities still exist in who gets special education.* Gaithersburg, Md., 1981.

VOGEL, S.A. On developing LD college programs. *Journal of Learning Disabilities*, 1982, *15*, 518–528.

WEIR, S., RUSSELL, S.J., & VALENTE, J.A. Logo: An approach to educating disabled children. *BYTE*, 1982, *7*, 342–360.

WEISS, B. Food additives and environmental chemicals as sources of childhood behavior disorders. *Journal of American Academy of Child Psychiatry*, 1982, *21*, 144–152.

WHITE, W.J., ALLEY, G.R., DESHLER, D.D., SCHUMAKER, J.B., WARNER, M.M., & CLARK, F.L. Are there learning disabilities after high school? *Exceptional Children*, 1982, *49*, 273–274.

WIEDERHOLT, J.L. Educating the learning disabled adolescent: Some assumptions. *Learning Disability Quarterly*, 1978, *1*, 11–23.

WINKLER, A., DIXON, J.F., & PARKER, J.B. Brain function in problem children and controls: Psychometric, neurological, and electroencephalographic comparisons. *American Journal of Psychiatry*, 1970, *125*, 94–105.

WONG, B.Y.L. Understanding learning disabled students' reading problems: Contributions from cognitive psychology. *Topics in Learning and Learning Disabilities*, 1982, *1*, 43–50.

WONG, B.Y.L., & JONES, W. Increasing metacomprehension in learning disabled and normally achieving students through self-questioning. *Learning Disability Quarterly*, 1982, *5*, 228–240.

WONG, B.Y.L., & WONG, R. Role-taking skills in normal achieving and learning disabled children. *Learning Disability Quarterly*, 1980, *3*, 11–18.

EMOTIONAL DISTURBANCE
4

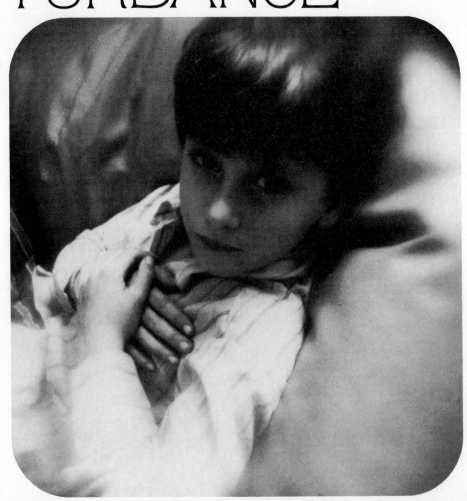

1. Our 8-year-old daughter Sarah has just been identified by the school psychologist for possible placement in a class for the disturbed. We've known for some time that Sarah has some behavior problems, but we always assumed that she really wasn't disturbed, since she isn't super bright, or anything. We had heard that disturbed children were very bright and high achievers. In fact, I don't know where I heard it, but I think I've even heard people say that there's a fine line between insanity and giftedness. If anything, our Sarah has learning problems. Could she be misdiagnosed? Should she be in a class for the learning disabled instead?

2. My sister's 2-year-old, Max, is quite aggressive. It's gotten to the point that I'm afraid to let Arnold, my 3-year-old, play with him. Max doesn't want to share any of his toys and even hits Arnold sometimes. I think Max is headed for some real problems. I've argued with my sister, but she doesn't seem to understand that Max needs therapy. What should I do?

3. Our 6-year-old son Ron has become a bedwetter. For the past few months there's hardly been a week during which he hasn't had an accident. In addition, he's starting to have nightmares on the average of about one a week. My wife thinks he's just going through a "stage" and will grow out of it. I think the boy's got serious problems and needs psychological counseling. Who is right?

4. My husband and I are planning to have children in the near future. What concerns me is the possibility that my child will have an emotional problem. My mother-in-law has been in and out of hospitals and clinics because of frequent nervous breakdowns. While my husband does not appear to have any signs of mental illness, his sister has had numerous problems throughout her childhood and adolescence. Is mental illness inherited? How can I tell if my children might be more susceptible to emotional problems?

5. My son Joshua is in a special class for children who have behavioral problems. Although he has made progress, it is sometimes difficult to control his behavior. Several times in recent months, Joshua has had tantrums at the homes of friends or in public places. What is most disturbing are the comments made by others. Their remarks suggest that I am to blame for Joshua's behaviors. My other children are embarrassed to have their friends over or go out with Joshua. Should I leave him with a sitter when we go on family trips? What can I say to people who comment on my "poor" discipline?

6. Yesterday, I was in a grocery store and saw a young mother with an adorable child who was about 3 years old. I spoke to the child, but he did not respond at all. It was almost as if he didn't hear me. The mother told me that her son did not talk with strangers. After I walked away, the child began shaking his hands rapidly, rocking and repeating sounds I couldn't understand. I've never seen such strange behavior. Is that child retarded? Is his behavior due to lack of discipline at home?

In Chapter 3 you read about an area of special education—learning disabilities—that is difficult to define. The task of defining emotional disturbance isn't any easier. If anything, it's harder. One of the primary reasons emotional disturbance defies clear and simple definition is the wide variety of behaviors found among disturbed individuals.

Attempts to describe the typical disturbed child are folly: There is no *typical* disturbed child. To illustrate our point, we'd like you to consider two children both of whom would be considered emotionally disturbed by most definitions.

VIVIENNE

Vivienne was the daughter of bright, professional parents. She had two perfectly normal siblings. She was a bright student with a special talent for writing poetry. Below is a representative example of her poetry:

You reach for a smile
But there is no one there
To reflect it.
You are utterly and absolutely
Alone.

Will there never be a hand
To grasp at yours within the mirror?
Will there never be an arm
To hold you tight amidst the terror?

The oddly methodical
Frenzy builds;
The terror of the moon is about you.
But it closes in
Only to stop and pause
And wonder why an arm lies empty.

Grasping hands flinch
In the pale, cool light of the moon.
And empty arms encompass it;
Blinding you for a moment.

But you will see
As you hold up your mirror
That it is only the empty sun
Which you have found.
You are alone. (Mack and Hickler, 1981)

As you might guess from her poetry, she was painfully shy and suffered from intense feelings of loneliness. At the age of 14 years and 4 months, Vivienne hanged herself in her mother's studio.

JOEY

I remember Joey, one of our first students, and the destruction resulting from his acts of aggression and hostility. There were days when everything within his reach was either thrown, torn, or smashed. Even with one teacher assigned exclusively to him, he created chaos. Here is a typical school day as described in excerpts from the teacher's anecdotal records:

Joey threw a tray with snacks on the floor . . . spilt the orange juice . . . upset two jars of paint . . . threw a pail at the window and broke a pane . . . swept food and dishes off the dining room table . . . kicked his heels through a wall. . . . (Fenichel, 1974, p. 64)

On the one hand, we have Vivienne, the sensitive, brooding poet. On the other, we have Joey, the destructive, hostile fireball. And these are not rare cases: There are thousands of Viviennes and thousands of Joeys, and there are thousands upon thousands of other children who fall somewhere between these two extremes. Is it any wonder that professionals have difficulty defining emotional disturbance? Is it any wonder that there is controversy over what causes emotional disturbance and how best to treat it? Is it any wonder that many find the area of emotional disturbance such a challenge?

More than any other group in special education, the emotionally disturbed population is the most difficult to define, identify, count, or assess. To begin with, there is substantial disagreement even over what we should *call* this group—emotionally disturbed, behaviorally disordered, socially maladjusted, deviant, psychologically impaired, educationally handicapped. We have chosen to use the term emotionally disturbed because it is the term used in PL 94–142 and other government directives.

The reasons for the lack of consensus in this area stems from the nature of the disorder itself. Human emotions and behaviors are richly varied, both among emotionally disturbed and "normal" people. Individuality, creativity, and innovative thinking are highly prized by some segments of our society. As William Rhodes, one of the outstanding leaders in the field of emotional disturbance, has been quoted as saying, "We must go beyond asserting our individuality to proclaiming and celebrating our deviance" (Wood, 1982, p. 235). If we were to follow Rhodes' advice, many fewer people would be considered disturbed.

Rhodes' position is an extreme one, but it does raise some interesting questions. How far can a person deviate from the average way of behaving before he or she is considered disturbed? How bizarre or excessive must behaviors be to classify one as emotionally disturbed? These questions have no definite answers. Most people have their own personal notion of what emotionally disturbed means, but these individual views may vary enormously, depending on personal values, previous experiences, age, present circumstances, and societal expectations.

The arbitrary nature of the concept of emotional disturbance creates substantial problems today in the major areas of definition, prevalence, assessment, causes, characteristics, and educational approaches. As you read through the chapter, you'll also see how this lack of consensus adversely affects social policy and provision of services.

TODAY'S DEFINITION OF EMOTIONAL DISTURBANCE

One of the major problems today is disagreement about how emotional disturbance should be defined. All categories of exceptional children are difficult to define in a clear and precise way, but problems peculiar to the emotionally disturbed make the difficulties here practically insurmountable. (In the Focus, Eli Bower vividly describes some of the aspects of emotional disturbance that make it especially resistant to a general definition.)

Not surprisingly, therefore, many theoretical and educational definitions have been proposed from a variety of perspectives and disciplines (Cullinan, Epstein, and Lloyd, 1983). The current official definition is comprised primarily of a definition developed by Bower (1969) with several significant modifications added by the federal government.

SOME THOUGHTS ABOUT DEFINING ED

Along with the hazards of street crime, drunk driving, and Christmas shopping is that of defining what is meant by "emotional disturbance." This is certainly no problem for a mental health worker with a client who hears voices and/or barricades himself in his house because he feels his neighbors are out to get him; or for a teacher facing a child with unpredictable periods of intense rage; or for a parent with an obviously autistic child. Definitions are usually clear and concise at the extremes of a condition. . .

There is no question that "emotional disturbance" is a particularly nasty and odious category for service and reimbursement purposes, especially as applied to schools. Most of the other handicaps such as physical, sensory, motor, and mental handicaps have quantitative linear criteria and measures to assist in defining populations in need of extra educational services. Emotion is nonrational, nonlinear, and so far has been pretty elusive to being pinned down by precise prose. One might point out that poets, artists, and musicians are better able to grasp and define emotional thought through their media than we are in words. Unfortunately, such "private" communications do not lend themselves to legislative or educational translations or to the language and mathematics that provide understandable guidelines to the nature and needs of the emotionally disturbed.

For many reasons, emotion is more clearly visible and identifiable where it is abnormal, as in psychoses . . . or rage. In many ways, emotional normality, to coin a phrase, is less amenable to description and measurement than is emotional abnormality. Define, for example, for a school board or State Legislature, the range of normal emotions, or what is meant by pride, jealousy, ambivalence, love, hate, love-hate, etc. . . . . A withdrawn quiet child may be a quiet child, a shy child, a new child, a retarded child, a bilingual child, or an autistic child. An adolescent who cries in class may be grieving about a death in the family or responding to inner feelings of despair and despondency . . .

With these and other difficulties contrived by Mother Nature, how does one go about defining "emotional disturbance" for educational purposes?

Source: E. M. Bower, Defining emotional disturbance: Public policy and research. *Psychology in the Schools*, 1982, *19*, 55–60. Reprinted with permission.

The federal government uses this definition in deciding for whom it should provide funds. The legal system and educators use it to determine placement.

The definition of seriously emotionally disturbed included in federal rules reads as follows (with significant changes to Bower's definition indicated by italics):

(i) The term means a condition exhibiting one or more of the following characteristics over a long period of time and to a marked degree *which adversely affects educational performance*:

(A) An inability to learn which cannot be explained by intellectual, sensory, or health factors;

(B) An inability to build or maintain satisfactory relationships with peers and teachers;

(C) Inappropriate types of behavior or feelings under normal circumstances;

(D) A general pervasive mood of unhappiness or depression; or

(E) A tendency to develop physical symptoms or fears associated with personal or school problems.

(ii) *The term includes children who are schizophrenic. The term does not include children who are socially maladjusted, unless it is determined that they are seriously emotionally disturbed.* (*Federal Register*, 1977, p. 42478) as amended in *Federal Register*, 1981, p. 463866.

Taking into account all the problems with the concept of emotional disturbance, this definition has several advantages and disadvantages over other definitions.

STRENGTHS OF THE FEDERAL DEFINITION

The definition does provide a general description of behavior without using jargon or technical terms. The conditions described are those school personnel would probably be able to observe and identify. In fact, Bower's substantial contribution to the federal definition is the result of extensive teacher surveys he conducted in California in the 1950s. The definition does not attempt to assign probable causes or define optimal treatment approaches. Definitions that have referred to causes or treatment approaches have never met with widespread acceptance because so much controversy surrounds the causes of emotional problems and the best treatment approaches. Finally, the definition conveys a relatively complete and vivid picture of the characteristics most likely to create adjustment problems for children, regardless of their age or environmental surroundings.

PROBLEMS WITH THE FEDERAL DEFINITION

There are, unfortunately, several major problems with the current definition. First, instead of clarifying the concept with precise terminology, the definition uses language that is general, vague, and open to different interpretations. For example, several key terms are quite subjective, such as "over a long period of time" (*how long?*), "satisfactory relationship" (*what is satisfactory?*), and "inappropriate types of behavior" (*what is inappropriate?*).

Second, most of the modifications to Bower's definition result in the restriction of services to a smaller number of children. Three major changes that have the potential for great impact on the provision of services and resources are these:

1. Addition of term "seriously" to "emotionally disturbed."
2. Addition that "educational performance" must be impaired.
3. Exclusion of children who are autistic or socially maladjusted.

SERIOUSLY EMOTIONALLY DISTURBED. The federal definition has changed the term "emotionally disturbed" to "seriously emotionally disturbed." In no other handicap category does such a designation appear, although all handicaps have levels of severity. This appears to be an attempt to justify not providing special services to individuals who are moderately disturbed. No such provision is made in any other category of PL 94–142. Should we provide services only to the "seriously" mentally retarded, the "seriously" speech and language impaired, or the "seriously" visually handicapped?

EFFECT ON EDUCATIONAL PERFORMANCE. The federal definition stipulates that, in order for children to be considered emotionally disturbed, one or more of the characteristics must not only persist for a long time and to a great degree, but must "adversely affect their educational performance." How adversely? How affected? What aspect of educational performance? This vague addition is, at best, repetitive and unnecessary. At worst, it can be used to exclude children from special services who show disturbed or deviant behaviors but who happen to be performing adequately on academic tasks.

EXCLUSION OF AUTISTIC AND SOCIALLY MALADJUSTED CHILDREN. In the 1977 federal definition, the category of emotionally disturbed included autistic children; in 1981, the definition was amended and autism was switched from the category of seriously emotionally disturbed to that of "other health impaired." Although this change makes sense since the relationship between autism and emotional disturbance is not clear (see Focus), many professionals fear that the intent is to be as restrictive as possible in order to serve fewer children.

FOCUS

LIKE THE CHILDREN THEMSELVES, THE CONCEPT OF AUTISM RESISTS "FITTING IN" ANYWHERE

From 1943, when Leo Kanner first identified it as a separate condition, the concept of **autism** has been almost as challenging to deal with as the autistic youngsters themselves. What is the mysterious condition that accounts for bizarre, severely handicapping behaviors, and why has it been resistant to definition, classification, assessment, and treatment?

Kanner initially emphasized that autism was a single, distinct set of behaviors which were markedly different from those exhibited by children with other problems. However, as researchers and practitioners worked with autistic youngsters, it became apparent that great variations existed in the behaviors of children identified as autistic. In addition, autistic children are frequently impossible to distinguish from children with serious handicaps such as mental retardation, sensory deficits, speech and language disorders, or psychiatric problems such as schizophrenia. Others have begun to attack Kanner's belief that classic autism is a unique entity (Wing, 1979).

DEFINITION AND CLASSIFICATION

When PL 94–142 was passed in 1977, autism was included under the definition of "seriously emotionally disturbed." This seemed to make sense, since the concept had shared a close relationship with childhood schizophrenia and other psychoses in terms of the professionals involved, classification systems, and treatment approaches.

However, the National Society for Children and Adults with Autism (NSCAA), an organization that functions as an advocacy group and a clearinghouse for information, argued with increasing vigor that emotional disturbance and autism were not so closely related. They believed that autism was not caused by emotional disturbance and that autistic youngsters often had less in common with children in the disturbed population than they did with children who had language problems or sensory deficits. As evidence of this thinking, the name of the *Journal of Autism and Childhood Schizophrenia* was changed to the *Journal of Autism and Developmental Disorders* in the late 1970s. The NSCAA worked for autism to be categorized in a way that addressed particular learning problems and increased the chances that appropriate services would be provided. In 1981, the inclusion of autism as a separate entity within the federal category of "other health impaired" was approved.

CHARACTERISTICS

Many autistic children share characteristics that nonautistic, severely handicapped youngsters display, such as lack of self-care skills, aggressive and self-injurious behaviors, and cognitive deficits. In addition, certain characteristics are considered to distinguish autistic children from other severely or multiply handicapped youngsters. The DSM-III (American Psychiatric Association, 1980) operational criteria include:

1. Onset usually prior to 30 months but up to 42 months
2. Lack of responsiveness to other human beings ("autism")
3. Self-isolation
4. Gross deficits in language development
5. If speech is present, peculiar speech patterns
6. Peculiar interest or attachments to animals or inanimate objects

WHAT CAUSES AUTISM?

In the 1950s and 1960s, psychoanalytic thinking dominated the prevailing theories on causation, and the behaviors of an autistic child were said to be the result of parental rejection and generally negative interactions with parents. However, as the study of autism continued, the initial theories became less credible. Today, the prevailing explanations for what causes autism are biological ones. For example, autistic behaviors are frequently seen in infants whose mothers were exposed to viruses during the early stages of pregnancy. [For a summary of the biophysical factors that seem to contribute to autistic symptoms, see Menolascino and Eyde (1979)].

INTERVENTION APPROACHES

Because of the similarities among autistic and retarded, language impaired, and sensory handicapped children, treatment programs designed for any of these groups are often appropriate approaches for autistic youngsters. Some of the language programs described in Chapter 5, such as the behavioral approach developed by Lovaas and his colleagues (Devany, Rincover, and Lovaas, 1981; Koegel, Rincover, and Egel, 1982) have been conducted primarily with autistic children. Total communication approaches with manual sign language training like that used with the hearing impaired have been effective in increasing the communication skills of autistic children (Brady and Smouse, 1978; Casey, 1978; Salvin, Routh, Foster, and Lovejoy, 1977).

Other language intervention programs stress a developmental approach that exposes the child to the sequence normal children follow (Richey, 1976). In addition to language, certain programs designed for autistic children stress sensory training (Des Lauriers and Carlson, 1969; Hermelin and O'Connor, 1970) and sensory motor training (Benaroya, Wesley, Ogilvie, Klein, and Meaney, 1977).

The major change in the way autism is approached today results from the newer view of the nature of the condition. Today autistic youngsters are seen as quite varied—ranging, for example, from profoundly retarded to not perceptibly retarded at all. Once thought to be a uniform group of children with relatively predictable behaviors and handicaps, today's autistic children show great differences in skills in all areas—motor, cognitive, language, and social.

PREVALENCE

As you might expect, the problems of defining emotional disturbance create equally large problems in estimating how many emotionally disturbed children there are. Estimates of prevalence have varied from as little as .05 to as much as 15 percent, depending

One of the many difficulties with defining and identifying emotional disturbances in children is the intensity and wide range of emotions which all children show. D. Grogan, U. Va./ CRC.

on the criteria used. As noted in Chapter 1, the federal government reports a range of 1.2 to 2.0 percent of the school-age population to be emotionally disturbed.

Within the category of emotional disturbance, three additional statements about prevalence can be made. First, boys outnumber girls in almost every classification of disorder, ranging from mild and moderate to severe and profound. Second, the majority of emotionally disturbed children fall within the mild to moderate category. Finally, the majority of emotionally disturbed children are identified or in some way come to our attention in the middle childhood and beginning teen years.

CLASSIFICATION

Classification systems help to organize information for us in ways that increase understanding. A man asks us at a party "So you're in special education—is special education only for the retarded or what?" We are able, if we choose to reply, to convey to him quickly the breadth of the concept by telling him the categories or subgroups included in special education, or by referring him to a well-organized treatise on the subject. Classification in special education helps to organize a body of knowledge into more comprehensible and manageable information.

The best effort in this area has been the work of Quay and his colleagues in the development of a **dimensional classification** (Quay, 1975, 1979). Quay and others have taken disturbed and disturbing characteristics reported by teachers and parents and, using computer-assisted statistical procedures, found that behaviors displayed by the disturbed cluster around four major dimensions. These four dimensions have emerged time and time again when similar analyses have been conducted. So they seem to be reliable, stable categories of the major types of behavior disorders a child is likely to develop. Here are the four dimensions and some representative characteristics:

1. Conduct disorder: disobedient, defiant, disruptive, assaultive, impertinent.
2. Anxiety-withdrawal: hypersensitive, self-conscious, depressed, lacks self-confidence, tense.
3. Socialized aggression: loyal to delinquent friends, steals in company with others, truant from school.
4. Immaturity: short attention span, messy, clumsy, fails to finish things, lacks initiative.

Autistic and seriously emotionally disturbed children frequently isolate themselves from other people. Arthur Tress, Photo Researchers, Inc.

However, even though this approach is the most accurate effort in the area of classification, it still does not classify emotionally disturbed children in ways that are directly tied to specific intervention approaches. Those who work with disturbed children need much more specific information about characteristics and behaviors.

ASSESSMENT

Comprehensive behavioral assessment should include information from a variety of sources—parent interviews, standardized tests, behavior observations, child self-reports, peer reports, teacher ratings, or any source that might contribute to the total picture of the child's feelings, behaviors, and experiences. Testing of a disturbed child is usually conducted for one of three specific purposes:

1. To screen children to find which ones might be disturbed.
2. To determine educational placement or eligibility for special services.
3. To determine which teaching or management approaches should be used, and their effectiveness.

SCREENING

A first step in the assessment of disturbed children is the identification of those who *might* be in need of further assessment and special services. Several screening tests are available. These instruments are designed to be given to entire schools in order to screen out those who are possible candidates for special services. One of the best known is Bower and Lambert's Process for In-School Screening of Children with Emotional Handicaps (1962), which combines three sources of information—teacher report, peer report, and self-report.

But neither Bower's screening device nor other screening instruments for the disturbed are widely used. Few school systems routinely conduct any type of systematic screening for disturbed children for two major reasons: (1) ease of teacher identification, and (2) economic limitations on available services.

EFFECTIVENESS OF TEACHER OBSERVATIONS. On the positive side, it can be argued that full-blown, schoolwide screening procedures are not necessary to identify the prime candidates for services for the disturbed. Teacher judgments and ratings are quite accurate, for the most part, in the identification of children with emotional handicaps (Fremont, Klingsporn, and Wilson, 1976; Grieger and Richards, 1976; Harris, King, and Drummond, 1978; Harth and Glavin, 1971).

ECONOMIC LIMITATIONS. On the negative side, in this post-PL 94–142 era, is the economic reality that school systems do not conduct such screening procedures because they may not be eager to identify more children who must then be provided with special services. Most school administrators feel they have enough such children identified by teacher referrals already without going through the added bother of a screening procedure and the identification of more children than can be adequately served.

EDUCATIONAL PLACEMENT AND SERVICES

To determine what educational placement is best for the child or what services are likely to be most helpful, it is often a good idea to find out how the child is different from or similar to other children. One common way to get such information is to test the child directly with standardized tests of intelligence, achievement, and/or personality. A second common way is to gather reported information, which can be furnished by the child, the teacher, parents, classmates, or anyone else who may know the child well.

STANDARDIZED TESTS. Standardized tests can provide important information about how a child might compare to other children the same age in general ability areas (intelligence tests), specific academic skills (achievement tests), and perceptions of himself and others (personality tests). Even if the instruments seem unrelated to the primary problem (abuse or abandonment by parents, for example), they are valuable in the judgment of how the child will do in a given placement or what benefits particular services might have.

The use of intelligence and achievement tests is a common procedure in assessing all exceptional children, and the controversies and cautions surrounding their use have been fully debated. More specific to the area of emotional disturbance is the use of instruments that attempt to measure elusive attributes—emotional problems, self-concept, self-esteem, peer relations, overall adjustment, home and school situations. The assessment of such factors is very important in gathering information about a disturbed child, but devising good instruments to measure them is extremely difficult. Available tests have serious limitations in terms of accuracy and are usually used only for experimental purposes. However, they can be valuable to the clinician or teacher who is trying to gain more information about a particular youngster.

One way of measuring emotional adjustment has been through the use of projective techniques that present children with fairly ambiguous stimuli in the hope that they will *project* inner conflicts or elaborate on problems affecting them. **Projective techniques** take many forms. For example, Barry might be asked to act out his fantasies with dolls, to draw a picture of himself, or to describe what he "sees" in inkblots (Aronow, Reznikoff, and Rauchway, 1979). The most useful projective technique appears to be the sentence completion tests (Watson, 1978). For a teacher who is interested in the information such a method might reveal, the Rotter Incomplete Sentence Blank (ISB) is one of the most valuable (Rotter and Rafferty, 1950). It consists of 40 brief items with clear instructions for scoring and interpretation. Here are some sample items:

I like _____ .

Back home _____ .

What annoys me _____ .

I can't _____ .

I secretly _____ .

One area of interest in the assessment of emotional disturbance is the measurement of self-concept. In many cases, it is important to get a better idea of how a child feels about herself and how she perceives her various strengths and weaknesses. Many efforts have been made to construct an effective measuring device (Goodstein and Doller, 1978). One of the most frequently used and best-known tests is The Piers-Harris Children's Self Concept Scale (Piers, 1969). The test consists of 80 items to be answered "yes" or "no." Here are some sample items:

My parents expect too much of me.

I get nervous when the teacher calls on me.

I sleep well at night.

I have a good figure.

I wish I were different.

REPORTED INFORMATION. In addition to the use of tests, assessment to determine educational placement or services often includes information reported by the child, teacher, parents, classmates, or anyone else who is familiar enough with the child to have relevant information. This information is most commonly retrieved in an interview situation in which specific questions about the child's behavior and experiences are asked. Occasionally, a teacher's report of the child's behavior will be structured around a behavior rating scale of sorts, the most common being Quay and Peterson's Behavior Problem Checklist (n.d.).

Since norm-referenced tests are not as accurate in the emotional-behavioral domain as they are in some other areas, subjective clinical judgment is important. Often, direct observation by an experienced clinician or teacher can be the most valuable part of the assessment of what services are appropriate for an ED child.

DETERMINING SPECIFIC APPROACHES

In determining which teaching or management approaches should be used, as well as their relative effectiveness when used, the best assessment involves direct observation and measurement of the problem behavior. Regardless of your perspective on the causes or the probable treatment approach, first-hand knowledge of the child's maladaptive behavior is essential in order to select an effective intervention. It is not enough to be told that 12-year-old Betty cries too much—you need to observe carefully how often she cries (frequency), for how long (duration), and under what circumstances. If possible, you need to make a judgment about *why* she cries.

In order to measure improvement, it is important to pinpoint precisely what behaviors you want to change. Several recording strategies for target behaviors are available (Kazdin, 1980). Depending on your approach, it may be necessary to record events that immediately precede and/or follow the behavior and to identify what might be reinforcing to the child. As we'll see later in the chapter, helping Betty herself become aware of her behavior and its surrounding events is important in certain treatment techniques. Self-assessment is often the first step in effective intervention.

CAUSES

Much attention has been given to attempting to identify the cause of emotional disturbance. However, in the vast majority of cases, ranging from mild to severe, the causes are not known. So many variables contribute to human experiences and emotions that

FOCUS

WHAT CAUSES CHILDREN TO BE DISTURBED?

Stress has always been with young people. Why suddenly have they gone wild, spewing terrifying statistics on us?

First of all, young people are more alone than they have ever been before . . . and stress increases without the touch of a calming hand. The family that used to be their mainstay has crumbled: aunts and uncles live in distant cities; cousins pass briefly at weddings and funerals; and for every two marriages in the United States, there is one divorce. It is hardly a joke that the nursery school story of Goldilocks today deals with Baby Bear, Mama Bear and Stepfather Bear.

More married women are working today than are staying home. More husbands are battering their wives; more parents are abusing their children. More husbands and wives have extramarital sex. A suburban housewife said the other day, "My child came home from school crying—he was the only one in his class living with both parents."

With the family shifting, where does the young person go for support? Not to church—he has not been raised as an attender. Not to school—the old teacher who cared has retired. Not to the community—the family has been transplanted so often in father's upward mobility that the child has no community.

No, today's youth finds support in his peer group. And these young people, like him, are scared and stress-burdened and themselves unsupported. They lean against one another like a house of cards.

Secondly, today's young people are pushed into greater competition than ever before. There are more of them in sheer numbers struggling for first place: to get the best mark, the most money, the highest football score, the most dates. They are rated by judges who set up the criteria for success, often arbitrarily. They are intelligent or slow according to Stanford-Binet's definition of IQ. They are popular according to the head cheerleader's or football captain's model. They get into college if their talents match those that Educational Testing Service holds up as important. So the struggle becomes one, not only for success, but also for conformity. The loner is doomed to the stress of failure. The group is doomed to the stress of competition.

For many of today's youth, the major emotional support and direction can only be found in peer group values and activities. Paul Conklin, Monkmeyer.

Society, which is merely a conglomerate of parents, teachers and community members, teaches young people to measure self-worth against success. So they dare not to be less than best. Some are lucky and learn to accept second-best.

Finally, never before have children been so indulged, so prized, so placated as today. The cause may be parental guilt or that old chestnut, "I want her to have more than I had." No matter—the result is the same: a generation of young people who cannot cope with the negatives the rest of us had to grow accustomed to. They get what they want—at no little expense to their parents—from birth through adolescence. They get what they see on television. They get what their friends have. Parents seem afraid to say "No."

The easy life leaves children with little sense of accountability. Parents team up to help them switch the blame. A child does poorly in school—Mother says the teacher is no good. A sixteen-year-old wants liquor at his party—Dad winks at the law. One mother boasted, "I will never let Rachel be upset if I can possibly prevent it." She prevented it, and Rachel is now at a psychiatrist's. She is six years old.

Now we find ourselves in the 1980s, in a world where the myth of childhood is being torn to bits . . . where children are beset with stress they are ill-equipped to handle . . . in a world where, unable to *scream* out, they *act* out their hurt . . . in a world where we adults, unable to interpret their screams, react only to their behavior. For we are deaf to our own cries of fear.

Source: Excerpt from CHILDSTRESS! Understanding and Answering Stress Signals of Infants, Children & Teenagers by Mary Susan Miller. Copyright © 1982 by Mary Susan Miller. Reprinted by permission of Doubleday & Company, Inc.

TABLE 4–1

TABLE 4–1
Conceptual Models and Causes

CONCEPTUAL MODEL	NATURE OF CAUSE	EMPHASIS ON CAUSE
Behavioral	Inappropriate learning of ED behaviors due to faulty reinforcement.	Underlying causes not important and do not relate directly to treatment; events immediately preceding behavior (that can be re-arranged) can be important to treatment.
Biological	Genetic, neurological, and biochemical factors.	Important but difficult to determine—relates directly to treatment when identified.
Ecological	Poor interaction of the child with the eco-system (social environment).	Important—relates somewhat to treatment. All parts of ecosystem (not just the causal ones) often receive intervention.
Psychoanalytic	Unresolved psychic conflicts due to im-balance of personality structures (id, ego, superego) or faulty passage through development stages (oral, anal, phallic, latency, genital).	Most important—essential to prescribing treatment; treatment often focuses exclu-sively on the elimination of causal factors.
Psychoeducational	Inner conflict cycle that includes child's personality structure, emotional reac-tions, and environmental events.	Important to know historical and symbolic causal factors, but treatment is broad enough to include aspects other than causes, such as academic instruction.

it is difficult to determine with any certainty what factors cause emotional problems. For example, many people think environmental experiences and circumstances alone create emotional disturbances. As the Focus shows, many situations today seem likely to create emotional problems in our young.

Yet, some children living in extremely undesirable circumstances end up as well-adjusted adults. We would all agree that the way parents treat their children is important to the children's mental health. Yet in one family one child may be emotionally disturbed, whereas all the other children are normal. Determining a specific cause of emotional disturbances is extremely difficult.

The theories we have can be grouped into five conceptual models. Depending on which model you follow, you tend to view different things as possible causal factors. As you can see in Table 4–1, not only is the nature of the cause seen as different, but the importance of knowing the cause is viewed differently, depending on the model.

CHARACTERISTICS

More than 100 characteristics are attributed to the population we call emotionally dis-turbed. They vary along a wide range of severity (mild to profound) and type (for example, withdrawn and aggressive).

Achenbach and Edelbrock (1981) administered Quay's Child Behavior Checklist to parents of normal and disturbed children aged 4 through 16 years. For the 112 behavior items, the behaviors that showed the greatest differences between normal and disturbed children were the following (in order of appearance on checklist and *not* in order of importance):

Acts too young
Argues
Can't concentrate
Obsessions
Hyperactive
Confused
Cries a lot
Cruel to others
Daydreams
Demands attention
Destroys own things
Destroys others' things
Disobedient at home
Disobedient at school
Poor peer relations
Lacks guilt
Feels unloved
Feels persecuted
Feels worthless
Fights
Impulsive
Lying or cheating
Nervous
Not liked
Too fearful or anxious
Feels too guilty
Poor schoolwork
Refuses to talk
Screams a lot
Secretive
Moody
Sulks a lot
Temper tantrums
Unhappy, sad, or depressed
Withdrawn

Several behaviors often mentioned by therapists as problems of the disturbed did *not* show up as significant differences between disturbed and normal children. Some of the surprising behaviors that did *not* seem different for disturbed and normal children are these:

Fears
Likes to be alone
Nightmares
Overeating
Aches or pains
Nausea, feels sick
Sexual problems

Shy or timid
Strange ideas
Too concerned with neatness or cleanliness
Bedwetting

The picture we get, then, of the emotionally disturbed is that of a heterogeneous group. James and Brad, who are in a special education class for the disturbed, are likely to display widely different behaviors. James may be rebellious, with a chip on his shoulder, whereas Brad may be withdrawn and nervous.

SOME COMMON CHARACTERISTICS

Three characteristics that *do* seem to be common to most mildly or moderately disturbed youngsters are these:

1. Poor academic achievement
2. Poor interpersonal relations
3. Poor self-esteem

POOR ACADEMIC ACHIEVEMENT. One common misconception is that the emotionally disturbed child is bright, motivated to perform in school, and an achiever (or even an overachiever). Although this does happen occasionally, it is much more likely that disturbed children, even those in the mild and moderate range, perform less well on intelligence tests and in all areas of academic achievement than their normal counterparts.

POOR INTERPERSONAL RELATIONS. As you can figure out from the lists of characteristics identified by Achenbach and Edelbrock, disturbed children are often described as, to put it bluntly, a pain in the neck. Their lack of social skills and pleasant personality traits impedes their ability to have satisfying relationships with parents, teachers, or peers. They are often disliked and rejected by most of the people they encounter.

POOR SELF-ESTEEM. In spite of disguising signs of bravado, the emotionally disturbed child frequently has a very poor sense of self-worth or self-concept. Measures of self-concept as well as teacher observations indicate that disturbed youngsters have far more problems with self-esteem. Some of the personal agony of a youngster with poor self-esteem and a serious eating disorder is described in the Focus.

SEVERELY AND PROFOUNDLY DISTURBED CHILDREN

So far, the characteristics we've been discussing apply mainly to the relatively mildly disturbed. A rather distinct set of behaviors is found among the severely and profoundly disturbed. Children who exhibit severe and profound behavior disorders have extreme difficulty functioning independently. These children are often called severely disturbed, multiply handicapped, or sometimes even severely retarded. Efforts directed toward debating what label should be used are not only pointless, but are better spent in the intensive

HOW IT FEELS TO HAVE ANOREXIA NERVOSA

Anorexia nervosa is an eating disorder most commonly seen in adolescent girls who refuse to eat or who alternately overeat (go on a ''binge'') and then induce vomiting. The result is gradual starvation which can cause serious physical damage and ultimately death. One of the major theories of causation for anorexia nervosa is that the girl has a very low self-concept and feels she has little control over any aspect of her life other than her body weight. Cherry Boone O'Neill, daughter of Pat Boone, recounts the horror:

Later that night, after my mother had gone to bed, I quietly snuck back to the kitchen determined to taste everything I'd missed. I grabbed a roll, dipped it into the gravy boat and crammed it into my mouth. Then I ate some stuffing. Then a bite of a vegetable casserole. Next some pecans off the pie. Suddenly, I realized I'd gone too far. In two minutes I had destroyed an all-day effort to avoid eating. Well, no need to get depressed. I might as well eat my fill of everything now. I'll just have to get rid of it later. I knew how. I'd done it dozens of times before.

Mindlessly, I began shoveling handfuls of food into my mouth. I devoured huge amounts of leftovers from Christmas dinner, breakfast, and even from days before. Some of my cookies (crumbs first and then broken pieces before whole cookies), slivers of cherry-cream pie, a piece of pecan pie, tablespoons of ice cream, chocolate chip and jamoca-almond-fudge, more rolls with quarter-inch layers of butter, globs of peanut butter followed by spoonfuls of jam, and egg nog straight from the pitcher.

My distended stomach ached—I must have looked six months pregnant. My food frenzy began to slow down when I could no longer walk without bending over. Did I get everything I wanted? I guess so—besides I can't eat any more.

But wait! Some chocolates! I'll chew on those on the way upstairs with a glass of punch.

Once in my bathroom, I completed the now familiar ritual I'd begun this time with that first bite of turkey. I forced my finger down my throat. After several gut-wrenching heaves I regurgitated as much as I could until nothing but small amounts of bile, tinged pink with blood, emerged. I wiped off the toilet and began rinsing my beet-red face when I was startled by a hard knock on the door.

''Cherry, what's going on?'' My father's voice was stern.

My heart pounded, ''I'm just going to the bathroom. Why?'' I quickly straightened my hair, sprayed air freshener, turned off the water.

''Open the door, Cherry. You know the rules about no locked doors in this house.''

''You and Mommy lock your door sometimes,'' I answered back.

''Open this door, Cherry! Right now!''

''All right! All right! Just let me get my robe on,'' I stalled, trying to open the window for fresh air. Then I calmly unlocked and opened the door.

''It doesn't take you fifteen minutes to go to the bathroom, Cherry.''

''I haven't been in here fifteen minutes,'' I lied.

''I was outside after taking a sauna and I looked up and saw your bathroom light on. I waited, listened, and I know I heard you vomiting.'' His eyes glistened with anger.

''I did not! I swear! I was just going to the bathroom and washing my face!''

''Look here, Cherry,'' he said, gripping my arm and pulling me back into the bathroom. ''Look at yourself! Your face is red, your eyes are bloodshot, the room stinks and you're telling me you didn't throw up?''

"I didn't Daddy! I promise I didn't! I was going to the bathroom. I've been constipated so my face gets red. Honest!" My voice quavered with fear. Tears welled up in my eyes.

"Cherry, I don't understand this. I know you're lying, but it's late and I have to get up early. We should both be in bed—it's been a busy day. But don't think we aren't going to discuss this when I get back from Chicago! Now go to bed, and don't you get up again—for any reason!"

Suddenly he was gone and I stood alone in front of the mirror. I stared at my gaunt face, then burst into tears.

God, what's wrong with me? Why can't I control myself? If I just hadn't tasted that turkey! Then I wouldn't have gorged and had to throw up and lie to Daddy. But I had to eat *something*. I hadn't eaten all day! I usually have a bit of dinner, at least.

I looked at my swollen eyes as tears streaked down my hollow cheeks. I leaned against the door and slid down slowly as my whining turned to heaving, uncontrollable sobs.

Source: From STARVING FOR ATTENTION by Cherry Boone O'Neill. Copyright © 1982 by the author. Used by permission of The Continuum Publishing Company.

treatment required to educate these children. Most of them have more than one of the following characteristics:

1. No speech
2. Meaningless speech such as repeating back exactly what is heard (**echolalia**)
3. Excessive self-stimulation behaviors
4. Self-injurious behaviors
5. Very few or no self-care skills
6. Nonresponsiveness (acting sometimes as if deaf and blind)
7. Intellectual retardation or lack of responsiveness to testing
8. Little or no warmth toward people
9. Extreme and unprovoked aggressiveness

TODAY'S EDUCATIONAL METHODS

As you can see from Chapter 1, the percentage of emotionally disturbed children receiving any services is far less than even the lowest figure in the range of prevalence estimates. Of the educational programs that are available, most are designed for the mildly and moderately disturbed child in the elementary school years. Relatively few services are available for the preschool or adolescent child.

PRESCHOOL PROGRAMMING

One of the reasons why few preschool services are available for young emotionally disturbed children is because, except for those who are severely disturbed, it is difficult to identify preschoolers who might be in need of some sort of intervention. This difficulty stems primarily from three aspects of *normal* child development:

1. Young children's range of behaviors is very limited. They do not have the motor or verbal ability to convey important information about their needs, motivations, fears, and so on. We can, at best, only guess about their feelings or make imprecise comparisons between them and children of the same age.
2. Much of normal young children's behavior is antisocial and disturbing to others. For instance, many normal toddlers appear to be hyperactive, engage in self-stimulating behaviors (thumb-sucking and blanket stroking), cling to mother in the presence of a stranger, have temper tantrums, and engage in many aggressive behaviors (grabbing toys from others, pushing, hitting). It is difficult to know how frequent or severe these undesirable behaviors must be to determine that the preschool child is disturbed.
3. Children's development in all areas—physical, cognitive, social—in the early years can be uneven and vary greatly. For example, John may be speaking with a vocabulary of 400 words at age 2½, whereas Rebecca at the same age barely speaks but demonstrates fine and gross motor skills far superior to John's. It is extremely difficult to make a judgment about what is "not normal."

An additional problem in the identification of young emotionally disturbed children is the wide diversity of expectations, values, and reactions parents bring to the situation. What is considered "too aggressive" or "too messy" in one home may not be so viewed in another home. Sam's parents may be able to tolerate jelly stuck to the handle of their refrigerator door; Beth's parents may be appalled to find a trace of mustard in the corner of their daughter's mouth while she's eating a hot dog. In addition to behavioral expectations, parents bring their own temperaments and personal styles to their childrearing experiences. Their approach may unwittingly neglect or increase their child's developing difficulties.

TELEVISION. Although home situations for preschool youngsters vary enormously, one major experience is common to most young children in this country—television.

Today's preschool children typically watch several hours of television a day—the effects of which are largely unknown. Vivienne, Photo Researchers, Inc.

Today's preschool child typically watches or is exposed to several hours of television a day.

There is much disagreement and uncertainty about what effect this has on young children, but what is especially relevant for disturbed children is the charge made by some authorities that television viewing is contributing to the increasing numbers of highly aggressive children in our culture.

It is estimated that by the time children are 5 years old they will have viewed 30,000 violently aggressive acts on TV. Since it has been demonstrated that the observation of aggression results in an increase in aggressive behaviors (Bandura, 1977), it follows that television, unless programs are carefully selected, may have an adverse effect on children's behavior.

It has been demonstrated that certain programs do have undesirable effects on social behaviors (Huston-Stein, Fox, Greer, Watkins, and Whitaker, 1981). Certain programs, on the other hand, seem to promote desirable social and intellectual responses (Ahammer and Murray, 1979). The culprit, then, may not be television in general, but certain programs young children perhaps should not see.

ELEMENTARY SCHOOL PROGRAMMING

The most common educational programs for the emotionally disturbed child in the elementary years are (1) the special self-contained class and (2) regular class placement with the assistance of a resource teacher. In the past, the more seriously disturbed were usually served in special classes, and those with milder handicaps were likely candidates for resource programs. Today, however, there is a push for the integration of even the more disturbed youngster into a resource room–regular class placement.

Educational methods for the emotionally disturbed have been largely determined by various theoretical perspectives (see Table 4–2). Historically, all these conceptual models have been important in the field of education for the disturbed and have influenced the various educational approaches. The majority of today's educational programs for the disturbed, however, are based on one of two models—psychoeducational or behavioral.

PSYCHOEDUCATIONAL METHODS AND PROGRAMS. **Psychoeducational methods** are based on psychoanalytic concepts concerning the child's unconscious emotions and inner psychic conflicts. The psychoanalytic approach uses various forms of psychotherapy (including art or play therapy) to uncover these unconscious internal problems. Bruno Bettelheim, a pioneer of the psychoeducational approach, proposed that disturbed children should not be restricted to the benefits of one hour per day or week of therapy. Instead, a therapeutic milieu should be created in which everyday activities and experiences are geared toward helping these children get better.

The psychoeducational perspective is, as its name implies, greatly concerned with *educating* the disturbed child. The role of the teacher is viewed as extremely important— it is thought that the teacher must establish a trusting, therapeutic relationship with the child. The teacher should be concerned with children's feelings and with their insight into their own emotions and behaviors. In addition, the psychoeducational teacher emphasizes academic instruction and performance.

Although the teacher strives to make the children feel accepted, today psychoeducational teachers convey to the children that not all their behaviors will be accepted.

TABLE 4–2
Conceptual Models and Educational Approaches

	GENERAL TREATMENT	SAMPLE METHODS	TEACHER'S ROLE
1. Behavioral	Rearrange environmental events.	Reinforcement, punishment, time out, contracts, modeling.	Selects and arranges consequences to behavior.
2. Biological	Change physiology.	Drugs, diet, megavitamins.	Has full knowledge of treatment, but considers educational treatment of equal or greater importance.
3. Ecological	Change the nature of the interaction between the child and the social environment.	Community involvement, teacher counselors, educateurs, family counseling.	Views the child in a comprehensive way and is concerned with all components in the child's life.
4. Psychoanalytic	Help the child to act out or talk out unconscious conflicts.	Art therapy, play therapy, catharsis (act it out).	Helps the child uncover unconscious emotions and work on them much like a therapist.
5. Psychoeducational	Create trust, accept feelings, and teach academics.	Life space interview, crisis intervention, antiseptic bouncing, planned ignoring.	Talks about feelings and instructs in academics.

Techniques for reducing undesirable behaviors in the classroom have been described by Nicholas Long and others (Long, Morse, and Newman, 1980; Long and Newman, 1976). They include strategies such as temporarily removing the child from the classroom, maintaining a predictable class schedule, holding the child when he seems unable to control his impulses, and removing objects such as paintbrushes that may entice the child to misbehave.

Because followers of the psychoeducational approach believe a child's emotional problems begin at an unconscious or hidden level, it is believed that a good time to intervene with therapeutic methods is when the child is in some sort of emotional "crisis." It is during these crisis periods, so the proponents say, that a child may be open to gaining insight into his or her behavior. There are methods for dealing with these crises. The first is what is called the **life space interview**. Created by Fritz Redl (1959), this technique has two broad goals: emotional first aid, or helping the child to regain quick control of emotions, and clinical exploitation of life events, or assisting the child to gain insight into a problem so it will be less troublesome in the future.

A second development in crisis intervention is the concept of a crisis-helping teacher model proposed by William Morse (1976). **Crisis-helping teachers** function in a school in much the same way that resource teachers do, except that they are especially well equipped to provide assistance at a time of child or child-teacher crises. The crisis-helping teacher is called upon to do a wide variety of tasks—diagnosis, teaching, counseling—and is expected to be able to work well with children, parents, and other teachers.

One representative psychoeducational program is that of the Hillcrest Children's Center in Washington, D.C. A residential and day school setting, Hillcrest provides a multidisciplinary approach to seriously disturbed elementary school children. During the 1960s, Nicholas Long, who is today one of the major proponents of the psychoeducational approach, was director of Hillcrest, and its program has served as a prototype for other psychoeducational programs throughout the country.

BEHAVIORAL METHODS AND PROGRAMS. Unlike the psychoeducators, behaviorists do not concern themselves with the treatment of underlying emotions. They focus instead on changing the disturbed or problem behaviors they can actually *see*. Behavioral methods change events that precede behavior (antecedents), or change events that follow (consequences) in order to improve the behavior. The changes consist of using reinforcers or rewards to increase desirable behaviors and punishment to decrease undesirable behaviors. Reinforcement may be given in the form of tangible items such as candy, classroom privileges, tokens, social attention, praise, stickers, or anything that is rewarding to a particular child. Punishment can be any of a variety of consequences a particular child dislikes. Behavioral methods have been shown to be very effective with the emotionally disturbed and have been widely used with elementary school youngsters.

TOKEN ECONOMY SYSTEMS. Perhaps the most widespread, specific method used with today's disturbed elementary school child is a behavioral method known as the **token economy**. This technique has been used to improve a large number of social and academic behaviors (see Kazdin [1977] for a review of specific behaviors). In a token economy, a classroom is set up so the children know that certain behaviors will gain them a certain number of "tokens." The tokens can actually be anything a child can see immediately following a desired behavior—stars, checkmarks, chips, buttons. Typically, the tokens are traded in for special privileges or tangible items, although the systems have been effective even when the tokens are not redeemable.

In many token classrooms, you can observe the teacher quietly but continuously distributing tokens or making checkmarks throughout the day. Usually, the teacher tells the child *exactly* what the token is for. As she passes Tom's desk, for example, she says: "I like the way you're sitting in your seat," and makes a checkmark on his tally sheet. It is important to convey clearly to the child what the desirable behaviors are. Using a token system with emotionally disturbed children not only clarifies behavioral expectations, but generally motivates them toward increasing desirable behaviors.

Many classrooms throughout the country, both self-contained and resource, use some type of token system. In addition, the majority of residential treatment centers for the more severely disturbed use a form of token economy. Programs can vary greatly in instructional content and administrative format and yet share the technique of token reinforcement. Much of its widespread adoption can be attributed to the fact that it is practical and generally produces quick, positive results.

One representative behavioral program is the well-known **engineered classroom** developed by Frank Hewett in the 1960s (Hewett and Taylor, 1980). Through the use of a token system and other behavioral procedures, Hewett "engineered" the classroom environment to decrease behaviors interfering with learning and increase behaviors needed in learning. Hewett's procedures were organized around a developmental sequence of goals. The classroom was highly structured in terms of scheduling and the arrangement of consequences.

Since Hewett applied these procedures in a public school setting—first in self-contained classrooms (the Santa Monica Project) and later in resource programs (the

Madison School Plan)—they have served as prototypes for other public school systems in providing services for the emotionally disturbed.

COGNITIVE BEHAVIOR MODIFICATION. A recent development within the behavioral approach is **cognitive behavior modification (CBM).** This approach uses behavioral techniques, such as reinforcement and precise measurement, but in addition the children themselves actively participate as their own therapists. The adults do not abandon their roles as teachers or therapists, but they train the children to use a variety of techniques, such as self-recording, self-instruction, and self-reinforcement. Randy, for example, might be instructed to note on a tally sheet every time he is out of his seat. Suzanne might be taught to decrease her impulsive, inaccurate responses by saying to herself throughout an academic task, "Am I going too fast? I need to slow down and think before I answer." And Mark might be instructed to give himself a token whenever he finishes a worksheet of math problems.

CBM procedures have been used successfully with different kinds of handicapped individuals to decrease a variety of undesirable behaviors (Meichenbaum, 1977). It seems to be a promising method for disturbed children, although evidence of its effectiveness in the social domain is just beginning to accumulate (Kneedler, 1980).

OTHER METHODS AND PROGRAMS. Some other educational approaches have also had an impact on educational programs for the emotionally disturbed. **Ecological approaches** (Rhodes and Paul, 1978) include a broad-based attack on the interaction of the child with all aspects of his or her environment. The best known ecologically based program is Re-ED, which was a project for elementary school children in two settings, in North Carolina and Tennessee. Re-ED was staffed by teacher-counselors who worked in conjunction with a multidisciplinary team of psychiatrists, psychologists, social workers, parents, and others in the community in an attempt to intervene in *all* areas of a child's life (Hobbs, 1978).

Humanistic approaches grew out of disillusion with and dislike for traditional, authoritarian schools which, according to humanistic advocates, harm a child's sense of self-esteem and self-direction. The atmosphere in a humanistic setting is open, with the children free to choose directions in their learning. Humanistic programs have some similarities with psychoeducational programs in that in both the teacher is concerned with the child's feelings and self-concept. However, the humanistic teacher plays a much more secondary role in the child's educational experience. The humanistic teacher is there to assist when needed in order to facilitate the child's learning, but is much less involved in direct academic instruction or therapeutic intervention than is the psychoeducational teacher. Humanistic programs are sometimes called alternative, open, nontraditional, experimental, or student-directed and are given in a variety of settings (Knoblock, 1983). The Focus gives some support to the humanistic approach.

PROGRAMS FOR THE SEVERELY DISTURBED. Although the majority of the severely disturbed are educated in residential settings or special class placements, following the passage of PL 94–142, parents and many professionals have pushed for greater integration of these youngsters into regular classes in the public schools. Specific procedures and programming for mainstreaming autistic and severely disturbed students into the public schools have recently been developed by psychoeducators (Knoblock, 1983) and behaviorists (Egel, Richman, and Button, 1982; Koegel, Rincover, and Russo, 1982).

THE MYTH OF "CAREFREE" CHILDHOOD

All adults, but especially parents and teachers and especially parents and teachers of the disturbed, should keep in mind just how difficult it sometimes is to be a child. No matter which educational approach you favor—psychoeducational, behavioral, humanistic—it is well to keep in mind that childhood isn't always easy. Children are vulnerable to all kinds of hurts. Since most of us made it through childhood and adolescence without too many emotional scars, we may have a tendency to forget just how much stress we faced in everyday situations. If you let your mind drift, however, you will no doubt see some of yourself in the following passage from M. S. Miller's book *Childstress*:

Until recently only a few adults have taken children's stress seriously. Perhaps we have been hoodwinked by the myth that childhood is a carefree time of life—"the apple tree, the singing and the gold." Or it may ease our own stress to cling to the make-believe child of nostalgia, even though that child is a figment of imagination. Have we so long concealed in the dark corners of our mind the child we actually were that we have lost her? If we listen, we may hear our own childhood cries for help misunderstood, ignored, like those of our children today. We may discover the real child we used to be.

Where is the three-year-old who held back tears as a new baby gurgled and got everyone's attention?

Where the five-year-old who, abandoned at the kindergarten door, faced a foreign land alone and alien?

Have we forgotten the ten-year-old praying to be picked for a team before the teacher assigned the stragglers that neither captain chose?

And the twelve-year-old who sneaked a nickel from his mother's purse to "buy" a best friend?

Remember the teenager whom no one invited to the dance?

Or the one whose father was too busy to attend Father's Day?

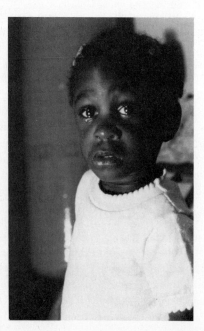

In spite of what we adults like to think, childhood is a time of many hurts and much stress. D. Grogan, U. Va./CRC.

Or the one who let his parents down by not getting into Colgate?

Where is the fat one? . . . The one with the funny dress? . . . Where is the one who can't read? . . . Who wears eyeglasses? . . . Whose skin is black?

Can't we find the child crying alone in her room? . . . and the child afraid of the dark? . . . and the child whose parents are fighting? . . . the child of divorce?

These are the real children we were before memory lost them.

More to the point, they are also our children—living with us, attending our schools, hiding their pain as we hid ours a generation ago. They are the children we overlook when we are busy . . . and scold for their failures (or for ours); the children for whom we set unattainable goals . . . whom we over-plan for and under-listen to. They are the children of love—and forget to let them know. They are our turtles and racehorses running at the wrong speed. In thirty years will they, too, create myths?

Probably. But what about today?

Source: M. S. Miller, *Childstress: Understanding and answering stress signals of infants, children, and teenagers*. Garden City, N.Y.: Doubleday, 1982, pp. 2, 3–4. Reprinted with permission.

SECONDARY AND POSTSECONDARY PROGRAMMING

The adolescents and young adults who have emotional or behavior problems are so varied that no single program can be chosen as the best. Although there are fewer secondary than elementary programs, the relatively few programs that do serve adolescents generally use methods and approaches based on the psychoeducational and behavioral models. For example, the psychoeducational method of life space interviews has been used with adolescents and young adults (Dembinski, 1978). The behavioral method of token reinforcement has been used successfully with disturbed adolescents for a variety of academic and social behaviors (Epstein and Cullinan, 1979; Epstein, Cullinan, and Rose, 1980). However, as we all know from our own experiences while growing up, adolescents are not simply bigger versions of younger children (see Focus).

FOCUS

TODAY'S TEEN: MORE VULNERABLE TO EMOTIONAL PROBLEMS?

Ask adults what their least favorite period of growing up was, and they'll often tell you it was their adolescent years. Ask parents what their least favorite period of parenting was, and they'll often point to the teenage years. There is little doubt that the teenage years can be a period of intense psychological turmoil. Many authorities are of the opinion that today's teenager is more likely than ever to experience psychological conflict because of pressures that threaten and weaken the traditional family unit. The following comparison presents a strong argument for the increased vulnerability of today's adolescent. As you read it, you might for the sake of argument think of possible alternatives to this point of view. Is it possible that today's teen is "stronger" because of these changes? Have there in fact been any real changes? Are the problems of today's teenager really the same as those of yesterday, only dressed in the fashion of the 1980s? Is today's punk-rocker yesterday's hippie?

When I was an adolescent the community was more stable and the news more muted. The radio was full of the adventures of Jack Armstrong and, although people were certainly killed, death was not served up as entertainment. Mr. Greeninger's drugstore always smelled of vanilla and he could be counted on to open the pharmacy at midnight if my mother had an emergency. I went to school with his son Ned. My grandparents lived with us. My aunts and uncles were only a brisk walk away. My father's siblings called him "Brother" and I grew up with cousins who always addressed him as "Uncle Brother." Strangers were noted in our neighborhood and only my old aunt May, who had never gotten over the death of Baby Rose, took drugs.

Aunt Claire, my mother's sister, knew everything: how to get grass stains out of a white shirt; what subway to take for obscure points in town; which shoes were practical and worth the money. It was always Aunt Claire who came when you were sick or sad.

My parents' friends had all attended school and college together and we called them Aunt and Uncle, though they were no blood relation. They came on our vacation sometimes where the oceans were always fresh and the air seemed pure and limitless. No one spoke of nitrites in the morning bacon or hormones in the Sunday roast. In our adolescent eyes, the world seemed safe and dependable. Couples celebrated golden wedding anniversaries and rarely moved from their houses.

Personal experiences have changed for adolescents. Divorce rates have soared. A family can move halfway across the country at a moment's notice and those that stay together are unusual. I notice this especially since I teach in a boarding school. More than half our students need two sets of grades and comments. I Xerox the required copies and send them to fathers in distant cities and mothers with new names. Sometimes, for our students, there is no one to turn to and so they often turn to each other to trade whatever physical closeness or substance they can. While adolescence has always been a time of change and anxiety, the outside world offers them little comfort. Young people seem more drastically unhappy, cynical and hopeless than they did even twenty years ago. The shrinking universe, the unthinkable possibility of nuclear war and the failing economy have all poisoned their future. The inner world of adolescence is difficult enough. When the impact of changing societies is added to it, young people sometimes flounder.

Source: H. A. Hickler, A teacher's view point. In J. E. Mack and H. Hickler, *Vivienne: The life and suicide of an adolescent girl.* Boston: Little Brown, 1981.

Certain characteristics and needs distinguish the developing adult who has emotional problems from the younger child:

1. Increase in antisocial and law-breaking behaviors
2. Increase in truancy
3. Increase in need for vocational/career training and information
4. Increase in need for counseling or instruction in matters such as drug abuse and sexuality

Today's successful intervention programs take these differences into account in treating the emotionally disturbed adolescent.

Psychoeducational services for the disturbed adolescent include a consultation model used with teachers (Newman, 1967), as well as psychoeducational secondary schools, such as the Mark Twain School in Montgomery County, Maryland (Fagen, 1979). As is the case at the elementary level, the behavioral approach is the most common with disturbed adolescents. An example of a well-known, successful behavioral intervention program is Achievement Place, which was a group home treatment program for delinquent youths begun in 1967 in Kansas. From this project evolved a teaching-family model that is in use in over 150 homes throughout the nation (Phillips, Fixsen, Phillips, and Wolf, 1979). The program, which uses a highly structured token economy, has demonstrated remarkably consistent success with this very difficult population.

In addition to psychoeducational and behavioral programs, other secondary programs for the disturbed have been developed on a much smaller scale. Alternative schooling for adolescents has been proposed by Knoblock (1983), who emphasizes that in these programs students can participate more fully in making educational decisions and determining a truly individualized curriculum. An example of this approach is the Ashland Senior High Learning Center for behaviorally disoriented adolescents in Oregon (Hoover, 1978).

Beyond the secondary level, very limited services are available for the disturbed adult. Unfortunately, most seriously disturbed or psychotic youngsters continue to exhibit disordered characteristics, do not develop into self-sufficient adults, and require continuous care or institutionalization. For the more moderately disturbed, occasional psychiatric care may be enough to allow them to lead self-sufficient lives.

TECHNOLOGICAL ADVANCES

So far, very few technological developments have been designed especially for the emotionally disturbed. In fact, the only technological advances specifically for the disturbed are for use with the communication problems exhibited by severely disturbed and autistic-like children. These developments are really offshoots from technology originally designed for the speech impaired. With the explosion of interest in microcomputers, however, it is only a matter of time until programs that deal specifically with interpersonal skill development are available.

The fact that high technology has not yet been applied to social and emotional difficulties does not mean that the emotionally disturbed cannot benefit from technological developments in other areas of special education. We've already noted that emotionally disturbed children experience more than their share of academic problems. The microcomputer programs mentioned in the chapter on learning disabilities can also be used by many emotionally disturbed students. In addition, special educators are beginning to look to videogame formats for ideas for developing exciting educational programs for exceptional children. What makes these efforts particularly suitable for the emotionally disturbed is that they focus on the motivational aspects of the games. Given the fact that many emotionally disturbed students are "turned off" to learning, any ideas for increasing their interest in academic learning are welcome.

Chaffin, Maxwell, and Thompson (1982) have developed educational games for basic arithmetic facts based on videogame formats. They based the games on the following four motivating features, which they believe are part of most successful videogames: feedback to the player, chance for improvement, fast-paced action, and unlimited ceilings on performance. There is no reason, of course, why these motivating features could not also be used in instruction that does not involve computers. In other words, perhaps the traditional mode of instruction could be spiced up too. In any case, it is nice to fantasize that someday we will be able to produce "academic junkies"—kids who will stand in line to get a chance to teach themselves academic skills for hours on end.

Not everyone, however, has embraced the use of computer-assisted instruction with the emotionally disturbed. Hofmeister (1982) warns that "If we take highly personalized aide [or teacher-] delivered tutorial programs and replace them with computer-delivered tutorial programs, we may reduce the opportunity to teach social-interpersonal skills simultaneously with other academic instruction." (p. 120). Hofmeister's fear is that if emotionally disturbed children end up interacting too much with computers rather than with human beings, their social-interpersonal problems may be intensified. Although the dangers of limited adult-child interaction are more apparent for emotionally disturbed children, Hofmeister's concern probably applies to all children who are exposed to computerized instruction. Computers, like all other human inventions, can be used or abused. When used wisely and moderately, however, current technological advances hold promise for the education of today's emotionally disturbed child and adult.

ANSWERS TO FREQUENTLY ASKED QUESTIONS
EMOTIONAL DISTURBANCE

1. It's a myth that disturbed children are always brighter than average children. In fact, one of the most common characteristics of disturbed children is poor school achievement. The notion of there being a relationship between giftedness and insanity is also a misconception probably based on a few highly publicized cases. In response to your concern about misdiagnosis, you might in fact have a point. It is often quite difficult to distinguish the disturbed from the learning disabled. However, a competent team of professionals working with you should be able to determine the best special education services for Sarah, should they be needed.

2. Although aggressive behavior such as you describe would definitely be cause for concern in a 6- or 7-year-old, chances are it does not indicate a problem in a younger child, especially one who is only 2. Many behaviors that are considered disturbed in older children are often exhibited by younger normal children. This doesn't mean, of course, that you and your sister shouldn't make an effort to eliminate or at least minimize Max's aggression. Probably the worst thing you can do would be to ignore it. He needs to be led to understand that what he's doing is inappropriate. If you consistently try to make this clear to him and if he's like most children, many of these behaviors will just disappear as he gets a little older.

3. Based solely on the behaviors you describe—bedwetting and nightmares—we'd tend to side with your wife. These behaviors are not at all uncommon among children Ron's age. If they increase in frequency or intensity, or seem to be making him increasingly unhappy, or continue to be a persistent problem when he is a little older, say 8 or 9, then you should become concerned and possibly consider professional help.

4. Your concern is something that occurs to many parents, particularly in families of children and adults with special problems. Research is currently being conducted to try to find links between genes and various emotional problems. Although there is some evidence for the idea that certain types of behavior disorders are influenced by genetic factors, you shouldn't be overly concerned. The evidence for a relationship between heredity and emotional disturbance is not strong.

5. Unlike some handicapping conditions, children with severe behavioral problems often appear "normal" physically, so people are shocked when some of their behavior is not normal. Those who are not familiar with emotional disturbance frequently mistakenly blame parents and teachers for the difficulties. This doesn't mean that there aren't things you can do to help keep the frequency of Joshua's misbehavior at a lower level. For example, it might be beneficial to reward Joshua in some way when he completes an outing without a tantrum. As his behavior improves, your other children might become less reluctant to go out with him. With regard to your friends, you could explain the reasons for his behavior problems to them. If they are truly your friends, they will understand. Regarding cruel comments made by casual acquaintances or strangers, you will save yourself unnecessary emotional wear and tear if you try to disregard them.

6. From your description of the boy's behavior, it seems he might be autistic. Children with autistic-like behaviors frequently do not respond to others, have language problems, and engage in repetitive behaviors. These behaviors make it hard to test their intelligence, so it is often difficult to determine if autistic children have average or below-average ability. Years ago, such behavior was erroneously thought to be the result of lack of affection and warmth in the home. The precise cause is not yet known, but parents are no longer blamed for these problems. Today autistic behavior is thought to be caused by biological rather than by environmental factors such as the parental discipline you asked about. Autism is no longer categorized as an emotional disturbance since there is no evidence of any link between the two. Various techniques are used to teach children with autistic behaviors, ranging from computerized communication devices to instruction in sign language.

SUMMARY

Because there is no typical disturbed child, one of the most difficult areas of special education to define is that of emotional disturbance. Disturbed individuals display a wide variety of behaviors and a wide range of levels of severity. There is no definite answer to the question of how far a person can deviate from the average before he or she is considered disturbed. So estimates of prevalence, assessment, causes, characteristics, and educational approaches all suffer from confusion and controversy.

The current official definition has been set by the federal government and is a modification of one developed in the late 1960s by Bower. It includes children who are schizophrenic, but not those who are socially maladjusted. It also no longer includes autistic children, whose problems make them especially difficult to place in any category of exceptionality. The federal definition focuses on behaviors and characteristics exhibited so continuously and to such a degree that they adversely affect educational performance.

Estimates of the prevalence of emotional disturbance range from .05 to 15 percent of the school-age population. Boys outnumber girls in every category from mild to severe, and the majority of children fall in the mild to moderate category. Most ED children are identified in the middle childhood and beginning teen years. According to a prominent classification system, the behaviors displayed by disturbed children cluster around four major dimensions: conduct disorder, anxiety-withdrawal, socialized aggression, and imma-turity.

Comprehensive behavior assessments include information from many sources: parent interviews, standardized tests, behavior observations, child self-reports, peer reports, teacher ratings. Testing is usually done for three reasons: to screen and identify children; to determine educational placement and eligibility for services; and to determine specific teaching or management approaches.

As with learning disabilities, the causes of the disturbance are unknown in the vast majority of cases. Current theories fall into five conceptual model groupings: behavioral, biological, ecological, psychoanalytic, and psychoeducational. These models affect educational approaches as well as the focus of attention in treatment and management.

The characteristics of ED children vary widely because they are such a heterogeneous group. Three characteristics common to most mildly or moderately disturbed children are poor academic achievement, poor interpersonal relations, and poor self-esteem. Severely and profoundly disturbed children show a different and distinct set of behaviors that cluster around extreme difficulty in functioning independently.

Most educational services are designed for mildly and moderately disturbed children in the elementary school years. Identifying preschool children is difficult, and the problems are compounded by the expectations, values, and reactions of the parents. The most common elementary programs are the special self-contained class and the resource room–regular class placement. With the passage of PL 94–142, the emphasis now is on integration of even the more disturbed into the resource room–regular classroom system.

Of the various educational approaches for the disturbed, two are currently dominant: Psychoeducational methods that focus on a child gaining insight into his or her behaviors through crisis techniques such as the life space interview; and behavioral methods, such as the widely used token economy. Other educational programs are based on ecological and humanistic approaches. All these approaches are used at both elementary and secondary levels. Services in the secondary and postsecondary areas are currently expanding as the impact of the new federal law begins to be felt.

Very few technological advances so far are aimed specifically at the emotionally disturbed, and those now in use are adaptations of devices designed for the speech impaired. But the future is bright: Microcomputers hold great promise, as do videogames, which have motivating features, such as immediate feedback and fast-paced action, that may be ideal for students who are often resistant to academic learning.

REFERENCES

ACHENBACH, T.M. & EDELBROCK, C.S. Behavioral problems and competencies reported by parents of normal and disturbed children aged four through sixteen. *Monographs of the Society for Research in Child Development,* 1981, *46,* Ser. No. .188.

AHAMMER, I.M., & MURRAY, J.P. Kindness in the kindergarten. The relative influence of role playing and prosocial television in facilitating altruisim. *International Journal of Behavioral Development,* 1979, *2,* 133–157.

AMERICAN PSYCHIATRIC ASSOCIATION. *Diagnostic and statistical manual of mental disorders* (3rd ed., DSM-III). Washington, D.C.: American Psychiatric Association, 1980.

ARONOW, E. REZNIKOFF, M.E., RAUCHWAY, A. Some old and new directions in Rorschach testing. *Journal of Personality Assessment,* 1979, *43,* 227–234.

BANDURA, A. *Social learning theory.* Englewood Cliffs, N.J.: Prentice-Hall, 1977.

BENAROYA, S., WESLEY, S., OLGIVIE, H., KLEIN, L.S., & MEANEY, M. Sign language and multisensory input training of children with communication and related developmental disorders. *Journal of Autism and Childhood Schizophrenia,* 1977, *7,* 23–31.

BETTELHEIM, B. *The empty fortress.* New York: Free Press, 1967.

BOWER, E.M. *Early identification of emotionally handicapped children in school* (2nd ed.). Springfield, Ill.: Charles C Thomas, 1969.

BOWER, E.M. Defining emotional disturbance: Public policy and research. *Psychology in the Schools,* 1982, *19,* 55–60.

BOWER, E.M., & LAMBERT, N.M. *A process for in-school screening of children with emotional handicaps.* Princeton, N.J.: Educational Testing Service, 1962.

BRADY, D.D. & SMOUSE, A.D. A simultaneous comparison of three methods for language training with an autistic child: An experimental cue analysis. *Journal of Autism and Childhood Schizophrenia*, 1978, *8*, 271–279.

CASEY, L.O. Development of communicative behavior in autistic children: A parent program using manual signs. *Journal of Autism and Childhood Schizophrenia*, 1978, *8*, 45–59.

CHAFFIN, J.D., MAXWELL, B., & THOMPSON, B. ARC-ED Curriculum: The applications of video game formats to educational software. *Exceptional Children*, 1982, *49*, 173–178.

CULLINAN, D., EPSTEIN, M.H., & LLOYD, J.W. *Behavior disorders of children and adolescents.* Englewood Cliffs, N.J.: Prentice-Hall, 1983.

DEMBINSKI, R.J. Psychoeducational management of disruptive youth. In D.A. Sabatino & A.J. Mauser (Eds.). *Intervention strategies for specialized secondary education.* Boston: Allyn and Bacon, 1978.

DES LAURIERS, A.M., & CARLSON, C.F. *Your child is asleep: Early infantile autism.* Homewood, Ill.: Dorsey, 1969.

DEVANY, J.M., RINCOVER, A., & LOVAAS, O.I. Teaching speech to nonverbal children. In J.M. Kauffman & D.P. Hallahan (Eds.). *Handbook of special education.* Englewood Cliffs, N.J.: Prentice-Hall, 1981.

EGEL, A.L., RICHMAN, G.S., & BUTTON, C.B. Integration of autistic children with normal children. In R.L. Koegel, A. Rincover, & A.L. Egel (Eds.). *Educating and understanding autistic children.* San Diego: College-Hill, 1982.

EPSTEIN, M.H., & CULLINAN, D. Education of handicapped adolescents: An overview. In D. Cullinan, & M.H. Epstein (Eds.). *Special education for adolescents.* Columbus, Ohio: Merrill, 1979.

EPSTEIN, M. H., CULLINAN, D., & ROSE, T.L. Applied behavior analysis and behaviorally disordered pupils: Selected issues. In L. Mann & D.A. Sabatino (Eds.). *The fourth review of special education.* New York: Grune & Stratton, 1980.

FAGEN, S.A. Psychoeducational management and self-control. In D. Cullinan & M.H. Epstein (Eds.), *Special education for adolescents.* Columbus, Ohio: Merrill, 1979.

FENICHEL, C. Carl Fenichel. In J.M. Kauffman & C.D. Lewis (Eds.). *Teaching children with behavior disorders: Personal perspectives.* Columbus, Ohio: Merrill, 1974.

FREMONT, T., KLINGSPORN, M., & WILSON, J. Identifying emotionally disturbed children: The professionals differ. *Journal of School Psychology*, 1976, *14*, 275–281.

GOODSTEIN, L.D., & DOLLER, D.L. The measurement of the self-concept. In B.B. Wolman (Ed.). *Clinical diagnosis of mental disorders.* New York: Plenum, 1978.

GRIEGER, R.M., & RICHARDS, H.C. Prevalence and structure of behavior symptoms among children in special education and regular classroom settings. *Journal of School Psychology*, 1976, *14*, 27–38.

HARRIS, W., KING, D., & DRUMMOND, R. Personality variables of children nominated as emotionally handicapped by classroom teachers. *Psychology in the Schools*, 1978, *15*, 361–363.

HARTH, R., & GLAVIN, T. Validity of teacher ratings as a subtest for screening emotionally disturbed children. *Exceptional Children*, 1971, *37*, 605–606.

HERMELIN, B., & O'CONNER, N. *Psychological experiments with autistic children.* New York: Pergamon, 1970.

HEWETT, F.M., & TAYLOR, F.D. *The emotionally disturbed child in the classroom.* (2nd ed.). Boston: Allyn & Bacon, 1980.

HOBBS, N. Perspectives on re-education. *Behavioral Disorders*, 1978, *3*, 65–66.

HOFMEISTER, A. M. Microcomputers in perspective. *Exceptional Children*, 1982, *49*, 115–121.

HOOVER, J. A rural program for emotionally handicapped students: Democracy in action. *Teaching Exceptional Children*, 1978, *10*, 30–32.

HUSTON-STEIN, A., FOX, S., GREER, D., WATKINS, B.A., & WHITAKER, J. The effects of TV action and violence on children's social behavior. *Journal of Genetic Psychology*, 1981, *138*, 183–191.

KANNER, L. The birth of early infantile autism. *Journal of Autism and Childhood Schizophrenia,* 1973, *3*, 93–95.

KAZDIN, A.E. *The token economy: A review and evaluation.* New York: Plenum, 1977.

KAZDIN, A.E. *Behavior modification in applied settings* (2nd ed.). Homewood, Ill.: Dorsey, 1980.

KNEEDLER, R.D. The use of cognitive training to change social behaviors. *Exceptional Education Quarterly,* 1980, *1*(1), 65–73.

KNOBLOCK, P. *Teaching emotionally disturbed children.* Boston: Houghton Mifflin, 1983.

KOEGEL, R.L., RINCOVER, A., & EGEL, A.L. (EDS.). *Educating and understanding autistic children.* San Diego: College-Hill, 1982.

KOEGEL, R.L., RINCOVER, A., & RUSSO, D.C. Classroom management: Progression from special to normal classrooms. In R.L. Koegel, A. Rincover, & A.L. Egel (Eds.). *Educating and understanding autistic children.* San Diego: College-Hill, 1982.

LONG, N.J., MORSE, W.C., & NEWMAN, R.G. (EDS.). *Conflict in the classroom* (4th ed.). Belmont, Calif.: Wadsworth, 1980.

LONG, N. J. & NEWMAN, R.G. Managing surface behavior of children in school. In N.J. Long, W.C. Morse, & R.G. Newman (Eds.). *Conflict in the classroom* (3rd ed.). Belmont, Calif.: Wadsworth, 1976.

MACK, J.E., & HICKLER, H. *Vivienne: The life and suicide of an adolescent girl.* Boston: Little, Brown, 1981.

MEICHENBAUM, D. *Cognitive-behavior modification: An integrative approach.* New York: Plenum, 1977.

MENOLASCINO, F.J., & EYDE, D.R. Biophysical bases of autism. *Behavioral Disorders,* 1979, *5*, 41–47.

MILLER, M.S. *Childstress! Understanding and answering stress signals of infants, children, and teenagers.* Garden City, N.Y.: Doubleday, 1982.

MORSE, W.C. The helpful teacher–crisis teacher concept. *Focus on Exceptional Children,* 1976, *8*(4), 1–11.

NEWMAN, R.G. *Psychological consultation in the schools: A catalyst for learning.* New York: Basic Books, 1967.

O'NEILL, C.B. *Starving for attention.* New York: Continuum, 1982.

PHILLIPS, E.L., FIXSEN, D.L., PHILLIPS, E.A., & WOLF, M.M. The teaching family model: A comprehensive approach to residential treatment of youth. In D. Cullinan, & M.H. Epstein (Eds.). *Special education for adolescents.* Columbus, Ohio: Merrill, 1979.

PIERS, E.V. *Manual for the Piers-Harris Children's Self-Concept Scale.* Nashville: Counselor Recordings and Tests, 1969.

QUAY, H.C. Classification in the treatment of delinquency and antisocial behavior. In N. Hobbs (Ed.). *Issues in the classification of children* (Vol. 1). San Francisco: Jossey-Bass, 1975.

QUAY, H.C. Classification. In H.C. Quay & J.S. Werry (Eds.). *Psychopathological disorders of childhood* (2nd ed.). New York: Wiley, 1979.

QUAY, H.C., & PETERSON, D.R. *Manual for the Behavior Problem Checklist.* Unpublished.

REDL, F. The concept of life space interviews. *American Journal of Orthopsychiatry,* 1959, *29*, 1–18.

RHODES, W.C., & PAUL, J.L. *Emotionally disturbed and deviant children: New views and approaches.* Englewood Cliffs, N.J.: Prentice-Hall, 1978.

RICHEY, E. The language problem. In E.R. Ritvo (Ed.). *Autism: Diagnosis, current research and management.* New York: Spectrum, 1976.

RIMLAND, B. *Infantile autism.* New York: Appleton-Century-Crofts, 1964.

ROTTER, J.B., & RAFFERTY, J.E. *Manual: The Rotter Incomplete Sentence Blank.* New York: Psychological Corporation, 1950.

SALVIN, A., ROUTH, D.K., FOSTER, R.E., & LOVEJOY, K.M. Acquisition of modified American sign language by a mute autistic child. *Journal of Autism and Childhood Schizophrenia,* 1977, *7*, 359–371.

WATSON, R.I. The sentence completion method. In B.B. Wolman (Ed.). *Clinical diagnosis of mental disorders.* New York: Plenum, 1978.

WING, L. Diagnosing autism and autistic-like conditions. *Proceedings of the 1979 Annual Meeting of the National Society for Autistic Children,* 1979.

WOOD, F.H. The antithesist vision of William Rhodes, *Behavioral Disorders,* 1982, 7, 234–243.

SPEECH AND LANGUAGE DISORDERS

5

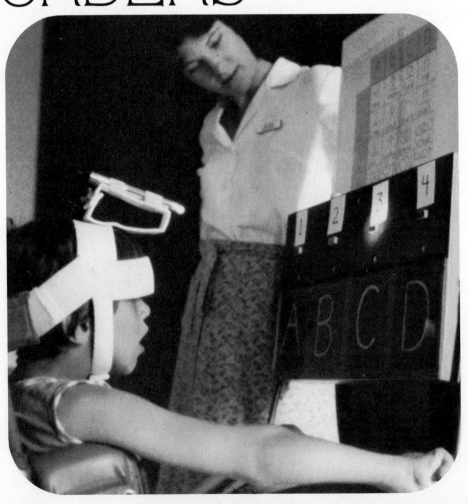

1. My friend has a son, Josh, who is 3½ years old. Josh was a "late" walker (2½), but still is not talking. Is he retarded, or does he have some kind of "emotional block" about learning to talk?

2. My 4-year-old son has problems with words. He says "fun" for "thumb," mispronounces *r* and *l* sounds, and can't say some words, like "measure." Should I have him tested? His teacher doesn't seem too concerned.

3. My next-door neighbor's father is recovering from a stroke. He sometimes stops by for a visit. The problem is that I find it extremely difficult to understand him. He speak words clearly, but they don't seem to make sense. His sentences have little meaning or content. Will he ever make sense when he speaks?

4. Last night I met my daughter Susan's teacher, Mr. Brown. Much to my surprise, Mr. Brown has some kind of speech problem. He has difficulty pronouncing certain words, speaks very slowly, and occasionally stutters. My daughter is very impressionable and thinks a great deal of Mr. Brown. I'm afraid that Susan might begin to imitate the way her teacher talks. I thought that people who stuttered grew out of it when they got older. How could the school employ someone with speech problems to teach young children?

5. My sister's 4-year-old daughter, Laura, was involved in an automobile accident. As the result of a brain injury, she is unable to speak. The doctors say she has average intellectual ability. Laura has been in speech therapy for about six months, and it is still extremely difficult to understand what she tries to say. She can't spell out words by pointing to letters because she has not yet learned to read. It might be a long time before her speech improves enough so that we can understand her. Is there something we could do to help Laura express her needs and communicate with us?

6. My grandson Tim is 1½ years old and can say only a few words, like "mama," "papa," and "bye-bye." I'm sure he understands what you say to him. He can point to objects and follow simple directions. What can we do about his problem? Where can my daughter go for help?

7. Jimmy, one of my second-graders, has a speech problem. It takes him a long time to answer questions because he stutters. The children become impatient waiting for him to answer. Sometimes they imitate his speech as a way of making fun of him. I don't want him to stop participating in class or to develop social or emotional problems because of the children's teasing. What can I do?

8. One of the girls in my class, Theresa, has a very low-pitched voice. She sounds so hoarse that on some days I think she has laryngitis. What also concerns me is that she is a cheerleader on Saturdays for soccer games. Will her voice always sound so strained?

9. My native language is English and my wife's first language is French. Our son is not yet a year old. Thus far, we have been speaking to him in both languages. Will this initial exposure to both English and French harm his language development? Shall we only speak English, since he will be using that language in school?

In many ways, today the outlook for the speech and language impaired is better than ever. The educational methods and technological advances available now were unknown even ten or twenty years ago. And many who require special services can receive them through local school systems at no cost.

With all these improvements, however, one major change has not happened—the attitudes of the nonhandicapped are still the same. We continue to be repelled by those with major communication defects. We continue to listen to the speech defect rather than the message. We continue to be in too much of a hurry to listen to slower forms of communication. And, as the following letter shows, we continue to fail to see the life-sustaining nature of communication:

August 10, 1979

Mr._____
Crippled Children's Services
Regular Medical Unit

_____

Re: "Jamie"
Dear Mr._____

Several months ago, your organization denied funding for a communication device for Jamie. She died Sunday, August 5, without ever receiving the benefits of an efficient means of communication. Her story will perhaps encourage you to place renewed emphasis on establishing funds for these much-needed systems.

Your rationale for not funding this system for this little girl was that this type of device is not a life support system; they are educational devices which do not fall subject to your generosity. Jamie's needs were not merely for a learning tool. Her needs were for a means to quickly communicate thoughts, feelings, and physical requirements to anyone. The communication notebook she did have required too much listener attention. The listener had to point for her and also remember the thought as the message continued word by word. Most people in her environment chose not to use the book. The only consistent yes-no response she had was a treadle switch attached to her wheelchair arm operated by her left foot. If she was out of her chair, which she was a great deal, this response was not even available.

Jamie acquired the skills of a normal child at her age level in spite of the physical handicaps she experienced, but she could not converse easily with her friends, foster parents, and strangers about life and daily needs.

Not being able to communicate her daily needs created some incidents that proved how essential to health support a communication system would have been for Jamie. Her extreme tone made it difficult for her to open her mouth far enough to eat. She was not able to tell people in new situations that she was too tight to open: she was misinterpreted as misbehaving and not allowed to finish her meal. The result of this was malnourishment in the form of insufficient caloric intake. When feeling discomfort, Jamie could not communicate this in any way but by throwing her body around, an action also frequently interpreted as bad behavior.

Jamie was hospitalized in September 1978 for surgery. She had no communication system to express pain, loneliness or to even let the hospital staff know that she understood the things they were telling her. The result of this was that the hospital staff treated her like a baby. What dignity do you think she had left?

Jamie had been moved by the state twice in the past year. Before her death, she was to be moved one more time. Her final anguish was the emotional reaction to having to be moved yet again into a new family without being able to communicate her needs to them.

She died after hours of physical discomfort. She died unable to communicate what her thoughts were or where the pain was. Yet you continue to insist that these devices are not life support systems.

Please respond to our plea to learn from Jamie's life. Nonvocal children need your help. Please listen to this child whose life never had a chance. With a means of communication, she could have lived to express herself as a beautiful human being.

Sincerely,

Friend of Jamie's
Communication Disorders Specialist

Reprinted from *Communication Outlook*, 1980, 2. Artificial Language Laboratory, Computer Science Department, Michigan State University, East Lansing, Michigan, 48824.

Today we see much that is improved due to technological and educational advances. Coupled with this, however, must be a concomitant shifting of priorities to make sure that such advances are applied in areas of human need. As John Eulenberg of the Artificial Language Lab at Michigan State observed:

> The world of mass market technology is so exciting to me because I know that's where the components are going to come from for us, for people to be able to speak. We need portable devices, we need micro-electronics, and I think that the motivation for that is coming through mass market products, like talking automobiles, or talking radar ranges, talking ovens, talking refrigerators, and that's fine. I have no problem with that technology and that mass marketing. But as long as there are going to be talking radar ranges and talking automobiles, let there be talking people first.

From NOVA, Finding a Voice,
1982 WGBH Educational Foundation

TODAY'S DEFINITION OF SPEECH AND LANGUAGE DISORDERS

Many people use the terms "communication," "speech," and "language" interchangeably. Some aspects of all three do overlap, and the differences can seem fuzzy. However, among speech and language professionals, these are all different terms.

Communication is a broad concept that includes any process of sharing or exchanging information. Communication can be verbal or nonverbal; it can convey any type of information, from the most abstract to the most concrete. Communication ranges from the emotional warmth of a loving caress to the facts given on a computer printout.

The two major components of communication are language and speech. **Language** is the code or system with which we communicate our thoughts. The code has certain structures and rules that organize our communication in a consistent and comprehensible pattern. **Speech** is the vocal or oral production of language.

DEVIATIONS AND DISORDERS

Speech and language are the major tools by which we human beings communicate. When deviations occur in either one, communication is affected. Depending on the severity of the deviation, interaction with others can be drastically altered and/or limited.

Speech and language disorders are disorders that interfere with communication and cause negative feelings in the speaker or listener. Some deviations in speech and language, such as regional dialects and accents, are quite obvious and may elicit negative reactions. But as long as communication is not disrupted, the deviation is not considered a disorder. Shirley, with her North Carolina drawl, may be considered to deviate from her Midwestern roommates at Ohio State, but she does not have a speech disorder. When the deviation interferes with communication, in addition to creating discomfort in the speaker or listener, it is serious enough to be considered a disorder.

DISORDERS DEFINED

As we can distinguish between language and speech, so we can distinguish between the disorders of each (see Table 5–1). **Language disorders** are handicapping deviances in the communication code or system, such as an apparent absence of verbal and/or receptive language. **Speech disorders** are problems in the intelligible production of language. Speech disorders are composed of specific characteristics or behaviors that hamper vocal production. As we discuss specific types of speech disorders, you will see that they can be quite different and have many different causes.

TYPES OF LANGUAGE DISORDERS

As Table 5–1 shows, a person can have four major problems with respect to language: (1) not have any (absence), (2) have begun acquiring it much later than others (delayed), (3) have had it and then lost it (interrupted), and (4) have inappropriate content (qualitative disorders).

ABSENCE OF LANGUAGE. Most children begin to understand and respond to spoken language in the first year of life. By the time they are 3, most children have both receptive and expressive language and already demonstrate an amazing understand-

---

TABLE 5–1
Types of Language and Speech Disorders

LANGUAGE DISORDERS. A handicapping deviance in the communication code or system.
    ABSENCE OF LANGUAGE: No recognizable receptive or expressive language.
    DELAYED LANGUAGE: Language acquired at a later point in time and at a slower than normal rate.
    INTERRUPTED LANGUAGE: A partial loss of language ability.
    QUALITATIVE DISORDERS: Bizarre or meaningless language that blocks communication.

SPEECH DISORDERS. Problems in the production of intelligible oral language.
    ABSENCE OF SPEECH: Total lack of intelligible speech.
    ARTICULATION DISORDERS: Errors and distortions in the way speech sounds are made.
    VOICE DISORDERS: Deviations in pitch, loudness, resonance, and voice quality that interfere with communication.
    FLUENCY DISORDERS: Problems in the rhythm, timing, and uninterrupted connecting of sounds and phrases.

ing of complex linguistic rules (Bangs, 1982; Tarver and Ellsworth, 1981). Some children, however, may show no signs of language comprehension. Children who have no recognizable language at the age of 5 years usually have other serious handicaps as well, such as profound retardation or autism.

DELAYED LANGUAGE. For some children, language development occurs at a later age. Bryan, who is 7, has the understanding and speaking vocabulary of a 4-year-old. Most authorities believe that a child with delayed language will learn language in the same way normal children do, only at a later time and at a slower pace. Delayed language frequently results from mental retardation or environmental deprivation.

INTERRUPTED LANGUAGE. Sometimes, an accident or infection can seriously affect the part of the brain relating to language. A dramatic example of this is seen in some adult stroke victims who seem to lose much understanding and language use following neurological damage. These persons are not just unable to speak; they no longer have the language they once had. A complete loss of language or drastically disordered language is called **aphasia**. A partial loss or disruption in language is called **dysphasia**. Dysphasia is more common, since language loss is rarely total.

QUALITATIVE DISORDERS. Certain youngsters may acquire language according to a normal timetable and may be able to produce sounds quite clearly, but select and arrange words in such a way that communication is impaired. In other words, the content of their language is disordered. An example of these qualitative disorders is echolalia, which is a robotlike repeating of exactly what is heard. Many autistic children have this disorder, which severely hampers their communication, interpersonal relations, and overall development.

Qualitative disorders can be less dramatic than echolalia. Rodney, for example, is not able to understand the meaning of a sentence like a normal child. Even though his speech skills are intact, he seems to have perceptual or comprehension problems which affect his ability to process language. Sheila's language comes out as bizarre nonsense; no one but Sheila knows what she means. These qualitative disorders are most often seen in children with severe emotional disturbance or mental retardation. Many children with learning disabilities also have language problems that prevent them from communicating easily with others (Hallahan and Bryan, 1981; Tarver and Ellsworth, 1981).

TYPES OF SPEECH DISORDERS

Many deviations, ranging from subtle to prominent, can distort or impair the actual production of language. But although speech disorders are quite diverse in terms of causes and characteristics, they can be organized into four major categories: (1) absence of speech, (2) articulation disorders, (3) voice disorders, and (4) fluency disorders. Figure 5–1 shows the major body parts that affect speech.

ABSENCE OF SPEECH. The child who has no discernible language because of profound retardation or severe autism would, of course, have no speech as well. Some exceptional individuals have language but, for a variety of reasons, cannot produce speech.

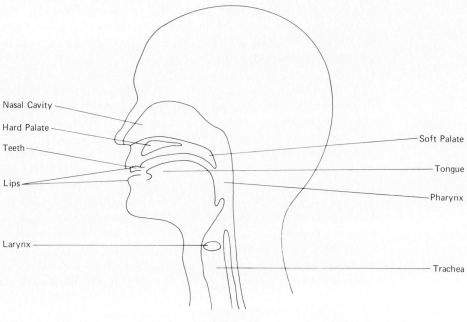

Nasal Cavity

Hard Palate

Teeth

Lips

Larynx

Soft Palate

Tongue

Pharynx

Trachea

FIGURE 5.1

Sarah, for example, is of normal intelligence and shows that she understands language and can read by pointing to words to ask and answer questions. But because of a severe case of cerebral palsy, she is unable to control the muscles needed to make intelligible speech sounds. Sarah has language, but she does not have speech. Thelma has had a stroke that damaged the nerves controlling her facial muscles. She cannot speak a single word, but her language comprehension is normal, as shown by constant note writing and gestures.

ARTICULATION DISORDERS. Disorders in the way speech sound is made are called **articulation disorders** and range from relatively mild defects to severe handicaps. Articulation disorders include the relatively minor errors of **omissions** ("I ove ou" for "I love you") and **substitutions** ("wed" for "red" and "thith" for "this"). We sometimes call these babytalk or lisping and, although they are distracting in a person's speech, they do not make the speech unintelligible. **Distortions,** on the other hand, include both close and remote approximations of what a sound should be. Severe distortions in articulation are often the result of one of these three biological factors: (1) **dysarthria,** lack of muscle control due to neurological damage (as in the case of cerebral palsy); (2) gross abnormalities of the facial structures necessary for speech, such as a cleft palate; and (3) severe hearing loss.

VOICE DISORDERS. Disorders of the voice have to do with deviations in such things as pitch, loudness, and quality. Two terms commonly used to describe voice quality are nasality and hoarseness (Perkins, 1980). A voice may be hypernasal if too much air passes through the nose while the person is speaking. This happens in cases of physical abnormalities of the oral cavity, such as cleft palate, or when there are hearing losses.

Chronic hoarseness often indicates serious pathology of the larynx, the structure in the throat containing the vocal cords. When the larynx must be removed, voice cannot be produced in the usual way. Individuals who have had their larynx removed can use an electromechanical device held against the throat or oral cavity. They may also learn to use esophageal speech, which is done by forcing air up from the esophagus to produce audible sounds.

FLUENCY DISORDERS. Disorders in fluency, which are also called rhythm, timing, and flow disorders, have to do with the problems a person has in producing smooth and uninterrupted sounds and phrases. All of us have moments when we struggle to produce a sound. When interruptions in the flow of speech become so frequent or obvious that they draw attention to the speaker, or seriously hamper the understanding of what is being said, then those interruptions are a **fluency disorder.**

The most common fluency disorder is **stuttering.** Although most of us are familiar with stuttering and its characteristics, there is much disagreement among speech pathologists regarding its definition, causes, and treatment. Among people who stutter, there are many differences in the nature and characteristics of their disability. For example,

---

FOCUS

COMMUNICATING WITH A PERSON WITH A SPEECH DISORDER

Regardless of whether the person stutters, has a cleft palate, uses a communication board, or has some other speech deviation, we who have normal speech often feel some degree of discomfort when trying to communicate. And yet, any negative feedback we give to them, such as embarrassment, avoidance, or rejection, can have a profound effect on their communication efforts and their social adjustment as well. Given the importance of interaction, how can we best help such people?

1. Slow down and be patient. This does not mean slow down in your talking, but slow down in your *listening*. Listen with full attention and try not to interrupt or otherwise act as if you are in a hurry. Speech-impaired people usually speak best with those who listen and talk in a relaxed and unhurried way.

2. Use nonverbal cues. To increase your understanding of the message the person is trying to convey, take into account other cues—facial expressions, gestures, context— as much as possible.

3. Continue to use your natural speech. Sometimes a speech-impaired person makes us feel self-conscious about our own speech, and we may change our rate, tone, or mannerisms. We should try to talk with as much ease as we do with anyone else. Except for being careful not to talk too fast (and possibly conveying a stressful expectation of similar speed), there is no need to alter our speaking style in any way.

4. Be receptive. Since individuals with speech problems often encounter avoidance and rejection from others, you may need to show extra encouragement or reinforcement for any communication attempts. Often a smile, facial expressions of interest and undivided attention, or a receptive verbal response can have a great effect on increasing the communication efforts of someone with speech problems.

Margot, whose conversation is plagued by frequent bouts of stuttering, doesn't stutter at all when singing or reading aloud; Jeffrey's entire body contorts with the struggle to form words in situations of stress; Suzanne can hide her stuttering for the most part by avoiding the words she knows she will block on. Although all three are considered to be stutterers, their characteristics affect their communication in three distinct ways. So although most of us have encountered stutterers and may feel familiar with the population we are describing, it is important to remember how different stutterers really are. This disorder, in the majority of cases, diminishes and disappears during late childhood or adolescence.

Another fluency disorder is **cluttering,** excessively fast and garbled speech character-ized by omitted and substituted sounds. Although the rate and articulation of the speech can make it unintelligible, the person with cluttered speech often seems unaware of or indifferent to any problems. Unlike the stutterer, the person with cluttered speech has no fear or shame about his or her speech and does not engage in struggle or avoidance behaviors (Perkins, 1980; Van Riper, 1978).

PREVALENCE

LANGUAGE DISORDERS

Because there are so many kinds of problems, it is extremely difficult to identify people with language disorders. For this reason, we do not have prevalence figures for language disorders as we do for other handicapping conditions.

SPEECH DISORDERS

Even though you would think speech disorders are apparent and so easy to pinpoint, there are still difficulties in estimating prevalence. One is disagreement on how severe a speech impairment should be before it is counted. In addition, specific speech disorders vary so widely in terms of characteristics, services needed, and specific prevalence figures that figures which lump all speech-related problems together are not particularly helpful or meaningful. The 1981 report noted in Chapter 1 estimates that 2.4 to 4 percent of school-aged children in this country are speech impaired. Within specific speech disorders, however, reports of prevalence figures contradict this figure. For example, about 1 percent of school-aged children are reported to have the disorder of stuttering (Perkins, 1980), 2 to 3 percent to have articulation disorders (Shriberg, 1980), and 3 to 5 percent to have voice disorders (Boone, 1980).

These problems are compounded by other factors. First, many speech impairments coexist with other handicaps (or may, in fact, be caused by these handicaps) in children who are counted as multiply handicapped or identified by a handicap *other* than their speech impairment, such as mental retardation. Second, counting children who have a certain speech-related handicap such as cleft palate may not give an accurate figure of children who are speech impaired or need services. For example, it is reported that one child in 800 will be born with some type of abnormal cleft (Wells, 1971), but for a variety of reasons (the main one being surgical repair), not all these children will have speech defects.

Unlike handicaps in some areas, such as vision and hearing, speech impairments do not show a significant increase with age. In fact, certain articulation and fluency disorders show a definite decrease as the individual enters the adolescent years.

ASSESSMENT OF LANGUAGE AND SPEECH DISORDERS

Because language and speech disorders are so diverse, assessment approaches vary according to each disorder. Every aspect of assessment—from the initial step of identification to the recommendations for intervention—is different for each disability. The processes involved in language and speech are so complex and interconnected that no two children have exactly the same problems. But although each assessment procedure must be tailor-made, we can make a few general comments.

LANGUAGE DISORDERS

In spite of the tremendous emphasis on dissecting the parts and processes of language, there is still much we do not know about how or why children learn language. The process continues to be studied intensely, with new areas of emphasis being pursued at different times (Schiefelbusch and McCormick, 1981). It may seem relatively simple to identify the presence of the four types of language disorders—absence, delayed, interrupted, or qualitative—but it is quite another task to try to assess exactly what the nature of a child's abilities and disabilities are within each category, and how best to correct the existing problems. Two major assessment approaches are used in the difficult area of language disorders—tests and scales, and clinical judgment.

TESTS AND SCALES. One evaluation technique uses standardized tests, nonstandardized tests, developmental scales, and behavioral observations. Example of standardized tests are the Illinois Test of Psycholinguistic Abilities (Kirk, McCarthy, and Kirk, 1968), the Peabody Picture Vocabulary Test (Dunn, 1965), and the Northwestern Syntax Screening Test (Lee, 1971). In selecting and using one of the many available language tests, you need to understand what the instrument you are using is designed to measure. Many tests examine only one kind of language behavior, such as comprehension. Naremore (1980) cautions against using test performance in one area to indicate deficiencies in other areas. A full evaluation of a child's language ability should include assessment of imitation, comprehension, and production skills.

CLINICAL JUDGMENT. A second major approach used in language assessment is the subjective judgment of a trained language pathologist. In this approach an experienced clinician selects the evaluation measures to be used, identifies the nature of each child's abilities, and pulls all the information together into a recommendation for treatment.

SPEECH DISORDERS

Like language, the process that results in speech involves many components that must work together simultaneously and intricately. Also, as is the case in language assessment, it is relatively easy to identify the existence of one of the four speech disorders—problems of no speech, articulation, voice, and fluency—but in many cases, it is quite difficult to decipher the precise source of these problems and to prescribe corrective steps.

LACK OF SPEECH. When there is no speech, assessment often involves identifying the factors that seem to cause or accompany the lack of speech. In most cases, absence of speech is accompanied by other serious handicaps, such as severe or profound retardation, autism, physical and motor disabilities, or deafness. Assessing the nature and extent of these other handicaps is an essential step in determining effective intervention approaches.

ARTICULATION DISORDERS. Most public schools screen all new pupils for this type of speech problem. Usually, if children continue to make articulation errors by third or fourth grade, they will be referred for further evaluation. According to Shriberg (1980), the most common methods of assessing articulation problems are (1) to compare the child's performance to that of children the same age; (2) to predict the severity or correctability of the problem; and (3) to monitor changes over time with or without intervention efforts.

Many articulation disorders result from biological and physiological problems such as cleft palate or other facial abnormalities, lack of voluntary control of the speech muscles due to neurological dysfunction, or severe hearing loss. In cases such as these, assessment must be conducted in collaboration with an interdisciplinary team of specialists. For example, in the case of articulation problems associated with a cleft palate, an assessment team might be made up of a language pathologist, a plastic surgeon, a dentist, a pediatrician, an audiologist, and a psychologist.

VOICE DISORDERS. According to Boone (1980), most children with voice disorders are identified in school screening programs, and most adults are self-referred or referred by physicians to a speech pathologist. The pathologist is trained to conduct sophisticated and highly technical measurements of such things as pitch, loudness, and breath control.

Because a large percentage of voice disorders are caused by physiological conditions such as infectious laryngitis or cancer of the larynx, a medical evaluation must be part of the total voice evaluation. In many cases involving voice disorders, the appropriate assessment by a speech pathologist involves referral to a physician, who may recommend rest, medication, and/or surgery. As in the case of articulation disorders, voice problems can also be associated with facial deformities, poor muscular control, or a hearing impairment. In such situations, assessment and intervention must include the appropriate specialist.

FLUENCY DISORDERS. Trying to measure the nature or severity of a fluency disorder is a very complicated procedure that does not lend itself well to a standardized measure, although such measures do exist. One evaluation method is a frequency count of dysfluencies. But this does not provide a complete picture: Some dysfluencies are of greater duration than others, and the severity of the disorder is not always related to the number of dysfluencies. For example, who has the most severe disorder—Janice, who chatters joyfully with numerous dysfluencies, or Charles, whose face contorts in a violent grimace for what seems like a very long single period of dysfluency? To obtain a more complete measure, there is equipment available that records both dysfluencies and elapsed speaking time (Perkins, 1980).

Regardless of the severity of the fluency disorder, it is sometimes of value to see to what degree the person is bothered by his or her impairment. In some cases, the person's perception of his or her speech and the resulting low self-esteem are worse than the speech impairment itself. For this aspect of evaluation, we have several rating scales that measure the person's attitude and opinion of his or her own disability (Erickson, 1969).

CAUSES OF LANGUAGE AND SPEECH DISORDERS

In many cases of language and speech disorder, the causes are unknown. For a small number, a description of the cause helps to clarify the nature of the disorder and to suggest treatment approaches, as in the case of deafness causing articulation and voice disorders. But for the majority of cases, the cause is impossible to determine.

LANGUAGE DISORDERS

The normal acquisition of language is still too much of a mystery for us to be able to separate out the factors that cause the process to go wrong. The best we can do is to identify problems that frequently coexist with certain language disorders and to suggest that there is a causal relationship.

Some such characteristics in a child with no language are deafness at birth, profound mental retardation, psychosis, autism, or gross neurological damage. Delayed language is thought to be the result of mental retardation, severe environmental deprivation, and hearing impairment. Interrupted language is typically caused by neurological damage resulting from an accident or infection, or by a hearing loss after some language has been acquired. Disorders in qualitative language are thought to result from conditions such as autism, severe emotional disturbance, mental retardation, learning disabilities, and hearing impairment. For many of these types of language disorders, the exact cause of the coexisting condition (such as severe emotional disturbance) is usually unknown.

SPEECH DISORDERS

As is the case with language disorders, the majority of speech disorders have unknown causes. A good example is stuttering. In spite of the enormous attention stuttering has received, there is no conclusive evidence about its cause. Stuttering has been accounted for by learning theories, psychodynamic theories, linquistic theories, and organic/biological theories. But there is no overwhelming evidence to support any one group of factors over any other (Perkins, 1980; Van Riper, 1978).

Some causes of speech disorders are apparent to the specialist and have important implications for the selection of an intervention approach. For example, articulation and voice disorders are sometimes caused by abnormalities of the face or mouth that can affect the use of the tongue, lips, nasal passages, ears, teeth, and palate. Even after corrective surgery, special educational methods are often needed to teach the child how to use the corrected facial structures. In some cases, the child must be taught other ways of making speech sounds.

Other distinct causes of articulation and voice disorders are deafness and impaired muscular control. Determining the cause in these cases is important for choosing corrective measures. Interestingly, in most cases the "causes" of these so-called causes of speech disorders (facial abnormalities, deafness, dysarthria) are unknown. The majority of these conditions are present at birth and have no determinable origin.

Voice disorders may also have physiological causes such as abnormalities or injury to the larynx resulting from growths, infections, or damage due to voice abuse. Infections of the tonsils, adenoids, and sinus cavity can affect voice production. In addition, psychological problems such as sex role identity problems and faulty learning patterns may be responsible for the persistence of a voice disorder.

CHARACTERISTICS ASSOCIATED WITH LANGUAGE AND SPEECH DISORDERS

Within the population of children with language and speech handicaps, a large number have additional handicaps of mental retardation, serious emotional disturbance, physical incapacities, and learning disabilities. Thus, taken as a group, language- and speech-disordered youngsters score lower than normal children on measures of intelligence, achievement, and adaptive social behavior. If we look at children who do not have accompanying handicaps, we can make few generalizations regarding their psychological and behavioral characteristics.

One that can be made is that our culture—perhaps more than any other—puts a tremendous value on speech ability and seriously discriminates against those who have speech problems. If we look around in our everyday life, there seems to be a correlation between a person's speaking ability and his or her vocational status, leadership opportunities, and general ability to influence others. The ways in which we as a society negatively view imperfect speech can be seen in two studies. Mowrer (1974) looked at whether the presence of slight or pronounced lisps in adult male speakers would affect businesspeople's ratings of their intelligence, education, masculinity, and social appeal. He reported that even a slight lisp resulted in lowered estimates in all areas. Silverman (1976) found that listeners who heard female speakers lisping and not lisping rated the lisper more negatively on 37 of 49 personality attributes even though the speaker was saying the same thing in both conditions.

In our fast-paced world, we reward the quick thinker and quick talker and penalize the person who has slow or imperfect speech. We become impatient, we avoid, we reject. The speech-impaired person in turn feels anxiety, guilt, and hostility. Children with speech problems often experience teasing by their friends. Adults with speech problems experience quiet (but equally as devastating) rejection and limited opportunities.

Language and speech disorders are frustrating in themselves, since they block the normal desire to organize and transmit our thoughts to others. But in our society, we impose the additional handicaps of rejection and alienation. Although not all handicapped people are harmed by the stigma to the same degree, for many it is a far greater handicap than the disorder itself.

TODAY'S EDUCATIONAL METHODS FOR THOSE WITH SPEECH AND LANGUAGE DISORDERS

PRESCHOOL PROGRAMS

Preschoolers with identifiable language or speech disorders requiring services are usually severely or multiply handicapped. Typically, they are developmentally delayed in other major areas needing intervention. As is the case in all areas of exceptionality, the most important influence in the preschool child's intervention program is the parents. The parents' interest and ability to extend therapeutic efforts in the home make an incalculable difference to the child's chances of improvement.

It is especially important in the preschool years to identify and correct factors that contribute to language problems, such as hearing loss and facial deformities. The earlier problems such as these can be corrected, the better the chances for normal language and speech development.

Much language and speech intervention for young children involves play activities to teach language concepts and usage, and to stimulate vocalization. Methods for specific disorders are provided later in the chapter.

ELEMENTARY AND SECONDARY PROGRAMS

Most elementary and secondary schoolchildren with language and speech disorders are educated in regular classrooms. Depending on the nature and severity of the particular disorder, these children may receive a variety of services from a specialist employed by the school system. Under Public Law 94-142, schools are required to provide identification and diagnosis, services for prevention and correction, and counseling to teachers and parents.

The specific methods used to correct language and speech disorders do not differ much among preschool, elementary, and secondary students. Instead, intervention approaches vary according to the kind of disorder. There are, however, some general steps teachers can take, as the Focus shows.

METHODS FOR THE LANGUAGE DISORDERED

The nature of language disorders—the fact that the trouble is in aggravatingly inaccessible parts of cognitive functions—makes the task of treatment especially difficult. As we noted earlier, the area of language disorders and, indeed, the processes of normal language development are not fully understood. Why a child may have a language disorder and what to do about it is still not an area of scientific precision. We cannot directly manipulate the parts of the brain that affect language operations. Although throughout this chapter we have maintained a distinction between language and speech, in fact treatment of language-disordered children focuses largely on the training and modification of speech. Speech is the part of language that is accessible, and it also reflects and affects language. Speech therapy can be used to change and improve the underlying language disorders.

Within the area of language disorders, intervention efforts have centered around two major approaches: (1) naturalistic or discovery language intervention and (2) behavioral intervention or, more specifically, operant conditioning.

NATURALISTIC INTERVENTION. One educational approach today for children with a language disorder is to duplicate the processes of normal language development in a more simplified, systematic, and stimulated way. Clinicians who use this approach may begin by creating a good atmosphere for communication. Their initial treatment sessions may consist of setting up the situation so that the child and the therapist interact in a relaxed, nonverbal way (as in play therapy, for example). The next step is typically the therapist's modeling of simple utterances appropriate to the developmental level of the child. As Bobby plays with a toy, for example, the specialist might say "car . . . car go . . . see car . . . see two cars? . . . see big car."

WHAT CAN A TEACHER DO ABOUT LANGUAGE AND SPEECH DISORDERS?

A large part of the intervention with a child who has language and speech problems seems to be the responsibility of a specialist in language and speech—often the school's therapist. But there are important ways in which a teacher can help the child's learning in these areas. Here are some:

1. Be alert to deviations in language and speech that may require services beyond those you are providing.
2. Refer children you suspect may have a problem to the specialist for evaluation.
3. If any of your children are in therapy, maintain contact with the specialist to understand the goals and new speech responses to be reinforced in the classroom.
4. Create a classroom atmosphere that is conducive to communication—that is relaxed and unpressured, yet filled with stimulating opportunities for the expression of ideas and feelings.
5. Reinforce a student's efforts to communicate, both verbal and nonverbal, with your attention. Many teachers unwittingly inhibit communication because they seem distracted.
6. Don't finish a child's sentence for him or her. How can you be sure you know what the child wants to say?

The language specialists in this approach usually arrange the intervention so that the *sequence* follows what is observed to be normal language development. Thus, first they try to develop receptive language comprehension and to elicit vocalizations, then one-word utterances, two-word utterances, simple sentences, and so on. The techniques for stimulating this receptive and expressive language vary greatly, but the sequence is for the most part shared by all specialists using this approach.

An important aspect of the naturalistic intervention is to get the parents to participate in home procedures. Two specific ways the parents can increase the child's exposure to receptive language is through parallel talk and self talk. In **parallel talk**, the parent verbalizes simple phrases that describe or note things from the child's perspective. For example, while Mother is mixing something at the stove, she could be watching what Joseph is doing and saying, "Joseph pats the cat. Soft kitty. Uh oh, kitty go away. Bye, bye kitty. Come see Joseph again." In **self talk**, the parents verablize aloud what they themselves are doing and feeling. Using the same example, Mother might be saying, "I will mix the eggs and milk. This will be a yummy cake. I love to eat cake. Daddy loves to eat cake. Joseph loves to eat cake too."

This simple modeling of speech by the parents is important in six ways: (1) It uses language with content that is relevant to the child's everyday world; (2) it offers labels at the very moment when a child might be needing them; (3) it organizes at a level of the child's understanding what might otherwise be confusing to the child; (4) it provides accurate language for the child; (5) it gives parents a constructive intervention method to use, replacing such anxiety-producing ones as "say this" commands; and (6) it provides behaviors for the child to imitate by the most important people in the child's life, which increases the chance of correct imitation.

Those who favor this approach insist that the objective is not to have children imitate successfully the sounds they hear, but to have the children discover how words and phrases connect together in meaningful communication. The emphasis on simple, sequential language models is to get children to discover the rules of the language code, which up until now they have not been able to do.

BEHAVIORAL INTERVENTION. For children who have major disorders, such as no apparent language or severely delayed language, the most promising educational approaches today revolve around operant conditioning. Major proponents of this perspective are Lovaas and his colleagues (Devany, Rincover, and Lovaas, 1981; Lovaas, 1977). The children with whom they have worked have serious deficits in receptive language and virtually no meaningful expressive language (they either have no speech or echolalic speech). Most of the youngsters are multiply handicapped. In addition to language disorders, they have minimal self-help skills, social interaction, or communication of any kind with the outside world. Because of their pathology, they are highly resistant to most intervention efforts.

Using the basic behavioral tools of shaping, prompt-fading, positive reinforcement, and punishment, the Lovaas program uses discrimination training to get the children to make a certain response in the presence of a particular stimulus, and to suppress that response when exposed to a different stimulus. Discrimination training enables Tommy to respond to questions such as "What is this?" (expressive response) or "Point to the ball" (receptive response) only when the correct item (ball) is present. The training, which requires many sessions, is essential if Tommy is to acquire language.

The initial objective in this method is to establish the verbal imitation skills that appear to be missing. Four steps are used to teach vocal imitation. (1) The teacher reinforces any vocalization that is made and will evoke sounds if necessary through stroking or tickling. In addition, the child is rewarded for looking at the teacher's mouth, since this is a required behavior for later training. (2) The teacher makes her speech a cue or signal for the child to respond by rewarding him whenever the child makes *any* vocalization within 5 seconds after the teacher has spoken. (3) The teacher reinforces the child when he follows the teacher's vocal sound with a close match of the same sound. The sounds should be selected according to visual traits that can be exaggerated by the teacher (*b*) or according to the ease with which they can be physically prompted (pushing the child's lips together to form *m*). (4) This step involves the same procedure as in step 3, but with the addition of a new sound. The teacher alternates the command to see if the child can discriminate between the old and the new sounds. After the child reaches a certain level of mastery of imitating new sounds at their initial presentation, he receives the same training procedure as in step 3 with simple syllables and later with simple words.

From this stage, the child proceeds through four additional programs. Program 2 emphasizes the semantics (meaning) of receptive and expressive language. Program 3 teaches abstract terms using prepositions, pronouns, time concepts and yes-no concepts. In program 4 the child is trained in conversational skills, including simple questions and answers, and in program 5 in grammatical skills such as verb tenses and plural forms.

The effectiveness of these procedures has been demonstrated (Devany, Rincover, and Lovaas, 1981; Lovaas 1977). Although the authors would be the first to caution that the procedures have not been successful with all children, they have worked far better than any other approach with children whose handicaps make them extremely resistant to language learning.

METHODS FOR THE SPEECH DISORDERED

Today most children with speech disorders are educated in regular classrooms. Even though an important part of the child's speech training is usually carried out by a specialist, today's teacher needs to be familiar with the major educational methods for each disorder.

LACK OF SPEECH. Unlike the other speech disorders, the severe disorder of no speech is not seen frequently in the regular school. Most children who have no speech have accompanying handicaps so serious they frequently require the services found in a residential institution. In those cases, educational methods for children who have the physical ability to speak would be similar to the behavioral procedures described above for language-disordered children. Modification would be needed based on the child's level of comprehension. It is important to keep in mind that some children with no speech also have no language understanding, but a good number of children who have no speech have a relatively sophisticated level of receptive language ability (including a skill such as reading).

Many of the children who have language but no speech have accompanying physical handicaps of such severity that no amount of intervention will enable them to produce speech. With conditions like extremely severe cerebral palsy, for example, they may never be able to overcome their physical limitations. For these children, intervention

A communication board enables this child whose speech is unintelligible to convey concepts by pointing to them.
D. Grogan, U. Va./CRC.

SPEECH AND
LANGUAGE
DISORDERS

159

efforts should be focused on teaching them some other means to communicate, such as gestures, sign language, or the use of a communication device. One such alternative might be a **communication board.** Although relatively simple to make, it must be tailored to match the intellectual and physical characteristics of the child. The child's intellectual level will indicate whether the board should contain pictures or words and, if words, at what level of complexity. The concepts the child needs most frequently are the ones displayed most prominently. Functional language reflecting the child's basic needs is often a good place to start—words or pictures depicting food, drink, bathroom, scratch, help, and so on.

Individualizing the communication device to match the child's physical attributes means enlisting the child's most controllable movement as the primary response mode. In other words, what physical response can the child control most consistently—a foot movement, an elbow jab, a pointing stick strapped to the head, eye movements in certain directions? Whatever seem to be the best responses should determine the size, positioning, and type of communication board used.

Communication devices for those with no speech have improved rapidly during the past decade because of technological advances, as we will see later in the chapter, and as the Focus shows.

ARTICULATION DISORDERS.   The first step in treating articulation disorders is to decide which error(s) to work on first. This decision may be made by choosing from several misarticulations those sounds that are (1) easier (*f* rather than *r*), (2) acquired first in normal language development (simple initial consonant sounds), or (3) of greater motivational appeal (such as the child's name).

The next step is to get the child to listen and hear the differences between correct and incorrect sounds. Then comes the crucial step of getting the child to produce the sound correctly. This step, which is the core of the intervention, is often taken with a variety of procedures and materials. Usually, speech therapists have the sound produced first by itself, then in a syllable, then in a word, and finally in a sentence. In order to get the child to change a mispronunciation, therapists give specific instructions in tongue and lip movements, model correct articulation, and provide whatever auditory, visual, and tangible cues might be necessary in getting the child to change a current speech pattern. The clinician may use operant conditioning techniques or helpful physical or verbal reminders.

To maintain interest during the necessary repeating of speech sounds, the therapist needs a "bag of tricks"—games, competitive drills, "I'll trick you" challenges, talking and writing practices, unison speech, role playing, catching the therapists' mistakes. Articulation therapy can often seem slow and laborious to a young child, especially to one who is easily frustrated. A good therapist can motivate the child to maintain effort throughout the sessions.

The goal of educational methods for articulation disorders is to have the child experience fewer errors not just in therapy sessions or in the classroom, but in ordinary conversation. Often, parents and teachers need to change their earlier pattern of responding to the child's errors or corrected speech in order to increase the chances that the child will maintain improved speech in all situations. Teachers can provide home assignments to encourage the child to work on errors in many situations. And depending on age and ability, the child may be able to use self-correcting techniques to monitor his or her own speech.

Focus

VOICE DISORDERS. Although our society is more tolerant of voice deviations than those of articulation or fluency, voices that are high-pitched, harsh and strident, hypernasal, too weak, or too loud can have a highly detrimental effect on social and vocational opportunities.

As noted earlier, in many cases of voice disorder, the proper intervention is medical. Treatments include rest, medication, or surgery. The major educational methods used today include counseling to help individuals recognize the nature of their disorders and training to enable them to change the way they use their voices.

A valuable first step in intervention is to have the person hear his or her own voice on a recording. Depending on the nature of the disorder, you may want to contrast the tape-recorded version with the normal speech of someone else. Hearing one's own voice in these cases seems to motivate the student to improve and clarify for the person what the problem is. A second step may be to identify and then decrease the amount of vocal abuse to which the person may be unwittingly subjecting his or her voice. Abuses such as excessive yelling, excessive smoking, or frequent throat clearing are bad habits that often must be eliminated. Sometimes just making the person aware of these behaviors will lead to a change in habit.

It may be helpful early in the intervention to have a child make gross variations in his or her voice, such as imitations of animals or fantasy characters. This lets the child see that he or she has control over his or her voice and choices among kinds of voice. As in the case of articulation disorders, training in voice disorders must be done by someone skilled in the voice problems, and often takes long practice to get the individual to make gradual approximations to the desired speech.

In training the person toward progressive approximations, Van Riper (1978) gives two examples of how the use of a tape-recorded passage can be effective:

> We also often make a tape recording which has on it, first, a vivid sample of the abnormal voice at its worst, then a series of graduated and numbered voice samples that progressively come closer and closer to the voice desired, which forms the terminal example. After the client becomes familiar with this "measuring tape," he is able, with fair consistency, to evaluate any vocal attempt in terms of its proximity to the desired new voice. Strong motivation is thereby procured. (Van Riper, 1978, p. 251)

> One of our favorite ways for using progressive approximation in voice therapy is to use a binaural auditory trainer. We then feed in the client's voice into one ear and our own voice into his other ear, thereby permitting simultaneous comparison. We usually begin by joining the client as he reads or phonates a tone, imitating him closely so both voices harmonize in unison, then gradually we change our own voice in small steps in the direction of the desired voice. Perceiving the difference, the client often shifts unconsciously to bring both voices together again, and so a progressive approximation has occurred. (Van Riper, 1978, p. 252)

The use of a "new voice" must be practiced enough so that its owner becomes very familiar and comfortable with it. Often it is a good idea to role-play everyday conversations in the therapy sessions to make sure the improved voice will not disappear in the "real world." Because friends and family members are often surprised to hear the changed voice, it is often suggested that practice conversations be conducted first in situations involving strangers. Every effort should be made to ensure that the person will continue to use the new voice and not regress to former patterns.

FLUENCY DISORDERS. Stuttering has been given a great deal of attention for hundreds of years, so every treatment imaginable has been reported as meeting with various degrees of success. In spite of the great variability among approaches, today's major intervention efforts come from three perspectives: psychotherapy, stuttering replaced by fluent speech, and fluent stuttering.

The most common approach with stutterers in the past has been psychotherapy. This approach grew out of the belief that people stutter because they are anxious, insecure, or neurotic in some way. By getting the person to resolve inner conflicts or some other personality problems, it was thought that the stuttering would decrease. Most evidence, today, however, indicates that the stutterer's anxieties are the *result* of the speech defect and not the *cause* (Van Riper, 1978). Although psychotherapy is still used as a treatment for stuttering, no one is able to produce scientific evidence of its effectiveness.

Stuttering replaced by fluent speech, or as Van Riper (1978) calls it, the "Don't Stutter" approach, uses behavioral principles to reinforce fluent speech. There are variations in specific techniques, but essentially the approach is to reinforce whatever fluent speech every stutterer has. Many behavior modification therapists use techniques that were used in the past in traditional stuttering therapy—rate control by delayed feedback, relaxation, modified breathing patterns, variations in phrasing, and so on. Critics of this approach argue that immediate and temporary improvement is relatively easy to get in any type of stuttering therapy, but that behavior modification techniques do not achieve any lasting improvement (Van Riper, 1978). Those who favor the approach report long-term improvement in a majority of cases and argue that competing therapies show no such results (Perkins, 1980; Perkins, Rudas, Johnson, Michael, and Curlee, 1974; Webster, 1974).

The third intervention approach emphasizes reducing the struggle and avoidance behaviors that plague the conversation of most stutterers. The idea is that, in all likelihood, a confirmed stutterer will continue to stutter in some form or another throughout life; therefore, don't fight it—accept yourself as a stutterer and slide through your stuttering as effortlessly and fluently as possible. What is often reported in this therapy is that once the stutterer relaxes and learns coping strategies, there is usually a dramatic decrease in stuttering. Equally as important, the stutterer does not continue to engage in as many time-consuming and emotionally draining avoidance behaviors.

In the fluent stuttering approach, the person is taught alternative ways to cope with stuttering behaviors—ways called by Van Riper (1978) cancellations, pull-outs, and preparatory sets. These strategies teach the person to replace previous stuttering behaviors with improved stuttering behaviors. In addition, the person works through required activities and assignments designed to help him or her face more realistically the reactions of others. Many stutterers exaggerate the negative reaction in others or anticipate harsher responses than they actually encounter. This approach retrains them to change their own reactions to situation fears, communicative stress, and frustration or hostility.

POSTSECONDARY AND ADULT TRAINING

Many of the educational methods described in previous sections can be used with adults who have language and speech disorders. The adult population seeking intervention generally comes from two major groups. The first is composed of self-referred persons who are extremely motivated to improve an embarrassing speech defect (articulation, voice, or fluency). For this group, the methods we discussed are typically used.

The second group are those who have physiological problems such as dysarthria, neurological damage, infections around the larynx, damage to or loss of part of the speech mechanism, or severe physical handicaps. For many of these people, alternatives to oral language seem to be the proper training. Due to their motivation, adults seem particularly well suited to use the electronic aids described in the following section.

TECHNOLOGICAL ADVANCES

It's difficult to imagine what it would be like not to be able to communicate with others through speech. Certainly you might be able to use other methods of conveying ideas. For example, you could use gestures or sign language. But suppose that the control of your arms, hands, and fingers was poor. Maybe you could point to letters on a board or tray. Think of the time, effort, and concentration needed to spell out even short, simple messages. Such a process is painfully slow for both listener and speaker. What about young children or individuals who cannot spell? How can they communicate with others?

As stated in a recent position paper on nonspeech communication published by the American Speech-Language and Hearing Association (ASHA, 1981), the number of children and adults who are nonspeaking as a result of some disability is over a million. So the importance of techniques and devices to enable these individuals to communicate and to take advantage of educational opportunities cannot be overstated. Rehabilitation engineers and researchers often work with the people affected to design useful and efficient devices. Efforts are made to keep costs low, to create portable devices when appropriate, and to develop aids that can be used efficiently. Noting the incredible advances that have been made, ASHA has gone so far as to state: "There is no nonspeaking person too physically handicapped to be able to utilize some augmentative communication system" (p. 578).

In addition to the devices themselves, switches and other equipment have been developed to allow access to the devices or to microcomputers. For example, electrodes

---

FOCUS

CONFESSIONS OF A CLOSET TECHNOCRAT

Michael Williams, a professional writer, gave the following speech at the Stanford University Rehabilitation Engineering Conference on March 19, 1982. The speech was made with a prototype VOCA (voice output communication aid) designed by Telesensory Systems Inc. (TSI). The VOCA, dubbed the TTS-X, was developed under a grant from the National Science Foundation. It is a text-to-speech device that can receive input through a keyboard, an Autocom, or an Express I. Sixteen pages of frequently used text can be stored on magnetic tape and accessed through codes chosen by the user. The voice synthesizer is capable of producing intonation patterns similar to those found in natural human speech.

I am a child of technology. I was struck by this thought one sweltering summer's evening as I sat listening to a poet . . . telling us how we all needed to get back to the land and get in touch with nature again. As he spoke, I tried to figure out how I could fit into the picture he was painting. I couldn't do it; in fact, as I listened to his words more closely, I decided that the picture he was painting would be remarkably free of people with disabilities.

Let's face it, folks, can you see me performing such earthly tasks as driving a four wheel drive stick shift truck, building a log cabin, chopping down trees and splitting logs for firewood, milking goats and slaughtering hogs? If any one of you can picture me doing all these things, all I've got to say is, "Boy have you got a vivid imagination."

The plain truth of all this is: had it not been for technology, I wouldn't be speaking to you today.

When I came tumbling out of my mother's womb, the doctors thought I was dead. I fooled them. But I had a two month hospital stay where I benefited from the then fledgling technology of premature infant care. In the early 1970's someone suggested I try out an electric wheelchair. I loved it. I was amazed at how much more freedom I had with it. For the first time in my life I could go down to the corner store under my own power and buy a candy bar. I was in my early thirties.

Four years ago a friend told me about something called a microcomputer. I didn't pay too much attention to this guy at the time. He's the type of fellow who often sees little green men crawling out of flying saucers at midnight. Besides, I was terrified of computers. Computers were out to rob everyone of their soul.

But I began to hear more and more about these things called microcomputers. I started hanging around computer stores in an effort to find out more about them. At first I felt like a virgin in a porno shop. But as I slowly picked up more and more computer lingo, I started to get some idea of what microcomputers could and could not do.

Then I got one and it changed my life. As some of you may know, I am a writer. I have been writing since I was twelve. I have pounded on all sorts of typewriters. I started out on an old Underwood, the kind with the glass keys, remember those? I've been through two manual and several electric typewriters. Now I write with a computer. If you haven't written with a computer equipped with word processing software, you just haven't written.

I no longer have to worry about stuffing paper in my typewriter. I can see everything I've written on a television screen. I can add, subtract, and modify things in my manuscript at will, and when my manuscript is perfect, I print it out exactly as I want it.

A bonus of writing with a computer which most people aren't aware of is: your room certainly neatens up when you start using one. You don't have all those papers strewn around. Everything is stored on little plastic discs.

Two years ago I was introduced to the most exciting technological development for disabled people I've ever seen: synthesized speech. If, when I was a little boy, someone had told me that I would grow up and make speeches to large groups, I would have called him either a fool or a madman. Yet, here I am.

When I first heard about synthesized speech I was immediately against it. Too mechanical sounding, I said. Besides, I get along fine with my letterboard. Then I tried a speech synthesizer and a new world opened up. I had no idea the worlds of speaking and writing were so different from each other.

When I use a letterboard to communicate, I am in an essentially private world. By this I mean I only feel comfortable communicating via letterboard with people who already know about letterboards and feel at ease with them. Try talking to someone who has never seen a letterboard before. It's sometimes a harrowing experience. A letterboard certainly limits the circle of people you can communicate with. You can't talk to a blind person with a letterboard. I have been a friend of Jeff Moyer for many, many years; yet Jeff and I had our first meaningful one on one conversation one afternoon last December when he brought the TSI synthesizer to my house for me to evaluate.

You can't communicate with people who are dyslexic with a letterboard. And when a small child comes up and asks why you are in that chair, you can't tell her if you're using a letterboard because she can't read . . . oh yes, I almost forgot, you most certainly cannot order a pizza over the telephone with a letterboard.

And so we come back to the poet and his efforts to renounce technology and get back to the way things were in the good old days. . . . As for me, I can only say this: modern technology has allowed me to release my creative spirit where it can soar, free, high above the clouds. Without the fruits of modern technology, I would probably be stuck in a room counting the hours until my death.

To some people, this synthesizer may be an ugly box with cables. To me, however, it is an analogue for freedom.

Let freedom ring.

Reprinted with permission from *Communication Outlook*, Artificial Language Laboratory, Computer Science Department, Michigan State University, East Lansing, Michigan 48824, Vol. 3, No. 4, 1982, p. 12.

attached to the skin can monitor electrical signals from muscle fibers. These signals can, in turn, activate devices that enable the individual to communicate (Silverman, 1980). The possibilities seem limitless.

AUGMENTATIVE DEVICES

Harris and Vanderheiden (1980b) suggest that nonvocal communication techniques be viewed as supplements rather than replacements for speech. The idea is that techniques or devices should be used to enhance or *augment* the vocal skills already possessed by the individual. Those techniques that do not require aids, such as manual or sign communication, are called unaided. Charts, pictures, communication boards, and electrical aids are said to be aided communication techniques. The primary focus of this section will be on the electrical aids that are currently used by nonvocal individuals.

The devices range in function and complexity. Lapboards or trays may include overlays of pictures, symbols, letters, words, or even groups of letters representing the most common English sounds (such as SPEEC, sequence of phonemes for efficient English communication, developed by Goodenough-Trepagnier). The descriptions that follow are arranged from least to most complex in terms of inputs, the device itself, and the various output capabilities.

PROVIDING INPUT TO THE DEVICES

There are three major techniques by which a person can activate the devices: direct selection, scanning, and encoding. Many of the aids require the **direct selection technique,** which means that the user points directly to elements of the message. This method requires the user to have a certain amount of control over some part of his or her body. A technique requiring a minimal amount of physical control is **scanning** (Harris and Vanderheiden, 1980a). An example of a simple scanning device is the Zygo-

A child uses a scanning device with the Zygo-Model 16C Communicator. Communication Outlook, 1979, 1 (4) p. 1.

Model 16C communicator, which contains 16 display areas with signal lights on which pictures or words can be placed. The elements are scanned in a specific sequence. By breaking the sequence, the user indicates the choice of message. A variety of control mechanisms can be used, and the speed at which the items are scanned can be modified.

The point and scan technique, as described by Harris and Vanderheiden (1980a) is useful for individuals who have limited pointing ability. After the user points to indicate a general area, the message receiver scans elements in that area until a specific element is selected. Although faster than the scanning technique, this approach may be confusing to the nonhandicapped individual trying to read the message. Harris and Vanderheiden noted that this technique allows the user to take a more active role in the communication process, as well as providing flexibility for the user, who can use direct selection "on good days."

Another strategy is **encoding**. A message is created using codes to represent elements of the message. For example, the sender might point to the number 3, which could stand for "I'm hungry." The code or pattern used may be memorized or referred to on a chart. An example is a device recently developed by Kelly and Smith (1982) in which the user enters Morse code (by means of a switch) into a microprocessor.

OUTPUT: PRINT

The Canon Communicator is a small battery-operated device that prints messages on a strip of paper. Keyboard covers (key guards) may be attached to it for use by persons operating the device with a headpointer or mouth stick.

OUTPUT: VOICE

Many aids now can be equipped with a voice output option. **Speech synthesizers,** which simulate the human voice, can produce words or sentences. Although voice quality and inflection are not always perfect, aids with voice output have greater advantages in simulating faster, more natural communication (Harris and Vanderheiden, 1980a).

Another voice output device is the Form-A-Phrase, available from Sci-Tronics,

This boy is touching the SAL board which can be individually tailored to his use by providing the pictures, words, or phrases that he needs most frequently. Communication Outlook, 1981, 23, 557.

Bethlehem, Pennsylvania. The device contains a vocabulary cartridge with 128 utterances that consist of one to five words. Custom cartridges are also available. The user may move a marker to the desired word or may enter a three-digit number to select words.

Eulenberg and Rahimi (1978) have described the Semantically Accessible Language (SAL) board, a computer-based talking-printing communication system they developed at the Artificial Language Laboratory at Michigan State University. Part of it is a communication board on which words, pictures, or phrases are placed. The items on the board can be changed to accommodate nonreaders. For example, for those individuals using **Blissymbolics,** a symbol system in which elements represent concepts, the SAL board becomes a talking Bliss board. The board is touch- or magnet-sensitive. The SAL board has voice output as well as a visual display, and user-created phrases can be stored.

A more sophisticated and flexible voice output device is the Phonic Mirror Handi-Voice, an electronic voice synthesizer available from Phonic Ear, Inc., in Mill Valley, California. It is portable, battery operated, and available in two models. One model has a preprogrammed keyboard and a visual display board consisting of 16 commonly used phrases, 373 words, 26 letters, 45 speech sounds, and 13 word prefixes and suffixes. In contrast to the rectangular board of the first model, the second model has a 16-button keyboard similar to a calculator. Three-digit codes are used to select phonemes, words (888), or phrases.

The Autocom (Auto-monitoring Communication Board) was developed by the staff of the Trace Center for the Severely Communicatively Handicapped at the University of Wisconsin—Madison. This device, now manufactured by Prentke Romich Company, is a portable, battery-charged microprocessor-based communication system. The board itself contains 128 locations (squares) for symbols, letters, words, phrases, or control of the Autocom. The vocabulary can be determined by the user, which gives the Autocom the flexibility to meet changing vocabulary needs. The Autocom has a built-in printer (32 characters) in addition to a 32-character lighted display (similar to displays found on some calculators). The board can be mounted on a wheelchair or connected to a computer. Although usually operated by a magnetic handpiece, other pointers can be used.

Harris-Vanderheiden (1977) described a field evaluation of Autocom use by seven students ranging in age from 7 to 19 years. Not only was progress in academic skills enhanced, but the teachers reported that the students took a more active role in class activities and social interaction.

Using a magnetic handpiece, this girl can select from 128 squares the symbols, words, or phrases that she needs with the use of the Autocom.
Courtesy, Telesensory Systems, Inc.

In addition to a communication aid, the Vocaid can be used as an instructional aid for young children with language and communication problems. Communication Outlook, 1982, 3 (3), p. 1.

A very recent advanced communication system available from Prentke Romich is the Express 3, which can be operated by direct selection, scanning, or encoding and has printer and display capabilities. The versatility of the Express 3 can be extended by using a speech output device or using it in combination with a page printer, television set, or computer.

In contrast to the very sophisticated Express 3, Texas Instruments now manufactures Vocaid, which is a voice output communication aid. The features of limited vocabulary and ease of use have led Eulenberg and Rosenfeld (1982) to suggest that the device would be most useful for persons with a short-term speech loss. Such a device could be used as an aid in therapy in addition to its primary use as a communication aid.

The Viewpoint Optical Indicator developed at the Trace Center enables persons with good head control to use certain communication devices. An incandescent lamp, mounted on a band, is used to point to items or control the communication aid.

The Jim Brooks Communication System is foot-operated. By using an 80-position pedal, Jim is able to access specific letters, words, or phrases stored in computer memory. Spoken output is obtained through the use of a voice synthesizer; output can also be printed. Finally, the device can be used to operate a standard computer terminal.

OBSTACLES TO USE

Often parents express some initial resistance to the use of nonvocal techniques or devices by their children. The belief that nonspeech techniques deter the development of oral communication is often given as a reason for this reluctance. Harris and Vanderheiden (1980b) say that clinical results indicate this is not the case. It appears that nonvocal communication techniques may enhance speech and oral expression by:

1. Increasing motivation to speak or communicate as a result of more successful communication experiences.
2. Reducing tension or pressures related to oral expression by providing a nonvocal communication mode to fall back on should the spoken message be unintelligible. (Harris and Vanderheiden, 1980b, p. 232)

Another obstacle to the use of many devices is availability. For the most part, we have restricted our discussion to devices that are commercially available. Many more aids are in the "development" stage, which could take years. At the major centers where research is being conducted, the engineers frequently have handicapped individuals on staff as consultants, developers, or field testers.

A third potential obstacle is financial. Justice and Vogel (1981) have discussed the procedures and regulations involved in looking for financial help to pay for a communication device.

Even if all these issues are resolved, there are still problems related to the establishment of effective communication through the use of devices. Vanderheiden (1978) thinks speed is the greatest barrier to widespread use. The effort expended by the listener as well as the nonvocal speaker is great and requires concentration. This probably influences the desire and/or motivation to communicate. The process of interaction is complex, so it is important to consider many factors as one sets up training programs or chooses systems to be used by the nonvocal speaker (Harris, 1982).

The selection of an appropriate augmentative communication system or device requires careful thought and consideration. Shane and Bashir (1980) have developed a decision matrix consisting of categories such as cognitive, emotional, age, motor capabilities, previous therapy, and environmental factors. Also, the type of input switches, strategy for selection (direct selection, scanning, encoding), symbols used, content/organization of the communication board, and output needed are issues to be addressed.

One final comment about communication devices. Harris (1982) suggested that these aids are sometimes incorrectly thought of as panaceas. A communication device does not immediately guarantee effective communication skills. Children and adults are likely to need training to help them develop interaction skills and to use the device effectively to augment their skills. Future technological advances will probably yield faster, more efficient devices. Along with this, more research needs to be conducted in order to determine which aids are effective with specific individuals so that the gift of speech can be extended to many more speechless individuals.

ANSWERS TO FREQUENTLY ASKED QUESTIONS
SPEECH AND LANGUAGE DISORDERS

1. There may be a number of different reasons why Josh does not talk. He might have a hearing loss, which would greatly affect his language development. If his hearing has not been tested, it should be. Many school districts have agencies or teams that evaluate preschoolers. While Josh's lack of spoken language is of primary concern, it will be important to assess other areas of development (since he walked late as well). Then appropriate instructional goals can be developed to stimulate Josh's language development.

2. Don't worry. Many kindergarten children make those substitutions. Sometimes it is not until the child is 6 or 7 years old that those sounds are produced accurately. Since you're concerned, talk with a school speech teacher. That person will be able to tell you more specifically what is "normal" or average for 4-year-old boys. Also, you might want to visit your son's class. Listen to the other children's speech. You might be surprised to find out that many other children have difficulty pronouncing certain words or sounds. Finally, if your son continues to misarticulate these sounds in late first or second grade, talk to your school speech teacher about a possible referral for testing.

3. It is hard to determine what specific problems the man has without more information. Sometimes after a stroke or brain injury, the ability to express oneself is impaired. In other cases, the ability to understand language is affected. Your neighbor is probably receiving speech and language therapy. The prognosis or amount of expected improvement depends on the type and extent of damage caused by the stroke.

4. You're right that stuttering is not as common for adults as it is for children. Mr. Brown probably does not stutter throughout the entire school day, but only in certain situations. His qualifications as a teacher are not changed because of his slow speech. It seems that if Susan thinks very highly of Mr. Brown, he is probably a very positive teacher who sets a good example for the students. This man, in spite of his speech problem, is capable of teaching Susan's class. As for the possibility of your daughter's imitating his speech, it is highly unlikely.

5. One thing your sister and Laura's speech teacher could try, if they haven't already, is a communication board. Because Laura is so young, you might place pictures on a board or lap tray that Laura could point to, such as "food," "drink," and "toilet." In this way, if Laura has enough arm control to point to pictures, she might be able to create sentences or carry on conversations. If Laura has adequate arm and finger/hand control, a gesture system such as sign language is also a possibility. Sometimes parents are hesitant to try communication boards or gestures. They are concerned that the use of such systems will inhibit the development of speech. Actually, in Laura's case, the use of a communication board might relieve the stress and frustration of not being understood by others and would probably further her overall language development. Your sister might ask Laura's speech therapist about the possibility of other communication devices or systems as well.

6. Don't be so sure he has a problem. The age at which children say their first words varies greatly. Some children begin to speak a few words at ages 8 to 10 months. Others might not talk until 24 months. The fact that Tim understands what is said to him is one reason not to be too concerned at this time. It's possible that he is a "late bloomer" with regard to his speech. If he is not saying many more words at 24 months, his parents should have him evaluated to see if he has a hearing loss or any other problem that might be affecting his speech. Tim's pediatrician should be able to refer them to the proper specialists for this testing.

7. One thing that you could do is try to note situations in which Jimmy's speech is more fluent, as well as situations in which he has more difficulty speaking. Call on him or otherwise arrange for him to talk in those situations when he speaks well and seems to be under less stress. It might also be helpful to explain to the class about his stuttering in a way that might increase their sensitivity to his feelings. Providing opportunities for him to be successful and helping him to gain better status with the other kids will go a long way in helping him over the problems associated with his poor speech.

8. First, you should refer Theresa to the speech and language therapist. Voice disorders are often the result of infections or growths on the larynx, and need to be treated. If this is the case, the speech and language therapist will refer her to a physician for the needed medical diagnosis and treatment. Often the recommended course of action is voice rest, training in correct vocal behaviors, medication, or surgery. She may need to modify her cheerleading activities until her voice returns to a more normal quality.

9. For some children, exposure to two languages does not present a problem. If you begin to notice some confusion or delay in the use of words, it might be a good idea to provide stimulation for vocabulary development in one language. It is a question of how well your son begins to pick up and use words. The use of two languages in the home does not automatically lead to language delay. Just continue to monitor his vocabulary development closely.

SUMMARY

Speech and language disorders today can present far less of an obstacle then they once did because of new educational methods and technology. The major problem, in fact, remains the attitudes of the nonhandicapped: We continue to listen to the speech defect rather than the message.

Defining speech and language disorders means distinguishing among three terms: communication, speech, and language. Communication includes any process or means of sharing or exchanging information. Language is the code or system with which we communicate thoughts. Speech is the vocal or oral production of language. Speech and language disorders are disorders that interfere with communication and cause negative feelings in the speaker or listener. Language disorders are handicapping deviances in the communication code or system; speech disorders are problems in the intelligible production of language.

Language disorders can be of four major types: absence of language, delayed language, interrupted language, and disorders in quality. Speech disorders are also of four main types: absence of speech, problems in articulation, disorders in voice quality, and fluency disorders.

Because the kinds of disorders vary so widely, it is extremely difficult to arrive at prevalence figures. The problem is compounded because many speech impairments coexist with (or may be caused by) other handicaps by which children or adults are already counted. Unlike other disorders, these impairments do not increase with age; some, in fact, show a definite decrease by adolescence and young adulthood.

Assessment approaches vary according to the disorder and the individual. The processes involved in language and speech are so complex that no two children have exactly the same problems. And there is still much we do not know about how or why children learn language.

Two major assessment approaches used in the area of language disorders are tests and scales, and clinical judgment. A full evaluation of language ability includes testing of imitation, comprehension, and production skills. Speech problems are also assessed with a variety of techniques. When there is no speech, the factors that cause or accompany the problem must be identified. Articulation disorders are usually discovered in routine school screenings, as are voice quality disorders. Most adults who have voice disorders are self-referred or referred by physicians. Fluency disorders do not lend themselves to standardized measures, and sometimes the person's perception of the difficulty is more important than the impairment itself.

Assessing speech and language disorders is difficult; identifying the causes is often impossible. The best that can be done usually is to identify problems that often coexist with certain language disorders and suggest a causal relationship, such as that between no language and deafness at birth, or that between speech disorders and facial abnormalities.

Since many children with language and speech handicaps have additional handicaps such as mental retardation, serious emotional disturbance, physical incapacities, and learning disabilities, as a group they tend to score lower than normal children on measures of intelligence, achievement, and adaptive social behavior. Children without accompanying handicaps show few common psychological and behavioral characteristics except the discrimination they suffer because of the tremendous value we place on speech ability and the penalties we impose for slow or imperfect speech.

Educational methods for very young children with speech and language problems begin with parental instruction. Most elementary and secondary schoolchildren are educated in regular classrooms, and the methods used to correct the disorders differ not by age, but by type of disorder. Because the parts of the brain that control language are inaccessible, most treatment focuses on the training and modification of speech.

Intervention efforts with language center on two major approaches: naturalistic or discovery intervention, and behavioral intervention, especially operant conditioning. Naturalistic procedures such as parallel talk and self talk can be used by parents in the home to help the child begin to discover how words and phrases are used to communicate. Operant conditioning is the technique of choice for children who have major disorders and multiple handicaps.

Speech disorders are also approached with many different methods. Those who have language but cannot physically produce speech must be taught other ways to communicate. Articulation disorders are worked on in sequence by means of slow and often laborious therapy. Voice disorders are also treated with therapy and with techniques to change abusive vocal habits that may be contributing to the problem. Often, the proper intervention is medical.

Fluency disorders, once considered "psychosomatic" and approached only through psychotherapy, are now also attacked by techniques that reinforce and seek to build on whatever fluent speech the person has, or to teach the person strategies to cope with the problem.

The revolution in technology has been of particular benefit to the speech and language impaired: Augmentative communication devices and new access devices have made it possible for almost anyone, no matter how handicapped, to communicate. Electrical aids for those who are nonvocal cover a wide range in function and complexity. They may be activated by three major techniques: direct selection, scanning, and encoding. The devices may produce output in print or in voice form. Speech synthesizers, which simulate the human voice, can produce words or sentences. Communication boards and computers can be adapted for readers and nonreaders, and can produce lighted displays as well as printouts.

These devices are not solutions to problems, but by increasing the person's motivation to communicate and to use whatever skills he or she has, they can enhance abilities and provide successful communication experiences.

REFERENCES

ASHA, Position statement on nonspeech communication. *American Speech and Hearing Association*, 1981, *23*, 577–581.

BANGS, T.E. *Language and learning disorders of the preacademic child with curriculum guide.* 2d ed. Englewood Cliffs, N.J.: Prentice-Hall, 1982.

BOONE, D.R. Voice disorders. In T.J. Hixon, L.D. Shriberg, & J.H. Saxman (Eds.). *Introduction to communication disorders.* Englewood Cliffs, N.J.: Prentice-Hall, 1980.

DEVANY, J.M., Rincover, A., & Lovaas, O.I. Teaching speech to nonverbal children. In J.M. Kauffman & D.P. Hallahan (Eds.). *Handbook of special education.* Englewood Cliffs, N.J.: Prentice-Hall, 1981.

DUNN, L. *Peabody picture vocabulary test.* Circle Pines, Minn.: American Guidance Service, 1965.

ERICKSON, R. Assessing communication attitudes among stutterers. *Journal of Speech and Hearing Research*, 1969, *12*, 711–724.

EULENBERG, J.B., & RAHIMI, M.A. Toward a semantically accessible communication aid. *Proceedings of the National Electronics Conference*, 1978, *32*, 278–283.

EULENBERG, J.B., & ROSENFELD, J. Vocaid—A new product from Texas Instruments. *Communication Outlook*, 1982, *3*, 1, 3.

HALLAHAN D.P. & BRYAN, T.H. Learning disabilities. In J.M. Kauffman & D.P. Hallahan (Eds.). *Handbook of special education.* Englewood Cliffs, N.J.: Prentice-Hall, 1981.

HARRIS, D. Communicative interaction processes involving nonvocal physically handicapped children. *Topics in Language Disorders*, 1982, *2*, 21–37.

HARRIS, D., & VANDERHEIDEN, G.C. Augmentative communication techniques. In R.L. Schiefelbusch (Ed.). *Nonspeech language and communication.* Baltimore: University Park Press, 1980. (a)

HARRIS, D., & VANDERHEIDEN, G.C. Enhancing the development of communicative interaction. In R.L. Schiefelbusch (Ed.). *Nonspeech language and communication.* Baltimore: University Park Press, 1980. (b)

HARRIS-VANDERHEIDEN, D. Field evaluation of the Auto-Com. In G.C. Vanderheiden & K. Grilley (Eds.). *Non-vocal communication techniques and aids for the severely physically handicapped.* Baltimore: University Park Press, 1977.

JUSTICE, R.L., & VOGEL, T. Speech prosthesis as a legal entitlement. *Communication Outlook*, *1981, 3*, 8–9.

KELLY, G.W., & SMITH, J.L. A programmable communicator for the speech impaired person. *Proceedings of the IEEE Computer Society Workshop on Computing to Aid the Handicapped.* Silver Spring, Md.: IEEE Computer Society Press, 1982.

KIRK, S., McCARTHY, J., & KIRK, W. *The Illinois test of psycholinguistic abilities* (rev. ed.). Urbana: University of Illinois Press, 1968.

LEE, L.L. Linguistic approaches to developmental language disorders. *Folia Phoniatrica*, *1974, 26*, 33–67.

LEE, L.L. *The Northwestern syntax screening test.* Evanston, Ill.: Northwestern University Press, 1971.

LOVAAS, O.I. *The autistic child: Language development through behavior modification.* New York: Wiley, 1977.

MOWRER, D. Social consequences of lisping in the speech of adult males. Paper presented to the Annual Convention of the American Speech and Hearing Association, Las Vegas, 1974.

NAREMORE, R.C. Language disorders in children. In T.J. Hixon, L.D. Shriberg, & J.H. Saxman (Eds.). *Introduction to communication disorders.* Englewood Cliffs, N.J.: Prentice-Hall, 1980.

PERKINS, W.H. Disorders of speech flow. In T.J. Hixon, L.D. Shriberg, & J.H. Saxman (Eds.). *Introduction to communication disorders.* Englewood Cliffs, N.J.: Prentice-Hall, 1980.

PERKINS, W., Rudas, J., Johnson, L., Michael, W., & Curlee, R. Replacement of stuttering with normal speech: III. Clinical effectiveness. *Journal of Speech and Hearing Research*, *1974, 39*, 416–428.

SCHIEFELBUSCH, R.L., & McCormick, L.P. Language and speech disorders. In J.M. Kauffman & D.P. Hallahan (Eds.). *Handbook of special education.* Englewood Cliffs, N.J.: Prentice-Hall, 1981.

SHANE, H.C., & Bashir, A.S. Election criteria for the adoption of an augmentative communication system: Preliminary considerations. *Journal of Speech and Hearing Disorders*, 1980, *45*, 408–414.

SHRIBERG, L.D. Developmental phonological disorders. In T.J. Hixon, L.D. Shriberg, & J. H. Saxman (Eds.). *Introduction to communication disorders.* Englewood Cliffs, N.J.: Prentice-Hall, 1980.

SILVERMAN, E. Listeners' impressions of speakers with lateral lips. *Journal of Speech and Hearing Disorders*, 1976, *41*, 547–552.

SILVERMAN, F. *Communication for the speechless.* Englewood Cliffs, N.J.: Prentice-Hall, 1980.

TARVER, S.G., & Ellsworth, P.S. Written and oral language for verbal children. In J.M. Kauffman, & D.P. Hallahan (Eds.). *Handbook of special education.* Englewood Cliffs, N.J.: Prentice-Hall, 1981.

VANDERHEIDEN, G. Technically speaking. *Communication Outlook*, 1978, *1*, 9.

Van Riper, C. *Speech correction: Principles and methods* (6th ed.). Englewood Cliffs, N.J.: Prentice-Hall, 1978.

Webster, R. A behavioral analysis of stuttering: Treatment and theory. In K. Calhoun, H. Adams, & K. Mitchell (Eds.). *Innovative treatment methods in psychopathology*, New York: Wiley, 1974.

Wells, C.G. *Cleft palate and its associated speech disorders*. New York: McGraw-Hill, 1971.

HEARING IMPAIRMENT

6

1. I am a third-grade teacher who has an 8-year-old hearing impaired child in my classroom. Patty seems to have great difficulty interacting with the other children. At first she had several friends, but now the others seem to exclude her from games and other activities. At recess, she sometimes plays with younger children. What can I do to help Patty develop friendships with children her own age? Should I just leave things alone and not interfere?

2. The doctor has just discovered that Ricky, my 4-year-old nephew, has a hearing loss, and he has just recently begun to wear a hearing aid. Ricky has always seemed in a world all his own and has never warmed up to anybody much except his parents. I understand now why he has been this way in the past and why he has not learned to talk like other kids his age. What I don't understand now is that since he has a hearing aid and can hear like everybody else, how come he still doesn't talk or play with others like his cousins do?

3. Soon John, a child from the class of hearing-impaired children in our school, will be mainstreamed into my classroom for several periods a day. John's teacher gave me some ideas as to possible modifications for him, but I'm concerned that I won't have enough time to implement them. Also, will I be responsible for checking his hearing aids?

4. Steven is an outgoing, personable fifth-grader in my classroom. In spite of his moderate to severe hearing loss, he is performing at an average or above-average level in all academic areas. He seems to have great self-confidence and does not hesitate to ask questions to clarify ideas or directions he does not understand. Except for the nasal tone in his speech, he really acts like his hearing friends in most ways. I thought children with hearing losses were always behind others in terms of language development and academic performance. Is there a problem with Steven that I may be overlooking?

5. The house next door has just been sold to a couple who must be deaf, because I've seen them use sign language when talking to each other and I think the woman wears a hearing aid. I want to be friendly, but I don't know how to communicate with them. What should I do?

6. Sandra is a child with a hearing loss in my class. She is able to keep pace with the class on math skills, but she has some problems with reading and social studies. Sandra attends speech and language therapy. I have tried to limit the amount of work she is required to complete, but she is still having problems. Should I refer her for more intensive special services?

Educational methods and experiences for today's hearing-impaired child differ in many ways from those of the past. As you will see as you read this chapter, improvements in technology and new information about teaching methods are some of the reasons for the many changes. One recent development allows a person with a severe hearing loss to use the telephone with the help of a teletypewriter connected to the phone by a special adapter. With this device, a deaf person can communicate with another person who has the special hookup. The phone conversation is typed out on one teletypewriter and transmitted across the telephone wire to a display screen connected to the other person's telephone.

Let's look in on a hypothetical telephone conversation between 20-year-old Mark and his 50-year-old father, both of whom are deaf. Mark is attending a special hearing-impaired program at a nearby college. In spite of the fact that Mark and his father have similar hearing disabilities, you get an idea of how their educational and social opportunities have been quite different. As you read this chapter, you will see what changes have occurred in the education of the hearing impaired and what further improvements seem likely for the future.

Mark: Hi, Dad. Sorry to call you so late. But I had to wait in line behind two other students to use the TTY. Seems like everyone wants to call home on Monday right before the football game. Are the Lions still ahead?

Father: No. Green Bay just scored on a punt return. Don't know who scored. Couldn't see the number. It's too bad live sports can't be captioned like programs that are prerecorded. How are your other classes?

Mark: Data processing is hardest. Instructor moves around too much while talking. Makes it difficult to understand what he is saying. For that class, I have an interpreter. She's good.

Father: Didn't you tell me you also had a person taking notes for you in that class?

Mark: Yes. I have both an interpreter and a notetaker. Can't decide which is more valuable. The course would be super hard without either one.

Father: How are other classes?

Mark: OK. Instructors are all good about writing down assignments and stuff to make sure I understand. Math is hardest. But I'm doing fine.

Father: Good. Try your hardest. But, if you do get behind, remember I said I'd be willing to pay for some extra tutoring.

Mark: Thanks Dad. But don't think I'll need it. The special program for the deaf here really provides a lot of stuff for you. If I can't make it with what they've got here, I'll never make it.

Father: I keep forgetting about all the special services. Still, if you need some tutoring, let me know. You know your mother is concerned.

Mark: She worries too much about me.

Father: I know. I know I've told you this before, but you have to remember that she and I have a hard time getting used to your being out there mixing with the hearing world.

Mark: I know. Keep forgetting that the only college program available for you and Mom was Gallaudet College way over on the east coast.

Father: Distance was only half the problem. Think I've mentioned this to you before, but the biggest problem was that I'd only been around other deaf kids all my life. Residential schools I attended gave no chance for me to mix with any of the hearing world. Your school experiences have been much different. Your residential school had a cooperative program with the public schools.

Mark: I think you're right. Couple of the guys who are having the hardest time adjusting here came from Bacon Hollow School for the Deaf. Their program was strictly residential. Nothing wrong with that except if you plan to mix with hearing society. College is really making me appreciate the mainstreaming I've already had. How's Mom?

Father: OK. Of course, she's a mother so she's worried that you'll starve to death or never wear clean clothes! She sends her love.

Mark: I need to go study. It's been good talking to you. Speaking of starving to death, Dad, I sure could use a little extra money.

TODAY'S DEFINITION OF HEARING IMPAIRMENT

There are many ways of defining and classifying hearing impairment. Hearing impairment is usually divided into two categories, the **deaf** and the **hard of hearing**. These two categories are defined differently by different professionals.

PHYSIOLOGICAL DEFINITIONS

Professionals who focus primarily on the physiological aspects of a handicap or on measurement prefer definitions that describe the severity of the hearing loss. Children who have the greatest hearing loss are classified as deaf, while children with a lesser hearing loss are considered hard of hearing.

EDUCATIONAL DEFINITIONS

Educators, on the other hand, may be most concerned with how the hearing impaired can be taught communication and other skills. They often make the distinction between the two categories by saying that the deaf child's development of speech and language is *visually based*, while the hard of hearing child develops basic communication skills through the *auditory channel*, generally with the use of a hearing aid (Ross, 1982). The deaf child is often instructed in sign language and fingerspelling, while the hard of hearing child is more likely taught lipreading and speech.

SEVERITY OF LOSS

The amount of hearing loss is measured by a unit of intensity or loudness of sound called a Bel (after Alexander Graham Bell). In order to make the scale more precise, Bels are further divided into 10 smaller parts known as **decibels** or **dBs**. Each decibel represents the smallest difference of loudness you can perceive in speech. The faintest sound a person with normal hearing can detect registers at zero decibels (0 dB). A whisper would be at about 30 dB, normal conversation at 60 dB, a loud shout at 90 dB, and the range in which sound begins to be uncomfortable and even painful at 120–130 dB. If Susan cannot hear a sound at the loudness of 90 dB or greater, she is said to have a profound hearing loss and is classified as deaf. Persons with a lesser hearing loss, such as Michael, who can detect sounds in the range of 60–70 dB, are considered to have a moderate hearing loss and are classified as hard of hearing.

AGE AT WHICH LOSS OCCURRED

Severity of loss is an important factor in diagnosis and educational approaches for the hearing impaired, but another factor is of almost equal importance: age at onset. Language development depends on hearing, so common terms used to describe the handicap in relation to age have to do with the relationship of language and speech acquisition. **Prelingual deafness** refers to deafness that is present at birth or occurs soon afterward— before the development of spoken language to any substantial degree. **Postlingual deafness** means the hearing loss occurred after the person had acquired language and learned to speak. As we will see in the section on characteristics, the time at which a hearing loss occurs has a tremendous influence on a number of characteristics.

Degree of loss and age of onset are two major factors that further define and delineate the categories of deaf and hard of hearing. Teachers should keep these factors in mind as they set out to understand the characteristics and determine educational approaches for a hearing-impaired student. For example, both Sharon, who has been hearing impaired since the age of 6 months, and Melanie, who suffered a hearing loss at age 4, can be taught to lipread and to speak. However, largely due to the difference in their ages at the time the loss occurred, there is a distinct difference in the sound of their speech. It is more difficult for Sharon to make her speech clear and comprehensible, since she had a shorter period in which to hear her own voice and the voices of those around her. Even if their hearing losses were identical in severity, age of onset would make a significant difference in their respective abilities.

PREVALENCE

Because of difficulties in identifying and testing persons who may have hearing losses, it is difficult to determine how many hearing-impaired individuals there are. As we noted in Chapter 1, a 1981 report estimates that 0.3 to 0.5 percent of school-aged children are hard of hearing and 0.075 to 0.19 percent are considered deaf. Unlike most handicaps (except a few, such as blindness), the prevalence of deafness increases with age. Some estimate that at least 14 million Americans suffer from a measurable hearing loss. This is three times the number of blind individuals in this country (Benderley, 1980). And yet most hearing people are not as aware of the handicap of a hearing impairment as they are of visual impairment because a hearing impairment is "invisible."

ASSESSMENT OF HEARING

The person who measures a child's or an adult's hearing ability is usually an **audiologist,** who is a professional trained in the detection and correction of hearing impairments. The audiologist can give a wide range of hearing tests. Which tests are selected can depend on such things as the purpose of the testing (screening or diagnosis), the suspected nature or degree of the hearing loss, and the age or general ability of the person to be tested.

SCREENING

The first step in an assessment procedure is often initial identification of a problem through some sort of screening test, administered either individually or in a group. Although children with severe hearing losses are more likely to be identified in the first years of life, youngsters with a less severe handicap may not be identified until they undergo a routine school screening. The most common screening instrument is the **sweep test,** which uses a portable audiometer to present tones at about 20 to 25 dB. An **audiometer** is a machine that produces tones of known pitch and loudness. If the child has a problem hearing these tones, he or she is referred for more extensive evaluation.

DIAGNOSTIC AUDIOMETRY

The next step in evaluating more precisely the extent and nature of the hearing loss can follow one of two general directions—pure-tone audiometry and speech audiometry. **Pure-tone audiometry** attempts to determine an individual's exact threshold for hearing pitch and loudness of various sounds. **Speech audiometry** is designed to test a person's detection and understanding of speech.

PURE-TONE AUDIOMETRY. Pure-tone testing is done with tones of various intensities (loudness) and frequencies (pitch). As we noted before, loudness is measured in decibel (dB) units. Frequencies are measured in units known as **Hertz (Hz).** These frequencies are known to us as **pitch.** The higher the frequency, the higher the pitch; the lower the frequency, the lower the pitch. Hertz are usually measured in the most relevant frequencies for speech—from 500 to 2000 Hz. Detection of tones within this range is the most important. The results of pure-tone audiometry can tell you at what precise levels of frequency and loudness an individual can detect sound.

SPEECH AUDIOMETRY. In contrast to pure-tone testing, speech audiometry measures the lowest level of decibels at which a person can detect speech and the level at which he or she can understand speech. Instead of using tones of various frequencies and intensities, spoken words are used at different levels of pitch and loudness.

There is a common problem in assessment which is especially acute in the assessment of hearing impairment: How do you test young or mentally or physically handicapped children so that their young age or handicaps do not interfere with the assessment of their hearing? Early detection and intervention are critical for language and intellectual development. It is extremely important that infants and children of any age who lack coherent speech be tested for suspected hearing losses.

TESTS FOR INFANTS AND MULTIPLY HANDICAPPED CHILDREN. The responses of infants and many handicapped children are too limited for the usual requirement in the testing of hearing, to speak or signal in some way when you hear a sound. Testing for these persons frequently makes use of reflexive behaviors as an indication that the child is hearing. Audiologists look for a number of **orienting responses,** which include eye movements directed toward the sound, head turning toward the sound, and an overall quieting of all body parts when a sound occurs. In the first few weeks of life, the baby responds to loud sounds with a whole-body startle known as the **Moro reflex.** One problem when using any of these reflexive behaviors as measures is that the child will not continue the behaviors indefinitely. In other words, 8-month-old Stephanie may show an orienting response to the sound of a ringing bell the first few times she hears it, but if it is repeated for too long she will lose interest and stop turning toward it, even though she continues to hear it. One way of increasing the number of times Stephanie will orient to the sound (and thus allow the audiologist to pinpoint her hearing ability) is to use visual reinforcers, such as animated animal figures that light up each time a sound is emitted.

Hearing assessment of infants and those unable to make voluntary responses can also be done by using physiological measures that detect changes in skin resistance and brain wave activity. These methods are more difficult to administer and interpret, but they can be very helpful in determining hearing disabilities in some cases.

TESTS FOR YOUNG CHILDREN. For children who are at least 3 years old and have receptive language skills, **play audiometry** can be used. This technique makes the testing more gamelike, with instructions to the child to do a certain activity, such

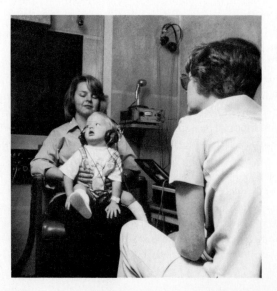

The assessment of a young child's hearing loss and abilities is an important, although difficult procedure. D. Grogan, U.Va./CRC.

as bounce a ball, when he or she hears a sound. In addition to tests for assessment of pure hearing ability, some tests designed for hearing-impaired youngsters measure various elements of communication. Most tests used in the evaluation of communicative and cognitive skills are not designed specifically for the hearing impaired, but they can be adapted for that use. An example of one of the few that are explicitly for hearing-impaired children is the SKI-HI Receptive Language Test, which measures language comprehension in the 2- to 4-year-old hard of hearing child (Longhurst, Briery, and Emery, 1975).

PARTS OF THE EAR

Figure 6–1 shows the major physical structures of the ear, and the Focus explains how the ear works when sound reaches it. The ear has three major parts: the outer, the middle, and the inner ear.

THE OUTER EAR

The outer ear, which is the most obvious and least important part, really does very little. Although the outer ear in other mammals serves useful purposes in pivoting and locating sound, the human outer ear acts only as a funnel through which sound passes. Other than that, it is most useful as a place to keep eyeglasses or sunglasses in place. The fleshy part of the ear, which supports eyeglasses and earrings, is called the **auricle.**

THE MIDDLE EAR

Sound enters the auricle and passes through the **ear canal** to the **eardrum** in the middle ear. The passageway of the ear canal contains protective hairs and a substance we call earwax, which helps to keep unwanted objects such as insects or dust particles from

---

FOCUS

HOW THE EAR WORKS

Figure 6–1 shows the major physical structures of the ear. Here is what happens when sound reaches it:

1. Sound enters the outer ear.
2. Sound strikes the eardrum, causing it to vibrate.
3. Vibrations are carried in the middle ear along a chain of bones (hammer, anvil, and stirrup) to the oval window of the inner ear.
4. Vibrations hit the oval window, causing movements in the fluid of the two major points of the inner ear—the vestibular membrane and the cochlea.
5. Fluid movements in the cochlea rearrange tiny hair cells, which signal electrical impulses to the brain.
6. Impulses are received and deciphered in the brain as sound.

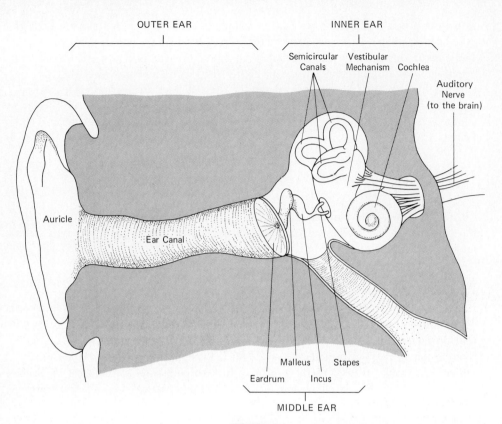

OUTER EAR

INNER EAR

Semicircular Canals

Vestibular Mechanism

Cochlea

Auditory Nerve (to the brain)

Auricle

Ear Canal

Malleus

Stapes

Eardrum

Incus

MIDDLE EAR

FIGURE 6.1

entering the middle ear. In addition to the eardrum, which is a membrane stretched across the opening of the ear canal, the middle ear consists of three tiny bones shaped like familiar objects called the **malleus** (hammer), **incus** (anvil), and **stapes** (stirrup). These three bones fit into one another in such a way that vibrations are carried along them.

THE INNER EAR

The third bone, the stirrup, attaches to the **oval window,** which marks the beginning of the more complex mechanism known as the inner ear. In contrast to the outer and middle ear, the inner ear is filled with fluid. Sound vibrations that started as movements in air hit against the inner ear and cause movements in the fluid. The inner ear has two main components, the **vestibular mechanism,** which registers changes in balance and body movements, and the **cochlea,** which receives the vibrations and converts these movements into electrical impulses that are sent to the brain. At this point, the brain takes over the primary function of the interpreting and sorting a myriad of sounds and giving them meaning.

CAUSES

The best way to classify the causes of hearing loss is according to the location of the problem—outer ear, middle ear, inner ear.

CAUSES IN THE OUTER EAR

Impairment in the outer ear can cause **conductive losses,** losses due to a problem in sound moving along the conductive pathway. Sound can be blocked in the external auditory canal of the outer ear by such things as malformation of the canal itself, excessive accumulation of earwax, presence of some undetected object in the ear, and the growth of tumors in the passageway.

CAUSES IN THE MIDDLE EAR

Impairment in the middle ear also results in conductive losses and is usually more serious than losses due to external ear problems. However, middle ear problems are generally not as serious as inner ear problems and are much more likely to be correctable with medical or surgical treatment. The most common cause of conductive hearing loss in the middle ear is **otitis media,** an infection of the middle ear involving the Eustachian tube. The position and size of children's **Eustachian tubes**—canals connecting the middle ear and the throat—make children more vulnerable than adults to middle ear infections. As a teacher, you should be aware that a child with constant ear infections should be watched carefully for any signs of hearing loss (see Focus).

FOCUS

SYMPTOMS THE CLASSROOM TEACHER SHOULD WATCH FOR

The teacher should consider further hearing assessment on a child in the classroom who *often*:

1. Does not follow directions accurately.
2. Does not interact with other children.
3. Does not attend to noises outside the room or in other parts of the room (traffic sounds, hall commotion, loud laughter).
4. Does not seem to listen unless you are facing him or her at a close distance.
5. Seems to be daydreaming.
6. Complains of earaches or is absent frequently due to colds and/or ear infections.
7. Makes incorrect speech sounds, such as omitting final consonant sounds.
8. Bends his or her head or leans toward the person who is speaking in a strained, unnatural position.

CAUSES IN THE INNER EAR

Children who have hearing impairments in the inner ear are said to have **sensorineural impairments.** Impairments in the inner ear are the most serious handicaps in two ways: (1) They frequently result in profound levels of hearing loss; (2) they are the most difficult to correct or improve with medical or educational treatment. Inner ear impairments result from damage to the cochlea or the auditory nerve. This damage is most often caused by viral infections (such as mumps and measles), bacterial infections (such as meningitis), prenatal infections of the mother (such as rubella), complications at birth such as lack of oxygen (anoxia), and unwanted side effects of certain antibiotics. Hereditary factors account for 25 to 50 percent of all childhood deafness (Hoemann and Briga, 1981; Moores, 1978). In some cases, a hearing deficit is only one of several handicaps in a genetic syndrome. Down's syndrome is an example of a genetic condition that may result in a hearing loss along with mental retardation, poor motor development, and other problems.

In addition to these causes of hearing loss in children, there are a number of inner ear problems that usually occur in cases of adult deafness. These are frequently caused by excessive exposure to noise, blows to the head, and deterioration caused by aging (see Focus).

FOCUS

BEWARE THE WALK ON THE LOUD SIDE

It's a real blowout—a walk on the loud side. But addicts of rock who use the headphones of a portable player like the Sony Walkman may pay a serious price for their constant musical fix: ear trouble.

The first warnings came from Japan, where 4 million people wear the stereo gadgets. Dr. Satoshi Koizumi of Hokushin General Hospital surveyed hearing acuity among 4,500 high-school students. Of 29 who had unexplained hearing problems, 21 turned out to be earphone addicts and played their cassettes one to four hours a day at an average of nearly 90 decibels (equivalent to a passing subway train). Dr. Kunishige Kambe, another ear specialist, subsequently described six youngsters with hearing loss who listened on headphones for up to five hours a day. Both doctors admit that their evidence is circumstantial, and Kambe notes that the hearing deficits among the students he saw disappeared when they reduced their listening.

Similar studies haven't been done in the United States. But Dr. Aram Glorig of the House Ear Institute in Los Angeles believes the portable stereos could cause problems if played at more than 80 decibels for long periods. Any permanent hearing loss would probably involve only the very-high-frequency range. Like the mad-dog riffing of Ted Nugent, fans.

Newsweek, September 13, 1982, p. 56. Reprinted by permission from Newsweek, Inc. Photograph by Ken Karp.

MIXED LOSS

Causes of hearing impairment can be attributed to conductive problems, sensorineural problems, or a mixture of both. Mixed hearing losses involve impairments along the conductive pathways as well as in the inner ear, and are particularly difficult to treat.

The popular habit of listening to loud music through earphones for an extended time can lead to hearing problems. Ken Karp.

CHARACTERISTICS

A hearing loss can have a great effect on some psychological and behavioral characteristics of a person and very little effect on other characteristics. Most people, when faced with the question, "If you had to be blind or deaf, which would you choose?" would choose deafness because we easily imagine how many things we rely on our sight for. We can blindfold ourselves to understand quickly how dependent we are on sight to get around and understand the world. It is much more difficult to imagine what it would be like to function without hearing. However, deafness is a greater handicap than blindness in our particular culture. Helen Keller, who had the burden of both handicaps, made this comparison:

> I am just as deaf as I am blind. The problems of deafness are deeper and more complex, if not more important than those of blindness. Deafness is a much worse misfortune. For it means the loss of the most vital stimulus—the sound of the voice that brings language, sets thoughts astir, and keeps us in the intellectual company of men. (Keller, 1933)

A hearing impairment, especially one that is severe and is present at birth, can have an impact in areas far beyond the primary handicap of the hearing disability. As Boothroyd (1982) points out, what begins as a sensory problem has consequences that can create:

1. A perceptual problem
2. A speech problem
3. A communication problem

4. A cognitive problem
5. A social problem
6. An emotional problem
7. An educational problem
8. An intellectual problem
9. A vocational problem

These problems are often compounded by:

10. Parental problems
11. Societal problems

FOCUS

HOW DOES IT FEEL TO BE DEAF?

No normally hearing person, of course, can ever experience the whole reality of deafness. To suggest otherwise is to insult daily, silent fortitude. A normally hearing person cannot ever know the awesome psychic permanence of deafness, but he can understand hearing loss on a superficial level, as a manner of physical being. All it takes is a few hours and a pair of hearing aids set to produce white noise (a general, featureless background). It's almost impossible to simulate profound deafness in a person with good hearing; the human audition is so maddeningly acute that enough noise to block out everything we hear would be positively harmful. But enough noise to muffle normal speech and drown out most ambient noise presents no real danger.

So, with two noisy hearing aids in place, we could set out on our way. We might walk, for example, down a familiar street. It looks the same, but in some way it yields less of itself. We are, in a sense, more alone, more closely inside ourself and cut off from our surroundings, although we watch closely and devour every visual detail with our eyes. There is no sound to tell us anything, not even that of our own steps or the rustle of our own clothing. No car noises. No birds. No airplanes overhead. No shaking leaves or barking dogs or human voices to populate the world around us with living things. A pair of pedestrians, deep in conversation, overtake and pass us. This is startling; we had no idea they were approaching, and we react clumsily. Not knowing their direction or speed, we can't tell which way to step to let them by. We grasp nothing of what they say. It's like being in a foreign country, but not really. There we would at least have heard them approach. . . .

Four friends are waiting for a lunch date at a restaurant. When we arrive at the table they're already deep in conversation. They nod and smile and someone tells us the topic. We don't catch it, but they plunge on ahead. The person on our right isn't talking at the moment, so we remark casually on the weather. The general conversation stops and everyone turns suddenly to us. Shouting again. Someone makes a joke—at least we surmise that from the fact that they all laugh—and the conversation starts up again. The person to our right asks, we think, whether it was hard to get here. We give an answer appropriate to the question we understood. It must not be quite right, because doubt flickers for a second in her eyes and she says something more slowly. We get even less of that, but nod and turn to take a roll. The conversation continues around us. If we could discover the topic, we decide, it would be easier to speechread some of what's being said. We watch intently, futilely, for almost an hour. Without a solid clue to what they're talking about, we could be, indeed we become, a piece of the scenery. Speaking directly to the person on either side, and watching and listening intently, we exchange some very simple ideas— the sandwich is good, the coffee is cold. But at last comes psychic withdrawal from the general conversation, the giving up of the pretense of following.

From *Dancing Without Music* by Beryl Lieff Benderly. Garden City, N.Y.: Anchor Press/Doubleday, 1980. Reprinted by permission.

Not all hearing-impaired children have problems in all these areas, of course. Much depends on the severity of the hearing loss and the age of onset. In addition, personality traits, effectiveness of intervention, and parental reaction can make a great difference in the adjustment and achievement of hearing-impaired children. However, regardless of the type or severity of the hearing loss, the area most affected by an impairment is the realm of language, speech, and communication.

LANGUAGE, SPEECH, AND COMMUNICATION

> The basic deprivation of profound congenital deafness is not the deprivation of sound; it is the deprivation of language. (Meadow, 1980, p. 17)

A hearing impairment has its most profound effect on the understanding and production of language. As noted earlier, the severity of the loss and the age of onset are the two most critical factors affecting the development of language and speech. Consider the case of Mark, a chubby, cute 8-month-old with a profound hearing loss. Unlike hearing babies, Mark is not reinforced by the sound of his own babbling, so he is less likely to continue it for as long as a hearing child. Mark does not respond to his mother's voice and therefore fails to reinforce her in her communication with him. He can not distinguish speech sounds of information (such as labeling a "car"), which hampers the development of his receptive language. And, obviously, if Mark is unable to hear speech sound, he will be unable to produce speech as a hearing child would.

LANGUAGE ACQUISITION. Children whose deafness precedes language receive their initial language experience in one of three ways: sign language, spoken English, or a combination of the two.

The deaf child who is born to deaf parents is typically exposed to the **American Sign Language (Ameslan)** as a first language. Although the use of sign language has been seen as a stigmatizing communication mode, deaf children of deaf parents using sign language usually experience language acquisition and family interactions earlier and at a greater rate than other deaf children. Their timetable of language acquisition is much closer to that of a hearing infant. Although as a group these children initially fall behind the other groups in spoken speech, their later speech ability is comparable. In addition, they enjoy greater academic and social success. Their emotional development is much more closely aligned with that of a hearing child, due largely to the greater ease with which early communication and parental acceptance is achieved.

The deaf child with either deaf or hearing parents may be exposed to both languages in the home, with varying emphasis on which is the primary mode. For example, in some families the deaf parents may use sign language with each other but spoken language with the child. In other families, the reverse may be true. This approach uses manual sign language (Ameslan), amplification, lipreading, and speech. Children who use bimodal receptive and expressive language show vocabulary growth, grammar complexity, and language comprehension like that of a hearing child. Their communication with hearing individuals is usually better than that of children in the first group.

The majority of deaf children have hearing parents who use spoken language as their only mode of communication. The first exposure the child has to language is usually spoken English, whether it is comprehensible or not. Hearing parents often support the position of teaching the child only speechreading and speech, with the idea that the greatest integration with the hearing community can be made only through spoken English. Although most deaf children can be taught to understand and produce spoken English, their understanding is severely delayed and the speech is often barely intelligible. There have been no systematic studies on the language development of these children, but it appears that their linguistic backwardness persists through adolescence and into adulthood (Meadow, 1980).

INTELLIGENCE AND COGNITIVE ABILITY

Because of the effect a hearing impairment has on language development, it has been assumed in the past that the deaf child's intellectual and cognitive abilities would be impaired. However, recent studies such as those conducted by Furth (1973) conclude that the cognitive abilities and thinking processes of deaf children are essentially the same as those of hearing children. When intelligence tests are given with a minimum of verbal instructions and spoken responses, hearing-impaired children perform within the normal range. For example, if the Performance Scale of the WISC-R is administered and the Verbal Scale omitted, deaf children score on a par with their hearing peers.

ACADEMIC ACHIEVEMENT

The normal intellectual capacity of most deaf children is not reflected in their academic achievement. The reading achievement of deaf children is repeatedly reported to be lower than that of their hearing peers (Conrad, 1977; Trybus and Karchmer, 1977). In addition, although there appears to be no connection betweeen degree of hearing loss and nonverbal intelligence, there is a significant relationship between degree of hearing loss and level of reading ability. The greater the hearing impairment, the poorer the reading ability. Interestingly, deaf children of deaf parents consistently perform at a higher level on tests of academic achievement than deaf children of hearing parents (Meadow, 1980).

SOCIAL ADJUSTMENT

Many separate and independent studies, conducted over several decades, have reported that hearing-impaired children are socially immature and deficient in interpersonal abilities. Unfortunately for such children, social skills in our culture largely depend on the ease, clarity, and attractiveness of verbal ability; the popular person is usually witty and outgoing, not inarticulate or withdrawn. The hearing-impaired child and adult is at a distinct disadvantage because of his or her language disability.

Although there is certainly no deaf personality type, some personality characteristics are described as occurring at a higher rate in the hearing impaired than in hearing individuals. For example, deaf adolescents are likely to be described as showing more impulsiveness and suggestibility than their hearing peers (Furth, 1973; Meadow, 1980). However, these behaviors probably exist not as personality attributes, but as a result of the hearing-impaired individual's limited experience. For example, greater signs of physical "impulsiveness" might occur because other avenues of responding are blocked, and

It is often difficult for the hearing-impaired individual to be assimilated into the social activities of the hearing world. Special efforts are needed to insure that social isolation does not occur. Barbara Alper, Stock, Boston.

physical reactions may have been successful in the past in helping the deaf individual get his or her ideas across. In addition, subtle signals of disapproval for not inhibiting such reactions were probably not received. Hearing-impaired adults may seem more suggestible because of their greater reliance on others to interpret or communicate events in their surroundings ("there goes the lunch bell"), and their greater dependence on visual cues.

Many of the behaviors essential in the deaf person's daily life happen to be considered negative or immature traits in our culture. For example, when two hearing people converse, they alternate between glancing at each other and looking away. Staring continuously at a companion's face, which is necessary to the deaf person's communication with the hearing, causes discomfort. Likewise, the physical gestures and facial animation that accompany the deaf person's speech are associated in our culture with people who are young or immature.

THE DEAF COMMUNITY

"Of all physical disabilities," writes psychologist Hans Furth, "deafness is the only one that makes its members part of a natural community" (1973, p. 2). "Unlike other disabled people, those who identify themselves as deaf form a true society, a genuine cultural group," asserts Beryl Lieff Benderly (1980, p. 12). Even though most deaf individuals have parents who can hear, the large majority spend their adult leisure time in the company of others who are also deaf. Regardless of whether they are trained in manual or oral communication, 80 percent choose to marry a hearing-impaired spouse. If they give birth to hearing children, these children learn to communicate in both worlds and are excellent interpreters for their parents, but go on to join their hearing peers when they become adults. They do not truly belong to the deaf community.

The deaf comprise a true "subculture," according to Meadow (1972), with its own language, publications, schools, social organizations, and art forms. In addition, the deaf community is a cohesive and fiercely proud group. When legislators were considering tax benefits for the deaf similar to those for the blind, organizations of the deaf voiced opposition; they did not seek or want any special favors.

TODAY'S EDUCATIONAL METHODS

Educational methods for today's hearing-impaired student are usually determined by the severity of the hearing loss, the age of onset, and the child's mode of communication. In general, children with mild to moderate hearing losses are educated in a regular classroom and are taught **oral communication,** which emphasizes auditory training, speechreading, and speech. Children with severe to profound hearing losses are more likely to receive their academic instruction in special classes or special schools and will frequently be instructed in **manual communication,** which uses sign language and finger-spelling.

ORAL LANGUAGE OR SIGN LANGUAGE?

Usually the first educational decision the parents of a hearing impaired child make is choosing the best way for their child to communicate. Instruction in oral communication emphasizes teaching children to make maximum use of whatever hearing they have. Due to technological improvements in amplification, the benefits of this auditory training can be extended to an increasing number of children. Instruction in speechreading includes teaching the child to use the visual cues of mouth movements (lipreading) and facial expressions to understand what is being said. Instruction in speech is a final and very important aspect of oral communication. Depending on the severity of the handicap, the acquisition of intelligible speech can be a laborious and frustrating task.

The manual communication approach teaches the child to use a standard set of signs known as American Sign Language (Ameslan). Ameslan is considered a true language in every sense. It has grammatical rules and a capacity for conveying both concrete and abstract ideas. An important complement to sign language is **fingerspelling,** which is used to spell out letter-by-letter those words not represented by a specific gesture in Ameslan (such as a proper name). Figure 6–2 shows the use of Ameslan to convey a whole word. Figure 6–3 depicts the finger position for one letter of the alphabet in fingerspelling.

PRESCHOOL PROGRAMMING

For the very young preschool child (birth to 3 years old), educational programming revolves around the family and focuses largely on parent counseling and training.

PARENTAL ADJUSTMENT. A critical first step for professionals working with a very young hearing-impaired child is to assist the parents as they cope with their initial reactions—denial, fear, sadness, anger. There is often a need for time for the parents

Manual communication enables a person to sign whole ideas or to spell words letter by letter. On the left, the woman is signing the abstract concept "language," while the picture on the right shows the sign for the letter "i."

TO SPEAK OR TO SIGN

Unfortunately, in the past, parents faced with the decision of which type of communication to select were not given an overview of the merits and drawbacks of oral and manual communication. Professionals working with the hearing impaired often were advocates of one approach or the other. Those supporting the oral language position argued that only by learning to speak could the hearing impaired be a part of society. Manual language was undesirable because it highlighted the deaf person's disability and separated him or her even more from the hearing world. Educational programs that favored oralism were extremely popular during the first half of this century. Children attending these programs were often forbidden to use physical gestures of any kind when attempting to communicate.

Advocates of manual communication argued that communication through the oral approach was slow, often unintelligible, and for the most part unsuccessful for many hearing-impaired individuals, especially those with a profound loss. The use of manual signs facilitates the acquisition of language and enables young deaf children to communicate language concepts at the same age as their hearing counterparts.

The controversy between oralism and manualism is still being argued today. However, one resolution to the debate has been gaining in popularity over the past decade: a combination of the two approaches called the **total communication approach** or **bimodalism** (Schlesinger, 1978). It uses speech, speechreading, amplification, and the manual sign system (usually Ameslan). Two variations on the total communication approach are the **Rochester method,** which uses spoken and fingerspelled language (Moores and Maestas y Moores, 1981), and **cued speech,** which uses hand shapes to represent specific sounds at the time spoken words are produced. At the present time, the total communication approach—speech, speechreading, amplification, and Ameslan—seems to be the most popular and efficient.

Although the infant pictured here is not deaf, parents of hearing impaired children need to respond to early vocalizations with similar positive attention. Teri Leigh Stratford.

to deal with feelings of inadequacy and anxiety before they are ready to begin to help the child.

Hearing-impaired babies, even those with a profound hearing loss, coo and babble like their hearing counterparts during the first five months or so. However, as auditory reinforcement begins to increase and affect the hearing infant's vocalizations, the lack of such reinforcement for the deaf child results in a decline in these efforts. Parents should be taught to reinforce the child's vocalizations by responding with obvious pleasure and attention through smiling, talking, and touching. In this way, the child becomes conscious of the effects of vocalizations and will continue the process in order to continue to receive positive responses.

PARENTAL EDUCATION. After the initial adjustment, the parents need to be instructed in the nature of the hearing loss, the stages of normal language development, and the attachment and use of a hearing aid. Horton provides five general categories of information needed by parents of very young hearing-impaired children, saying that an ideal program should (Horton, 1974, p. 483):

1. Teach the parents to optimize the auditory environment for their child.
2. Teach the parents how to talk to their child.
3. Familiarize parents with the principles, stages, and sequence of normal language development and how to apply this frame of reference in stimulating their child.
4. Teach parents strategies of behavior management.
5. Supply effective support to aid the family in coping with their feelings about their child and the stresses that a handicapped child places on the integrity of the family.

FORMAL PRESCHOOL PROGRAMS. As the hearing-impaired preschooler approaches the age of 3, intervention procedures should extend beyond those implemented by the parents in the home. The child at this point needs to have his or her social development and independence fostered by greater exposure to peer-group situations. In addition, hearing-impaired children are usually ready at this age for structured learning experiences to teach them the language comprehension and speech skills they lack. A number of resources are available to parents and professionals who want to work with hearing-impaired infants and preschool children (Hasenstab and Horner, 1981).

A longitudinal survey of seven different types of early education programs for hearing-impaired youngsters was conducted by Moores, Weiss, and Goodwin (1978). They found that the children in programs with the greatest academic orientation (direct instruction of specific skills) performed better on measures of academic achievement and readiness, psycholinguistic abilities, and receptive communication than did children in a more traditional nursery model (a more natural approach through language enrichment experiences). In addition, children in programs that used manual language components in teaching communication were more successful on measures of receptive communication and articulation than children whose programs did not incorporate manual language. Early manual communication appeared to have no discernible positive or negative effects on the use of speech or residual hearing.

ELEMENTARY SCHOOL PROGRAMMING

Hearing-impaired children may spend their elementary school years in any one of the following programs:

1. Residential or day school specially designed for the deaf. Typically, classes are small (8 to 10 hearing-impaired children) and a full range of auditory, speech, and language services are a regular part of the program. Instruction in oral or combined oral and manual language is usually emphasized.
2. Special classes for the hearing impaired within a regular elementary school. Small classes (8 to 10 children) are taught by a teacher trained in education of the hearing impaired. Although the class is operated on a self-contained basis, mainstreaming opportunities are available in the public school setting. Speech, hearing, and language services are provided. Language instruction is oral or total communication.
3. Regular class placement with resource room assistance. The child is placed in a regular classroom with hearing children, but spends at least one hour each day in a resource program with a specialist teacher. In addition, the child is provided with the services of the school speech, hearing, and language therapist.
4. Regular class placement with itinerant special teacher. The child is in the regular classroom with hearing children most of the time, but spends a prescribed time (usually one to three times per week) in small group with a specialist resource teacher who often assists in more than one school. In addition, services of the school speech, hearing, and language therapist are provided.
5. Regular class placement with access to regular services. The child is in the regular classroom and is provided all the services available to any hearing child—remedial reading teacher, school speech therapist, resource teacher, and so on.

With the push during the past decade toward mainstreaming and the least restrictive environment, more and more hearing-impaired children are being placed in regular classrooms for at least some portion of the day. An increasing number of teachers who were not formally trained in the education of the hearing impaired are faced with the task of integrating and educating these children. Although much depends on the severity

A teacher often needs to signal to a child in order for her to focus visual and auditory attention on what is being said. New York League for the Hard of Hearing.

of the hearing loss, the age and level of functioning of the child, and the availability and quality of other services in the school, the following suggestions can assist teachers who are meeting their first hearing-impaired student.

1. Seat the child in a good listening and viewing position. This will depend on your classroom seating arrangement and where you stand when teaching. Often, this is near the front of the classroom, in which case you need to encourage the child to turn around to look when other children are speaking.

2. Signal the child before speaking if necessary to have him or her focus visual and auditory attention.

3. Have a hearing buddy assist the child in situations such as following a group discussion or understanding an assignment.

4. Remember when presenting new material orally to the class that visual material is needed in the acquisition of *new* skills. Write key words or phrases on the board or give written handouts to everyone.

5. Don't say instructions or give information while writing on the board, looking in a closet, reading from a book.

6. Avoid standing with your back to the windows or any bright light—this makes speechreading especially difficult.

7. Be aware of problems the child may have whenever the speaker is not visible—loudspeaker announcements, recordings, television programs, longer-distance playground calls.

8. Be aware that when noise levels are not kept low—such as during group activities or in the cafeteria or auditorium—the child will probably experience greater difficulty understanding what is being said.

9. Speak clearly and not too fast, but do not exaggerate your lip movements or drastically slow the rate of your speech—that makes the speech more difficult to understand because it does not resemble natural speech.

10. Keep a diary for the parents to clarify assignments, inform them of hearing aid problems, make study suggestions, and generally keep them up to date on their child's progress. When communicating with parents, include aspects of the child's performance or behavior that are not directly related to the hearing disability.

11. Establish positive attitudes toward the hearing-impaired child. Help the class to understand hearing loss by discussing some of the following topics: the ear and the hearing process, hearing aids, and famous people who are or were hearing impaired, such as Kitty O'Neill, the deaf movie and TV stuntwoman who also happens to be champion diver and skier and the holder of the female land speed record. Various resources are available to help convey information in a positive way to the hearing classmates (see Focus).

FOCUS

LISA AND HER SOUNDLESS WORLD

When Lisa grew up some more, her parents began to worry about her. When they talked to Lisa, she would only look at them. She did not say anything. Lisa could not hear what they were saying. So how could she understand them? She did not know what they were telling her. Lisa did not know what anybody was telling her.

Do you want to know how it feels to be like Lisa? Not to know what people are saying to you? Not to hear them?

Go over to the television set and turn it on to your favorite program. Then turn off the sound.

What happens?

You can see the program fine. But you can't hear anything. So you don't know what the people are saying. You don't know why they are laughing. You don't know what they are telling you.

Everything is all mixed up.

But when you turn on the sound again, everything is all right. You know what the people are saying. You know why they are laughing. You know what they are telling you. You know what the program is all about. You *understand*. Because you can hear.

And that is what it is like not to hear. It is like television with the sound turned off. You can turn the sound on again whenever you want to. But nobody could turn on Lisa's hearing. Lisa lived in a soundless world. And because she did, Lisa could not talk.

From E. S. Levine, *Lisa and her soundless world*. New York: Human Sciences Press, 1974. Illustrated by Gloria Kamen. Used with permission.

12. Familiarize yourself with the child's hearing aid enough so you can check its functioning and determine when there is a problem. You don't have to be an expert in hearing aids—however, you should take the relatively small extra time required to be able to discriminate between minor problems (dead battery) and more complex ones requiring other professional personnel such as the audiologist.

13. Help the hearing-impaired child develop a good self-concept by including him or her in classroom activities and chores. Don't lower your expectations—demand the same type of effort and responsibilities as you do of children who do not have hearing handicaps.

14. Inform the child about the handicap and limitations in a straightforward way. Too often, we assess and teach these children without telling them what we know about their disability and their skills. Making them more knowledgeable will make them seem more confident and mature in dealing with situations and people. Resources designed for the hearing-impaired child at all age levels are available through organizations such as the Alexander Graham Bell Association for the Deaf in Washington, D.C.

SECONDARY AND POSTSECONDARY PROGRAMMING

SECONDARY PROGRAMS. The school programs described for the elementary school child are available for the most part for the older hearing-impaired child. In other words, residential schools, day schools, special classes in regular schools, and regular classes with special services typically extend to the completion of high school.

As is the case with nonhandicapped persons, the needs of the hearing-impaired adolescent are quite different from those of the younger child. The teenage years are characterized by major biological, psychological, and social changes. Helping the hearing-impaired adolescent make the best possible adjustment to these changes is an important concern for the secondary teacher. In addition, teachers working with hearing-impaired adolescents should encourage the following:

PEER RELATIONS. Counseling hearing-impaired students in order to improve their acceptance by their peers can be valuable to the student. Even if they profess not to care, they usually do. The counseling, of course, varies according to the individual's particular characteristics and interests, and may take many directions. The teacher may point out a subtle dress code deviation that may be contributing to peer rejection, or help the student to shrug off harmless, routine teasing in order to decrease the likelihood of future teasing.

EXTRACURRICULAR ACTIVITIES. Often there is a reluctance by both the hearing-impaired student and the other students to have the hearing-impaired student participate in school and community activities. The teacher can help not only by encouraging the student to become involved, but also by providing specific information to the student regarding the activities. These activities provide experiences that are important to the adolescent's sense of belonging.

VOCATIONAL TRAINING AND COUNSELING. Hearing-impaired students should be helped to assess their strengths and interests and to begin to make decisions about what to do after high school. As a teacher, you can help provide information about job opportunities for them to consider. Do not advise them only about those vocational areas the deaf have frequently pursued in the past (such as woodworking). Help them to see the broadest array of options, and if their interests lie in areas that have less

HUMANE ASSOCIATION IS TEACHING ABANDONED DOGS
TO HEAR FOR DEAF

When the doorbell rings, or the telephone, or one of Joanna Nash's three children cries out, her miniature gray poodle Reddie nudges her on the leg and leads her to the source of the sound.

And suppose the smoke alarm goes off in the middle of the night? "Reddie would jump on my bed and wake me up by licking my face or walking all over me until I wake up," Mrs. Nash explains by teletype. "Then he would get off my bed and lay down fast so I know there is a fire somewhere in this house."

Hearing dogs. The deaf need them, in their way, as much as blind people need seeing-eye dogs. Life is full of signals—and hazards—that depend on hearing. The nonprofit American Humane Association and some other organizations are training about 150 hearing dogs a year, using dogs from animal shelters.

"There's the double benefit of aiding those who have perhaps the most neglected handicap, because it's invisible, and saving homeless animals," says Carolyn Bird, executive director of the Red Acre Farm Hearing Dog Center in Stowe, Mass.

Joanna and David Nash's young children have normal hearing, but they both are deaf. That makes them prime candidates for hearing dogs, which are in short supply. Other preferred recipients are college-age people out in the world on their own for the first time, and the elderly.

Trainers say mutts make the best hearing dogs. They select dogs that are intelligent, attuned to people and sharp of hearing. Most of those used are a year or so old. The basic course of 12 to 14 weeks trains them to listen for certain sounds and to alert their owners. When a dog goes to a home, a handler goes along for five to seven days of custom training on the spot. The total cost of training a dog is $3,500 to $5,000.

The dogs are taught to give gentle nudges. Though many deaf people have special lights or other devices to alert them to sounds, the dogs still have a place. The Nashes had a special light rigged to their son Jason's crib, but "sometimes the lights wouldn't work or the sun would block us from seeing them," says Mrs. Nash.

Hearing dogs can help at the office, too. John Dutton, who works at Massachusetts Maritime Academy, uses his collie-Labrador retriever Tanya to let him know when his amplified telephone rings. "She is truly the most intelligent animal I've ever owned, or seen for that matter," he says.

Old people living alone get an extra benefit from the dogs, Mrs. Bird points out: "companionship and a sense of security."

A hearing dog can be trained to alert hearing impaired individuals when certain sounds occur such as alarm clock buzzes, telephone rings, and baby's cries. Red Acre Farm Hearing Dog Center.

certain success (such as drama), try not to discourage their interest. As with any adolescent, these students should have a major responsibility in deciding their future. Counseling may range from advising a student to take a particular high school course that teaches a desired vocational skill (such as clerical typing) to providing information about postsecondary programs that match the student's interests and needs.

POSTSECONDARY PROGRAMS. For many years, the only educational program designed for the hearing impaired after high school was Gallaudet College, a liberal arts school in Washington, D.C. In the late 1960s, the picture began to change as more and more colleges and vocational schools opened their doors to hearing-impaired students. The National Technical Institute for the Deaf at the Rochester Institute of Technology trains students from all over the country in technical fields such as computer systems, photography, architectural drafting, business administration, mechanical engineering, and medical technology. In addition, over 60 colleges and centers provide postsecondary programs in a variety of areas designed or modified for the hearing-impaired student. Many special services are available in these programs, such as sign language interpreters, tutoring and notetaking services, manual communication training for instructors, supervised housing, and assistance in vocational placement. A directory of college and career programs for deaf postsecondary students is available (Rawlings, Trybus, and Biser, 1978).

TECHNOLOGICAL ADVANCES

With the recent developments in computers and electronic information processing has come a number of electronic devices that are particularly well suited to the needs of the hearing impaired. Television, which is probably the most powerful and effective communicator of information and social mores, can now become a critical factor in the integration of the hearing impaired into the world.

TELEVISION CAPTIONING AND TELETEXT

TELEVISION CAPTIONING. **Open captioning,** which means that captions can be seen on all television sets, was used with selected programs during the 1970s. Hearing audiences found the captions distracting, and since only a small number of programs were captioned, the hard of hearing were left with most of their television viewing uncaptioned and largely incomprehensible. In 1980, **closed captioning** for the hearing impaired became available on a large number of PBS and commercial network television programs. Closed captioning means that the captions are visible only on sets equipped with a decoder. Today, in the lead-in credit of numerous TV shows, a symbol and message indicate if closed captioning is available.

TELETEXT. **Teletext** is a means of presenting information on a standard television screen which the user can view whenever he or she chooses. Teletext requires a decoder and keypad for retrieving the information. Although teletext is available more widely in Europe than it is in the United States, it seems likely that with the current demand

Teletext captioning has great capabilities for providing captioned information for both entertainment and educational purposes. Alexander Graham Bell Association for the Deaf, Inc.

for electronic information processing and with teletext's mass-market appeal, it will become an affordable home convenience in this country within the next decade. Teletext is more easily updated than printed information such as the daily newspaper. It can provide, at a moment's notice, information such as news, sports, entertainment listings, cultural calendars, and community announcements. In addition, teletext can be used as a captioning system with far greater capabilities than those of current systems (Blatt, 1982).

TELEPHONE ADAPTIONS

Besides television, a second vital communication device that has historically been cut off from deaf people is the telephone. Even persons wearing hearing aids can have major problems using the telephone because of acoustic feedback and noise from contact or closeness of a telephone receiver and a hearing aid. Although electronic advances show promise for the development of aids that will overcome this problem, a practical solution available on the market today is the TTY, a teletypewriter connected to a telephone by a special adapter. Although the TTY requires that both callers have the hookup, over 25,000 are currently in this country, and a directory of people and businesses equipped with the device is available.

According to Stoker (1982), current developments in technology will enable a hearing-impaired person to telephone people who do not have the TTY hookups in the near future. The **Superphone,** developed by Dr. Robert Engelke, can be used by a deaf person to communicate with anyone who has a pushbutton phone. The Superphone changes the keyboard message typed by the deaf person into an intelligible electronic voice. The person can hear the machine speaking to them and may then respond by pushing the touch-tone keys to type a message that will appear on the character display of the deaf person's TTY.

OTHER COMMUNICATION AIDS

HEARING AIDS. A very important technological aid for the hearing impaired continues to be hearing aids themselves. Progress is being made in the quality of the amplification and the reduced size and increasing convenience of these devices. Unfortunately, because of the relatively small demand, advances in this area have not kept pace with those in the mass market areas of computer technology and electronic communication devices.

The four basic types of hearing aids are named according to location of attachment. The **body aid** is used by very young children and by the physically handicapped or elderly who cannot manipulate the tiny controls in the ear-level instruments. The receiver, which is inserted in the ear, is attached by a cord to a larger box worn on the person's chest. The chest box contains the microphone, battery, and volume and tone controls.

The **behind-the-ear hearing aid** is worn by the largest percentage of hearing-impaired persons. Technical improvements in this type of aid now make it suitable for severe impairments that in the past could only be helped by body aids. As a result, almost 60 percent of all aids sold in a six-month period in 1980 were behind-the-ear aids (*Hearing Aid Journal*, 1980).

The **eyeglass hearing aid** is more commonly used by adults than by children. In some eyeglass models, the aid is contained in the side parts that fit over the ears. In other models, the frames contain some of the parts (usually the battery, tone and volume controls, and microphone), but the earmold part of the hearing aid is a separate attachment. Although the number of eyeglass aids in use seems to be declining (Sanders, 1982), they are preferred for both convenience and cosmetic reasons by many individuals who must wear corrective lenses.

The **in-the-ear hearing aid** has benefited greatly from recent improvements that have reduced mechanical feedback problems. With the improvement in the quality of amplification as well as the cosmetic appeal of being the least conspicuous aid, the in-the-ear aid should have the greatest increase in sales of any aid in the future (*Hearing Aid Journal*, 1980). Although not as common as the behind-the-ear version, at this point, the in-the-ear aid has shown the greatest increase over the past two decades. Sanders (1982) notes that purchases have increased fivefold since 1965.

FUTURE AIDS. Some extraordinary technological devices are currently not available to the average hearing-impaired person due to cost, distribution problems, lack of sufficient demand, or a combination of these factors. An example is the **Autocuer,** a portable minicomputer that mechanically "hears" words spoken to a deaf person and projects symbols onto the lens area of a pair of eyeglasses. The symbols, shown in Figure 6–6 for the phrase "He can go," act as visual cues to reduce the ambiguity of words that look similar to a person who is lipreading.

Another example of advances resulting from the current explosion in computer technology is a typewriter developed by IBM that "hears" speech and converts it to a

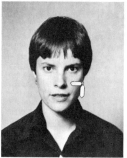
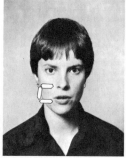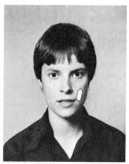

In the top pictures, the girl is saying "He can go." In the bottom pictures, the girl is saying "Get a coat." To a lipreader, some parts of the statements look similar. Note the similar mouth positions in "He" and "Get" and "go" and "coat." An Automatic cuer, the Autocuer, can flash symbols onto the wearer's eyeglasses lenses to aid in the deaf person's understanding of what is being said. Public Information Office, Research Triangle Institute, Research Triangle Park, North Carolina. Reproduced by permission.

typed format. This product should be available at an affordable price by the 1990s (Branscom, 1980).

Even though not specifically designed for the deaf population, by the next century computer technology will be providing more sophisticated tools for everyone in a variety of areas. The hearing impaired will be able to purchase and use these aids to gain access to information and communication in ways that were hard to imagine fifty years ago.

ANSWERS TO FREQUENTLY ASKED QUESTIONS
HEARING IMPAIRMENT

1. There are some things you might try in order to encourage Patty to interact with her classmates. Don't worry about "interfering," because interaction with hearing children is extremely beneficial to the hearing-impaired child for the development of communication skills.

First, the class might need an explanation of Patty's hearing loss. Patty's parents, her speech therapist or audiologist, or you could explain the loss to the children. Perhaps Patty herself could talk about her hearing aids. This might help the children to know why Patty needs directions or statements repeated or said when she is looking at the person's face.

Second, small group activities like art projects could be used to encourage social interaction. One reason why Patty feels more comfortable with younger children might be that she finds them easier to understand. They probably are closer or more similar to her in level of language development. Still, structured activities within the classroom setting should be provided to assist Patty in developing communication skills. As the children become more knowledgeable about Patty's hearing loss and have positive interactions with her in the classroom setting, friendships will be more likely to develop.

2. Give Ricky some time. It takes time to adjust to a hearing aid and for the doctor to determine exactly what level of amplification will work best for Ricky. Hearing aids do not permit people to hear *exactly* as a hearing person does—only the intricate, miraculous human ear can do that. A hearing aid mainly makes sounds louder, but Ricky (depending on how great his hearing loss is) will most likely still have problems in hearing some sounds. In addition, Ricky needs time to relearn and understand the meaning of sounds he may have missed all his life.

You can help Ricky by interacting with him and by trying to include him in activities with his cousins. Don't ignore him. Even if you are uncomfortable, just think how "left out" and uncomfortable he probably feels. Speak clearly to him when he can see your face, and gesture to him with smiles or pats to reaffirm to him that you are interested in him and like to be with him.

3. Having a special child mainstreamed into your class will require some extra time and effort. The time spent with John may seem like a great deal of effort at first, but gradually you will find that methods like visual aids and simplified written directions will probably fit well into your classroom routine. One thing you might do is assign a classmate to help John with directions on tasks. Be sure to try to encourage him to ask for clarification or repeated instructions. Keep in close contact with John's teacher and parents regarding John's performance in class.

You should speak with John's parents about his hearing aids. They probably check his aids daily for appropriate volume and sound quality, and they could familiarize you with that procedure. Sometimes feedback in the form of a high-frequency whistle occurs. If this happens frequently, inform John's parents. He might have a poorly fitted earmold. You do not have to be a technical expert in the care of the aids, but be on the lookout for potential problems. Erratic performance or distractibility could signify problems with the aids or excessive reverberation of noise within the classroom setting. In either case, checking classroom acoustics and/or possible problems with the aids would be a good idea.

4. Probably not. Steve sounds like an exceptional young man. He probably had intensive speech and language therapy during preschool years. We've known of one child who had a moderate to severe loss who played the piano. This child was so capable of coping with his learning impairment that a teacher once remarked he must be faking his hearing loss!

Skills such as those developed by Steven probably resulted from early detection of the hearing loss and intensive special help, along with years of hard work. Just as all hearing children are very different from one another, so are those with hearing losses. Steven is a good example of how heterogeneous the hearing-impaired population is. Such children differ in severity of hearing loss, age at which loss occurred or was detected, amount of special services received, personality traits such as motivation and assertiveness, and home or other environmental conditions.

5. Your desire to be friendly is well-intended, and these kind intentions will no doubt come through as you approach your neighbors. Go over and welcome them as you would any neighbor: with a smile and a handshake. Remember that they have had years of experience of having to communicate their needs and ideas to hearing people in some form or other. They will most likely indicate to you what mode of communication works best for them by gesturing, or speaking to you, or writing a note. An important thing to keep in mind is that, with the exception of their handicap, they are like any other couple moving into a new neighborhood. They will probably have the ordinary questions regarding local stores, services, and so on. You can be an invaluable help to them as they settle in to their new home.

6. Not yet. First, talk with the speech therapist about the specific concepts that give Sandra the most problems. Use as many visual cues as you can to illustrate new ideas. Often, explanations using objects and actions are beneficial. If Sandra is having difficulty with directions, try to rephrase or have a buddy check her understanding of them. Ask the speech therapist or other school personnel for suggestions for classroom modifications. Also, be careful about lowering expectations. That can be harmful in a number of ways—it can lower motivation and self-esteem. If she continues to have difficulty, check into the availability of itinerant or special resource teachers or the advisability of some part of the day being spent in a special class placement. If her problems continue but are not very different from the weaknesses in reading and social studies of some of her hearing peers, then continue placement in the regular class.

SUMMARY

Much has changed and improved in educational methods and social experiences for the hearing impaired over the past two decades. New devices and techniques are allowing the hearing impaired to live more easily and more fully in a hearing world.

Hearing impairment is usually divided into two categories, deaf and hard of hearing. The deaf are those with the greatest hearing loss whose development of speech and language is visually based. The hard of hearing are those with a lesser hearing loss who develop basic communication skills through the auditory channel. Severity of hearing loss is measured in terms of decibels, units of loudness or intensity. As important as the extent and kind of the loss is the age at onset—whether the loss is prelingual, (present at birth or soon afterward), or postlingual (after the person had acquired language and learned to speak).

Estimates of prevalence among children vary, but the official estimates are all under 1 percent of the school-age population. Prevalence for this handicap increases with age. Some experts estimate that at least 14 million Americans suffer from hearing loss, and that this figure is three times the number of those who suffer from visual impairments.

Hearing ability is usually measured by an audiologist, a professional trained in the detection and correction of hearing impairments. Assessment tests and techniques vary. The first step is usually a screening such as a sweep test; then comes diagnostic audiometry, in which more precise measurements of loss are made. Pure-tone audiometry is used to determine the person's exact threshold for hearing pitch and loudness; speech audiometry is used to test detection and understanding of speech. Special techniques have been developed for testing young or mentally and physically handicapped persons: there are tests for infants and the multiply handicapped, and play audiometry for young children.

The usual way to classify the causes of hearing loss is according to the location of the problem—outer ear, middle ear, inner ear. Impairment in the outer ear can cause conductive losses, as can impairment in the middle ear, but middle ear losses are usually more serious. The most common cause of middle ear impairment is infection. Losses because of inner-ear impairments are the most serious and are called sensorineural impairments. They often cause profound losses and are the most difficult to treat and correct.

The consequences of a hearing loss extend far beyond the physical handicap: there can be perceptual, speech, communication, cognitive, social, and emotional problems; there can also be educational, intellectual, and vocational difficulties. The area that is always most affected is communication, particularly the understanding and production of speech. Here, severity of loss and age at onset are the critical factors.

Children whose deafness is prelingual learn language through signing (American Sign Language), spoken English, or a combination of the two. The intellectual and cognitive abilities of hearing-impaired children appear to be essentially the same as those of hearing children, although academic achievement, especially in areas such as reading, may be lower. Social adjustment generally presents the most difficulty because verbal ability is rewarded in our culture, and because the experiences of the hearing impaired have been limited. In addition, the hearing impaired suffer from a naivete that comes from being dependent on others or on visual cues for information. Many of the behaviors essential to a deaf person's daily life are considered negative or immature traits in our culture.

Unlike other disabled people, the deaf identify themselves as a cohesive cultural group and spend a great deal of time with other deaf persons. The deaf have their own language, publications, schools, social organizations, and art forms.

Educational methods for the hearing impaired vary according to severity of loss, age of onset, and the person's mode of communication. Oral communication, which emphasizes auditory training, speechreading, and speech, is usually given to those with mild to moderate losses in a regular classroom; those with severe losses are instructed in manual communication, which uses sign language and fingerspelling. Once, the decision was oral versus manual communication, and for a long time educators favored the oral approach and discouraged the use of signing. Today there is a combination of the two called the total communication approach, which uses speech, speechreading, amplification, and the manual sign system (usually Ameslan).

Work with the young hearing-impaired child begins with parental training in a variety of techniques, after a period of adjustment to and understanding of the child's impairment. Formal preschool programs focus on social development and independence as well as language skills. Elementary and secondary programs range from special residential or day schools to regular class placement with resource room assistance, itinerant special teacher, or regular services. In secondary and postsecondary programming there is usually special emphasis on peer relations, extracurricular activities, and vocational training and counseling. Today, there are many more opportunities and programs than there were even in the recent past, opening up many new careers to the hearing impaired.

Technological advances are also opening up opportunities by making the hearing world more accessible. Television captioning and Teletext bring programs and information into the home; and new telephone devices have now given the hearing impaired access to this vital link with others. The primary technology for the hearing impaired, however, remains the hearing aid. These devices have been much improved in quality and reduced in size by technological advances. Hearing aids are of four major types: body aids, behind-the-ear hearing aids, eyeglass hearing aids, and in-the-ear hearing aids. Extraordinary new devices are waiting for proper marketing and distribution, along with affordable prices. All of them should give the hearing impaired access to the wider world in ways undreamed of fifty years ago.

REFERENCES

BENDERLY, B.L. *Dancing without music: Deafness in America*. Garden City, N.Y.: Anchor Press/ Doubleday, 1980.

BLATT, J. Teletext: A new television service for home information and captioning. *The Volta Review*, 1982, May, 209–217.

BOOTHROYD, A. *Hearing impairments in young children*. Englewood Cliffs, N.J.: Prentice-Hall, 1982.

BRANSCOM, L.M. *And man created the chip*. Newsweek, June 30, 1980, 50–56.

CONRAD, R. Reading ability of deaf school-leavers. *British Journal of Educational Psychology*, 1977, *47*, 138–148.

FURTH, H.G. *Deafness and learning: A psychosocial approach*. Belmont, Calif.: Wadsworth, 1973.

HASENSTAB, M.S., & HORNER, J.L. *Comprehensive intervention with hearing-impaired infants and preschool children*. Gaithersburg, Md.: Aspen Systems, 1981.

Hearing Aid Journal. 26th annual facts and figures, 1980, *34*, 3.

HOEMANN, H.W., & BRIGA, J.S. Hearing impairments. In J.M. Kauffman & D.P. Hallahan (Eds.). *Handbook of special education*. Englewood Cliffs, N.J.: Prentice-Hall, 1981.

HORTON, K. Infant intervention and language learning. In R. Schiefelbusch & L. Lloyd (Eds.). *Language perspectives: Acquisition, retardation, and intervention*. Baltimore: University Park Press, 1974.

KELLER, H. *Helen Keller in Scotland*. London: Methuen, 1933.

LEVINE, E.S. *Lisa and her soundless world*. New York: Human Sciences Press, 1974.

LONGHURST, T., BRIERY, D., & EMERY, J. *SKI-HI Receptive Language Test*, Project SKI-HI. Logan: Utah State University, 1975.

MEADOW, K.P. *Deafness and child development*. Berkeley: University of California Press, 1980.

MEADOW, K.P. Sociolinguistics, sign language, and the deaf subculture. In T.J. O'Rourke (Ed.). *Psycholinguistics and total communication: The state of the art*. Washington, D.C.: American Annals of the Deaf, 1972.

MOORES, D.F. *Educating the deaf: Psychology, principles, and practices*. Boston: Houghton Mifflin, 1978.

MOORES, D.F., & MAESTAS Y MOORES, J. Special adaptations necessitated by hearing impairments. In J.M. Kauffman & D.P. Hallahan (Eds.). *Handbook of special education*. Englewood Cliffs, N.J.: Prentice-Hall, 1981.

MOORES, D.F., WEISS, K.L., & GOODWIN, M.W. Early education programs for hearing impaired children: Major findings. *American Annals of the Deaf*, 1978, *123*, 925–936.

RAWLINGS, B.W., TRYBUS, R.J., & BISER, J. *A guide to college/career programs for deaf students*. Washington, D.C.: Office of Demographic Studies, Gallaudet College, 1978.

ROSS, M., with BRACKETT, D., & MAXON, A. *Hard of hearing children in regular schools*. Englewood Cliffs, N.J.: Prentice-Hall, 1982.

SANDERS, D.A. *Aural rehabilitation: A management model* (2nd ed.). Englewood Cliffs, N.J.: Prentice-Hall, 1982.

SCHLESINGER, H.S. The acquisition of bimodal language. In I.M. Schlesinger & L. Namir (Eds.). *Sign language of the deaf: Psychological, linguistic, and sociological perspectives*. New York: Academic Press, 1978.

STOKER, R.G. Telecommunications technology and the hearing impaired: Recent research trends and a look into the future. *The Volta Review*, 1982, 147–155.

TRYBUS, R.J., & KARCHMER, M.A. School achievement scores of hearing impaired children: National data on achievement status and growth patterns. *American Annals of the Deaf*, 1977, *122*, 62–69.

VISUAL
IMPAIRMENT
7

1. I'm a sixth-grade teacher and am about to have Brian, a blind student, placed in my classroom. My principal and the director of special education have both assured me that I'll be getting help from a special teacher who travels from school to school, but I still have questions about how this blind student will ever be able to get along in my class. Two of my biggest concerns relate to Brian's reading material and his ability to get around in my classroom. First of all, I've been told that Brian is "legally" blind but that he is able to read print by using a magnifying glass. In fact, the director of special education told me that Brian doesn't even know how to read Braille. I thought legally blind meant you couldn't see anything.

Second, I'm concerned about how Brian is going to get around in the school. I've heard he doesn't have a seeing-eye dog, but instead relies on a cane. Besides having to go to the lunchroom, gym, and bathroom outside my class, I'm also worried that he'll have difficulty in my class. I like to have the students move from one area of the room to another frequently. I'd really like to have Brian in my class, but I wonder if he won't have too hard a time here.

2. My wife and I have always heard that blind people develop an extra sense that helps them to sense objects in their way. Our new neighbors have a teenage daughter, Karen, who has been blind and deaf from birth. We've watched her closely over the past couple of months and don't think she has this ability. She gets along all right with her cane, but when she doesn't have it, she often walks into things. We don't want to meddle, but perhaps there's something more wrong with Karen than her parents realize. Maybe she's retarded too, since she hasn't got this extra sense.

3. My daughter has a 5-month-old baby, Jeffrey, who is blind. I'm greatly concerned about both the baby and my daughter's reaction to him. He's not cooing or smiling yet like her other two boys did at that age. In addition, my daughter doesn't seem to be interacting with Jeffrey as she did with her other babies. I don't want to be a meddling grandmother, but should I be concerned about the lack of responsiveness on the part of both the baby and the mother?

4. My wife and I are recently divorced, and she has custody of our 3-year-old son, J. C. When I went to visit J. C. last weekend, he had a patch over his left eye and my wife told me the doctor had told her he should wear it for different periods of the day. She said the doctor had told her J. C. has something called a "lazy eye." My wife's not one to go in for weird health fads or anything like that, but I thought I'd better check into this lazy eye business. It seems to me J. C.'s awfully young to be having an eye patched. Is this lazy eye diagnosis legitimate, and how serious is it?

5. I work as a secretary in a large office building in downtown Detroit. I've become acquainted with another secretary who works on the same floor as I do. She is almost totally blind, but has a special machine that enables her to do her work in Braille as she types on the typewriter. What I'm most concerned about is whether or not I should offer her help in getting around the building. I don't want to offend her, but it seems at times, particularly when work lets out, that she might need some assistance. Our office building is in quite a congested area, and I'm afraid she might have difficulty getting to the bus stop. What should I do?

6. I'm a ninth-grade teacher of English and have recently been informed that a totally blind student will be entering my classroom. All I know about her is that she writes and reads English. What special adjustments should I be prepared to make? Will I be expected to learn Braille?

Today the educator of the visually impaired has many new and different skills. In recent years there have been a great many changes in how we approach the education of the visually impaired child and adult. With the 1980s have come a number of exciting new ideas and methods. To give you a glimpse of how much has changed in this field in the past few years, here is an imaginary conversation between Tom, a 15-year-old student, and Mr. Oldsight, a 38-year-old former student at the Pineview Residential School for the Blind. Oldsight has returned to Pineview for a class reunion.

The outlook for Tom's future is much brighter than it was for Mr. Oldsight when he was 15. What you'll find as you read this chapter is that the outlook for today's visually impaired child is more optimistic than it was in the past. You'll also find, however, that there is much room for improvement. Researchers and educators are just beginning to make real headway in discovering the best ways to educate the visually impaired.

Oldsight: You know I've heard about some of these new inventions, but I've not actually had the opportunity to use any of them. This laser cane that you use, exactly how does it work?

Tom: Well, I don't know all the scientific background, but basically it sends out infrared light beams—one goes up, one goes down, and the other goes straight ahead. When one of the beams hits something in my way, the light beam is converted into sound.

Oldsight: So it's sort of like hearing what's out there in front of you. Amazing!

Tom: Yeah. It's really a big help. Although I've got to admit it did take some getting used to.

Oldsight: How?

Tom: Well, it took months of practice before I got comfortable with it, and I could still use some improvement in my technique. The hardest part is using it when it's raining or snowing. Don't get me wrong. I really like it, but it isn't foolproof by any means. One thing I'd really like to try some time are sonic glasses. Have you tried them?

Oldsight: No. What are they?

Tom: They're worn like glasses on your face and send out ultrasound.

Oldsight: Isn't that sound so high in frequency humans can't hear it?

Tom: Right. Anyway, the ultrasound bounces off objects and comes back to you converted into sound you can hear. The pitch of the echo tells you how far away things are.

Oldsight: Sounds to me like the expression "Blind as a bat" isn't too far off the mark.

Tom: Actually, a lot of the research behind the sonic glasses is based on studies of the ability of bats to use echoes.

Oldsight: Amazing. I really envy you and the other students here. When I was here we didn't have any of these mobility devices. In fact, twenty years ago we didn't get all that much in the way of mobility training.

Tom: No kidding. Boy, we sure do. If anything, these new devices have made mobility instruction all the more important.

Oldsight: Say, let me ask you this. I've heard that Pineview bought a Kurzweil Reading Machine.

Tom: Yes. Now talk about electronic wizardry—there's the machine. You put your book down on the scanner and bingo, "Kurt" (that's what we call him) reads the book to you out loud. It sure beats Braille for speed.

Oldsight: I'd guess so! How much do you use Braille anyway?

Tom: Myself? Well, I'm pretty fluent in it, and still use it quite a bit. But some of the younger students don't use it so much.

Oldsight: I suppose a lot of them, besides the Kurzweil, are using cassettes.

Tom: Right. The compressed speech devices have really been perfected. The computer slices out parts of the tape but still leaves it intelligible.

Oldsight: I've just begun using one of those things. It's about three times faster than reading Braille. Listen, how much are they teaching you here now about independent living skills? We got some training, but I've always felt we should've gotten more. The first jobs I got after I left here were real disasters for me because I didn't feel capable of living by myself. It wasn't until I met Mary, my wife, who's sighted, that I really was able to take on job responsibilities. Before that I was overwhelmed. . . .

Tom: I've heard other older blind people say the same thing. I think the situation has changed a lot since you were here. They really stress independent living skills now. And after graduation I can live in an apartment downtown with three other blind people while I hold down a job.

Oldsight: What about those who are going to go on to college? Is there any kind of preparation for that?

Tom: Yes. I was just about to say that we also have a model apartment here at Pineview. Starting in the tenth grade, we're scheduled into the apartment in groups of four along with a teacher. The experience of living in the apartment really helps prepare us for independent living, like living at college. We live there for two weeks every year and learn things like cooking, laundry, washing and drying dishes. That kind of stuff.

Oldsight: That certainly sounds like a good arrangement. . . . Say, I know what I wanted to ask you. How's the arrangement with the public schools working out?

Tom: What do you mean?

Oldsight: Well, when I was here at Pineview we took all our classes right here. I understand from your principal that for the past few years students have been taking the bulk of their academic subjects in the public schools. That's a big change from when I was here. Boy, the folks in town rarely saw any of us. Occasionally we took a field trip into town, but that was about it.

Tom: "Mainstreaming"—that's what they call it—is really a big deal now.

Oldsight: Well, what do you think of going into the public schools for your classes?

Tom: I really like it. I get my Braille instruction here and my mobility training. I also get special tutoring for the classes in town, but all my academics I take at the local high school. Of course, the thing that makes it work so smoothly is that our teachers here at Pineview are in constant contact with the teachers at the public school. They provide them with special materials and give them helpful suggestions and things like that.

Oldsight: That's great. When I was growing up I guess I just never would've thought about trying to cope with it. The whole idea probably would've scared me to death.

Tom: Well, it's no bed of roses. I mean it's different . . . you know, to change other people's attitudes. But all in all, I think it's good for us and good for the sighted.

TODAY'S DEFINITION OF VISUAL IMPAIRMENT

There are two classifications of visual impairment you should know—blind and partially sighted. In addition, there are two different definitions for determining when a particular individual is blind or partially sighted—the legal definition and the educational definition.

THE LEGAL DEFINITION

The legal definition is used to decide whether an individual is entitled to legal benefits, such as tax benefits and money for special materials. You have no doubt heard people say that they do or do not have 20/20 vision. When people have 20/20 vision it simply means they have normal visual acuity—they can see at 20 feet what a person with normal vision can also see at 20 feet. A legally blind person, however, has visual acuity of 20/200 or less in the better eye even with correction (such as glasses). A partially sighted person, under the legal definition, has visual acuity between 20/70 and 20/200 in the better eye with correction. In other words, if a person has visual acuity no better than being able to see at 20 feet what an individual with normal vision sees at 200 feet, that person would be considered legally blind. A person is also classified as legally blind if he or she has an extremely narrow field of vision. If a person's field of vision is so narrow that its diameter is no greater than 20 degrees, then that person is considered legally blind.

THE EDUCATIONAL DEFINITION

At first glance, it would seem that the legal definitions would be acceptable to most professionals. After all, measuring visual acuity is a relatively straightforward matter. Most educators, however, find the legal classification scheme inadequate. Knowing that

Because this child is classified as legally blind does not mean that he is totally blind. Very few visually impaired individuals are totally blind. Ken Karp.

John's visual acuity is 20/150 (partially sighted) and Martha's is 20/250 (blind) does not enable us to predict with very much accuracy that John will function better than Martha on visual tasks. *The fact of the matter is that visual acuity tells us nothing about how a person will use his or her remaining sight.* Martha, even though she may be classified as legally blind, may actually be able to read regular print books. John, who may be legally classified as partially sighted, may rely on Braille. An indication of just how irrelevant the classification of legal blindness can be is highlighted by Willis's (1976) large-scale survey of reading methods. She found that 52 percent of legally blind students use large- or regular-print books as their primary method of reading. In addition, she found that only 18 percent were totally blind.

Most educators, recognizing the limitations of the legal definitions, favor a definition based on educational considerations. For educational purposes, the blind person is one whose sight is so severely impaired that he or she must be taught to read by Braille or by aural methods (audiotapes and records). The partially sighted person can read print even though magnifying devices or large-print books may be needed.

FOCUS

HOW THE EYE WORKS

Figure 7–1 depicts the major physical structures of the eye. When we look at an object in our visual field, if our vision is normal the light rays from the object end up being focused on the back part of the eye, the retina. This sends an electrical impulse via the optic nerve to the visual center of the brain, and the result is that we "see" the object. Before the light rays from the object make it to the retina, however, they must journey through and by a number of other structures and substances within the eye. The light rays:

1. Pass through and are bent (refracted) by the transparent **cornea**
2. Pass through the **aqueous humor** (a watery substance)
3. Pass through the **pupil**
4. Change the size of the opening to the pupil by having the **iris** (the colored portion of the eye) open or close depending upon how much or how little light is hitting it
5. Pass through and are bent some more by the **lens**
6. Pass through the **vitreous humor** (a jellylike, transparent substance)
7. Come to focus on the **retina** (the back portion of the eye containing nerve fibers connected to the **optic nerve**)

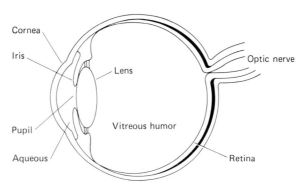

FIGURE 7.1

PREVALENCE

As we noted in Chapter 1, somewhere between .05 and .16 percent of the school-age population is visually impaired—either partially sighted or blind. Most prevalence estimates, however, indicate that about one out of every 1,000 children, or 0.1 percent of the child population, is visually handicapped. Unlike most other areas of exceptionality, the prevalence of visual impairment increases dramatically with age. Most estimates, for example, indicate that blindness is ten times more prevalent among adults. But even these figures still make the visually impaired one of the least prevalent groups of handicapped individuals in the United States.

ASSESSMENT OF VISION

Visual acuity is most often assessed by using a Snellen chart, the chart you see in practically every physician's office. It consists of rows of letters or of *E*s for individuals like young children who do not know the alphabet. In the latter case, the child is asked to point in the direction the "legs" of the *E*s are facing. Each row of letters or *E*s corresponds to the distance at which an individual with normal vision can identify the letters or the direction of the legs on the *E*s. For example, if at 20 feet (the normal distance for testing) you can identify the letters in the 20-foot row, you have

---

FOCUS

SYMPTOMS THE CLASSROOM TEACHER SHOULD WATCH FOR

Behavior

Rubs eyes excessively
Shuts or covers one eye, tilts head or thrusts head forward
Has difficulty in reading or in other work requiring close use of the eyes
Blinks more than usual or is irritable when doing close work
Holds book close to eyes
Is unable to see distant things clearly
Squints or frowns

Appearance

Crossed eyes
Red-rimmed, encrusted, or swollen eyelids
Inflamed or watery eyes
Recurring styes

Complaints

Eyes itch, burn, or feel scratchy
Cannot see well
Dizziness, headaches, or nausea following close eye work
Blurred or double vision

20/20 central visual acuity for far distances. If you can distinguish only the much larger letters in the 70-foot row, you have 20/70 central visual acuity for far distances.

Note that in the statements above we used the terms *central* visual acuity and *far* distances. This is because the Snellen chart tells us little about peripheral vision or visual acuity for *near* distances. Visual acuity for far distances is not always an accurate predictor of how well an individual can see at near distances—distances that are more important for academic tasks such as reading. Your near vision can be measured by using a special Snellen chart, to be used at a distance of 14 inches, or the **Jaeger chart,** another test designed for measuring near vision.

For school screening purposes, the Snellen chart is usually used. A child doing poorly on the Snellen should be tested further by an **ophthalmologist,** a physician trained to diagnose and treat eye diseases. School screening should be considered only a gross method of detecting visual problems. A child may still have significant vision problems (such as peripheral problems or specific difficulties with near vision) that might be missed. School screening will not pick up every child who has a visual impairment. For this reason, teachers need to be aware of possible indicators that a child may have a visual impairment (see the Focus).

CAUSES

REFRACTIVE CAUSES

The most common causes of visual impairment are refraction errors, which are errors related to the bending of the light rays by the eye. These errors most often result in reduced central visual acuity. **Nearsightedness (myopia), farsightedness (hyperopia), astigmatism** (blurred vision), and **cataracts** (clouding of the lens) are all examples of refraction errors resulting in reduced central visual acuity. If you're nearsighted, you're able to see things up close all right, but have difficulty in seeing things at a distance. Nearsightedness results when light rays from objects come into focus in front of rather than on the retina. The opposite is true for farsightedness. If you're farsighted, you're able to see things at a distance but have difficulty seeing things up close. Farsightedness results when light rays from objects come into focus on a point behind rather than on the retina. Irregularities in the cornea or lens result in astigmatism, which causes light rays to hit the retina in a distorted or blurred manner. Cataracts are caused by a clouding of the lens that results in light rays not coming into proper focus on the retina.

Fortunately, most refractive errors, particularly nearsightedness, farsightedness, and astigmatism, are correctable. Eyeglasses or contact lenses can help the person with nearsightedness, farsightedness, or astigmatism. Surgery can usually correct problems caused by cataracts.

MUSCULAR CAUSES

Strabismus and nystagmus are caused by improper muscle functioning. **Strabismus** is a condition in which the eye (or eyes) is (are) directed inward toward the nose or outward toward the ear. If left untreated, strabismus can lead to blindness (see Focus). **Nystagmus**

EYE AND BRAIN: A DELICATE BALANCE

A most unfortunate interaction between eye and brain can occur in the person who has strabismus in one eye and does not have it corrected. Such a person has what is called a "lazy eye." Traci, who has a lazy eye, has a hard time focusing on objects in her environment. If, for example, she wants to look at a tree, she will see two trees (she will see "double") rather than one because the one "good" eye will be focused on the tree, but the lazy eye will not. Unfortunately, unless Traci has her lazy eye corrected in some way, she may end up actually losing sight in it. This is where the brain comes into play. The brain, being a highly adaptive organ, will over time actually try to "fix" the double image by rejecting the image from the lazy eye, so that Traci will see one rather than two images. If no treatment intervenes, lack of use may result in loss of vision in the eye (this loss of vision is called amblyopia).

Fortunately, there are ways to strengthen Traci's lazy eye. The ophthalmologist may recommend that the stronger eye be patched for periods of the day to force Traci to use the impaired eye. Traci can also do special eye exercises. If patching and exercising fail to remedy the problem, surgery can be performed to align the eye muscles correctly. In most cases, early treatment or surgery can bring the lazy eye back into alignment and thus avoid any loss of vision.

is a condition in which there are rapid, jerky, involuntary movements of the eye or eyes. This can result in dizziness or nausea. Nystagmus is sometimes a sign of brain malfunction and/or inner ear problems.

BIOLOGICAL CAUSES

A number of biological factors can result in visual impairment. Most of these conditions involve damage to the retina and produce some of the most severe cases of visual impairment. Fortunately, one of these causes, **retrolental fibroplasia (RLF)**, has been on the decrease ever since the 1950s, when it was discovered that the administration of high levels of oxygen to premature babies to prevent brain damage was resulting in damage to their retinas. To avoid RLF, hospital staff are now more careful in administering oxygen to premature infants. RLF has not disappeared, however; recent medical advances allow many more very premature babies to survive, but only if high levels of oxygen are used.

Other medical conditions that can result in damage to the retina are retinitis pigmentosa, diabetic retinopathy, coloboma, and glaucoma. **Retinitis pigmentosa** is a hereditary disease resulting in deterioration of the retina. Diabetes can result in loss of blood supply to the retina, a condition that is called **diabetic retinopathy. Coloboma** is a degenerative disease in which parts of the retina are not completely formed. **Glaucoma** results from excessive pressure within the eye; if left undetected, it can result in damage to the retina and optic nerve and total blindness. Because its appearance is much more likely in older adults, many ophthalmologists recommend that all adults have periodic eye examinations after age 35.

CHARACTERISTICS

SOME GENERAL GUIDELINES

Before discussing some of the specific effects visual impairment can have on the individual, we need to make a few general statements.

AGE AT ONSET AND DEGREE OF IMPAIRMENT. Age at onset and degree of impairment can affect the subsequent development of the visually impaired person. Brad, who became blind at 2 years of age, is probably much better off than someone who has been blind from birth. Those two years of sight may have allowed Brad to begin the formation of visually based concepts and provided him with basic visual information that enables him to travel about his environment relatively independently. Kelli, who is legally blind but has enough vision to be able to read large-print books, is no doubt further ahead in many areas of functioning than if she were totally blind.

This does not mean that a child who is blind from birth or who is totally blind will always be less able to function than the child who becomes blind later or who has some useful vision. Differences among people in how they adjust to a visual impairment and in how handicapped they are as a result of it are due to other factors as well, such as intelligence, motivation, and parental attitudes, to name but a few.

TOUCH VERSUS VISION. Visually impaired individuals must rely heavily on touch to gain information about their environment. But although even the totally blind can achieve a sophisticated understanding of objects in their environment, there is no doubt that they have a more difficult time than if they had sight to help them. There are at least two reasons why touch is not as efficient as sight. First, when we use touch we perceive things successively, whereas with vision we are better able to perceive things

FOCUS

TOUCH: THE SUCCESSIVE AND NOT SIMULTANEOUS SENSE

Vision allows us to perceive various aspects of an object all at once, or simultaneously. This is true of even relatively large things in our environment, such as automobiles or buildings. To perceive an automobile through touch, however, we would need to piece together a number of sensory impressions obtained from exploring the car's parts. That touch is more time-consuming and less accurate is understandable. Try it yourself. Close your eyes and ask a friend to give you an object to explore tactually and see how long it takes you to identify it. If it is a large object, you'll probably have even more difficulty identifying it than if it's small. This is because with the large object, you must put together more successive impressions. Even though you realize how difficult it is to identify things by touch, remember that you have a number of years of sight to help you identify what it is you're touching. Think how difficult it is for a child sightless from birth who cannot fall back on visual experience. Consider too how difficult it is for the blind child to understand things so large or so small that they cannot possibly be perceived appropriately through touch. Imagine, if you will, how difficult it must be for the blind child to arrive at a full appreciation of Mount Everest or the human cell.

Blind infants should be encouraged to explore their environment through touch. This blind child is coming to know more about his baby brother through the sense of touch. Inger Abrahamsen, Rapho/Photo Researchers, Inc.

simultaneously (Griffin and Gerber, 1982; Lowenfeld, 1971). In other words, vision allows us to "take in" large objects all at once, whereas touch can only provide information in a piecemeal fashion. We gain an understanding of what we touch by touching one part of an object after another and then putting these separate impressions together to arrive at a concept. Second, as Lowenfeld (1973) has observed, touch compared to vision requires a great deal more conscious effort on the part of the person. Another way of saying this is that our eyes, and particularly our ears, rarely "shut down"; they are constantly taking in information. To gain information through touch, however, we must make a specific effort to attend to tactual perceptions (see Focus).

Touch, while not as efficient as vision, can still provide a wealth of information. The blind child can be taught touch strategies. Teaching the child strategies is important (Berla, Butterfield, and Murr, 1976), and the earlier the training the better (Berla, 1981). One general strategy that is especially important for tactual development is the ability to focus tactual exploration on the critical features (such as shape, size, softness or hardness) that help to distinguish one object from another (Griffin and Gerber, 1982).

INTELLECTUAL ABILITY

In general, intelligence as traditionally defined by IQ tests is unaffected by the lack of sight. IQ tests specifically designed for use with the visually impaired, such as the Hayes-Binet (a special adaptation of the Stanford-Binet IQ test), or the verbal portion of the Wechsler Intelligence Scale for Children—Revised (WISC-R), show that blind children do not have lower IQs than sighted children (Hayes, 1950). These IQ tests, being heavily verbal in nature, do not put the visually impaired at a disadvantage. Researchers have found that, except for a few minor aspects of communication, such as gestures that accompany talking, the visually impaired do not differ from the sighted in language ability (Anderson and Olson, 1981; Bateman, 1965; McGinnis, 1981; Rogow, 1981).

Although general intelligence may be unimpaired by the lack of sight, some specific areas of development are affected by visual impairment. As you would expect, the visually impaired have particular difficulty with abstract concepts, concepts about things or ideas that cannot be touched (Gottesman, 1973, 1976; Hall, 1981; Stephens and Grube, 1982; Suppes, 1974). Fortunately, these problems are not insurmountable. Through special training, educators have been able to overcome many of these conceptual difficulties (Friedman and Pasnak, 1973; Stephens and Grube, 1982).

SPATIAL CONCEPTS. Even though we've been able to find ways of improving most conceptual abilities of the visually impaired, one area that continues to remain a problem is that of space. Although advances are being made in understanding the best ways to teach spatial concepts, the visually impaired person is still likely to experience great difficulty in understanding his or her environment. You can imagine how difficult it would be for you, if you had never had sight, to figure out how to go to a house you had never before visited. It is not surprising that some visually impaired individuals, particularly the blind, have problems in spatial orientation. It is also not surprising that these problems lead to difficulties in the next area we will consider—mobility.

MOBILITY

As used by professionals working with the visually impaired, **mobility** refers to the individual's ability to travel about in his or her environment (see Focus). Mobility skills are closely linked to spatial ability. In the 1980s there has been a dramatic increase in research into the spatial orientation and mobility skills of the visually impaired. We are a long way from a complete understanding of the interplay between these two areas, but we do know three things:

1. A variety of authorities agree that, in general, the visually impaired process spatial information in two different ways—as a sequential route or as a map that depicts the overall relationship among various points in the environment (Casey, 1978; Dodds, Howarth, and Carter, 1982; Fletcher, 1980, 1981; Rieser, Gurth, and Hill, 1982). In the following quote, Fletcher (1980) captures the essential differences between the two and also highlights why the ability to "map" the environment is preferable:

   A route-type representation encodes only the sequential relationships among objects. Thus people who represent information as a route learn a series of movements that connect landmarks. For example, a woman might learn that to get to the shopping center from her house, she has to turn right at the front gate, proceed along the street for two blocks, turn left at the gas station, continue for one more block, and then turn right at the church. People who represent spatial information as a map, however, extract an overview of the area and thus are aware of the relationships among objects even though they have not experienced all these relationships directly.

   In terms of the ability to navigate in an environment, the implications of these different representational modes are obvious. To go back to the previous example, suppose the road between the gas station and the church were closed to traffic. The woman with the route-type representation would have to rely on trial-and-error methods to reach the shopping center (unless, of course, she had previously learned an alternate route). A person with a map-type representation would immediately be able to formulate another route. This person's knowledge of the relationships among all the parts would enable him or her to select an appropriate equivalent path. (p. 381)

2. Although there are certainly exceptions, in general those who lose their sight at a very early age or who are blind at birth are less able to build spatial maps. They rely on a sequential route representation of their environment and are thus more handicapped in terms of mobility.

3. Intelligence is related to the ability to build spatial maps. Those visually impaired individuals who are high in intelligence are usually better travelers because they are able to make and use spatial maps.

FOCUS

MOBILITY IN THE BLIND: ARE THEY AIDED BY AN EXTRA SENSE OR BETTER ACUITY IN THEIR OTHER SENSES?

Two related myths have been connected with the mobility skills of the blind. A blind person walking along the street often seems able to "sense" an object in his or her path. This ability has come to be known as an "obstacle sense." This is an unfortunate term, since it gives the impression that the blind have an extra sense. As any blind person will tell you, this is not true. A number of experiments have demonstrated that, *with practice*, the visually impaired can learn to detect subtle changes in the pitch of high-frequency echoes as they move toward objects.

Related to the myth of an extra sense is the common misconception that the blind actually have better acuity in their other senses, such as touch and hearing. This is not true either. Again, *through practice*, the blind do learn to make very fine discriminations based on touch and hearing.

As the blind person will tell you, there's nothing magical about either the obstacle sense ability or the ability to notice very subtle differences based on touch or hearing. These skills are learned through hard work and concentration. Furthermore, the blind individual would be the first to tell you not to overrate their importance. The obstacle sense, for example, cannot by itself make a person a highly proficient traveler. It is just an aid. Weather and environmental conditions (noises of rain, wind, traffic, talking) can make it useless.

One of Marvel Comics most popular superheroes is Daredevil, a character who although blind has superhuman sensory powers. His radarlike sense enables him to negotiate his environment like no ordinary, sighted mortal. Through the use of his extraordinary powers, he outwits villains and rescues damsels in distress. But as Jerry Miller of the Commission for the Blind and Visually Handicapped for the New York State Department of Social Services notes (Miller, 1981), it is difficult to decide whether Daredevil, whose monthly circulation approaches half a million, is a help or hindrance when it comes to attitudes toward the blind.

Although the writers periodically point out that Matt Murdock, Daredevil's alias, received both his blindness and his supersensory powers because of a radioactivity accident, Miller notes that the casual reader might not always be aware of the causes of Daredevil's superskills. If the reader has already heard myths about the sensory powers of blind people, Daredevil might reinforce them. On the other hand, Daredevil can also be a potentially positive influence. As Miller points out, surveys have shown that the disabled have traditionally been portrayed in comics as evil rather than good (Weinberg and Santana, 1978). That a blind superhero can be "just one of the superguys" might be having a positive impact on how young people view the blind. Because of the low incidence of blindness, few of us are exposed to very many blind people. *Daredevil* puts before its readers a blind person who is not only not evil or totally dependent, but a genuine superhero.

ACADEMIC ACHIEVEMENT

We must be cautious in drawing conclusions about the academic achievement of the visually impaired because they often must be tested under modified conditions. For example, the visually impaired are usually allowed a longer time on tests that require reading. The reading of Braille takes much longer than print, and even those who do read print do so at a slow rate (Nolan and Ashcroft, 1969). Authorities, however, do agree on the following:

1. Both the partially sighted and the blind are often behind their sighted peers in academic achievement (Suppes, 1974).
2. The achievement of the visually impaired is not as seriously affected as that of the hearing impaired.

SOCIAL ADJUSTMENT

Research has not provided us with a clear answer to the question of whether or not the visually impaired are less well adjusted than the sighted. Some studies show the blind to have poorer self-concepts and some show them to have better self-concepts than the sighted (Cook-Clampert, 1981). Of one thing we can be fairly certain: Social

THOSE LOVELY LAMPS . . . THOSE WINDOWS OF THE SOUL
Guillame deSalluste, duBartas
Divine Weeks and Works, 1578

Poets, playwrights, and songwriters have long recognized the special part the eyes play in revealing emotions. In everyday life, we are apt to take eye contact for granted. To see just how much we depend on visual contact in talking with another person, try this experiment. When talking with a friend, purposely avoid making eye contact and observe how this affects the person's behavior. You will notice that it is altered in some way. More than likely, your friend will feel uncomfortable and unsure of how to respond to you. This is because we depend to a great degree on the expressiveness of the other person's eyes to judge how he or she is responding to what we are saying. Think of how often you have heard someone say, or you yourself have said, that you prefer to talk face to face on an important matter rather than over the telephone.

Research has established that sighted people tend to reject the blind socially (Bateman, 1964; Jones, Gottfried, and Owens, 1966). Sighted people apparently have a tendency to feel awkward in the presence of a visually impaired person. It would be interesting to know how much of this social rejection is due to the fact that the sighted person does not get the usual feedback from the eyes of the visually impaired person.

adaptation problems are less likely to be due to the blindness itself than to society's reaction to the blindness (see Focus). Our own reactions to the visually impaired child can be important determinants of how he or she adjusts. Sam, who has been rejected by his sighted classmates and overprotected by his parents, may be a prime candidate for social adjustment problems. The best thing for Sam would be for his peers to learn to treat him as they would any other child in the class. It is important for peers to realize that Sam is not inherently different because he lacks sight; he has the same needs and feelings they do. His parents would help him considerably if they would strike a balance between providing for his special needs and working toward making him as independent as possible.

TODAY'S EDUCATIONAL METHODS FOR THE VISUALLY IMPAIRED

Today's visually impaired child, whether blind or partially sighted, is educated for most, if not all, of the school day in a regular classroom. Residential programs for the visually impaired are much less popular than they once were (Spungin, 1982), and the same can be said of special classes. Most authorities recognize that, with proper teaching and curriculum modification, the best place to teach the visually impaired child is in the regular classroom. Multiple handicaps, of course, may require concentrated special services that can best be obtained in a residential setting. But regular class placement does not mean that the regular class teacher receives no help in coping with some of the special problems presented by visual impairment. A resource or itinerant teacher will also work with the child and the teacher to develop an appropriate educational program. The itinerant teacher, who travels from school to school, is the most practical and most frequently chosen model of assistance by school districts because there are so few visually impaired students in any one school.

PRESCHOOL PROGRAMMING

Today's special educator recognizes the importance of working with the visually impaired as early as possible. Because of the recent work of psychologists who specialize in infancy research, we now know that sighted infants begin to learn about their environment through the visual system within the first few weeks of life. So even in the first few weeks after birth, visually impaired babies will be slower to explore their environment. They may be delayed in learning what kinds of things exist outside their own bodies (Warren, 1981). This lack of awareness of the external environment may explain why blind infants crawl later than sighted babies. It may be that until the child learns there is something "out there" that might be worth going after, he or she will not crawl (Fraiberg, 1977). There are a number of preschool programs for the visually impaired that can help the child to "catch up" and to begin to learn necessary skills. These programs can be home- or school-based.

HOME-BASED PROGRAMS. Selma Fraiberg's educational program for preschool blind children is probably the best known of the home-based approaches (Fraiberg, Smith, and Adelson, 1969). Her orientation is toward fostering a strong emotional attachment between parents and child. She believes that the early relationship between infant and parents can be very important for later social and intellectual development. The blind infant may be especially difficult for the sighted parent to learn to accept. Fraiberg believes a major problem is that parents are often overwhelmed by the prospect of rearing a child with no sight. Another key problem may be that the visually impaired infant does not respond in the usual way to the parents.

SCHOOL-BASED PROGRAMS. School programs are designed to provide the visually impaired child with a variety of exploratory activities. Young visually impaired children are often reluctant to investigate their environment. The more we can encourage them to explore their environment and objects within it, the better off they will be. Active manipulation of objects and exploration of the environment does two things: it promotes intellectual growth and independence.

Because of the low prevalence of visual impairment, preschool teachers usually do not have much experience with visually impaired children. It is thus understandable that their first reaction when faced with the prospect of teaching a blind preschooler is often one of uncertainty. With help from a resource or itinerant teacher, however, the preschool teacher can provide a rich and meaningful program for the visually impaired child. Scott (1982) has a number of tips for the preschool teacher, some of which we adapted for the list below:

1. Although sighted preschoolers do not tend to react negatively, they will be curious about a blind child in the class. You should give simple, factual answers to their questions. Turn it into a learning experience for all the children.
2. The blind child may need considerable help in the early weeks in finding his or her way about the classroom and/or building. It is all right to assign other children to help in

guiding the child to other places, such as the bathroom. In addition, as early as possible the teacher should give the child a tour of the room and the building, pointing out the major landmarks.

3. Having children sort is a favorite activity of preschool teachers. Usually, however, it is done on a visual basis, such as by colors or shapes. The visually impaired child can sort on the basis of touch by using blocks and textures.

4. Having children color with crayons is another favorite preschool activity. Depending upon how much sight he or she has, the visually impaired child can also enjoy this activity. A piece of window screening placed underneath the paper will help the child feel outlines as he or she colors.

5. If the preschool child is totally blind, reading readiness materials for Braille, available from the American Foundation for the Blind and the American Printing House for the Blind, should be used. These can be supplemented by teacher-made materials. Scott (1982) suggests pasting small gummed shapes onto construction paper or drawing with a ballpoint pen on a sheet of bond paper placed over a window screen. The latter technique results in raised dots on top of the paper.

ELEMENTARY SCHOOL PROGRAMMING

Four special areas must be considered when educating the visually impaired child: (1) Braille, (2) the use of remaining sight, (3) listening skills, and (4) mobility training. How much the child will need instruction in each of these areas depends on the severity of the impairment. Totally blind children, for example, will undoubtedly benefit from Braille instruction. Partially sighted children, on the other hand, may not need Braille, but may benefit from techniques that encourage them to use their remaining sight.

BRAILLE. Today's visually impaired child is less likely to be taught Braille as the primary method of reading than once was the case. Recent technological innovations enable print to be converted into sound, and recordings are much more widely available. And the prevailing philosophy today is that even if an individual has only a little sight, it should be used to its fullest.

Braille, however, is still used, particularly by the totally blind. One good reason for teaching children Braille, even if they have access to and use other methods of reading, is that it is a common medium through which they can communicate with other blind individuals. Not all blind individuals have at their disposal the sophisticated and costly computer devices that are now available. Braille, however, is accessible to all who have an unimpaired sense of touch.

Braille is a complex system used for writing and reading. The basic unit is a quadrangular "cell" containing anywhere from one to six raised dots. There are different types of Braille. The system that is most often used because of its flexibility is, unfortunately, quite difficult to learn. It contains many contractions and abbreviations. How fast children can read and write using Braille varies considerably, with reading and writing rates much slower than those of sighted students writing and reading print. Learning to read Braille, like learning to read print, depends upon language ability (Griffin and Gerber, 1982). In addition, the reading of Braille requires smooth coordination of perceptual and motor skills. The child must gain perceptual information from touching the raised dots while at the same time moving his or her hands over the line of Braille (Wormsley, 1981). There are different ways of reading Braille. The one some authorities believe is most efficient requires that readers coordinate the movements of

This boy is using a Perkins Brailler and on his desk are a slate and stylus. In spite of recent technological developments, these two devices continue to be the major ways to write Braille. Irene Bayer, Monkmeyer.

both hands (Wormsley, 1981). The left hand reads the left half of the line of Braille. Once the left hand reaches the middle of the page, the right hand takes over and finishes the line while the left hand locates the next line.

Although there are some recent innovations (discussed in the Technological Advances section later in the chapter), the two primary ways of writing Braille are still the Perkins Brailler and the slate and stylus. The **Perkins Brailler** has six keys, one for each of the dots of the cell. When the person depresses the keys, they leave raised dots on the paper. The **slate and stylus** are more portable than the Brailler, but more difficult to use. The person presses the stylus through the openings of the slate, which holds the paper between its two halves. One of the reasons the slate and stylus is so slow is that the person must write the cells in reverse order, from right to left.

Because of the special knowledge required to teach Braille, school systems have special Braille instructors. These instructors coordinate their efforts with those of the regular classroom teacher.

USE OF REMAINING SIGHT. Today's special educator of the visually impaired knows that visually impaired children should be encouraged to use what sight they have. If at all possible, visually impaired children should be taught to read print. If they cannot read ordinary print, they may be able to use large-print publications and

Many blind individuals are able to take advantage of magnifying devices. United Nations, Photo by P. Strange.

magnifying devices. Large-print books and newspapers are available. Most are printed in a type size about twice the size of the text you are now reading, although much larger sizes are also available. The drawback to large-print material is that it is of limited availability and takes up a great deal of storage space. Visually impaired individuals can use magnifying devices in conjunction with large-print material or with normal-size print. These devices range from simple hand-held lenses and eyeglasses to closed-circuit TV screens that reproduce enlarged images of printed matter.

LISTENING SKILLS. Listening skills are vital for the visually impaired. Unfortunately, some people assume that the blind automatically develop superior listening abilities. Listening is a skill that must be taught (Bischoff, 1979). The teacher with a visually impaired child in his or her classroom should take every opportunity to provide that child with listening experiences. There are a variety of ways of doing this—one good example is the game "Simon Says." An additional benefit to teaching activities designed to increase listening skills for the visually handicapped is that they are usually of great value to sighted children as well.

The growing quantity of material available on audiocassettes also means that the visually impaired child must be a good listener. With audiotapes, visually impaired children can "read" at a much faster rate than if they use Braille or large-print materials, especially if they use **compressed speech devices.** A compressed speech device automatically discards small segments of speech so the speech is more rapid but still understandable. In a comparison of the three reading methods for the blind, Tuttle (1974) found listening to a recording at normal speed to be twice as fast as Braille, and compressed speech three times as fast. In addition, evidence indicates that comprehension of the material is actually superior with compressed speech as opposed to speech at a normal rate (Bancroft and Bendinelli, 1982).

THE MOBILITY AND ORIENTATION SPECIALIST

The mobility and orientation instructor can be of enormous benefit to the visually impaired. Because we are sighted, we take for granted the ability to travel from one place to another. The complexities of travel for the visually impaired are considerable. For this reason, the instructor must be well versed in a variety of detailed techniques. To give you the flavor of this detail, below is an excerpt from the mobility instructor's bible—Hill and Ponder's (1976) *Orientation and Mobility Techniques*. This particular lesson deals with how to negotiate revolving doors.

From Hill, E. W. & Ponder, P. *Orientation and mobility techniques: A guide for practitioners*. New York: American Foundation for the Blind, 1976, p. 90.

H. REVOLVING DOORS

PURPOSE: ■ To enable the student to utilize revolving doors safely, efficiently and independently.

1. BASIC METHOD

1.1 Procedure

1.1.1 The student approaches the door from the right side, parallel to and near the wall.

1.1.2 The student trails the wall, cane in right hand, employing the upper hand and forearm with the opposite arm.

1.1.3 The student contacts the revolving door with his left hand, makes a right turn and quickly follows it inward.

1.1.4 The student trails the wall of the door with his right elbow, and when contact is lost, he exits, quickly turning slightly to the right while using appropriate cane technique.

1.2 Rationale

1.2.1 This positions the student away from pedestrian traffic and facilitates location of the door.

1.2.2 Trailing the wall facilitates locating the revolving door.

The upper hand and forearm provides protection and facilitates detection of the vertical features and rhythm of the door.

1.2.3 Contacting the door with the left hand provides leverage for negotiating the door.

The student makes a right turn and quickly follows the door inward to maintain the door's rhythm and avoid pedestrian congestion.

1.2.4 The student trails the wall of the door to detect the appropriate time to exit. The student exits quickly to avoid pedestrian congestion and turns slightly to the right to reestablish his intended line of travel.

1.3 Observations

1.3.1 The student may utilize temperature changes, pedestrian traffic, auditory clues, or landmarks to locate the revolving doors.

1.3.2 The student should always approach the door from the right side to avoid injury to himself or others who may be exiting on the left because of the door's counterclockwise movement.

1.3.3 The student may slide his hand down to locate the push bar of the door. The student may choke up on the cane and hold it in a vertical position to facilitate movement while traversing the door.

1.3.4 The student may utilize his hand or the cane's crook for trailing the inside of revolving door.

It is important for the student to execute a slight right turn to maintain orientation.

Temperature and auditory clues may inform the student that he has traversed the door.

GENERAL OBSERVATIONS

■ Revolving doors are usually located in larger downtown areas in older buildings.

■ Automatic or pneumatic doors may be located on either side of the revolving door, and the student should utilize those if possible.

■ When walking with a sighted guide, the student should break contact and negotiate the door independently, because of the narrow width of the door opening.

■ Congenitally blind students may have unfounded fears of getting their hand trapped between the canvas flap and the wall.

■ If pedestrian traffic through the revolving door is light, the instructor may push the door and have the student negotiate it independently for practice.

■ If the panels of the revolving door are not in motion, the student quickly steps inside, locates the push bar, and applies pressure to negotiate the door.

MOBILITY TRAINING. Although mobility training should certainly start during the preschool years, it begins to receive heavy emphasis during the elementary years. In training visually impaired individuals to become more mobile, we are concerned with increasing their own sensory skills as well as making them better able to use external travel aids (see Focus). In addition to devices we will describe later in the chapter, there are three external travel aids: (1) human guides, (2) the Hoover cane, and (3) seeing-eye dogs.

HUMAN GUIDES. A sighted human guide affords the visually impaired person the safest and most flexible means of travel. It is also the most impractical of the three types of travel aid, since it requires the assistance of another person. For this reason, it is not wise for the student to become too dependent on such help.

HOOVER CANE. Sometimes called the long cane, the **Hoover cane,** simple as it looks, can be of enormous help to the visually impaired individual. It is the external aid used by most blind people. The long cane makes it possible to detect obstacles and changes in terrain. A great deal of practice is required before a person is skilled in the use of the long cane.

The Hoover cane, sometimes called the long cane, is the type of mobility aid used by most blind people. United Nations, Photo by L. Solmsen.

GUIDE DOGS. Most of us think that guide dogs are extremely useful and may wonder why we do not see more of them. The fact is that even though they do offer some protection against walking into dangerous areas, the dogs cannot actually "take" a person anywhere: you must first know where you are going. In addition, guide dogs are impractical for children, since they need to be cared for and tend to walk too fast.

SECONDARY AND POSTSECONDARY PROGRAMMING

The first priority for today's educator of older visually impaired individuals is to encourage their independence. Most authorities agree that the blind are susceptible to becoming dependent on others and that this susceptibility is often fostered by society at large. We have a tendency to view the blind person as dependent. These feelings may be rooted in our own fears of blindness. Think of the last time the lights in your house or apartment went out because of a power failure. You no doubt suddenly felt a sense of helplessness. We tend to forget that the blind have usually had the opportunity to adjust to their condition and to learn how to live with it.

One major means of achieving independence is to hold a worthwhile job. Unfortunately, surveys show that only about one-third of working-age blind adults are employed (Pfouts and Nixon, 1982). In addition, many of those who are employed are overtrained for the jobs they have. The ability to live independently is a major factor in determining how well the blind person will do in the job market. Things that we take for granted because we are sighted must be taught to the blind. Besides travel, which we have

---

FOCUS

TO HELP OR NOT TO HELP, AND HOW BEST TO DO SO IF THE ANSWER IS YES

At some time or another we have all encountered a blind individual who looks as though he or she might need some aid. Some of us have probably hesitated, not knowing whether an offer of help would be taken as rude. There are two relatively common mistakes you should try to avoid in this kind of situation:

1. Unless the person is in immediate danger, do not impulsively rush to his or her aid. Stop and watch the individual for a minute or two and see whether or not help is needed.
2. If you decide assistance might be needed, be sure to *ask* the person if he or she needs help. As any blind person will testify, there is nothing quite as aggravating as being suddenly manhandled by a stranger. If the visually impaired person declines help, do not persist in your efforts. Assuming there is no immediate danger and that the person is old enough to judge whether aid is required, there is little point in arguing. Visually impaired people are fully capable of making their own decisions. We tend to forget that such people are constantly faced with their disability and know best how much help they need.

There are times, of course, when assistance is appreciated. Even the best blind travelers will get into situations where help is needed. If you are called upon to serve as a sighted guide, here are some points you should keep in mind. Your first tendency will probably be to hold the arm of the blind person. In fact, the opposite is the correct way of aiding the blind person. The blind individual holds your arm just above the elbow and walks about a half step behind you.

If you become confused in your efforts to help, remember that the person you are assisting is undoubtedly used to such lack of expertise. Relax. In our anxiety not to lead him or her into the path of an onrushing auto or a low overhanging sign, we have a tendency to forget that we can ask the person we are guiding whether or not our efforts are a help or a hindrance. Talk to the person; he or she can tell you what you are doing right or wrong.

already considered, imagine how much more difficult it would be for you to do the following if you had limited or no sight: laundry, grocery shopping, finding the right clothes in the morning, and preparing a meal. We can easily appreciate the need for training in independence for the visually impaired. Today, visually impaired adolescents are being trained in those skills that will allow them to function independently in society.

One other area that has received a great deal more attention than previously is sex education. It is interesting to note, in talking with older blind people, how often they mention that they felt as they were growing up that they were not given the appropriate degree of information regarding sexual matters, particularly anatomy. Stop and think of how much we learn about sex through the sense of sight. The best method of teaching human sexuality to the visually impaired is a matter of considerable debate. The fact that some have suggested the use of live human models whose bodies can be explored gives some idea of why there has been so much controversy. No matter what the method of instruction, the fact remains that sex education for the visually impaired deserves more attention than it has been given so far.

TECHNOLOGICAL ADVANCES

Today's visually impaired child is likely to be exposed to a variety of electronic devices. This new technology can be classified into two broad categories, depending on the particular function of the equipment involved. Some devices are for use with academic-type tasks such as reading, writing, and math; some are for use as mobility aids.

DEVICES FOR USE ON ACADEMIC-TYPE TASKS

One of the first of the special technological devices for the blind was the Optacon. The **Optacon** converts individual letters of print into information that is delivered to the fingers by vibrating pins. The Optacon's major disadvantage is that one cannot

The Kurzweil Reading Machine converts print into speech. Here a student places his book face down on the Kurzweil scanner and hears it being read by an electronic voice. Kurzweil Computer Products, Martin L. Scheider/Associates.

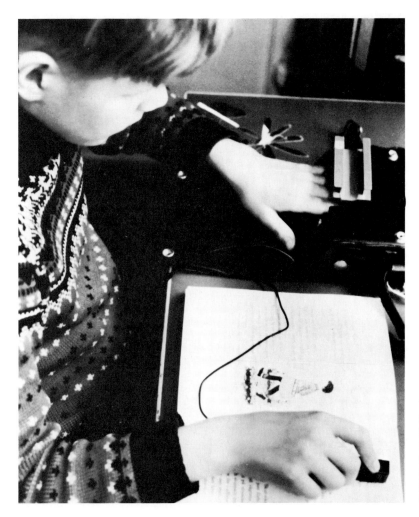

The Optacon, made by Telesensory Systems, Inc., helps the blind read printed material by converting individual letters of print into information that is delivered to the fingers by vibrating pins. Courtesy, Telesensory Systems.

"read" very fast with it. It does, however, allow the person to read a variety of different materials, such as newspapers and magazines, as well as books.

Although the Optacon was, and still is, an amazing piece of machinery, it is being overshadowed by an even more sophisticated device—the **Kurzweil Reading Machine,** which converts print into speech. If printed material is placed face down on the Kurzweil scanner, the person will hear it being "read" by an electronic voice. The Kurzweil, unlike the Optacon, allows the person to read at least as fast as human speech.

Paperless Braille recorders are among the most recent innovations for the blind. Two commercially available paperless Braille recorders are the Microbrailler and Versabraille. These instruments encode Braille onto tape and provide a readout in Braille. One of the major advantages of the Microbrailler and Versabraille systems is that they are tremendous space savers. As Ashcroft and Bourgeois (1980) point out, an 800-page novel requires approximately seven Braille volumes, each one of which is about 11 × 13 × 2 inches. Using a paperless Braille system requires only about four ordinary tape

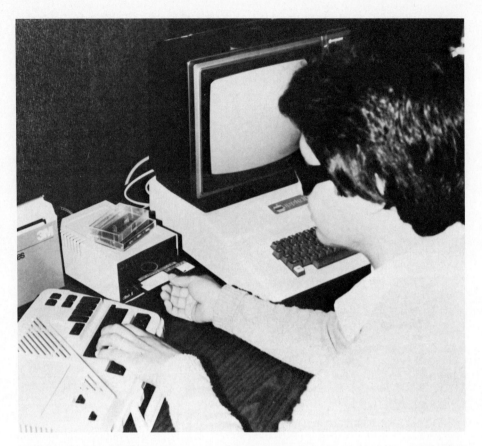

VersaBraille turns braille into electronic impulses and records them on ordinary cassette tape. It plays tapes back in Braille and also converts materials from computers into Braille. Printers, modems (phone couplers), talking terminals, teletypers, word processors, electronic mail—these are some of the electronic devices which can be used with VersaBraille, made by Telesensory Systems, Inc. Courtesy, Telesensory Systems.

cassettes to store the same novel. In addition, these machines can be connected to other devices, thus opening up a variety of employment opportunities for the blind. For example, they can be hooked up to an IBM typewriter so that a blind secretary can read his or her own typing in Braille. In addition, a sighted typist who does not know Braille can type on the typewriter and the result will automatically be stored as Braille.

DEVICES FOR USE IN MOBILITY

A number of highly sophisticated electronic mobility aids are now being produced. Although most of them are still undergoing further refinement, they can be of great benefit to the blind traveler. Two examples are the laser cane and Sonic glasses. The

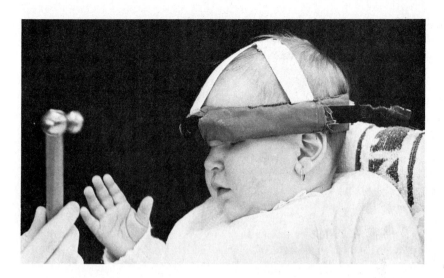

A blind baby, with the help of an ultrasonic device worn on the head, learns to locate an object held by an adult. T. Bower, New Scientist, February 3, 1977. Ric Gemmel for *New Scientist,* London. This first appeared in *New Scientist,* London, the weekly review of science and technology.

laser cane can be used like the long cane, or as a sensing device to detect objects in the environment. Used as a sensing device, it emits beams of light that are converted into sounds when they strike objects in the person's path. **Sonic glasses** operate on the principle that human beings, like bats, can learn to locate objects by means of echoes. Sonic glasses send out ultrasonic sound (sound that can't be heard) which bounces back off objects and is then converted into audible sound. The person can determine the distance of objects by the pitch of the echo that is sent back.

If these developments are not amazing enough, consider the work of Dr. Tom Bower of the University of Edinburgh, Scotland (Bower, 1977). Bower has been working on developing the **Sonicguide,** a device for use by blind infants. As can be seen in the above figure, the device is worn on the head. It emits ultrasonic sound which then bounces back off objects like an echo and is converted into audible sound. The infant learns about objects in the environment by hearing three different characteristics of the sound: (1) Pitch indicates distance of the object—the higher the pitch, the farther away the object. (2) Loudness indicates size—the louder the sound, the bigger the object. (3) Clarity of sound indicates texture—the fuzzier the sound, the softer the object. Here is an example of a "lesson" using the Sonicguide:

> A favorite activity was to talk to the child from a distance of three feet, then slowly move in and kiss the child, maintaining verbal contact. As the child learned to stand, the parent would kneel about four feet away and wave an arm, while the teacher encouraged the child to "Find mommy/daddy." Reaching without prior object contact was also encouraged, as well as tracking a moving object, playing peek-a-boo, trailing, paralleling walls, hiding behind curtains. . . . (Ferrell, 1980, p. 213)

The Sonicguide is still experimental. Research that has been done on it indicates that not all babies benefit from its use. One important factor is the age at which it is introduced. In general, the earlier the better (Aitken and Bower, 1982; Ferrell, 1980). If the baby is already more than a year old, its effectiveness is diminished.

A NOTE OF CAUTION

Although devices such as the Kurzweil Reading Machine, Sonic glasses, and the Sonicguide have already begun to revolutionize special educators' approaches to the visually impaired, some cautions are in order. Since we all want these devices to reduce the handicaps imposed by blindness, it is easy for us to be overly optimistic about their value. But although these breakthroughs are truly astounding technological achievements, they do not cure all the problems visual impairment presents. Most of these devices, particularly those for mobility, are still in the developmental stages. Many "bugs" need to be worked out. Strelow (1982) has perhaps best stated the reason why these mobility devices have not proved to be cure-alls. He points out that the development of these machines for the blind came because the devices were already being developed for other purposes. For example, many of the mobility devices for the blind are spinoffs of research on naval sonar and the scientific study of bats:

> In other words, rather than a situation in which blind users, or some expert who speaks for them collectively, say "Here is what we need. Have you anything to meet this specification?", it is one in which designers say, "Here is what we have. Can you use it?" (p. 241)

Nevertheless, many of these devices are already benefiting the visually impaired. Future discoveries and refinements will undoubtedly produce even greater changes in how we go about educating them. Today's special educators must keep abreast of these advances in order to be of the greatest service to their students.

ANSWERS TO FREQUENTLY ASKED QUESTIONS
VISUAL IMPAIRMENT

1. The concerns you've raised are not at all uncommon. First, what many people don't realize is that the term "legally blind" is not a precise one. Legal blindness is determined by how poorly one does when asked to "read" the letters on a Snellen chart, the chart you've seen in physicians' offices. The cutoff on this chart for legal blindness is such that only a small percentage of those who are classified as legally blind cannot see anything at all. In addition, there's a great deal of variability in how well people who are legally blind can use the sight they have remaining. It's not all that unusual for a legally blind person not to use Braille.

Second, although we can't assure you from the information you've provided that Brian won't have any mobility problems, there's no reason to expect that mobility is going to be difficult for him. Don't worry about his not having a guide dog. They're actually inappropriate for children, because the normal pace of the dog is faster than that of a child. If his needs are being attended to, Brian should be receiving (or should have received) instruction from someone trained in mobility and orientation instruction. You will undoubtedly need to give Brian a ''tour'' of your classroom and the building at the beginning (or, preferably, before) the school year. In addition, you might also want to assign him to a child who can act as his guide for the first few weeks of school. As he becomes used to the building and the routine, he will become more and more independent.

We don't want to leave you with the impression that Brian will not require special attention on your part. He undoubtedly will. How much depends a great deal on his attitude and skills as well as the attitude and skills of those around him, especially his itinerant teacher and you. Working as a team, the three of you should be able to create a good learning environment for Brian.

2. There's no assurance, from what you say, that Karen isn't retarded. However, neither is there any reason to suspect that she is. It's actually a myth that the blind automatically develop an extra sense. With lots of practice, they can learn to take advantage of echoes that result when they walk. They learn to listen for subtle changes in these echoes to indicate obstacles in their path. In the case of Karen, the reason she doesn't have this ability is simple—her deafness prevents her from being able to learn this skill. Even if she could, however, we should point out that the ability to detect obstacles is not all that useful to the blind. It is merely one aid. Environmental noises such as wind and traffic can make it useless. In addition, you have to be walking at a fairly slow speed in order to be able to stop in time if something is in your way.

3. Yes and no. In one sense, it is quite natural for both the baby and the mother to react differently toward each other because of the blindness. It would be very normal for your daughter to feel depressed and for this to affect how she interacts with her baby. Even if she isn't depressed, her natural reaction might be to act less responsive toward the child because he is acting less responsive toward her. As parents we rely a great deal on such things as cooing, smiling, and eye contact to make us feel good about being a mother or father. If a baby doesn't do that, it's more difficult for us at first to enjoy the child and to feel competent as parents. Research shows that blind babies are slower to coo and smile and may never make appropriate eye contact.

On the other hand, your daughter should be encouraged to stimulate Jeffrey as much as possible through the other senses, such as hearing and touch. There's reason to believe that the vicious circle between her and Jeffrey can and should be broken. Because she is the adult, it is up to your daughter to initiate a change in the way she interacts with Jeffrey. Our society tends to have a touch taboo of sorts. If she can overcome this, she'll probably discover that fondling and cuddling Jeffrey can be a pleasurable experience for her and for Jeffrey.

4. Although we obviously can't testify to the accuracy of your son's diagnosis, we can assure you that such a diagnosis is not at all uncommon. There is such a thing as ''lazy eye,'' and if left untreated it can develop into something serious, possibly even resulting in blindness. A lazy eye occurs when one of the eyes does not look at what we want it to look at, but instead drifts inward toward the nose or outward toward the ear. It is a muscular problem. With proper treatment, the problem is relatively easy to correct. A common treatment for lazy eye is patching the stronger of the two eyes so that the ''lazy'' one has to work harder.

5. It sounds as though you have already done the most logical thing. Observe your friend and judge whether she needs help. If it looks as though she might need aid, ask her if she would like you to provide assistance. It may be that she is quite satisfied with her mobility, or it may be that she would appreciate some assistance, especially when work lets out and everyone is rushing out of the building.

6. First, be ready to spend extra time with both the student and the resource or itinerant teacher who will be assigned to the child. The special education teacher should have a number of suggestions for you. Although not all of the following may be necessary, be prepared to:

a. Give the student extra time for assignments and tests. It will take longer for her to read and write in Braille. Although it would certainly be helpful if you learned some Braille, it isn't necessary. The itinerant teacher should provide help in having materials prepared for her in Braille and having her Braille translated into print for you.

b. Read her exams to her or record them on tape.

c. Say aloud whatever you write on the chalkboard.

d. Have other students in the class serve as notetakers for the blind student. They can make carbons of any notes they take.

SUMMARY

The education of the visually impaired today is very different from what it was even twenty years ago. New approaches and techniques—and new technology—are giving the visually impaired much better chances of leading full, independent lives.

The term visually impaired covers two broad classifications—the blind and the partially sighted. It also includes two kinds of definition, the legal and the educational. But no matter what definition or classification is used, visual impairment is one of the least prevalent handicaps in the American population, especially among children.

The first screening for visual problems is usually done in school by tests of visual acuity such as the Snellen chart or the Jaeger chart, and by teacher observation of certain behaviors and symptoms. Most visual impairment is caused by refraction errors in the eye. The results—nearsightedness, farsightedness, astigmatism, and cataracts, are usually easily corrected. Impairment from muscular or biological causes sometimes requires long and specialized medical treatment. Conditions such as strabismus (lazy eye) and glaucoma can result in blindness if left untreated.

But the severity of the visual impairment does not automatically predict the person's ability to learn or to function. Much depends on age at onset of the condition and degree of impairment, as well as proper training for mobility and the attitudes of the person and of those around him or her.

Intellectual ability is generally not affected by visual impairment, and physical difficulties in learning can be overcome by training in the other senses through which information about the environment can be gained: touch, smell, and hearing. Techniques to teach spatial ability can increase mobility and therefore access to education. Academic problems are usually caused by the slower rate at which the visually impaired can acquire and process information. Social adjustment problems, although the evidence is not yet clear, seem to come more from society's reaction to the impairment than from the impairment itself.

Educational programs for the visually impaired today use information from psychological research and electronic technology as well as teaching techniques to help the visually impaired to become independent adults leading lives as close to those of the sighted as possible. There are infant and preschool programs, both home- and school-based, to begin the learning and training process. Elementary school programs focus on four areas: use of Braille, use of remaining sight, listening skills, and mobility training. Secondary and postsecondary programs are concentrated on encouraging independence through training in living and vocational skills.

All these educational efforts are supported by many new electronic devices, such as the Optacon, the Kurzweil Reading Machine, paperless Braille recorders, the laser cane, sonic glasses, and the Sonicguide. The devices, many of which are still experimental, do not solve all problems. But they are revolutionizing the way special educators approach the teaching of the visually impaired.

REFERENCES

AITKEN, S., & BOWER, T.G.R. The use of Sonicguide in infancy. *Journal of Visual Impairment and Blindness*, 1982, *76*, 91–100.

ALS, H., TRONICK, E., & BRAZELTON, T.B. Stages of early behavioral organization: The study of a sighted infant and a blind infant in interaction with their mothers. In T.M. Field, S. Goldberg, D. Stern, and A.M. Sostek (Eds.). *High risk infants and children: Adult and peer interactions.* New York: Academic Press, 1980.

ANDERSON, D.W., & OLSON, M.R. Word meaning among congenitally blind children. *Journal of Visual Impairment and Blindness*, 1981, *75*, 165–168.

ASHCROFT, S.C., & BOURGEOIS, M.S. Recent technological developments for the visually impaired: State of the art. *Journal of Special Education Technology*, 1980, *3*, 5–10.

BANCROFT, N.R., & BENDINELLI, L. Listening comprehension of compressed, accelerated and normal speech by the visually handicapped. *Journal of Visual Impairment and Blindness*, 1982, *76*, 235–237.

BARTAS, G. *His divine weekes and workes*, 1598. J. Sylvester (trans.). London: Humfrey Lownes, 1605.

BATEMAN, B.D. The modifiability of sighted adults' perceptions of blind children's abilities. *New Outlook for the Blind*, 1964, *58*, 133–135.

BATEMAN, B.D. Reading and psycholinguistic processes of partially seeing children. *Research Bulletin: American Foundation for the Blind*, 1965, No. 8.

BERLA, E.P. Tactile scanning and memory for a spatial display by blind students. *Journal of Special Education*, 1981, *15*, 341–350.

BERLA, E.P., BUTTERFIELD, L.H., & MURR, M.J. Tactual reading maps by blind students: A videomatic behavioral analysis. *Journal of Special Education*, 1976, *10*, 265–276.

BISCHOFF, R.W. Listening: A teachable skill for visually impaired persons. *Journal of Visual Impairment and Blindness*, 1979, *73*, 59–67.

BOWER, T.J.R. Blind babies see with their ears. *New Scientist*, 1977, *73*, 255–257.

CASEY, S.M. Cognitive mapping by the blind. *Journal of Visual Impairment and Blindness*, 1978, *72*, 297–301.

COOK-CLAMPERT, D. The development of self-concept in blind children. *Journal of Visual Impairment and Blindness*, 1981, *75*, 233–238.

DODDS, A.G., HOWARTH, C.I., & CARTER, D.C. The mental maps of the blind: The role of previous visual experience. *Journal of Visual Impairment and Blindness*, 1982, *76*, 5–12.

FERRELL, K.A. Can infants use the Sonicguide? Two years of experience of Project VIEW. *Journal of Visual Impairment and Blindness*, 1980, *74*, 209–220.

FLETCHER, J.F. Spatial representation in blind children. 1: Development compared to sighted children. *Journal of Visual Impairment and Blindness*, 1980, *74*, 381–385.

FLETCHER, J.F. Spatial representation in blind children. 3: Effects of individual differences. *Journal of Visual Impairment and Blindness*, 1981, *75*, 46–49.

FRAIBERG, S. *Insights from the blind.* New York: Basic Books, 1977.

FRAIBERG, S., SMITH, M., & ADELSON, E. An educational program for blind infants. *Journal of Special Education*, 1969, *3*, 121–139.

FRIEDMAN, J., & PASNAK, R. Accelerated acquisition of classification skills by blind children. *Developmental Psychology*, 1973, *9*, 333–337.

GOTTESMAN, M. Conservation development in blind children. *Child Development*, 1973, *44*, 824–827.

GOTTESMAN, M. Stage development of blind children: A Piagetian view. *New Outlook for the Blind*, 1976, *70*, 74–100.

GRIFFIN, H.C., & GERBER, P.J. Tactual development and its implications for the education of blind children. *Education of the Visually Handicapped*, 1982, *13*, 116–123.

HALL, A. Mental images and the cognitive development of the congenitally blind. *Journal of Visual Impairment and Blindness*, 1981, *75*, 281–285.

HAYES, S.P. Measuring the intelligence of the blind. In P.A. Zahl (Ed.). *Blindness*. Princeton, N.J.: Princeton University Press, 1950.

HILL, E.W., & PONDER, P. *Orientation and mobility techniques: A guide for practitioners*. New York: American Foundation for the Blind, 1976.

JONES, R., GOTTFRIED, N., & OWENS, A. The social distance of the exceptional: A study at the high school level. *Exceptional Children*, 1966, *32*, 551–556.

LOWENFELD, B. Psychological considerations. In B. Lowenfeld (Ed.). *The visually handicapped child in school*. New York: John Day, 1973.

LOWENFELD, B. Psychological problems of children with vision. In W.M. Cruickshank (Ed.). *Psychology of exceptional children and youth* (3rd ed.). Englewood Cliffs, N.J.: Prentice-Hall, 1971.

McGINNIS, A.R. Functional linguistic strategies of blind children. *Journal of Visual Impairment and Blindness*, 1981, *75*, 210–214.

MILLER, J. DAREDEVIL: Blind superhero—Affirmative action or negative image? *Journal of Visual Impairment and Blindness*, 1981 *75*, 341–343.

NOLAN, C.Y., & ASHCROFT, S.C. The visually handicapped. *Review of Educational Research*, 1969, *39*, 52–70.

PFOUTS, J.H., & NIXON, D.G. The reality of the dream: Present status of a sample of 98 totally blind adults. *Journal of Visual Impairment and Blindness*, 1982, *76*, 41–48.

RIESER, J.J., GURTH, D.A., & HILL, E.W. Mental processes mediating independent travel: Implications for orientation and mobility. *Journal of Visual Impairment and Blindness*, 1982, *76*, 213–218.

ROGOW, S.M. Developing play skills and communicative competence in multiply handicapped young people. *Journal of Visual Impairment and Blindness*, 1981, *75*, 197–202.

SCOTT, E.P. *Your visually impaired student: A guide for teachers*. Baltimore: University Park Press, 1982.

SPUNGIN, S.J. The future role of residential schools for visually handicapped children. *Journal of Visual Impairment and Blindness*, 1982, *76*, 229–233.

STEPHENS, B., & GRUBE, C. Development of Piagetian reasoning in congenitally blind children. *Journal of Visual Impairment and Blindness*, 1982, *76*, 133–143.

STRELOW, E.R. Sensory aids: Commercial versus research interests. *Journal of Visual Impairment and Blindness*, 1982, *76*, 241–243.

SUPPES, P. A survey of cognition in handicapped children. *Review of Educational Research*, 1974, *44*, 145–175.

TUTTLE, D. A comparison of three reading media for the blind: Braille, normal recording, and compressed speech. *Research Bulletin: American Foundation for the Blind*, 1974, *27*, 217–230.

WARREN, D.H. Visual impairments. In J.M. Kauffman & D.P. Hallahan (Eds.). *Handbook of special education*. Englewood Cliffs, N.J.: Prentice-Hall, 1981.

WEINBERG, N., & SANTANA, R. "Comic books": Champions of disabled stereotype. *Rehabilitation and Literature*, November-December, 1978, *39*, 327–331.

WILLIS, D.H. *A study of the relationship between visual acuity, reading mode, and school systems for blind students—1976.* Louisville, Ky.: American Printing House for the Blind, 1976.

WORMSLEY, D.P. Hand movement training in Braille reading. *Journal of Visual Impairment*, 1981, *75*, 327–331.

PHYSICAL
DISABILITIES
8

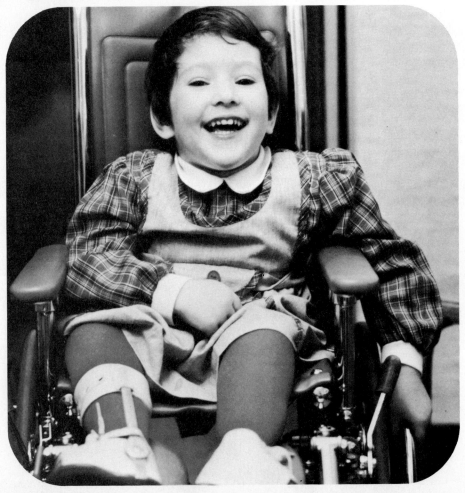

1. Will there ever be a cure for cerebral palsy?

2. Some authors, I've noticed, discuss teenage pregnancy as a type of physical disability. Personally, I think that's sort of strange. How can anyone consider being pregnant a physical disability?

3. A lot of the physically disabled people I've seen seem to me not to be very "with it." In fact, I think a lot of them might be retarded. Is the IQ of most physically disabled people lower than average?

4. I've heard that federal laws now require all parts of all public buildings, including schools, to be accessible to the physically handicapped. Is that actually true?

5. I get the impression that before long physical disabilities won't really be disabilities as we know them today. New medical and surgical techniques and new developments in artificial body parts will make it possible for almost every "disabled" person to look and act like everyone else. Is that just a dream, or could it really happen?

Barriers—things that keep us apart from others or block our achievement of goals—are familiar to all of us. Exceptional individuals, however, are confronted by barriers most of us seldom experience. The barriers faced by the physically disabled person are particularly difficult—they are educational, occupational, legal, personal, and spatial (Bowe, 1978). All these barriers to self-realization and personal fulfillment are important in any disability, but the barrier of others' attitudes is perhaps the most important consideration for the physically disabled.

You may have tried to imagine what it is like to be disabled. For most of us, the prospect of being visibly different, so we cannot hide our disability under any circumstances, is the most frightening disability we can imagine. Not every physical disability is visible, and some visible disabilities are not obvious to the casual observer. Yet because physical disabilities tend to be among the most difficult to hide exceptionalities, we easily make the error of thinking that the physically disabled person is more different from us than like us. Our attitudes become barriers to accepting people who are physically different because our attention is drawn to their disabilities rather than to their abilities. Bowe (1978) points out that nondisabled peoples' attitudes toward the disabled, and disabled peoples' attitudes as well, are very diverse, but that "one central, tragically wrong assumption seems to pervade most of these attitudes: that disabled people are different from us more than they are like us, that their disabilities somehow set them apart from the rest of us" (p. 109).

Today, physically disabled people are set apart by fewer spatial barriers than in the past. Laws and court decisions have removed many of the educational, occupational, and legal barriers that formerly blocked their paths. Nevertheless, life is still far from free for a physically disabled person in our society.

To get a better idea of how some things have changed and other things have not changed, let's listen in on a hypothetical conversation between two people confined to wheelchairs. Ed is a 15-year-old with spina bifida, a birth defect in which the spinal cord may be damaged (sometimes meaning that the individual has no use of his or her legs), and Sally is a middle-aged counselor who lost the use of her legs when her spinal cord was injured in a car accident when she was in junior high school. Their conversation begins in a hallway of the rehabilitation center where Sally provides counseling for young people who come there, as Ed has, for evaluation and rehabilitation.

Ed: Bet I can beat you to your office!

Sally: Who cares? I'm not your P.E. teacher, you know. What's on your mind today . . . besides speed?

Ed: Hey, listen, I told you I'm not doing any drugs. I know a lot of kids who are, but I'm not.

Sally: Did I say anything about drugs? I was referring to your chair.

Ed: Oh, yeah. This is a new racing chair they're letting me try out. It's made of this experimental material that's super lightweight. And these levers I push to turn the wheels are a lot more efficient than the hand rims you have. I can really torque it up. I just wish they'd let me keep it. Man, I tell you I'd clean up at the Special Olympics if they'd let me race this chair!

Sally: You seem to be awfully interested in competition.

Ed: I guess I am. But I really don't get to compete that much. When I'm here, I can do lots of sports and things, but at home the schools don't provide much activity for kids in wheelchairs. Small town. People who don't understand. Know what I mean?

Sally: Yes, I know.

Ed: Here, I always have something exciting to do. Next week I'm going to the beach with a new "beach buggy" chair some guy in rehab engineering invented. It's got big, fat tires on it instead of thin wheels, and you can take it just about anywhere. It's got a really long wheelbase to help you keep from getting stuck. They told me I could even go right into the ocean with it. Just think of that! Crash! This big wave breaks over me, and I'm just sittin' there in that chair! They tell me the chair will actually float because of the air in the tires.

Sally: You're making me jealous. In high school, when everyone else was going to beach week, I couldn't go. There was no way for me to get on the beach in my wheelchair, much less in the water.

Ed: How was it for you in high school? I mean, did you go to a regular high school like I do?

Sally: Don't I wish I had! No, I went to a special school for the physically handicapped. When I was in high school in the early 1950s, most people just assumed that a kid in a wheelchair didn't belong in a regular high school. Besides, if I had been able to go to our high school, I wouldn't have been able to get to many of the classes or use the bathrooms.

Ed: Well, at least I can get around to all the classrooms and use the bathrooms at school. That's really no problem. But what's frustrating is that people don't seem to think of me as just another kid, only one who can't walk.

Sally: Tell me what you're talking about.

Ed: Oh, you know. Like the P.E. teacher, Mr. Rich. If he had his way, all I'd ever do is archery and darts. He doesn't want me to play pingpong because he's afraid I'll hurt myself by running into the edge of the table or something, or back my wheelchair over another kid's toes. And the athletic director doesn't want me on the basketball court. She's afraid my wheels will ruin the floor. Then there's the principal. Last month I went to a dance at school. I was having a great time because I was out on the floor moving my chair around to the music and some other kids were starting to dance with me. He came out and made a big scene and told us to stop because he couldn't be responsible if my chair tipped over or somebody tripped and got hurt.

Sally: The other kids . . . how do you feel about them?

Ed: They're all nice to me, really. They're OK. They try to include me in things, and they don't always assume I can't or shouldn't do things like the teachers do.

Sally: Do you have any special friends? Is there someone who is your best friend?

Ed: No, not really. I get along fine with everybody.

Sally: Why do you think that's so? Why do you get along fine with everybody but don't have any really special friends, and no best friend?

Ed: I don't know. I wish I knew.

Sally: Lots of people are afraid to get too close to someone who is disabled, Ed. They know they want to be compassionate and help us, and they can see that in most ways we are just like them. But they get hung up on the way we're different. Our difference scares them because they don't understand it. And they're afraid to overlook it completely because if they did, they wouldn't be like everybody else. Then they'd be different too.

Ed: Maybe. All I know is I don't have any real buddies and I can't ask any girls to go out with me. I don't really have anybody to go out with.

Sally: It's tough. Really tough. I remember my own high school days. In some ways, attitudes haven't really changed much in the past 30 years.

Ed: So maybe someday I'll meet a kid who isn't afraid to accept me for just what I am.

Sally: I'm certain you will. But remember one thing about that. Acceptance is a two-way street. Someone who doesn't let your disability affect the way he feels about you—or she feels about you—is just about as unusual as someone in a wheelchair. It might not be so easy for you to accept them, either. I can tell you, it's sort of scary to believe that's the way they really feel, because you want so much not to be let down or disappointed. It's hard not to be afraid of being hurt. It's hard not to play it safe and keep your distance emotionally.

TODAY'S DEFINITION OF PHYSICAL DISABILITY

When special educators speak of the **physically disabled,** they are referring to children and youth who have a physical impairment (other than a visual or hearing impairment) that interferes with school attendance or learning to such an extent that special services are required. The disability or impairment handicaps the child or youth educationally. Such disabilities may be present at birth or acquired later. They may be caused by genetic defects, injury, disease, or unknown factors. The physically disabled child or youth may have other handicaps (for example, mental retardation) or be gifted or talented. The feature that defines a physically disabled child for special education purposes is a problem of health or a lack of bodily function that puts the child at a significant disadvantage at school.

The specific physical disabilities that may require special education are extremely varied (see Verhaaren and Connor, 1981a). We will not attempt to list them all; in the section of this chapter on characteristics, we will describe just three categories of disability—neurological impairments, musculoskeletal conditions, and other defects and disorders—and give a few examples of each.

PREVALENCE

Government estimates of the percentage of children needing special education because of physical disabilities range from 0.2 to 1.5 percent (General Accounting Office, 1980). About half the children included in this category have cerebral palsy or some other crippling condition; and about half have chronic health problems or diseases of some kind that interfere with their education.

Getting precise estimates of the number of children who have particular disabilities is not as easy as you might imagine. Some disabling conditions, such as cerebral palsy, range from severe to mild. Some of the mild cases may go unidentified, especially if the child receives very poor health care. Other conditions, such as arthritis or asthma, tend not to be constant. Screening at a particular time is likely to miss some children because they are not having an episode of the disability. Furthermore, a particular child's condition may be considered disabling or handicapping by one physician or special educator and within the normal range by another. So the estimated number of children and youth thought to be physically disabled varies considerably, depending on the source you consult.

ASSESSMENT

Two major considerations must be kept in mind in assessing the physically disabled: (1) Assessment must be done by a team of specialists representing a variety of disciplines, and (2) the focus of assessment must be on the individual's abilities rather than on the disabilities.

FOCUS

RETHINKING WHEELCHAIRS

A rehabilitation engineer works with disabled persons as a colleague of physicians, physical therapists, and other specialists. Colin McLaurin is the engineering director of the Rehabilitation Engineering Center at the University of Virginia. He and his colleagues have given special attention to the problems of wheelchair users and have come up with some designs that show special promise. Recently, a graduate student in special education at the University of Virginia asked McLaurin about some of the new developments.

Q: Could you tell me a little about the all-terrain wheelchair I've read about in the newspaper?

McLaurin: We started on it about four years ago when the director of a wildlife refuge on the Eastern Shore of Virginia told us he was concerned about people in wheelchairs having access to the beach. Of course, if you get an ordinary wheelchair on sand it's completely hopeless. So we got some of these big fat tires—all-terrain tires—and built a model. We took it to one of the staff members of the refuge who is a paraplegic (has paralyzed legs) and he tried it out. With a few changes in the original design, we found it worked pretty well.

Q: It's being used now?

McLaurin: It's been used every summer for several years now by a class of marine biologists who are disabled. They've had a lot of fun with it, and they actually go into the water with it as well as use it on the beach and in the swamps and so on. That has been a good experience for us as far as design is concerned. We learned about how bearings corrode and things like that. We also made it so that you can take it apart and put it in the trunk of a car easily. In addition, we have an option on wheels. Instead of the fat tires that are used on sand, we can put on wheels that are more like big bicycle tires—stump jumpers, I think they call them.

Q: Has there been much interest in what you've designed?

McLaurin: We've had more response to this than anything else we've done—hundreds of letters from all over from people who want one. So it showed us there's a big need for recreational vehicles for people in wheelchairs.

Q: Can every disabled person use it?

McLaurin: Almost anybody, not quite everybody. If they have good use of their arms, they can propel it themselves. If they don't, then somebody can push them. Most people off the beaten track won't be alone. The all-terrain chair can be pushed, and it also has handles so it can be pulled like a sulkie. Farmers, I think, would have use for it, too, because the ordinary wheelchair isn't very good in the fields and around the barn. But farmers, if they have good use of their arms, are going in for these three-wheeled Honda motorcycles that can be modified.

Q: You're working on a stowaway wheelchair. What's that?

McLaurin: Disabled people and those who work in the field of rehabilitation are concerned about someone in a wheelchair not being able to get to the washroom on long flights. So we designed a chair that can be stowed in a small space on an airliner and that is small enough to be maneuvered up and down the aisle of an airliner in flight.

Q: What do you see in the way of future innovations or different designs for the wheelchair?

McLaurin: One of our biggest concerns is function. We want to make them light, strong, and efficient to operate. We've been testing various models for efficiency now for about four years. We make changes in the seating position and the type of handrims and gear ratios and things like that. The ordinary wheelchair is only about 5 percent efficient, so you're wasting a lot of energy. A good bicycle rider is about 20 to 25 percent efficient. By using levers instead of handrims, we're getting up to around 15 percent efficiency. That's pretty exciting, I think, that you can triple your performance in a wheelchair just by making some mechanical innovations!

Rehabilitation engineers are redesigning wheelchairs for use in off-the-street recreational and work environments. These all-terrain wheelchairs allow disabled persons to engage in work and play that formerly were difficult or impossible for them. Rehabilitation Medical Center, Information Services, University of Virginia.

Besides special educators, the team of professionals assessing a physically disabled student often consists of physicians, physical therapists, occupational therapists, speech-language therapists, social workers, psychologists, counselors, and others who specialize in the design or construction of artificial body parts or equipment that help the person function more normally (see Focus). Not every case will require all the specialties we just mentioned, though some will. However, without the close cooperation of all the disciplines relevant to a student's disability, important aspects of his or her problems and abilities are likely to be overlooked. Together, the disciplines involved in assessment and treatment will be concerned with achieving three aims: (1) education—teaching the child skills that will make life as normal as possible; (2) prevention—keeping any further disabilities or deformities from developing if at all possible; and (3) correction—reducing disabilities or deformities as much as possible (Verhaaren and Connor, 1981b).

Developing an individual education plan for a physically disabled student requires not only information about the nature of the physical problem and how it may affect ability to perform at school, but also careful assessment of what the student can do. Assessment of intelligence, academic performance under optimal conditions, and ability to perform everyday functions (walking, dressing, eating, and using the toilet, for example) is required. Information regarding the student's attitude toward the disability and the support provided by family members will be important in determining realistic goals and objectives. The emphasis must be on the abilities that have not been affected by the disability, on developing intact abilities to the maximum extent possible, and on alternative ways of performing tasks with which the disability interferes.

CAUSES OF PHYSICAL DISABILITIES

The causes of physical disabilities are numerous and varied. As we mentioned previously, some defects are **congenital**—children are born with them. Other defects are **adventitious**—individuals acquire them, through accident or disease, after they are born.

CONGENITAL DEFECTS

Many things can cause a child to be born with a physical defect. Some defects are caused by genetic factors, meaning that the child is destined to have a physical disability from the moment of conception. Muscular dystrophy, for example, is a genetically transmitted disease in which the child's muscles become progressively weaker because the muscle fibers slowly degenerate. Although the symptoms of muscular dystrophy are not apparent at birth, the child is born with the problem. Some defects are congenital but not genetic. That is, something causes a defect in the fetus during its development. Spina bifida is a congenital defect that is the result of incomplete closure of the spinal column during fetal development.

The causes of many congenital defects are not known. Often it is known that certain factors *could* have caused the defect, but in a given case the cause is often impossible to pinpoint. Factors known to have caused or suspected of causing defects in unborn children include the following:

Viruses or bacteria that infected the mother during pregnancy

Exposure of the mother and fetus to radiation (such as X rays) during pregnancy

Drugs taken by the mother during pregnancy

Physical illness of the mother during pregnancy

Physical injury to the fetus

Malnutrition of the mother during pregnancy

Lack of sufficient oxygen to the mother and/or fetus

Alcohol consumed by the mother during pregnancy

The list of drugs, other chemicals, and viruses and bacteria that can cause birth defects is growing constantly.

ADVENTITIOUS DISABILITIES

After a child is born, disabilities can be acquired through a variety of diseases and accidents. Any disease that results in extremely high and prolonged fever or lack of sufficient oxygen to the brain can result in brain damage. Accidents resulting in trauma to the brain or damage to other parts of the body can, of course, cause disability. A variety of physical conditions in which an organ system of the body does not function properly may result in disability. In some cases, the cause of the organ dysfunction is not known. For example, a child may have cancer that affects a particular organ system or may develop diabetes (lack of proper functioning of the pancreas) for unknown reasons.

HIGH-RISK SITUATIONS

Some circumstances carry a particularly high risk of a child being born with or acquiring a physical disability. The genetic makeup of one or both parents in some cases means that the child will probably or even certainly be born with a defect. Genetic counseling of prospective parents, particularly those from families in which there is a history of congenital defects, is an important factor in assessing the risk of having a defective child.

When the mother is a teenager or over the age of 39, the chances that the child will be defective are considerably higher than when the mother is in her late twenties or early thirties. Teenage pregnancy is a serious problem not only because of risk that the baby will be defective, but also because of risk to the health of the mother. The younger the teenager who is pregnant, the greater the risk to both mother and child. Furthermore, teenage mothers are more likely than mothers over 20 to be abusive toward or neglect their babies. And the teenage mother is not likely to finish high school (see Nye, 1977; Scales, 1978).

Child abuse is a serious cause of adventitious physical disabilities. At least one of every 100 children in the United States under the age of 18 is seriously abused or neglected (*Children Today*, 1982, p. 27). Neglect and abuse take a variety of forms and include failing to provide adequate nourishment, leaving young children unattended for long periods, sexually abusing children, beating and burning children and inflicting other cruelties. As a result of such treatment, hundreds of children are killed and many thousands are left scarred, crippled, or unable to learn. Contrary to popular belief, adolescents are abused and neglected more often than preschool children. And although parents who are poor more often abuse or neglect their children than parents who are well off financially, abuse and neglect of children are found at every economic level and in all social classes.

CHARACTERISTICS

The physically disabled all have one obvious characteristic: a physical condition that interferes with normal functioning. But beyond that single common feature, we cannot describe a "typical" physically disabled person. The physically disabled may vary in intelligence from profoundly mentally retarded to intellectually gifted and in achievement from completely obscure to eminent. No particular type of personality is associated with physical disability (Lewandowski and Cruickshank, 1980; Newman, 1980). The reactions of parents, siblings, teachers, peers, and the public to an individual's physical disability are critical for the development of the disabled child's emotional and behavioral characteristics, just as they are for the nondisabled child (Bigge and O'Donnell, 1977; Verhaaren and Connor, 1981a). Research has not linked most types of disability to depression or suicide (Bryan and Herjanic, 1980). However, teenage mothers attempt suicide several times more frequently than teenagers who do not have children (Nye, 1977).

We do not want to give you the impression that physical disabilities do not cause psychological problems for children. Learning to live with limitations, especially if they are severe, permanent, and acquired after a period of normal development, is not easy for a child or a family. Coping with pain and confronting the prospect of increasing disability or early death is not easy for children or adults. Being separated from parents during hospitalization and being subjected to medical procedures are bound to cause a child considerable anxiety. Clearly, physical disabilities are laced with emotional stress and full of possibilities for psychological disorders. Sensitive and skillful intervention is called for on the part of all who work with the physically disabled child and his or her family.

Disabled persons often make a good psychological adjustment to their physical limitations and learn to make maximum use of their remaining abilities. Frequently, they are able to offer significant psychological help to others who are similarly disabled. Consider the example provided by 10-year-old Michael Eades, who became quadriplegic after his spinal cord was injured (see Focus).

FOCUS

PARALYZED BOY BECOMES ROLE MODEL

A paralyzed 10-year-old Bristol boy who relies on a respirator to breathe has been given the chance to be a hero.

For months, home for Michael Eades has been a brightly decorated University of Virginia Hospital room stocked with toys, games and autographed pictures of the Virginia basketball team.

But now he has a roommate, a younger boy in a similar condition. And doctors hope the younger boy can learn from Michael that life goes on.

They say Michael enjoys being a role model for his "little brother." For instance, even though he is so paralyzed that he has to operate his computer with his chin, Michael can score 71,000 points on Pac-Man.

Michael's story hits close to home for many University students who were involved in fundraising events organized last year to help offset some of the boy's medical costs.

Last month, 5-year-old Jonathan "Jon-Jon" Magpie joined Michael in his room. Jon-Jon arrived from Children's Hospital in Washington, D.C., where he was brought following a June 1981 auto accident which left him with a paralysis nearly identical to Michael's.

Michael was left a quadriplegic when two cars struck him as he played on a Bristol street three years ago.

Jon-Jon underwent the same operation Dr. Stanton P. Nolan, a thoracic surgeon at the hospital, performed on Michael. The operation installed a phrenic nerve pacemaker.

It is anticipated that Jon-Jon's pacemaker will enable him to breathe without the help of a respirator for up to 16 hours a day. Nolan placed a pacemaker above one of Jon-Jon's lungs last month and installed a second pacemaker above the other lung several weeks ago.

The two-part operation was only the second of its kind performed at the University, and one of only several hundred performed in the country, according to Dr. John W. Hoyt, director of the Surgical Intensive Care Unit (SICU).

Like Michael, Jon-Jon's neck was broken so high that the nerves which stimulate the diaphragm—and trigger breathing—were permanently damaged. The phrenic nerve pacemaker works like a heart pacemaker, with electrodes triggering the diaphragm's movement by taking over for the damaged nerves.

"Michael has been very excited about Jon-Jon's arrival and he knows he's going to be a big brother to Jon-Jon," Hoyt said.

Hoyt expects both boys to benefit from the experience of rooming together because "Jon-Jon will see how independent Michael is, and it will give him some role model to go towards. I think it will benefit Michael just to see someone else whom he can help and serve as a role model to," Hoyt said.

Much of Michael's independence is due to getting his wheelchair last summer, a wheelchair modified for him at the University's Rehabilitation Engineering Center. Another factor is a recreational and educational computer, which he operates with a mouthstick or his chin.

"The wheelchair has made him more extroverted," Hoyt said.

"There's no reason Michael couldn't grow up to become a computer operator and programmer," Hoyt added.

From United Press International Wire Service, Monday, January 24, 1983.

Because physical disabilities and the psychological and behavioral characteristics of students who have them are so different, we will describe three major categories of physical disability: (1) neurological impairments, (2) musculoskeletal conditions, and (3) other defects and disorders. We will discuss nonphysical characteristics only if the disorder is clearly associated with certain psychological or behavioral features.

NEUROLOGICAL IMPAIRMENTS

Neurological impairments involve damage to or dysfunction of the brain, spinal cord, or nerves that supply muscles and other organs. The most common and serious impairments are those in which there is damage to the central nervous system (the brain or spinal cord).

BRAIN DAMAGE. Damage to the brain can cause a variety of disabilities, including impairment of the ability to hear, see, speak, or control muscles. It may also cause mental retardation. Sometimes the nerve cells in a part of the brain show an abnormal discharge of electricity, either because of known damage or for some unknown reason. The abnormal discharge is called a **seizure,** and it sends the person into a convulsion in which muscles twitch and jerk uncontrollably.

When the brain is damaged before, during, or shortly after birth and the ability to control muscles is impaired, the condition is called **cerebral palsy.** Cerebral palsy, or CP, may result in the weakness of or inability voluntarily to control the muscles of any part of the body. When both legs are weakened or paralyzed, the condition is known as **paraplegia.** Quadriplegia means there is paralysis or weakness of both arms and both legs. Other technical terms are used to refer to involvement of one limb or one side of the body. The most common effect of CP is **spasticity,** which is the term for involuntary contraction and tight, jerky motion when the person tries to use the muscles. Athetosis and other technical terms are used to refer to different types of awkwardness and poor coordination associated with brain damage.

Cerebral palsy is a multiple disability. Very seldom is difficulty in controlling muscles the only symptom of the brain damage. Typically the child has additional disabilities, such as mental retardation, impaired vision or hearing, seizures, or speech and language problems (Cruickshank, 1976). Children with CP usually have many educational problems. However, you should remember that CP can range from very severe to very mild in its effects. Furthermore, severe impairment of muscle control does not always

Geri Jewell, a comedian who has cerebral palsy, has overcome many of the limitations associated with her disability. Her work is helping to change attitudes toward the physically disabled. © 1981 Daniel H. Birman.

mean the child's intelligence is impaired. Some individuals with CP are highly intelligent, even though they are severely crippled. Areas of the brain involving muscle control may be damaged, while those having to do with the ability to think are left undamaged. One example of someone who has cerebral palsy but is highly intelligent and talented is Geri Jewell. Her wit and charm, and her candid descriptions of what it is like to have CP, have delighted audiences and given many of us a better understanding of what it is like to be a disabled person in our society (see Focus).

Not all damage to the brain results in a physical disability. Furthermore, some physical disabilities resulting from brain damage are not considered cerebral palsy. If the brain is damaged when the child is older than 6, then any resulting disability is not usually called cerebral palsy. However, a child who suffers brain damage after the age of 6 may show symptoms very similar to those shown by a child who is said to have CP.

People who have seizures may or may not have brain damage that can be identified. More important is the fact that they may or may not have *recurrent* seizures. If a person has recurrent seizures, he or she is said to have **epilepsy.** Only about 0.5 to 1.0 percent of Americans have epilepsy, but about 8 percent can expect to have at least one seizure at some time during their lives. If a person has epilepsy, it is likely that the seizures will begin before 2 years of age or in old age. In fact, few people have a seizure after they become adults but before they reach old age, unless they have epilepsy (Hauser and Kurland, 1975).

Seizures can be caused by high fever, drugs or poisons, or other trauma to the brain. In most cases, however, the cause of the abnormal discharge in the brain is unknown. Sometimes seizures can be set off by certain stimuli, such as flashing lights. Fortunately, the seizures of most people who have epilepsy can be controlled by medication.

Seizures may take a variety of forms. Those in which the person typically falls, loses consciousness, and goes through a period of involuntary movements are known as **grand mal seizures.** Grand mal seizures may last for several minutes or longer and may be accompanied by loss of bowel or bladder control, drooling, unusual noises, and other effects. **Petit mal seizures** (sometimes called **absence seizures**) are typically very brief (a second to a half minute in duration). Petit mal seizures are a clouding or lapse in consciousness in which the afflicted individuals suddenly stop doing whatever they are doing for a short time and then resume their activities. During their "absences" they may stare, blink, or twitch slightly. Such seizures can occur very frequently (sometimes 100 or more times a day). Other types of seizures, all of which are comparatively rare, may result in specific involuntary movements and/or sensations.

Seizures can be very frightening to people who do not understand them. There are many misconceptions about seizures and epilepsy, and it is important to educate the public about them. The person who has a seizure typically is not harmed by it, and epilepsy is not "catching" in any way. Neither an isolated seizure nor epilepsy is a sign of impaired intelligence. Most people who have epilepsy are completely normal between seizures, and often they can be completely free of seizures with proper medication. Although severely retarded children and those with other severe developmental disabilities tend to have seizures more frequently (due to the frequency with which they have suffered brain damage), the seizures do not have educational implications. The teacher must be aware of them and of techniques for their management, and give the child ample opportunity to respond to educational tasks that may have been missed during attacks.

CEREBRAL PALSY CANNOT CRIPPLE THIS YOUNG COMIC'S WIT OR WILL

FOCUS

On TV, where even the newsmen and women are supposed to be physically flawless, Geri Jewell is a stunning anomaly. She walks with a lurch and a shuffle, has difficulty hearing and sometimes slurs her speech. Like 700,000 other Americans, Jewell suffers from cerebral palsy, a condition caused by brain injury and resulting in spastic movement and other disorders. Yet for Geri, who may have suffered prenatal brain damage when her mother jumped off a porch to avoid an out-of-control car, CP has not been an insurmountable obstacle. After two years of college, she launched a career as a stand-up comic at L.A.'s Comedy Store in 1978, using her own handicap as a source of material. Spotted by producer Norman Lear, she made her debut last season in the Lear sitcom *The Facts of Life*. Off-camera, Jewell, whose mother is a mail carrier and whose father is a hotel security chief, drives her own car and lives by herself in a one-bedroom home in Toluca Lake, California.

I've spent many frustrating years dealing with people who don't know how to deal with me. I don't have epilepsy or muscular dystrophy or multiple sclerosis. I was born prematurely with cerebral palsy. Although some people become CP victims because of an accident during delivery, you don't necessarily get it at birth. It just means your head was injured in some manner and the motor part of the brain damaged.

When I was little, my palsy was severe. My parents taped a spoon to my hand, sandbagged my arm to eliminate the shaking and let me try to feed myself. Naturally, I'd throw every other spoonful over my shoulder, so my parents, my two brothers and my sister would sit at one end of the table and put me down at the other end where the dog would stand behind me, waiting for his dinner. They'd do this for about 15 or 20 minutes every meal before they'd feed me, so I had to work for that food.

I got used to having neighborhood kids make fun of me, walk and talk like me, and ape my movements. God, it was tough. They used to think I was mentally retarded, and I had to live with that. Once when I was about 9 I went to my speech therapist and burst into tears. I told her I wanted a pair of canes, those metal crutches with arm braces, and she asked why. I said if I had those canes, then people would know my problems were physical and that I wasn't mentally retarded. I wanted to look like I had cerebral palsy so people would understand.

I knew that I was different, but oddly enough, I didn't see my handicap the way other people did. Even now, the only time I see it is when I'm walking toward a glass door or see my reflection in a mirror, because in my own mind I don't look like that. Also, I developed a sense of humor about myself. I was a clown. My parents never told my brothers and sister not to laugh at me, so they'd laugh and say, "Oh, look, Geri just spilled her third glass of milk." I learned to play to the audience real young, and many times I'd deliberately spill my milk to get their reaction.

In high school I went through my first experience with self-pity. I thought I'd be as popular as I had been in my special ed classes for the handicapped. I expected to go out with the quarterback. I expected to go to the prom and the parties and the football games, but it didn't happen. Also, it didn't help that my younger sister was extremely popular and strikingly beautiful. A lot of the guys in my class would sit next to me only to talk about Gloria. I became emotionally hungry for a friend, and if I did make one, I'd hold on too tightly. I used to be so afraid of offending, and I'd apologize for everything.

Source: G. Jewell, Cerebral palsy cannot cripple this young comic's wit or will. *People Weekly*, February 8, 1982, pp. 111–113.

SPINAL CORD INJURY. If the spinal cord is seriously injured or severed, impulses from the brain cannot reach the nerves that supply the muscles below the injury, and weakness or paralysis is the result. Spinal cord injury can result from direct trauma (as when the spine is broken in a fall or car wreck), disease, or malformations of the spine.

Poliomyelitis (or polio, an infectious viral disease) was a common cause of paralysis until an effective vaccine was invented in the mid-1950s. Accidents in which the spine is injured are now the most common cause of spinal cord injury. The most common congenital condition is spina bifida. **Spina bifida** means that the bones of the spine did not close completely at the midline of the body during fetal development. In some cases of spina bifida, the spinal cord or part of it protrudes from the opening in the spine into a tumorlike sac on the child's back. When the spinal cord protrudes into such a sac, the deformity is called a **myelomeningocele.**

The myelomeningocele may be located anywhere between the child's head and the lower end of the spine, though it is usually located in the lower back. Nerve impulses are partially or completely blocked at the point of the myelomeningocele, resulting in weakness or total paralysis of muscles below that point. The child may be unable to use his or her legs or control bladder and bowel. The fact that the spinal cord protrudes through the spine means that a myelomeningocele also contains spinal fluid. Often there are complications such as hydrocephalus (an enlargement of the head caused by excessive pressure of the cerebrospinal fluid—see Chapter 2).

A baby born with spina bifida usually undergoes surgery very early in life to correct the defect as much as possible. With proper medical treatment, most children with spina bifida do not develop complications that cause mental retardation or hydrocephalus. Usually the child can use braces, crutches, or a wheelchair to get about and can attend regular public school classes. Frequently, the greatest problems for the school are the child's lack of bowel or bladder control.

Some children with spinal cord injury require clean intermittent catheterization (CIC), a simple procedure in which a tube is used to drain the bladder. The issues of who should perform this procedure, where it should be done in the school, and who should pay for the cost have sometimes been difficult to resolve. However, the U.S. Department of Education has determined that CIC is a related service (under PL 94–142) to which children who need it are entitled at no cost to the parents.

OTHER TYPES OF NERVE DAMAGE. Diseases and hereditary conditions of various kinds can damage nerves and cause physical disabilities. Multiple sclerosis (MS) is one of the better known diseases of this type, although its cause remains a mystery. MS is a slow, progressive hardening or scarring of the protective covering of nerve fibers. The course of the disease is unpredictable, and the symptoms are extremely varied. It may produce muscle weakness, spasticity, speech difficulties, visual impairments, and other problems. Usually, it affects people in their late teens or early adulthood, and does not affect intelligence.

MUSCULOSKELETAL CONDITIONS

Some children are disabled by diseases or other conditions that affect their muscles or bones. As a result, they may have difficulty walking, standing, using their hands, and so on. The conditions may affect their legs, arms, joints, or spine. Some of the conditions are congenital and some are adventitious. They may involve genetic defects, diseases, accidents, or developmental disorders with unknown causes.

Two of the most common musculoskeletal conditions affecting children and youth are muscular dystrophy and arthritis. **Muscular dystrophy** is a hereditary disease characterized by progressive weakness caused by wasting away of the muscle fibers. The biological reasons for muscular dystrophy are not understood, and there is no cure for the condition. In some forms of the disease the child appears to be healthy and strong, but fatty tissue has actually replaced the muscle fibers. One form of the disease affects only boys. Its symptoms are usually detected about the time the child is learning to walk. By the time the child reaches adolescence, he usually is confined to a wheelchair, and he is not likely to live beyond early adulthood.

Contrary to what many people think, **arthritis** is not a problem only for older people. About 8 in 10,000 children under the age of 17 have arthritis (U.S. Department of Health, Education and Welfare, 1974). Girls more often have arthritis than boys, and the symptoms may range from mild to severe. Inflammation and pain in muscles and around the joints is the main problem, although complications such as eye infections, fever, and heart problems sometimes occur. The disease can be severely crippling. Arthritis tends to be episodic, sometimes getting better and sometimes worse, often for unknown reasons. The causes are not known.

OTHER DEFECTS AND DISORDERS

A wide variety of physical disabilities besides the ones we have mentioned so far can be present at birth or acquired during childhood or adolescence. Some children are born with missing or deformed limbs, faces, or internal organs. Diseases and disorders affecting respiration, digestion, kidney function, or circulation may require medical intervention, hospitalization, and special education. In the case of any physical disability, the objective of special education is primarily to make the child's experience of school as normal as possible and to help the child achieve the highest possible level of self-sufficiency and academic proficiency.

TODAY'S EDUCATIONAL METHODS

In the past, the common practice was to keep physically disabled children at home or send them to special schools to segregate them from nonhandicapped children. Today, most children with physical disabilities attend regular public school classes unless their condition requires medical treatment or therapy for which they must be confined to the home, a hospital, a clinic, or a rehabilitation center. Then, if their condition permits, they are taught in that confined setting by a visiting, itinerant, or hospital teacher and other specialists until they are able to return to regular classes. Sometimes the student may spend part or most of the day in a regular class and the rest of the day in a special class for children with orthopedic problems or other disabilities. Some children with multiple handicaps that include severe physical disabilities spend the entire school day in a special class in a public school, or attend a special day school or institutional school.

For some children with physical disabilities, special equipment is required for their effective and therapeutic participation in classroom activities. Here, children are using standing tables that allow them to get out of their wheelchairs, use their legs for support, and work at a regular table. Ken Karp.

Regular class attendance has been made the norm for physically handicapped children and youth because of the requirements of Public Law 94–142 and the Rehabilitation Act of 1973, advances in medical and rehabilitation technology, removal of physical barriers, and gradual changes in professional and public attitudes. School buildings now must be planned to accommodate students confined to wheelchairs and to meet the needs of other handicapped students (Bednar, 1981).

Unless the child has other handicaps, educational goals and curriculum should be the same as for a nonhandicapped student. However, additional training in mobility, daily living skills, and/or career skills may be required. That is, rehabilitation training may be necessary to allow the student to be as independent as possible and to prepare for a normal, self-sufficient adult life. A physical therapist may be needed to evaluate the child's physical capacities and limitations and to plan a therapy program that will prevent, minimize, or correct physical deformities and build strength, mobility, and general health. An occupational therapist may be needed to plan a program of instruction in daily living skills (eating, dressing, cooking, using the telephone, and other activities essential to achieving independence).

Specialists may be needed to design and build artificial limbs, braces, or other equipment that will help the disabled individual function more normally. Social workers and psychologists are often needed to help the child and the family deal with the stresses of disability and treatment and to continue the treatment and education programs after they have been initiated. Speech-language therapists are often required to help the child learn to communicate effectively. Specialists in adaptive physical education must plan a program of activity designed to help the student make maximum use of

Animals are increasingly being used for therapeutic purposes with the disabled. Handling and caring for animals has psychological benefits for many people, and horseback riding can help correct some of the physical problems that accompany certain neurological and musculoskeletal conditions. Top right and bottom photos by D. Grogan, U.Va./CRC. From *Smithsonian Magazine,* July 1981. Top left photo by Eugene Richards, Magnum Photos, Inc.

MORE THAN "MAN'S BEST FRIEND"

Only recently have professionals who work with handicapped individuals begun to observe the special therapeutic effects that interaction with animals can have. Patricia Curtis, who writes mainly about animals, noted the benefits animals can provide for physically disabled children. Her observations were made at Children's Memorial Hospital in Chicago, where pet animals are welcome.

Children in bathrobes trot up and down the halls, are pushed in wheelchairs or carried about by parents. They lie in beds, bandaged, in traction, surrounded by toys. A blond toddler reels about the floor of his room with his toys, cheerfully dragging a long cord by which he is attached to a machine that keeps him alive. A six-year-old strolls by wearing a baseball cap that keeps falling over his eyes. ("Some of the children in chemotherapy lose their hair, so they are given caps to wear," someone explains.)

Even though many of the children are very sick or badly injured, almost all are eager to hold the pets. A beautiful child in pigtails sees us in the hall and her eyes grow wide. Her mother props her up. The little girl cannot speak and lacks motor control of her arms, but she manages to draw Miss Anderson's hand close to her face so she can nuzzle a kitten.

A quadriplegic boy of about 12 is asked if he would like to see a dog. "Yep," he whispers. The pup's warm body is held against the boy's cheek. He smiles.

A wisp of a child attached to bottles and machines lies in her mother's lap in another room. Quietly we ask the mother if the child would like to pet a kitten. We are abashed in the presence of so much pain. But the child smiles, raises her hand to run it over the kitten.

Source: P. Curtis, Animals are good for the handicapped, perhaps all of us. *Smithsonian*, July 1981, 48–57.

whatever physical abilities he or she has for recreational purposes (Adams, 1981; Winnick, 1982).

Physical disabilities tend to interfere with children's educational progress in two ways. First, they often keep children from having certain educational experiences, such as outdoor play and travel. Second, they may prevent children from manipulating educational materials the way nondisabled children can. A special education teacher and the other professionals involved must seek ways to make the child's experience as normal as possible and to devise efficient alternative ways for the disabled child to respond to educational tasks.

One example of recent efforts to normalize the experiences of physically disabled children is the introduction of animal pets in hospitals and treatment centers (see Focus). Until recently, few people recognized the value of animals in therapy for the disabled. As a volunteer hospital worker put it:

When we first got permission to bring pets here, some of the doctors and nurses disapproved. . . . They envisioned mess, noise, germs, all sorts of problems. Now, they welcome us because the pets do the kids so much good. (Curtis, 1981, p. 52)

New technologies are opening up an increasing number of alternative ways for disabled students to respond to educational tasks. Most important are those technologies having to do with communication (see also Chapters 1 and 5). Computer technology, particularly, holds great promise for allowing the physically disabled to achieve their full educational potential. Aside from the new technologies, however, the teacher of physically disabled students must be aware of simple, inexpensive, reliable adaptations of materials and equipment that make them usable by the handicapped (Verhaaren and Connor, 1981b).

A child who has a weak grasp may be able to use a pencil if it is thrust through a sponge or rubber ball; a clipboard fastened to the desk may make it possible for a student who has difficulty stabilizing the paper to write. Creativity and ingenuity in analyzing problems and finding simple solutions are required.

Teachers of physically disabled children of any age must be prepared not only to deal with instruction in appropriate skills, but also to respond to the child's pain and emotional stress (Verhaaren and Connor, 1981a). They may need to learn how to teach children techniques for the management of pain and to deal intelligently and sensitively with fears of separation from parents, abandonment by friends, and death. Integration of the severely physically disabled into the mainstream of education means that more terminally ill children attend public schools. The teachers who work with them may need special training in managing their own as well as their students' attitudes toward death and dying (Shell, 1981).

EDUCATION IN THE HOME AND PRESCHOOL

For infants and preschoolers, the two most critical considerations are early identification and handling and positioning. Early identification of the child with cerebral palsy or other disability allows treatment to begin before the problem has caused needless deformity or loss of function. Early treatment increases the chance that the child will achieve the greatest possible degree of independence. Handling and positioning—how the child is picked up, held, and placed in relation to what he or she can see and manipulate—will make a great difference in how the child can use his or her body and learn about the environment. Correct handling and positioning will strengthen normal reflexes and encourage perception and exploration of the environment. The child should, as much

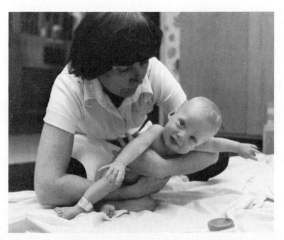

Early identification, handling, positioning, and physical therapy are extremely important for handicapped infants. How much progress the infant makes often depends on the extent to which parents carry out a program of stimulation and therapy at home. D. Grogan, U.Va./CRC.

as possible, be enabled to see, touch, mouth, and manipulate things the way nonhandicapped children do.

SPECIAL EDUCATION FOR THE ELEMENTARY SCHOOL CHILD

When the child enters school, emphasis should be placed on making the experience as normal as possible. The child's condition, abilities, and limitations should be explained to other children matter-of-factly. Pushing the child beyond his or her limitations must be avoided, but so must overprotection. If the child must be hospitalized or kept at home for a period of time, the teacher must make every effort to help the child keep up with academic work by sending assignments and materials to the parents, the hospital, or itinerant teacher.

SECONDARY AND POSTSECONDARY EDUCATION

Besides the usual academic concerns of high-schoolers, physically disabled adolescents and young adults have special concerns about social acceptance, sexuality, and career choices. Opportunities for social interaction with peers and for warm physical contact are important for the physically disabled adolescent. Depending on the student's past experience and typical behavior, instruction in social skills may be required. The physically handicapped need to be made aware that their own sexuality is acceptable and that they have the same rights to sexual expression and gratification as the nonhandicapped (Edmonson, 1980; Lewandowski and Cruickshank, 1980). For many disabled adolescents and young adults, dating is a frustrating and disappointing experience. One enterprising young woman recently started a dating service for the disabled (see Focus). The fact that she herself is mildly cerebral palsied illustrates the fact that the disabled are increasingly becoming advocates for themselves and demonstrating their abilities to manage their own lives.

Career choices for the physically disabled should be limited only by the individual's preferences and disabilities that preclude competent performance on the job. Career planning and placement requires careful assessment of the student's specific abilities and disabilities, motivation, preferences, and performance in a training program (Fonosch, Arany, Lee, and Loving, 1982; Ryan, 1979). The aims of secondary and postsecondary education should not be altered for a student simply because he or she has a physical disability. That is, the aims should be to allow students to pursue whatever courses of study interest them and in which they can perform successfully, and their study should prepare them to assume the duties, responsibilities, and freedoms of adult citizens.

Self-sufficiency and independence become focal concerns of adolescents and young adults with severe disabilities. Total self-sufficiency may not be a realistic goal for all severely disabled adults, but any technological advance or creative idea that lessens dependence on others represents hope. The most realistic first approach for most severely disabled individuals is the training offered by occupational and physical therapists. The use of animal assistants described in the Focus and the technological advances described in the next section can bring new independence to some people with severe physical limitations.

HANDICAPPED WOMAN STARTS DATING SERVICE FOR DISABLED

Cynthia Van Horne knows the sting of the "one-date" syndrome that often afflicts the social lives of the handicapped.

So Ms. Van Horne, who has a mild case of cerebral palsy that left one leg shorter than the other, is starting up a special dating service just for the disabled.

"My handicapped friends all say they've gone out with 50 people—once," said Ms. Van Horne, 28, a government office receptionist from nearby Mount Lebanon.

"It can be a real hassle to get dates," she said. "It's happened to me a few times. I thought, 'Good heavens, all I do is limp. If they treat me like that, what about people in wheelchairs?'"

Ms. Van Horne, who now has a steady boyfriend, said handicapped people who resort to traditional dating services are discriminated against.

"The dating services don't discriminate. But people go out one time and that's it. You know the reason has to be your disability. The date will say, 'I didn't know you were disabled,'" she said.

Ms. Van Horne and a friend, Karen Staver of Pittsburgh, are compiling a list of clients who will pay $30 for three months of "Specialized Dating Service," which has yet to prompt its first matchup.

"So far we've had 50 or 60 people contact us—mostly women—but we need more men before we distribute the list (of clients) to the people," said Ms. Van Horne.

Ms. Staver, who is not handicapped, thought up the idea, and Ms. Van Horne took it to local radio stations. The brisk interest in the service has come without the need for advertising.

Ms. Van Horne said some dating services charge $400, but the $30 fee was calculated based on "what handicapped people can afford." She said she hopes similar services spring up nationwide.

"I've never heard of one anywhere especially for disabled people," she said. "This is for just physically disabled people."

The service will be open to the overweight who feel "disabled for a normal dating life," or someone who is not disabled and would like to date a handicapped person, she said.

Ms. Van Horne said many social agencies help the handicapped in employment or other important areas but ignore "the social realm."

"Basically, disabled people are like everyone else and have the same attitudes and desires. I'd like people to start realizing that—to look past the disability to the person."

Source: From United Press International Wire Service, Friday, January 7, 1983.

MORE THAN "MAN'S BEST FRIEND"

Several years ago Dr. Mary Willard, who was working with the famous psychologist B. F. Skinner, started training Capuchin monkeys as personal assistants for quadriplegics. Capuchin monkeys are about a foot and a half tall, are fairly easy to train, and live as long as 30 years. They are the kind of monkeys typically associated with organ grinders. Dr. Willard thinks that Capuchins might become as valuable and well accepted as assistants for paralyzed people as guide dogs have become for the blind. The following excerpt from *The New Yorker* magazine highlights the problem of dependence faced by quadriplegics and their families, and illustrates some of the problems and potentials of Capuchin assistants.

Greg, the patient we were going to see, who is now eighteen, hurt himself two years ago diving into a river. The river at that point was much shallower than he expected—some companions, who had dived in close by, did not hit bottom and were not injured. For a time, the family coped, though with the greatest difficulty, with moving him around, even getting him to school—Greg has just graduated from high school—but it couldn't go on. "One of his brothers has been an invaluable help, and Greg's got an electric wheelchair that he can activate with his mouth," said the Doctor. "But, as you can perhaps imagine, it's pretty rough. It's very hard on all of them. After the accident, they decided they would have to move, and they did—from their two-story house to this one, where it's been possible to adapt a whole wing for Greg and his wheelchair. But his mother has never been able to get away. She once told me that for all those months she herself became a quadriplegic—that's what it amounted to. There are so many things a person needs all the time. They didn't have a great deal of money, so a nurse—that is, a human nurse—who could stand by all day was out of the question. We hope the capuchin will fill in on a lot of the little duties, and in many ways she already does, after about five weeks with the patient. She can fetch cold drinks from the refrigerator, for instance, and bring books. Greg is taking a computer course right now, and is studying hard. It would be wonderful if he could hold a job, and there is really no reason he can't."

Greg is a good-looking blond boy with a mustache. His brother, who was with him when their mother, Beverly, led us into Greg's room, looks remarkably like him. Willie, the monkey (female, in spite of her name), lives in a cage in one corner, but she was out and about when we entered. She immediately darted at Beverly's ankles.

"She's been developing that behavior only lately," said Dr. Willard. "Greg, you should give her a shock every time she does it. It won't take long to eradicate it."

"I know," said Greg. "But something's wrong with the handle here."

They studied the mechanism and discussed what was needed. We, too, looked at it, and at other electric fitments and levers that Greg can handle with his teeth. Among them is one that enables him to aim a laser light at whatever nearby object he needs—a book or a cup, say. What looks like a red spark shows the monkey what is wanted. Chirruping, trilling, and twittering, Willie leaped about the room. She exhibited her skills: following directions, she opened a little refrigerator door and brought Greg a plastic container of water, put a tube in the water and placed the tube's other end in his mouth; she brought him a book that he indicated with the red spark, and put in his mouth a mouthstick, tipped with rubber, with which he can turn pages; and, theoretically, she did these things while avoiding places marked with white stickers like the ones we had seen in Dr. Willard's office. She didn't accomplish all the tasks perfectly or at the first try.

"It takes a few weeks," said Dr. Willard, "but in time a genuine attachment develops—on both sides."

TECHNOLOGICAL ADVANCES

Recent technological developments are making great changes in the lives of physically disabled individuals. And disabled persons themselves are contributing to the design and testing of new technological devices. Some researchers and developers of new equipment now hire disabled persons to help design aids and devices that are reliable, flexible, comfortable, and simple to use.

Devices considered in the realm of science fiction only a few years ago are now realities:

Programmable robotlike arms, attached to worktables, that can be used for feeding, turning book pages, and providing access to a telephone or personal computer (Schneider, Schmeisser, and Seamone, 1981).

A device that reminds its user to take medications and calls for help if the user fails to respond within 5 minutes to the question "Are you OK?" (Rush, 1982).

Wheelchairs designed for use on the beach; others that can be controlled by humming or turning the head slightly (McLaurin, 1982; Myers, 1982; Stamp and McLaurin, 1982).

Miniature pumps used to regulate glucose and/or insulin levels in the blood of diabetics (Albisser and Spencer, 1982).

Electrical stimulation devices that provide exercise for the muscles of people who are paralyzed (Phillips, 1982).

All these devices have been built, but several are still in the experimental stage. That is, before these aids are manufactured and marketed, they must be carefully evaluated by engineers, as well as by those most likely to use them. Technology for the physically disabled applies to nearly every aspect of their lives. We will give you examples of recent developments in just two categories: aids for independent living, and techniques for making muscles work again.

AIDS FOR INDEPENDENT LIVING

Try to imagine what it would be like to rely on another person for almost every one of your needs. Just think of the number of times you move from one room to another, change your clothes, turn on your stereo or television, grasp a pencil and write, get a snack or drink, comb your hair, brush your teeth, turn the pages of a book, and so on. For some physically disabled persons, every one of these everyday tasks is an insurmountable obstacle. For every physically disabled person, every small increase in independence is highly valued. Anything that enables a person to control any part of the environment is a significant aid.

Environmental control systems do exactly what their name implies. They provide a means of control over one's environment. An environmental control system typically consists of a control switch, a control unit, and devices to be controlled (doors, TV, telephone, bed, personal computer, feeding device). Control switches can be operated in a number of ways, including very slight movements, breath control (sips and puffs), or muscle contractions. The Abilityphone™, a telephone-microprocessor system, is an example of an advanced environmental control system. Besides its communication features, the Abilityphone can control as many as 15 different lights or appliances. That is, it can be programmed to turn them on or off at specified times (Eifert, Griesemer, and Piekenbrock, 1981).

TECHNIQUES FOR MAKING MUSCLES WORK AGAIN

Electrical stimulation has been used in medical treatment for many years. Pacemakers are routinely implanted surgically to control the heart beats of heart attack victims by small pulses of electricity. Now scientists are experimenting with electrical stimulation of muscles in the legs and arms of people who have been paralyzed. Researchers at Rancho Los Amigos in California have investigated the use of implantable stimulators to correct weakness in muscles controlling the feet of patients who have suffered brain damage due to strokes. In Yugoslavia, braces with muscle stimulators attached to them have been used with persons who are paralyzed on one side of the body to improve their ability to walk normally (Vodovnik, Stanic, Kralj, Acimovic, Gracanin, Brobelnik, Suhel, Godec, and Plevnik, 1977).

At Case Western Reserve University, this type of stimulation has been used to increase hand function for quadriplegics. Instead of attaching electrodes to the skin, investigators at Case use a different technique. First, they insert needles through the skin. Electrodes attached to the needles are activated by a shoulder control switch. One of the participants in the study at Case is now able to hold a cup and grasp a pen for writing (Phillips, 1982). At Wright State University, computer-controlled electrical stimulation has allowed a young woman paralyzed from the ribs down to take her first, halting steps (see Focus).

These are just a few examples of the use of electrical stimulation for persons with paralyzed limbs. The closely monitored studies are still highly experimental. Huge harnesses and tangles of wires like those linking Nan Davis and the computer that controlled the stimulation of her muscles are not very practical for everyday use. Neither are the needles through the skin used to stimulate hand function in the experiments at Case University. Yet, with current interest and research into these techniques, who knows what might be developed in the next 20 years?

FOCUS

GIANT STEPS

Nan Davis, 22, hesitantly lifted her right leg a few inches above a laboratory floor in Ohio. She put her foot down jerkily and listed to the side, then recovered her balance. She raised her left leg, let it down, and paused. Guided by parallel bars and enmeshed in a tangle of wires, Davis had just taken the first two of six steps that carried her ten feet—and into scientific history. Davis, a student at Wright State University near Dayton, has been paralyzed from the ribs down ever since she injured her spine in a car accident the night she graduated from high school four years ago. Now she was moving her legs, however haltingly, entirely in response to electrical impulses from and to a computer—the first person ever to do so.

The heart of the miracle walker was a 2,000-command computer program masterminded by WSU bioengineer Jerrold Petrofsky (DISCOVER, July). Carefully modulated electrical signals delivered by electrodes to Davis's skin from the computer stimulated her leg muscles to contract, while—going beyond similar experiments elsewhere—sensors fed back continual information to the machine on the position of her ankles, knees, and hips. . . . When spinal injury blocks the brain's signals to the legs, the computer not only must supply substitute "messages" electrically; to assure smooth motion, it also must monitor the effects of those instructions.

For Petrofsky, Nan Davis's walk was the culmination of 13 years of experiments, during which he developed a computer-assisted, muscle-operated exerciser, wheelchair, and tricycle. "This is just another step," he says. The next one: to make the system portable. . . .

Petrofsky warns that without months of building up weakened muscles beforehand, computer walking could lead to broken bones and serious strain on the heart. Moreover, even when the apparatus becomes commercially available—at least a decade from now—it will be useful only to victims of spinal injury and stroke, not to those suffering from degeneration of leg nerves or leg muscles. Still, as many as 2 million patients in the United States alone could benefit from it.

Meanwhile, Nan Davis was happy just to be a little closer to her goal of walking again. "It was fantastic," she said. "After all, the body was made to walk."

Source: Discover Magazine © 1983, Time Inc.

Nan Davis, a paralyzed Wright State University student, is shown here walking under her own muscle power with computer assistance, in the biomedical engineering labs at Wright State University in Dayton, Ohio. University Communications/Wright State University.

ANSWERS TO FREQUENTLY ASKED QUESTIONS
PHYSICAL DISABILITIES

1. No, there will never be a "cure" for cerebral palsy. CP is not a disease in the usual sense of the word. It cannot be transmitted, and it never goes away. CP is damage to the brain that occurs before, during, or shortly after birth. The result of the brain damage is weakness or paralysis of certain muscles. Sometimes the brain damage also causes other disabilities, such as mental retardation or visual impairments. Although there is no way to repair the damage to the brain—and it is extremely unlikely that there ever will be—various therapies can help the individual to overcome some or all the disabilities caused by the brain damage, depending on how severe the damage is. Although CP cannot be "cured," we are finding more and more ways to lessen the disabilities it causes. Prevention of the conditions that are likely to result in brain damage and early identification of the child who has CP, so that effective therapies can begin while the child's brain and muscles are developing most rapidly, probably are the best we will ever be able to provide.

2. Being pregnant can be considered a temporary physical disability if it prevents a girl from participating in activities that are very important for her social-psychological welfare or if her physical health is endangered. Pregnancy very often has serious negative consequences for the social and psychological development of teenagers who have not finished high school. Furthermore, the younger the teenage mother, the greater the risk to her health. You must consider the implications for the baby, too. Teenagers are much more likely than women in their twenties to give birth to underweight babies (who are "at risk" for a variety of developmental problems), to have children with disabilities, and to be neglectful and abusive mothers. Thus, pregnancy of teenagers often results in physical disabilities for the young mother and for her baby; and the younger the mother, the greater the risk for both mother and child.

3. We don't know where you have observed physically disabled people, but we think you are probably the victim of some misconceptions. True, some physical disabilities are often accompanied by lower than average intelligence (cerebral palsy, for instance, because it is the result of brain damage). But most have absolutely nothing to do with intelligence. The range of intelligence among the physically disabled is as great as it is among the nondisabled. A casual observer may guess that a physically disabled person is not "with it" or may get a false impression of the person's intelligence because he or she feels threatened by the disability and/or simply does not understand how a person can demonstrate intelligence in spite of severe physical limitations.

4. No. Every public building, including every school, must be accessible to the handicapped, but not every part of every building must be accessible. The rule of thumb is that school programs and public functions and activities must be available to all, including those confined to wheelchairs. New buildings are to be designed to provide maximum accessibility and old buildings modified to yield enough accessibility to allow someone confined to a wheelchair to participate in public functions held in them.

5. We are constantly amazed by the technological developments that improve the ability of physically disabled persons to overcome limitations. But we are not of the opinion that all or nearly all physical disabilities will be eliminated through technological advances in the next 50 years. Some of the serious limiting factors in the application of technology to the elimination of disabilities are the cost and reliability of the innovations, and the severity and complexity of some disabilities. But perhaps we underestimate the rate of technological development and the commitment of our society to rehabilitation of the disabled. We hope we do.

SUMMARY

Today the physically disabled are set apart by fewer physical barriers than ever before; the barrier of others' attitudes, however, remains high. Friendships and relationships with other people remain difficult mostly because we often make the error of thinking the physically disabled are more different from us than like us.

Special educators define the physically disabled as children and youth who have a physical impairment (other than a visual or hearing impairment) that interferes with school attendance or learning to such an extent that special services are required. The specific physical disability that may require special education may be any of a number of conditions.

The federal government's estimates of the prevalence of physical disabilities requiring special education range from 0.2 to 1.5 percent of all children, about half of whom have cerebral palsy or some other crippling condition. Estimates are difficult because the conditions range from mild to severe, and because some tend to be episodic rather than constant.

Assessment of the physically disabled child must be done by a team of professionals, and the focus must be on abilities rather than disabilities. Developing an educational plan for a physically disabled child requires information about the nature of the disability and careful assessment of what the individual is able to do. The emphasis is on developing intact abilities and alternate ways of performing tasks with which the disability interferes.

The many causes of physical defects fall into two major categories: congenital defects (those with which children are born) and adventitious defects (those acquired after birth through accident or disease). Some congenital defects, such as muscular dystrophy, are genetically transmitted; others are the result of accident or injury to the fetus. Certain situations may cause a child to be at greater risk of a physical disability: a family genetic history of disability; a teenage mother or one who is over 39; and child abuse or neglect.

Beyond the physical disability, those who are handicapped in this way have no common or "typical" characteristics. They are, however, grouped into three categories by type of disability: neurological impairments, musculoskeletal conditions, and other defects and disorders. Neurological impairments involve damage to or dysfunction of the brain, spinal cord, or nerves that supply muscles and other organs, and include conditions such as cerebral palsy and various types of epilepsy, paralysis due to accident, spina bifida, and diseases such as multiple sclerosis. Two common musculoskeletal impairments are muscular dystrophy and arthritis.

Educational methods for the physically disabled are far different now from those of the past. Most such children attend regular public school classes instead of being segregated in special schools or kept at home. Regular class attendance has been fostered by PL 94–142 and the Rehabilitation Act of 1973, by advances in medical and rehabilitation technology, by removal of physical barriers, and by changes in professional and public attitudes. And unless a child has other handicaps, the goals of education for the physically disabled are the same as for the nonhandicapped. Programs often include additional training in mobility and daily living and/or career skills and involve health professionals as well as educators.

Two important goals are to make the child's experiences as like those of the nonhandicapped as possible and to provide alternate ways for a disabled child to fulfill educational tasks. Teachers of the physically disabled must also be sensitive to and learn to deal with the child's pain and emotional stress.

For infants and preschoolers, two critical factors are early identification and handling and positioning. When children enter school, the most important concern is making the experience as normal as possible. Physically disabled adolescents and young adults have special concerns about social interaction, sexuality, and independence in addition to the usual academic concerns.

The technological advances of recent years have played a large role in giving more of the physically disabled hope for greater independence. The disabled themselves work with researchers and developers of new equipment to help design aids and devices that are reliable, flexible, comfortable, and simple to use. Technology for the physically disabled applies to nearly every aspect of life. Two important areas in which significant advances have been made are aids for independent living, and electrical techniques for making muscles work again. Some devices and techniques are still in the experimental stages, but the promise for the future is bright.

REFERENCES

ADAMS, R.C. Adapted physical education. In J.M. Kauffman & D.P. Hallahan (Eds.). *Handbook of special education*. Englewood Cliffs, N.J.: Prentice-Hall, 1981.

ALBISSER, A.M., & SPENCER, W.J. Electronics for the diabetic. *IEEE Transactions on Biomedical Engineering*, 1982, 29, 239–248.

BEDNAR, M.J. Architectural planning for special education. In J.M. Kauffman & D.P. Hallahan (Eds.). *Handbook of special education*. Englewood Cliffs, N.J.: Prentice-Hall, 1981.

BIGGE, J., & O'DONNELL, P. *Teaching individuals with physical disabilities*. Columbus, Ohio: Charles E. Merrill, 1977.

BOWE, F. *Handicapping America: Barriers to disabled people*. New York: Harper & Row, 1978.

BRYAN, D.P., & HERJANIC, B. Depression and suicide among adolescents and young adults with selective handicapping conditions. *Exceptional Education Quarterly*, 1980, *1*, 57–66.

Children Today, January–February, 1982.

CRUICKSHANK, W.M. (Ed.). *Cerebral palsy: A developmental disability*. Syracuse, N.Y.: Syracuse University Press, 1976.

CURTIS, P. Animals are good for the handicapped, perhaps all of us. *Smithsonian*, July 1981, 48–57.

EDMONSON, B. Sociosexual education for the handicapped. *Exceptional Education Quarterly*, 1980, *1*(2), 67–76.

EIFERT, F., GRIESEMER, V., & PIEKENBROCK, L. Abilityphone terminal adapts to users. *Proceedings of the Johns Hopkins first national search for applications of personal computing to aid the handicapped*. Los Angeles: IEEE Computer Society, 1981.

FONOSCH, G.G., ARANY, J., LEE, A., & LOVING, S. Providing career planning and placement services for college students with disabilities. *Exceptional Education Quarterly*, 1982, *3*, 67–74.

GENERAL ACCOUNTING OFFICE. *Disparities still exist in who gets special education*. Report to the chairman, Subcommittee on Select Education, Committee on Education and Labor, House of Representatives of the United States, September 30, 1980. Gaithersburg, Md.: Author.

HAUSER, W.A., & KURLAND, L.T. The epidemiology of epilepsy in Rochester, Minnesota, 1935 through 1967. *Epilepsia*, 1975, *16*, 1–66.

LEWANDOWSKI, L.J., & CRUICKSHANK, W.M. Psychological development of crippled children and youth. In W.M. Cruickshank (Ed.). *Psychology of exceptional children and youth* (4th ed.). Englewood Cliffs, N.J.: Prentice-Hall, 1980.

McLAURIN, C.A. Wheelchairs: Technical design. *Engineering in Medicine and Biology Magazine*, 1982, *1*, 28–30.

MYERS, W. Personal computers aid the handicapped. *IEEE Micro*, 1982, *2*, 26–40.

NEWMAN, J. Psychological problems of children and youth with chronic medical disorders. In W.M. Cruickshank (Ed.). *Psychology of exceptional children and youth* (4th ed.). Englewood Cliffs, N.J.: Prentice-Hall, 1980.

NYE, F.I. School-age parenthood: Consequences for babies, mothers, fathers, grandfathers, and others. *Extension Bulletin 667*. Pullman: Washington State University Cooperative Extension Service, January 1977.

PHILLIPS, L. Increased function on the horizon through functional electrical stimulation. *Paraplegia News*, 1982, *36*, 26–28.

RUSH, W.L. The Abilityphone™. *Byte*, 1982, *7*, 240–46.

RYAN, P.A. Widening their horizons: A model career development program for severely physically disabled youth. *Rehabilitation Literature*, 1979, *40*, 72–74.

SCALES, P. *Teenage pregnancy—A selected bibliography*. Baltimore: Teen Project, National Organization for Non-Parents, August 1978.

SHELL, P.M. Straining the system: Serving low-incidence handicapped children in an urban setting. *Exceptional Education Quarterly*, 1981, *2*(2), 1–10.

SCHNEIDER, W., SCHMEISSER, G., & SEAMONE, W. A computer-based robotic arm/worktable system for the high-level quadriplegic. *Computer*, 1981, *14*, 41–47.

STAMP, W.F., & McLAURIN, C.A. *Wheelchair mobility: A summary of activities at the University of Virginia Rehabilitation Engineering Center 1976–1981*. Charlottesville, VA: University of Virginia, 1982.

U.S. Department of Health, Education and Welfare. *Prevalence of chronic skin and musculoskeletal conditions—United States 1969 vital and health statistics*, Series 10, No. 92, 1974.

Verhaaren, P., & Connor, F.P. Physical disabilities. In J.M. Kauffman & D.P. Hallahan (Eds.). *Handbook of special education*. Englewood Cliffs, N.J.: Prentice-Hall, 1981. (a)

Verhaaren, P., & Connor, F.P. Special adaptations necessitated by physical disabilities. In J.M. Kauffman & D.P. Hallahan (Eds.). *Handbook of special education*. Englewood Cliffs, N.J.: Prentice-Hall, 1981. (b)

Vodovnik, L., Stanic, U., Kralj, A., Acimovic, R., Gracanin, F., Brobelnik, S., Suhel, P., Godec, C., & Plevnik, S. Functional electrical stimulation in Ljubljana: Projects, problems, perspectives. In F.T. Hambrecht & J.B. Reswick (Eds.). *Functional electrical stimulation*. New York: Marcel Dekker, 1977.

Winnick, J.P. (Ed.). Adapted physical education. *Exceptional Education Quarterly*, 1982, *3*(1).

GIFTEDNESS
9

1. Two friends of ours recently married. Both are intellectually brilliant. Both come from families in which everyone is extremely intelligent and highly successful in a profession. Is it true that their children are certain to be gifted?

2. I have a friend here in the college who says he wants to work with gifted kids. He's not a good student now, and he wasn't a good student in high school either. Can people like him, who don't seem particularly bright themselves, be good teachers of the gifted?

3. My cousin and her husband have a 10-year-old child who is very, very bright but really obnoxious. The teachers are trying to get the parents to agree to placing the kid in a regular seventh grade. He's a fifth-grader now. But his parents don't want any part of that. They want him to have some sort of enrichment program that means he'll stay in fifth grade and go to some special classes or activities once or twice a week. They say the reason he's obnoxious is that he's one of the youngest kids in his class. Placing him two grades ahead would just make him more of a misfit, they feel. What should they do?

4. Steve, a 17-year-old who is dating our daughter, is really an incredible fellow. He's a junior at the university already. He's a chemistry major and apparently one of the best students the chemistry department has ever had. Obviously, he'll be going on to graduate school right away. According to our daughter, he's already made some sort of discovery chemical companies are interested in. What we're concerned about is that at the rate he's going, he'll burn himself out and be ready for retirement before he's 40. Is there any truth to the saying "early ripe, early rot?"

5. It's always seemed to me that this gifted education stuff is pure bunk. I don't understand why smart kids need something special. If they're really so smart, why do they need special help? Sure, we've got to recognize that these kids are smart, but that doesn't mean we have to treat them any differently. Why can't we just try to make schools better for everybody and forget all this nonsense about special education for the gifted and talented?

Special education has been regarded primarily as an effort to help children who do not have the ability to perform well in school. One goal of special education is to help handicapped children perform more like the average nonhandicapped child. In recent years, federal law has required that priority be given to handicapped students who have been excluded from school and to those students who are least able to achieve at school—the most severely handicapped. Quite predictably, education of the gifted and talented has gotten lost in the federal priorities. Education of the gifted and talented is designed to help the best students perform better. It is inconsistent with the idea that the purpose of special education is to help children get closer to the average in their school performance.

Fortunately, special education does not mean *only* helping those students who are below average. It can be interpreted to mean making special provisions for any child who is markedly different from the average, even if this difference is positive or desirable. As long as special education is guided by the philosophy that every exceptional child (not just every handicapped child) is entitled to an appropriate education, education of the gifted and talented will have a place in the special education profession and its literature.

Compared to education of the handicapped, education of the gifted and talented is a small enterprise. It is not mandated by federal law or funded by the federal government. The amount of money spent for it is extremely small compared to that spent on education of the handicapped, and there are few teacher training programs. Nevertheless, progress is being made, primarily at the state level, in giving the most capable students in our schools an education appropriate for their abilities.

The University of Virginia is fortunate to have a special summer enrichment program for gifted and talented students directed by a leader in special education for such children, Professor Carolyn M. Callahan. In a recent interview, one of our doctoral students in special education asked Callahan about what is happening today in this area.

Q: You've been able to observe changes in the past 10 years in how gifted and talented kids are treated in schools. How is education for these students different today from what it was in the past?

Callahan: I think there are four major differences. First, gifted education is oriented more toward benefiting the children involved rather than solving all the ills of society. People are recognizing that gifted children have a right to an appropriate education, and this is probably an outgrowth of the general special education movement in this country. Second, gifted education has expanded to include not only intellectually gifted children—those with high IQs—but also children who have gifts in specific areas. Third, more than one approach is being used to serve gifted children. Depending on their individual needs, they may be served in special schools, resource rooms, or cluster groups in their regular classrooms. For some kids, acceleration is most appropriate. Rather than debating the relative merits of enrichment and acceleration, people are examining multiple options to meet the needs of the individual gifted children. Finally, attention is being given to special populations within the gifted group. We are concerned about children who are, for example, female, handicapped, or from minority ethnic groups. We cannot claim to be serving all gifted children until we are meeting the needs of these special populations.

Q: What about different age groups? What about preschool gifted children? And what happens to these kids when they get to high school?

Callahan: Until three or four years ago, almost all gifted programs were limited to the fourth through eighth grades. Now, preschool and primary school gifted programs have become more widely accepted. In addition, there has been a big push to develop secondary gifted programs; many of the kids who've completed the fourth through eighth grade programs have found, upon entering junior and senior high school, that their classes no longer meet their needs. So students and their parents are demanding more appropriate services.

Q: I know parents of the handicapped have had a big influence on special education, but I haven't heard about parent action for the gifted.

Callahan: In the late 1950s and 1960s, in response to the launching of Sputnik, the Russian satellite, the federal government provided most of the impetus in the gifted movement. But that has been lost now. Today it is parents who are pushing for new programs for their children, and they've been aided in their efforts by local and state level support groups.

Q: I can imagine that some people react very negatively to pressure from parents or anyone else to make special provisions in public schools for students who are gifted and talented. How do you respond to the charge of "elitism" in gifted programs?

Callahan: The charge is primarily a result of mistakes that were made in the past in the name of gifted education. Numerous privileges were given to kids in the gifted programs. Besides that, we separated gifted kids from others and implied that they were "better." We weren't careful enough to tell them they were only better *at certain things*. Some of them apparently thought we felt they were better human beings than nongifted kids. The emphasis is now on using special education services to meet the individual needs of gifted students. The gifted don't necessarily need more or better resources; rather, they need *different* resources.

Q: Wait a minute. How can you have a special program without more and better resources? I don't understand.

Callahan: Well, it depends partly on how you define more and better. Often these kids just need access to programs or materials or instructional opportunities that are already available to older students or that can be provided by specially trained teachers or the community.

Q: You mean that one approach to programming is letting them make use of things that are already there in the public education system?

Callahan: To a large extent, yes.

Q: I hope that tactic will work. Where do you see gifted education going in the future?

Callahan: As with other educational services for exceptional children, gifted programs are being affected by limited financial resources. One consequence of the funding shortage involves direct services. Although more children may be identified as gifted, not all of them will receive all types of services or receive services all the time. Some may be identified as gifted in specific areas and be provided enrichment or acceleration only in those areas. In addition, more gifted students will be served in their regular classrooms, while their teachers cooperate more directly with special resource and itinerant teachers. Another change will be an increase in research and program evaluation. If gifted education is going to survive, we must make a commitment to extensive research. We are also seeing a growing interest in innovative programming at the state level. For instance, North Carolina—a leader in such programming—has established residential schools for the gifted, both in the fine arts and in science and math. In that state, support for the gifted and talented has not adversely affected the funding of education for the handicapped.

Q: You say that North Carolina is a leader. But I know you have an exciting summer program here at the University of Virginia. I'd like to hear about that.

Callahan: The UVA Summer Enrichment Program, which we started in 1980, consists of three two-week sessions each summer. It has two primary functions: to provide gifted children with a unique learning experience, and to train teachers to work with gifted students. Two hundred children in grades 5 through 10 are selected for each session from throughout the state of Virginia. The fifth- through eighth-graders are admitted on the basis of aptitude and achievement test scores or other evidence of outstanding achievement, expression of creativity, and high motivation. They're given the option of enrolling in classes in math, science, language and social studies, or fine arts. The ninth- and tenth-graders are required to submit proposals in which they identify a problem they would like to investigate at the university and devise a 10-day plan for pursuing their research. Each three-hour morning class of 17 to 18 students is supervised by a master teacher and an intern. Master teachers are selected on the basis of superior recommendations and experience with gifted children; interns are regular teachers who participate for college credit and experience. The teachers are responsible for developing curriculums that will provide their students with experiences they are not likely to have in school; they must therefore use their own skills as well as university resources. Early afternoon classes consist of one-hour presentations by university faculty members and students of research or information in their specialty areas. We take the kids to the labs and offices, and to local facilities such as the observatory and the nuclear reactor, to see demonstrations of ongoing research. Later in the afternoon, 90-minute seminars are taught by graduate students who are skilled in such diverse areas as water color painting, astronomy, medieval history, and computer science. In the evenings and on weekends, university student counselors arrange and supervise recreational activities. The students sleep in dormitory suites, with one counselor responsible for each group of eight kids.

Q: Sounds like a program that could be highly successful.

Callahan: It has been—for the kids and for the adults.

GIFTED AND TALENTED:
A DIFFERENT KIND OF CATEGORY

The quality of our lives is obviously improved by gifted and talented people. Stop for a moment to consider what your life would be like if there were no brilliant or exceptionally talented musicians, painters, athletes, writers, physicians, comedians, mathematicians, biologists . . . if your life did not include any of the exciting or useful performances or products of gifted and talented individuals. It is true that every person has intrinsic value and that handicapped individuals may enrich our lives. But it is also true that the quality of our lives is improved primarily by the discoveries, inventions, and creative performances of people who have demonstrated remarkable gifts or talents.

PUBLIC ATTITUDES

In spite of the fact that we owe a great deal to the gifted and talented for making our lives healthier, easier, longer, safer, and more interesting and exciting, American public education has done relatively little to encourage the development of such persons. In 1978, the United States Congress passed the Gifted and Talented Children's Act, in which it was stated that

> (1) The Nation's greatest resource for solving critical national problems in areas of national concern is its gifted and talented children,
>
> (2) unless the special abilities of gifted and talented children are developed during their elementary and secondary school years, their special potentials for assisting the Nation may be lost.

Even though the need for special education of the gifted and talented has been recognized, there is no federal law requiring appropriate education for them. The federal Office of Gifted and Talented, which was established in 1972, has been disbanded. Federal allocations of money for education of the gifted and talented have never been large. In the early 1980s, the federal budget for education of the gifted and talented was a very small fraction (about $\frac{1}{200}$) of the federal budget for education of the handicapped. Congress never did actually provide the full amount it authorized for educating the gifted (Lyon, 1981). Currently there are no federal funds designated for education of the gifted and talented; these funds are now part of block grants to the states for education. States may spend part of the money they receive for education of the gifted, but there is no requirement that they do so. State and local budgets for educating the gifted and talented also are very small in most cases. Today the prevailing attitude is that education of the gifted and talented is a state and local concern. And most states and localities are not concerned enough to give much emphasis to it, although interest in educating gifted and talented children seems to be increasing (Mitchell, 1982).

THE MAJOR DIFFERENCES

The category of gifted and talented is different from all other categories of exceptionality in three major ways:

1. Being gifted or talented is generally thought to be highly desirable.
2. Many different types of gifts and talents can be identified, yet the gifted and talented typically are considered as a single category.
3. No federal law requires free, appropriate public education for the gifted and talented.

These differences between the gifted and talented category and categories involving handicaps are important to your understanding of special education in today's schools. Therefore, we will explain each of them briefly.

BEING GIFTED OR TALENTED IS DESIRABLE. No one wants to be handicapped or disabled, but nearly everyone would like to be gifted or talented. Handicaps often stigmatize a person; special gifts or talents typically increase a person's attractiveness and social status. Special education is intended to overcome or prevent handicapping conditions. But in the case of special gifts and talents, special education is designed to increase or even create the individual's special characteristics (that is, to help the child become *more* rather than less exceptional or to develop special gifts or talents). Special education for the handicapped involves helping children who have a disadvantage to become more like the average child. But for the gifted and talented, special education involves helping children who are already much better at something than the average child to become even better (more unlike the average). Our society places relatively little value on developing the gifts and talents of the best performers in school, except in competitive athletics. So it is not surprising that the gifted and talented tend to be a neglected group in special education.

GIFTS AND TALENTS OF MANY KINDS. When we speak of the handicapped, we recognize that we are speaking of several categories of exceptionality (learning disabled, physically disabled, mentally retarded, hearing impaired, and so on). In fact, we often speak of specific categories of handicapping conditions. Perhaps children can be gifted or talented in as many ways as they can be handicapped. But special educators do not often give much emphasis to specific categories of giftedness or talent (for example, children with special gifts or talents in music, mathematics, dance, or languages). Consequently, generalizations about the education of gifted and talented youngsters are difficult to make. Federal and state programs for exceptional children tend to be funded and administered according to specific categories of disability, but to treat gifted and talented as a single, separate category. A much smaller percentage of the population is considered gifted or talented than is considered handicapped; and much less money is spent for educating the gifted and talented (less per child and a smaller total) than for educating the handicapped.

EDUCATION FOR THE GIFTED AND TALENTED AND FEDERAL LAW. As we have already mentioned (Chapter 1), federal law requires special education and related services for all handicapped children. Gifted and talented children are not mentioned in Public Law 94–142, even though they have long been included in the federal categories of special education. This omission in the most important and comprehensive federal legislation governing special education means that the needs of gifted and talented children can easily be ignored in some states. Handicapped children and their parents have rights under federal law that gifted and talented children and their parents simply do not have. The only way federal guarantees of a free, appropriate public education can be made to apply to a child who is gifted or talented is to have the child classified as handicapped. A journalist recently wrote one of us,

> My wife and I have been frequently frustrated by school systems' inability and unwillingness to respond in any direct and effective way to the special needs of their specially talented children. In fact, it is at times difficult to get individual educators to accept the idea that bright children are different and do have personal and educational needs unlike those of "average" children. Our solution has been to call [our especially bright 11-year-old seventh-grader] and others like her "handicapped"; that gets an educator's attention, believe me. . . . Perhaps one day the educational goal, in policy and in law, will be education appropriate to *all* pupils, not just those with handicaps that slow their education.

TODAY'S DEFINITION OF THE GIFTED AND TALENTED

Before defining the category of gifted and talented, we need to clarify some of the terms often encountered in the literature. "Gifted and talented" is in some ways a redundancy, because a dictionary will likely tell you that gifted means talented and talented means gifted. But the history of these terms in education suggests that **gifted** has traditionally been used to refer to very high intelligence, whereas **talented** has been used more often to refer to remarkably high ability in a particular skill or art. Of course, a person can have intellectual talent or be a gifted violinist. But the term **gifted and talented** is used today to cover especially high ability or potential in one or more of several valued areas of performance. The term "talented" was added to the term "gifted" in federal legislation and publications to counter the idea that concern should be shown only for those students whose IQs are very high.

Other terms you will frequently encounter in the literature on gifted and talented children are precocious and genius. **Precocious** means developing or maturing very early. **Genius** may mean extremely intelligent (for example, IQ 180 or higher) or highly innovative or creative. "Creative" also is frequently used to describe the gifted and talented. In fact, as we will see, creativity is probably as important as intelligence in determining whether someone is gifted or talented. **Creativity** refers to the ability to see and do things in ways that most people don't, to come up with novel ideas that are useful or stimulating to others in a productive way.

Defining persons as gifted or talented after they have done something remarkable or spectacular is easier than identifying them before they have done it. In fact, it has

Gifted children learn quickly, are creative, and exhibit leadership qualities. But in typical classrooms, it may be difficult to identify the children who are gifted. Paul Conklin, Monkmeyer.

not been uncommon for a person's special talent or gift to be recognized only after he or she has died. We can recognize that someone *has* done something to show he or she is gifted or talented much more accurately than we can predict that someone *will* show a gift or talent. It is not surprising, then, that defining gifted and talented children for special education purposes is a difficult problem. After all, one of the major purposes of special education for such children is to find and provide extra opportunities for those who seem likely to become gifted or talented adults. Most of the children served in special programs have already demonstrated special abilities of some sort— but it is anybody's guess what kind of contribution to society any one of them may make later.

Gifted and talented children are defined in the Gifted and Talented Act of 1978 as

> . . . children and, whenever applicable, youth, who are identified at the preschool, elementary, or secondary level as possessing demonstrated or potential abilities that give evidence of high performance capabilities in areas such as intellectual, creative, specific academic, or leadership ability, or in the performing and visual arts, and who by reason thereof, require services or activities not ordinarily provided by the school. (Public Law 95–561, section 902)

If you think about what this definition says, you will see it leaves a lot of room for guesswork. How do you recognize potential ability, and how do you measure leadership ability, for example?

Another definition has been suggested by Renzulli (1977). He based his definition on the characteristics of adults who are known to be gifted or talented. He noted that three things are necessary to become known as a gifted or talented person: (1) high ability, (2) high creativity, and (3) high commitment to a task. Someone does not come to be recognized as gifted or talented just because he or she has great ability (intelligence or skill), is highly creative (sees things in unusual ways), or is very committed to an accomplishment (has tremendous motivation to do something). In fact, unless a person has all three characteristics (high ability, creativity, and commitment), she or he is not likely to do anything very remarkable. Therefore, Renzulli suggests that gifted and talented children should be defined as those who have demonstrated or show potential for ability, creativity, and task commitment that are clearly superior. Renzulli's definition does not resolve the problem of identifying *potential* gifts and talents, and it leaves open the possibility that any sort of performance or ability valued by society can be included. Nevertheless, it may point to the essential characteristics that define a gifted or talented person.

Today's definitions of giftedness are significantly different from those used 20 or more years ago. In the early 1900s, when systematic studies of gifted children were just beginning, high intelligence was the only factor taken into account in identifying the gifted. Children were identified as gifted if and only if they scored exceptionally high (usually 140 or higher) on an IQ test. But in the 1950s and 1960s, psychologists began studying the various facets of intelligence and investigating the relationship between intelligence and creativity. Many experts realized that IQ tests alone were not adequate for identifying giftedness, and researchers began assessing creativity and motivation as well. Nowadays, it is recognized that an adequate definition must include factors that will identify gifts and talents of all kinds and that will not overlook gifted and talented women, minorities, the handicapped, or economically disadvantaged youngsters.

We are beginning to recognize not only that there are many facets to being gifted and talented, but also that giftedness and special talents can change with time or circumstances. True, some people exhibit superior abilities nearly all their lives. But others make a remarkable achievement or contribution to society only during a particular phase of their development. So researchers and special educators who deal with the gifted and talented are beginning to make provision for students who may be (or show the potential for being) gifted or talented at one time but not at another, or in one particular type of school activity but not in another (Renzulli and Smith, 1980).

IDENTIFYING THE GIFTED AND TALENTED

An adequate system of identification of gifted and talented students requires both testing and observation. In this sense, identification of gifted and talented children is no different from identification of children with handicapping conditions. For example, children are not identified as mentally retarded simply on the basis of a low score on an intelligence test; they must be observed to have deficits in adaptive behavior as well (see Chapter 2). Children should not be identified as gifted or talented simply on the basis of a high score on an intelligence test; they should show high motivation and creativity as well. According to the model suggested by Renzulli (1977), adequate identification procedures are based on multiple criteria: the child's intelligence, creativity, and motivation.

MEASURES OF INTELLIGENCE

Intelligence tests were at one time the only means used to identify gifted children. It was assumed that intelligence was measured very precisely by IQ tests, that a person's IQ never changed, and that IQ was the only really important factor in determining who was gifted.

Gifted and talented children's intelligence often is demonstrated in situations that call for creative problem-solving and communication, as exemplified by this classroom game of charades. Ken Karp.

Attitudes and beliefs regarding intelligence and intelligence tests have changed dramatically since the tests were first developed. Today, we realize that an IQ test does not necessarily give us an accurate, unbiased estimate of a person's intelligence. A person's IQ can change over a period of years, and appropriate education might result in significant improvement of some children's intelligence. Furthermore, high intelligence is not the only characteristic of gifted people.

In the early decades of the twentieth century the public was awed by IQ tests, and psychologists perhaps placed too much confidence in them. Today, many professionals have attacked standardized tests of all kinds, especially IQ tests. Critics argue that the tests are biased against certain racial or ethnic groups, that they do not really measure what they are supposed to measure, and that the results are used inappropriately to classify individuals or provide them with special treatment.

In spite of the heavy criticism of IQ tests in recent years, they remain an important part of identification procedures for gifted and talented students (Gallagher, 1975). Ignoring IQ tests as a tool for assessing children's intelligence and identifying gifted children just because the tests have certain limitations makes no sense. After all, these tests are still the best, most unbiased means we have of estimating people's intelligence. And although a high IQ is not by itself enough to identify someone as gifted, we do know that above-average intelligence is a *necessary* characteristic of intellectual giftedness. Note, however, that high artistic ability, but not necessarily high IQ, is a necessary characteristic of the artistically talented.

MEASURES OF CREATIVITY

Devising a truly valid standardized test of creativity may be impossible. Petrosko (1978) notes that measuring creativity presents a special paradox: Creativity means that a person sees things in a nonstandard way; so how can a test for creativity be standardized?

Nevertheless, tests of creativity have been devised by Torrance (1962, 1966) and others (see Khatena, 1982). On these tests, people are asked to think of as many novel responses as they can to certain problems or questions (see Focus). Tests of creativity have been rather widely used, but also widely criticized for their limitations (Gallagher, 1966; Treffinger, Renzulli, and Feldhusen, 1975). Their biggest limitation is that they sometimes have little to do with a person's creative performance on everyday tasks.

Another approach to measuring creativity is to measure it in terms of specific types of responses that can be counted reliably. Researchers have measured creative responses in block-building (Baer, Rowbury, and Goetz, 1976), story writing (Brigham, Graubard, and Stans, 1972), and easel painting (Goetz and Salmonson, 1972). For example, Baer et al. counted the number of different forms children constructed in playing with blocks. Children were considered more creative to the extent that they made a higher number of different forms with a given number of blocks.

Experts do not often agree about how creativity should be defined, and they agree even less about how it can best be measured. However, nearly everyone agrees that creativity is a key characteristic of the gifted and talented. Creativity is assessed sometimes by someone's subjective judgment of an individual's behavior or what he or she produces, sometimes by objective observations, and sometimes by tests.

TEST YOUR CREATIVITY

Tests of creativity are based on the concept of **divergent production.** Divergent production has been described by psychologist J. P. Guilford (1959) as a mental operation in which a person suggests many possible answers to a question or problem, as opposed to **convergent production,** in which a person must arrive at one best or correct answer. Intelligence and achievement tests require convergent production almost exclusively; tests of creativity require divergent production.

The ability of someone to think divergently (creatively) is usually assessed by noting the extent to which their responses to questions or problems reflect fluency, flexibility, originality, and elaboration. Fluency refers to the ready flow of ideas, the speed and ease with which one can suggest possible answers or relationships. Flexibility involves the ability to change perspectives or directions in thinking without being instructed or required to do so. Originality is the ability to give answers that are almost never given by anyone else and to come up with responses that are clever or do not seem at first to be related to the question or problem. Elaboration means ability to fill out an idea with many details.

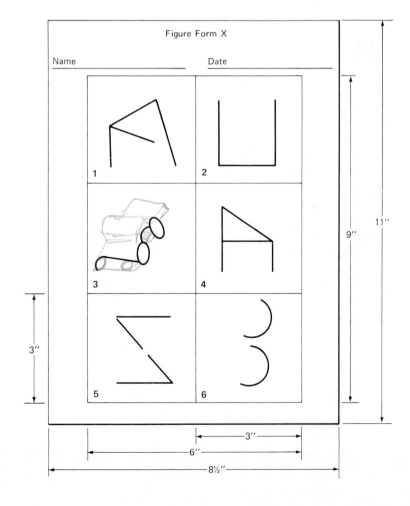

Numerous tests of creativity have been devised. The Torrance Tests of Creative Thinking, by Torrance and his colleagues, are among the best known. The Torrance tests consist of a variety of verbal and nonverbal tasks designed to measure the creativity of students in kindergarten through graduate school. Scoring criteria for each task include the fluency, flexibility, originality, and elaboration of a person's responses. Here are some tasks similar to those used in Torrance's early work (1962).

INCOMPLETE FIGURES TASK

Note: Two forms of this task were available. Only one is reproduced here. The figures actually presented in the test were larger than the ones shown here. Time to do the task was limited to 10 minutes.

Instructions: By adding lines to the six figures on page 281, sketch some object or design that no one else in the class will think of. Try to include as many different ideas as you can in your drawing. In other words, don't stop with your first idea for completing the figure; keep building on it. Make up titles for each of your pictures, and write one at the bottom of each block next to the number of the figure.

UNUSUAL USES TASK

Note: This task is limited to 5 minutes.

Instructions: Now try to think of some unusual uses of cardboard boxes. List the cleverest, most interesting, and most unusual uses you can think of for cardboard boxes. The boxes may be of any size, and you can change them in any way they can be changed.

Source: From Torrance, E. P. *Guiding Creative Talent*. Malabar, Fla.: Robert E. Krieger Publishing Co., 1976, p. 214.

MEASURES OF MOTIVATION

To some extent a student's **motivation,** or tendency to perform a task or accomplish a goal, is reflected in achievement. A student's performance on a standardized achievement test and/or grades achieved are often taken as measures of motivation. Sometimes achievement is compared to intelligence; if students achieve at or above what one would expect of those with their intelligence, they are assumed to be adequately motivated.

Another feasible way of measuring motivation is through observation by teachers and/or parents. A rating scale may help teachers or parents in making judgments about a child's motivation. The scale should help them look for characteristics like "stick-to-it-iveness," completing tasks, going beyond what is requested, and maintaining interest in a project without much encouragement or supervision.

Ideally, identification of the gifted and talented should involve standardized tests of intelligence and achievement, assessment of creativity, and assessment of motivation. Teachers' judgments are necessarily involved in identification. But unguided teacher judgment has not been found to be very reliable (Gallagher, 1966). Without assistance in what to look for and how to look for it, teachers are not very good at selecting students who are truly superior. With the assistance of a rating scale, however, teachers can provide valuable information in the identification process. Renzulli, Hartman, and Callahan (1975) have prepared a scale on which teachers rate pupils on a series of

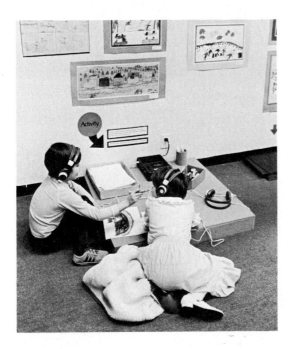

One characteristic of gifted and talented children is high motivation to pursue creative activities independently. Robert A. Isaacs/Photo Researchers.

items related to learning, motivation, creativity, and leadership. This scale helps teachers make more objective judgments about characteristics that are related to gifted and talented performance.

PREVALENCE

Some people say that each one of us can do something better than anyone else in the world. You don't need to think about this notion very long to realize that it is a meaningless exaggeration. Probably it reflects the common desire to excel, to be considered gifted or talented in some way. But to be rational, we must define giftedness and exceptional talents in such a way that only a relatively small percentage of the population is included. Using the federal definition, 2 to 5 percent of the population probably could be considered gifted or talented.

Of course, more children will be identified if the criteria for identification are lowered, and fewer children will be identified if the criteria are raised. What the criteria for identification of gifted and talented children should be is merely a matter of opinion and tradition—a matter of what people consider reasonable and useful. The IQ criterion for identification of gifted children has often been set at 130 because only about 2 percent of the school population will score that high or higher. About 15 percent of all children will attain an IQ of 115 or higher, and most educators and psychologists apparently do not believe that 15 percent of our school children should be considered gifted.

Renzulli (1982) points out that a prevalence estimate based strictly on IQ is very misleading. The typical 3 to 5 percent prevalence estimate appears to be based on an

IQ criterion alone and does not include some highly motivated and creative children whose IQs fall below the typical cutoff score. Still, it is sensible to believe that only a relatively small percentage of the school population is gifted or talented to such an extent that special programming is necessary for them. We'd be as silly to consider a very large percentage of the population gifted as we would to consider a very large percentage mentally retarded.

A final point to keep in mind about the prevalence of gifted and talented children is that the percentage may vary from place to place. Giftedness is something we "make" by comparisons. If we make comparisons only among children in each school building, then obviously we'd expect to find about the same percentage of gifted and talented children in every school. If we compare individual children to a larger group—all other children in a large city, for example—then we may find a larger percentage of gifted and talented students in some schools and a smaller percentage in others. As you might guess, the decision regarding who the comparison group should be in defining and identifying gifted and talented children is a point of controversy.

FACTORS THAT CAUSE GIFTEDNESS

Like mental retardation, giftedness and special talents sometimes run in the family. And just like mental retardation, giftedness and talentedness cannot be explained simply on the basis of genetic, neurological, or environmental factors. That is, the nature versus nurture controversy applies to the gifted and talented as well as the retarded. Common sense tells us that an unstimulating environment in which the child has little opportunity to learn will not increase the likelihood that the child will develop superior abilities. But some gifted or talented children do overcome serious environmental disadvantages. Brilliant parents are more likely than slow-learning parents to have brilliant children; yet some gifted children are born to parents who are intellectually below average. We know that both genetic and environmental factors are involved in determining whether a child will be gifted. We don't know, however, exactly how or to what extent these two factors work in a given case.

BIOLOGICAL FACTORS

The idea that genetic factors play an important role in determining how intelligent people are has always been controversial. Studies of twins and other blood relatives have, over the years, led researchers to the conclusion that the genetic influence on intellectual ability is very strong (Bouchard and McGue, 1981; Freeman, 1981; Scarr-Salapatek, 1975). The evidence points clearly to the conclusion that some children inherit the capacity for superior performance and others do not. What remains a complete mystery is exactly what gifted and talented children inherit—which specific genes or combinations of them account for gifted and talented children's special abilities? And, of course, the extent to which these genetic factors can deliberately be passed along to future generations at this point is anyone's guess (see Focus).

Other biological factors besides inheritance may play a part in the development

SHOULD WE—IF WE CAN—BREED GIFTEDNESS?

In the late 1970s Robert K. Graham, an industrialist and optics expert who was then in his seventies, organized a human sperm bank. His organization, known as the Repository for Germinal Choice, collects and stores sperm from male Nobel Prize winners and other highly intelligent, creative men and makes the sperm available to highly intelligent, creative women who are unable to be impregnated by their husbands. On May 24, 1982, the Repository announced the birth of the first baby conceived through the services of its sperm bank.

The hope of Mr. Graham and others who support the idea of such sperm banks is that the genes that account for Nobel Laureates' and others' special gifts and talents will be passed along to more children than would otherwise be possible. Nobel winner William Shockley and others who have contributed to the sperm bank argue that they are increasing the chances that more gifted and talented children will be born (see "Playboy Interview: William Shockley," *Playboy*, August 1980, pp. 69–102). Their ideas are controversial and are frequently attacked both in the professional literature and in the popular press. The following editorial from the *New York Times* (May 27, 1982) reflects the common reaction:

BANKING ON VANITY AND GENES

A California sperm bank has announced its first birth, a child born last month after her mother was inseminated with sperm from an "eminent mathematician." The bank, which accepts deposits from Nobel Prize winners, was founded as "a means of breeding higher intelligence." Recipients who buy for that reason should realize they are chasing a chimera.

Intellectual quality in families may often seem to be inherited, as with the musicianship that appeared in generation after generation of Bachs. But the family relationship is bound by culture as well as by genes; the cultural impact of having a J. S. Bach as a father was doubtless far stronger than any influence he transmitted in the genes.

Simple traits like the Hapsburg lip may pass from parent to children over several generations, but more complex attributes, like intellect, are probably mediated by many genes and are not inheritable in any straightforward way. In any case, genes only sketch the possibilities that culture can bring to fruition.

The four Nobel Prize winners whom the California sperm bank claims as donors should know better than anyone the full depth of the fallacy they are endorsing. There is a well-documented relationship between Nobel Prize winners, but it has nothing to do with genetics: it is a master-apprentice relationship. Many scientists who have won Nobel Prizes learned their trade under other Nobel Prize winners, attesting yet again to the surprising power of environment in setting the stage for human intellectual achievements.

The actress Ellen Terry once advocated mutual parenthood to George Bernard Shaw with the argument that any child of theirs would be blessed with her beauty and his brains. Shaw, resisting the proposal, ungenerously remarked on the calamity if, in the lottery of procreation, their respective contributions were reversed.

If intellectual qualities were inheritable in any simple fashion, those who conceive with the help of the Nobel sperm could count on offspring endowed with a great deal of vanity and a plain dearth of sense. Chances are, however, they will get themselves just children.

of special gifts and talents. For example, optimum nutrition and freedom from disease and injury might improve the chances that a child will be gifted or talented. But studies so far have not indicated that this is the case. Fisch, Bilek, Horrobin, and Chang (1976) studied the physical and intellectual characteristics of over two thousand babies, whom they continued to study for a period of years.

They found that neurological and physical abnormalities, infections, anoxia (significant lack of oxygen to the brain), and other injuries occurred with nearly equal frequency in groups of newborn babies who later (at age 7) had low, average, or high IQs. Children who showed neurological abnormalities at age 1 and at age 7 or who had inadequate speech, language, or hearing when they were 5 were found with nearly equal frequency in average and high IQ groups. But children in the low IQ group showed these characteristics more often than children whose IQs were average or above. The measure that was the best predictor of which babies would later show high intelligence was head circumference—babies with bigger heads tended to have higher IQs by the time they were 7 years old. Keep in mind, however, the fact that head circumference could be a result of genetic *or* environmental factors, or both.

Studies by Fisch and others (1976) suggest that the biological factors which contribute to giftedness are not simply the opposite of those which contribute to mental retardation or other disabilities. Absence of brain trauma (at least during infancy) does not seem to improve a child's chances of being gifted or talented. We just are not able to say exactly what biological factors, aside from inheritance, contribute to the development of special abilities.

FACTORS IN THE SOCIAL ENVIRONMENT AND CULTURE

Children's abilities might be correlated with their parents' abilities because of genetics, but the correlation might also be accounted for by the learning environment provided by the parents. The belief that environmental factors are the most significant and powerful forces in intelligence is deeply rooted in American ideals and politics and lends support to programs designed to promote social equality. The reasoning of those who believe environment is more important than genetics is this: If children's environments can be improved dramatically, then their IQs can be increased dramatically as well; given the proper learning environment, as many gifted and talented children will be found among one social class, race, or ethnic group as any other.

Although there is no reliable scientific evidence to support the idea that environmental factors play the most important role in determining intelligence, children's social and cultural environments obviously do affect how they learn and respond to opportunities. Studies of the intelligence of family members indicate that environmental factors, not just genetics, determine intelligence (Bouchard and McGue, 1981). Homes and cultures are more likely to produce gifted and talented children if they provide stimulation, encouragement, recognition, and reward for accomplishments that are valued by the dominant group in society. Furthermore, recent studies of the gifted and talented (such as Bloom, 1982; Bloom and Sosniak, 1981; see also Callahan and Kauffman, 1982) indicate that parents and families play a very important role in the emergence of children's special abilities.

Whether or not a child will be gifted depends on more than genetic factors. A stimulating environment in which adults demonstrate and teach problem-solving skills increases the likelihood that a young child will exhibit superior performance. Janet Charles/United Cerebral Palsy/NYC.

CHARACTERISTICS

One old idea that is dying slowly is that the gifted and talented tend to be "oddballs"—emotionally unstable, weak or sickly, not able to perform well except in one narrow intellectual pursuit. This mistaken notion of what the gifted and talented person tends to be like came from several sources. First, in the late 1800s and early 1900s, books were written about how genius and insanity were closely linked (Lombroso, 1905; Sanborn, 1885). These ideas found their way into the popular press and were accepted as established fact. Second, some of the early studies of the gifted included only children with extremely high IQs (Hollingworth, 1942). These studies did not deal with children who are representative of the gifted as a group. Third, one can find cases in which a person's giftedness or special talent was accompanied by eccentricity or emotional disturbance (for instance, the Dutch painter Vincent Van Gogh). These cases capture people's imagination and lead to the erroneous conclusion that gifted and talented people are always odd.

We know today that the gifted and talented tend to be healthy, both physically and emotionally, and that they often excel in more than one special area. Now we are in danger of developing a new stereotype of the gifted or talented person, a stereotype of someone who can do everything exceedingly well and never has any serious emotional or physical problems. We must remember that although the gifted and talented tend as a group to be superior to most of us on a variety of characteristics, individuals who are gifted or talented may range from those who are well adjusted, well rounded, and physically superior to those who are emotionally ill, narrow in their interests, or physically disabled.

One of the leading scholars who studied gifted children over a long period of time was Lewis Terman. Beginning in 1926, he and his colleagues published a series of reports on the characteristics of a large group of the gifted (Terman, 1926; Terman and Oden, 1959). As a group, gifted children tended to be taller, heavier, stronger, more energetic, and healthier than the average child. Furthermore, many of these children excelled in athletics; and they tended to maintain their physical superiority in adulthood. Not only were they superior academically at school, but they tended to become successful professionals in very demanding occupations.

Terman's work has been criticized because of the procedures he used to obtain subjects. Critics argue that his sample of gifted students was biased because he relied only on teacher nomination as a screening method, relied exclusively on the Stanford-Binet IQ test for selection, and chose only children from white middle-class schools in California (see Khatena, 1982). Nevertheless, Terman's research and the research of others has shattered the myth that giftedness is associated with negative characteristics.

Since the 1950s, scholars have recognized that some highly creative individuals do not score extremely high on IQ tests. Getzels and Jackson (1958) were among the first to point out that the most highly creative students may not be the ones who are highest in IQ and that the highly creative may exhibit behaviors and emotions quite different from those of highly intelligent but comparatively uncreative students. In a series of studies in which they compared students who scored in the top 20 percent on tests of creativity but not on tests of intelligence and those who scored in the top 20 percent on IQ tests but not on tests of creativity, they found that high creative and high IQ students performed about the same academically. But teachers rated the high IQ students as more desirable than those who were highly creative. And the high creative students appeared to enjoy risk-taking, independence, and uncertainty more than their high IQ peers, to be better able to produce new ideas, and to prefer unconventional, high-risk occupations.

A recent follow-up study by Torrance and Wu (1981) suggests that high creativity may be at least as important as high intelligence in achievements during high school and in adulthood. Most scholars now recognize that adequate consideration of the characteristics of the gifted and talented must include study of individuals who show great creativity but do not necessarily score very high on IQ tests.

Thus, while we have good reason to believe that most gifted and talented children and youth are socially, emotionally, and educationally successful (Tidwell, 1980), we know too that they are a diverse, heterogeneous group (Treffinger, 1982). Perhaps more important than the fact that the gifted and talented often show an array of desirable characteristics in addition to their remarkable performance or potential in a specific area is that they tend to be overlooked if they possess certain other characteristics.

FEMALES. Most of the adults who have been recognized as gifted or talented are men. Although there may be inherent sex differences in particular types of abilities, cultural stereotypes and social barriers often have restricted females' choices in career preparation. Callahan (1981) has noted the social and cultural expectations that may keep gifted and talented females' abilities from being recognized, developed, and displayed. As Schwartz (1980) stated:

Like many members of minority groups who have experienced discrimination, many gifted females have internalized the majority view of themselves. They have accepted the socially approved roles assigned to them, believing that maybe they are less competent than men even with equivalent skills and training; that it is wrong to assert their abilities. Indeed, they are frequently reinforced from childhood on for conformity and docility. The first task facing educators and others, therefore, is to help gifted females to gain the self-confidence, the sense of independence, and the positive image of themselves necessary for continuing achievement. (p. 115)

UNDERACHIEVERS. Many females may underachieve compared to males and compared to what they might achieve if there were no social or cultural barriers to their achievement. But much **underachievement** (failure to achieve at a level consistent with one's ability) cannot be explained simply by sex discrimination, for many boys also are underachievers. Underachievement of gifted and talented children can result from any of the factors that lead to underachievement in any group (e.g., emotional conflicts or a poor home environment). A very frequent cause of underachievement is an inappropriate school program—school work that is unchallenging and boring because the gifted child has already mastered most of the material. And gifted underachievers often develop negative images of themselves and negative attitudes toward school (see Delisle, 1982; Whitmore, 1980). When a child shows negative attitudes toward school and self, any special abilities he or she may have are easily overlooked.

Delisle (1981) cautioned that underachievement must not be confused with nonproductivity. That is, we have the expectation that the gifted or talented child will constantly be producing something remarkable, and we may easily misinterpret a lapse in productivity as underachievement. Delisle's caution points up some of the difficulties in defining giftedness: Is a highly able person, child, or adult gifted only at those times when he or she is being productive? How much time must elapse between episodes of productivity before we say that someone is no longer gifted or is an underachiever?

CULTURALLY DIFFERENT CHILDREN. Different cultural and ethnic groups place different values on academic achievement and areas of performance in which talent is important. Stereotypes can easily lead us to overlook intellectual giftedness or talents or to over- or under-rate children on any characteristic because they do not conform to our expectations based on their race, socioeconomic status, or religion. Special care must be taken in identification procedures and educational programming to ensure that bias does not result in the exclusion of gifted and talented children who do not fit the pattern of the dominant culture (Callahan, 1981; Sisk, 1981). (Note the problems described by a minority gifted student in the Focus.)

FOCUS

A MINORITY WITHIN A MINORITY: THE CULTURALLY DIFFERENT GIFTED AND TALENTED

In 1975, a special conference was held to which 20 gifted and talented high school juniors and seniors were invited. One outcome of the conference was publication of a book, *On Being Gifted*, which was written entirely by the 20 young participants. The reflections of these young people on their experiences and feelings and their recommendations for other gifted and talented youths make fascinating reading. One of the topics dealt with by several of the contributors is the problems of cultural minorities. A young native American wrote:

ARE YOU A MINORITY WITHIN OUR GIFTED AND TALENTED MINORITY?

Our Indian culture views gifted and talented youth in a type of religious manner. For our part, it takes quite a bit of intelligence to understand what goes on around us—such as the religious ceremonies. The elderly people believe you are nothing unless as an Indian you know you *are* an Indian and are fully aware of your culture.

But, in retrospect, we have the same interpretations of various aspects in life, whether it be of old legends or of religious beliefs.

Sometimes I am quite confused over certain things because of my two different cultures. I feel you have to adjust yourself to completely understand society *now*.

Educational opportunities for gifted and talented native Americans are a lot stronger now. There are more chances for higher education at more institutions, but we definitely need an even greater force to educate the rural gifted and talented native American.

Living in a rural area is undoubtedly different from living in an urbanized residence. I don't have much of an opportunity to increase my learning ability. Libraries and various other learning centers are situated in distant places requiring transportation and time for further studying. Yet, living in a rural area does have a basic learning value also, such as studying in secluded places where "city noise" is non-existent or sometimes just studying life itself. We have time and a place to do that without distraction.

Although I feel I have matured quite fast in the last several months since early admission to the local university, my life has not changed much because of my so-called "unique learning needs." Other than that, our school requires the usual classes to be taken in order to graduate with a certain amount of credit hours. This is where kids become bored. We all need a change of environment which goes along with selecting a wider variety of chosen fields. I myself became very depressed when higher educational opportunities were non-existent for students with unique learning needs. In addition, our community also fails to cooperate. *I mean, there are all these organizations helping the underachieving students, when I feel I need help, too*!

Source: On being gifted. New York: American Association for Gifted Children. Copyright © 1978 by the American Association for Gifted Children. Used by permission of Walker & Co.

HANDICAPPED. A substantial percentage of eminent persons have been handicapped (Porter, 1982). In spite of this fact, the special abilities of handicapped people are often overlooked (Maker, 1977). Today we must be certain that a handicapped person's abilities are not underestimated because of a disability. Technological advances that can be used to assist disabled persons might result in more reliable identification of their gifts and talents.

We want to make one final point about the characteristics of the gifted and talented. Although they exhibit enviable characteristics and tend as a group (with exceptions, as we have noted previously) to be happy, healthy, popular, and productive, their lives are not all fun and games. Being gifted or talented has its burdens and disadvantages. A gifted or talented person is under constant pressure to perform. Sometimes this pressure comes from others; often it is self-imposed. But regardless of the source of the pressure, the gifted frequently feel driven to be not just better, but best. For some, the constant demand for excellence becomes a heavy burden. And being gifted or talented can be a stigma, even though most people are in some ways envious of others' special gifts

Giftedness among the disabled sometimes goes unrecognized. Handicapped people with special gifts and talents must be given the opportunity to develop them to the fullest possible extent. United Nations, photo by Jan Corash.

and talents. The envy of peers and the stigma that goes with being "too good" at something or a "smarty" makes some children hide their abilities and/or withdraw from others their own age. Consider the feelings of gifted and talented students expressed in the Focus and see if you can suggest ways in which special educational provisions for these students might have helped them be happier and more productive.

FOCUS

BEING GIFTED: SOME UNHAPPY FEELINGS

On Being Gifted, written by 20 gifted and talented high school students, also contains a few brief comments by fourth-, fifth-, and sixth-graders from Norwich, Connecticut. Their comments illustrate the negative self-perceptions and social stigma that gifted and talented students sometimes experience.

PEER PRESSURE

To many with exceptional talents a problem arises concerning their peers and contacts with other people. Of course the gifted student is proud of his powers but his peer group makes it very difficult for him.

People with special gifts get a great deal of attention from the society around them. For me it is not as great a problem as for others simply because I am in my own age group. However, prodding, teasing, and resentment do present themselves as foolish obstacles.

Students in my peer group are jealous about my ability. I do my best to share with them my knowledge and I try to help them whenever possible but all this is to no avail. (Jealousy stirs teasing—which gets to be a drag.) (p. 21)

CAUGHT IN THE MIDDLE

As I sit in a classroom of a smalltown high school, I am listening to the teacher begin a lecture for the day. He asks a question regarding the assigned homework, chapter 25 in our book. I raise my hand and respond correctly to his query. He continues to ask questions and I continue to answer them. After a couple of rounds I begin to look around sheepishly to see if anyone else has his hand raised. No one does so I answer again. I hear annoyed mutterings from my classmates. I just know they're thinking, "She thinks she knows everything." So in a futile effort to conform and satisfy them, I sink down in my seat just a little and let the rest of the questions slide by. The teacher becomes angry that no one has read the assignment and feels he must repeat the chapter. And another day is wasted.

So goes it, and unfortunately, too often. As a result, I do not feel challenged nor do I attempt to be when I find myself in such a class. One alternative, which in my school is extremely limited, is to sign up for those courses which are designed for people planning to major in that specific area. But alas, not enough teachers, nor enough money in the budget for books or supplies. So suffer, kid! (pp. 24–25)

PRESSURES FROM TEACHERS

Often our peers get their cues when our teachers begin to reject us. This often happens when an instructor feels threatened by the exceptional student. In my school this takes the form of neglect. The teacher does not fill my needs because he will not devote extra time to me and often totally ignores my suggestions.

Often, instructors, though not actually threatened, feel that the gifted student has had enough recognition and therefore bypass him. Many times one of my teachers has preferred to work extremely hard with his favorite remedial workshop student than to talk to me. This sort of behavior has caused me to doubt my priorities concerning education.

WHO'S ON OUR SIDE?

Occasionally teachers seem to be foes rather than allies. Unfortunately, many times teachers are on an ego trip, preferring to help slower students so that they might appear to be all-powerful and all-knowing.

If a student happens to learn rapidly or already has a knowledge of the subject from prior exposure, the teacher develops a deep resentment for the child.

In my case, I had a teacher of algebra who developed this type of resentment. I understood the material because of previous contact with the subject. I seldom missed problems on tests, homework or on the board; when I did, I caught his wrath.

I don't know the psychological reasons; I only know this situation shouldn't exist. (pp. 28–29)

Source: *On being gifted*. New York: American Association for Gifted Children, 1978.

TODAY'S EDUCATIONAL PROGRAMMING

Trends in education of the gifted and talented are toward local and state initiatives and a wide variety of programming options that are an integral part of the public education system. In the past, programs for the gifted and talented tended to be patched into regular education and to be obtrusively separate; today they are increasingly integrated with the regular system as one more of the many options available to meet students' individual needs. We do not mean to give the impression that all programs for the gifted and talented are now an indistinguishable part of comprehensive educational services for children in all communities or states, merely that the trend is in that direction.

Although most states and many localities may be making progress in providing appropriate education for their most capable students, resistance to the very notion of special educational programming for these children still is easy to find. Some educators fear that any special programming for especially capable children will be discriminatory and foster destructive elitism. And although strong arguments can be made in favor of special education for the gifted and talented, opponents of such education can point to an almost complete lack of research showing that special programs of any kind are effective in helping gifted and talented children become more productive adults (Weiss and Gallagher, 1982).

SPECIAL EDUCATION FOR THE GIFTED AND TALENTED: A GOOD IDEA?

Advocates for special provisions for gifted and talented children use two basic arguments: (1) The children have special needs that can be met only if they are given an educational program that is different from that of the average child, and every child, including the gifted and talented, is entitled to education designed to meet her or his needs. (2) We all stand to profit from special education of the gifted and talented, since their achievements will improve our quality of life and have the best chance of solving our society's most pressing problems. Khatena has said that "it is the creative potential of the gifted and talented that excites us and that removes the issue from some kind of educational frill to the central question of whether our society can maximize creative performance in its adults soon enough to avoid disaster" (1982, p. 2).

But not all educators or social commentators agree. Consider the following perspectives:

> Aside from the fact that our methods for identifying the gifted are highly unreliable, we must consider two fundamental questions at the heart of this controversy: Do gifted children deserve special treatment, and do they merit more societal resources than "average" children? If we begin from the premise that all children deserve a "suitable publicly supported education," then we could possibly justify special gifted programs on the basis that all children should be afforded the opportunity to develop their talents to the fullest. Again, the fact that all children do not have the opportunity to develop their talents—e.g., the poor, and those from ethnic and racial minorities—renders any simple justification of gifted programs quite spurious. Perhaps if *all* children were guaranteed an education that would be tailored to fit their individual needs, then special gifted programs would not be discriminatory, and all children would then have the opportunity to fulfill their capacities. . . .
>
> Objections to programs for the gifted . . . fall into two categories:
>
> *Access.* Gifted children from backgrounds other than white middle class may be denied access to the programs based on low test scores or other forms of institutional discrimination that camouflage their giftedness.
>
> *Suitability of Education.* Providing innovative and exciting programs for an elite few, while the rest of the class meanders through tedious drill or seatwork, is hardly the best way to insure that all children receive an excellent education. What logic is there to grouping the top 1% or 2% in gifted programs, while the rest of the children receive essentially the same education they have always received? Certainly the variety of interests, motivation, and creativity represented among the nongifted is as great as the diversity between these two groups. Might not all children benefit from a "gifted" curriculum that emphasizes integration of knowledge and embraces new points of view and ways of looking at the

world? Teachers, then, must see as their task the broadening of *all* children's knowledge, not a select few upon whom we heap extra resources. Programs for the gifted are suitable for all children; making them exclusive deprives most children of the special opportunity to develop their individual talents and enhance their lives (Baer, 1980).

No matter how giftedness is defined, then, the unreliability of our judgments of one another is bound to cause mistakes in classification. These mistakes are tolerable when giftedness is used merely as a category in research studies—say, on the origins of creative talent. But such arbitrariness becomes pernicious when schools use giftedness as a standard for labeling and grouping children. . . .

The separation of gifted from nongifted apparently magnifies the relative advantage of those already socially advantaged. Half a century of educational research, however, has not shown that ability grouping actually produces substantial academic benefits—only that it generally reinforces de facto segregation of socioeconomic classes and, to some extent, of ethnic groups.

Americans are not ignorant of the real differences in inherited ability and motivation among children. Rather than structure an intellectual aristocracy, however, we prefer to give children many fresh chances to demonstrate their abilities. Egalitarian values restrain us from judging and classifying people lest we establish an academic caste system. This is only wise. Children who are exceptional in reading, after all, are not always exceptional in math, and those who are exceptional today may not be so exceptional tomorrow (Myers and Ridl, 1981, p. 32).

These and similar comments reflect a great fear of elitism and an anti-intellectualism that runs deep in America. As Gallagher and Weiss (1979) have pointed out, American society's relationship with the gifted and talented has been both loving (of the good things they have produced) and hateful (of special recognition of their superior performances). Segregation, special grouping, special resources, special privileges, selection of the ablest without concern over leaving someone out—all the supposedly un-American and inhumane practices condemned by Baer and Myers and Ridl—are not only tolerated, but enthusiastically supported and defended if the talent a school is fostering is related to athletic competition.

Consider this as well: The arguments Baer and Myers and Ridl use against special education for the gifted and talented can be turned with equal force against special education for any group. That is, handicapped children in several categories (especially MR, LD, and ED) (1) cannot be identified with great reliability; (2) are more often found in some social classes or ethnic groups than in others; (3) receive educational resources that are not provided to others, although many other children might profit from them; (4) may be handicapped in one area but not in another or at one time but not at another; and (5) are distinguished from their peers in a way that risks stigmatization of children. We believe that to argue against special education of the gifted and talented is to argue against special education for anyone.

TEACHING THE GIFTED AND TALENTED

Gifted and talented children need something other than the usual educational program if they are to realize their potential to the same degree as average learners. A reasonable deduction from this assumption is that they may need special teachers. What kind of teachers should they have? Surprisingly little research has been done on this question. A high level of knowledge of the content they teach, above-average intelligence and

Gifted and talented students, regardless of their age, need frequent opportunities to use all their abilities to explore real-life problems.
Ken Karp.

creativity, ability to stimulate children's curiosity, and other seemingly obvious characteristics have been suggested.

Whatever the characteristics of teachers of the gifted and talented, they are not immune to the problems of teacher burnout (Dettmer, 1982). Their professional role has high visibility. Often they serve as itinerant or resource teachers. And gifted and talented children and youth, especially underachievers who may be skilled at challenging the "system," can often be verbally caustic. These factors make teaching the gifted and talented a high stress vocation, even for teachers who are gifted (see Focus).

WOULD YOU MAKE A GOOD TEACHER OF THE GIFTED AND TALENTED?

Some teachers are better suited to teaching gifted and talented children than others. High intelligence and creativity are characteristics one obviously would look for in teachers of such children (see Callahan, 1981). But what other characteristics are important? Lindsey (1980) lists the following:

PERSONAL CHARACTERISTICS

Understands, accepts, respects, trusts, and likes self; has outstanding ego strength

Is sensitive to others, less concerned with self; supports, respects, trusts others

Is above average intellectually; exhibits an intellectual style of conceptualizing, generalizing, creating, initiating, relating, organizing, imagining

Is flexible, open to new ideas

Has intellectual interests, literary and cultural

Desires to learn, increase knowledge; has high achievement needs

Is enthusiastic

Is intuitive, perceptive
Is committed to excellence
Feels responsible for own behavior and consequences

PERSONAL–PROFESSIONAL PREDISPOSITIONS

To guide rather than to coerce or pressure
To be democratic rather than autocratic
To focus on process as well as product
To be innovative and experimental rather than conforming
To use problem-solving procedures rather than jump to unfounded conclusions
To seek involvement of others in discovery rather than give out answers

TEACHING BEHAVIORS

Develops a flexible, individualized program
Creates a warm, safe, and permissive atmosphere
Provides feedback
Uses varied strategies
Respects personal self-images and enhances positive ones; respects personal values
Respects creativity and imagination
Stimulates higher-order mental processes
Respects individuality and personal integrity (pp. 13–14)

Many of these characteristics are desirable for all teachers. Yet the average teacher is not likely to provide the stimulation and challenge necessary to help gifted and talented children learn as much as they can. These students make particularly high demands on the energies and talents of their teachers. Good teachers of such children should be role models, demonstrating high intelligence, creativity, and commitment to the task of helping students learn.

As Lindsey points out, all teachers need training in how to identify and teach especially able students. But research (Bloom, 1982; Bloom and Sosniak, 1981) clearly indicates the importance of special teachers or mentors—often, but not always, the child's parents—in developing special gifts and talents.

TYPES OF PROGRAMS

Not much research has been done to show that special programs of a particular kind are effective. But we can predict with confidence that the usual education provided to average children will do nothing to spur the gifted and talented on to greater achievements. Furthermore, program evaluations and subjective judgments of parents and children have frequently indicated the value of special programs (Weiss and Gallagher, 1982).

Many different types of programs have been tried over the years. Weiss and Gallagher (1982) group them into three major categories: those that focus on (1) training in certain thinking skills, (2) modification of curriculum content, or (3) modification of the learning environment. Each of these types of programs or strategies has been

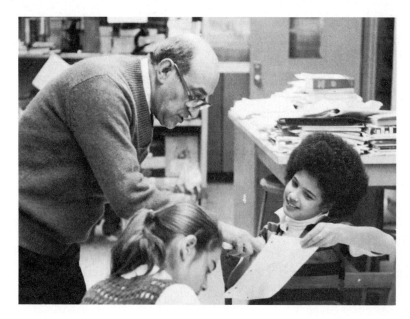

A good teacher of gifted and talented children must be highly intelligent and creative, have unusual depth of knowledge of the subject taught, be able to stimulate and guide students' curiosity, and have a high level of energy and commitment to teaching. Ken Karp.

tried in schools somewhere in the nation, from the preschool level through high school.

Training in thinking skills has emphasized creativity, problem solving, independent study, and leadership. The training may be done as a separate, special set of activities or as part of the curriculum in an academic subject. Children might be given exercises designed to teach them to produce more divergent responses when confronted with a problem or task. They might also be given instruction in problem solving designed to improve their ability to think convergently—to arrive at a correct answer through logical deduction. Independent study programs are designed in part to teach children study and work skills, including how to set goals, find and use resources for their work, and evaluate their progress. Leadership training includes identifying and practicing the characteristics of leaders and helping students to recognize and deal with ethical and moral dilemmas. Programs designed to train such thinking skills have been evaluated favorably as far as students' performance on training exercises is concerned. Unfortunately, research has not shown that the skills students acquire during training transfer to everyday situations or academic tasks.

Curriculum modifications may involve presenting work at an advanced level in only one academic area; in some cases, advanced study may be provided in a wide array of content areas. Advanced study usually means making available to the child the same curriculum content typically presented to older students. That is, the child is advanced through the usual graded curriculum in one or more academic area at a faster than normal rate. Providing access to an advanced curriculum requires an administrative plan for modifying the child's learning environment.

Weiss and Gallagher (1982, pp. 47–48) describe seven administrative plans for providing special curriculum modifications for the gifted and talented:

1. *Enrichment in the classroom*. Provision of a differentiated program of study for the gifted by the classroom teacher within the regular classroom, without assistance from an outside resource or consultant teacher.

2. *Consultant teacher program*. Differentiated instruction provided within the regular classroom by the classroom teacher with the assistance of a specially trained consultant teacher.
3. *Resource room/pullout program*. Gifted students leave the classroom on a regular basis for differentiated instruction provided by a specially trained teacher.
4. *Community mentor program*. Gifted students interact on an individual basis with selected members of the community for an extended time period on a topic of special interest to the child.
5. *Independent study program*. Differentiated instruction consists of independent study projects supervised by a qualified adult.
6. *Special class*. Gifted students are grouped together and receive instruction from a specially trained teacher.
7. *Special school*. Gifted students receive differentiated instruction in a specialized school established for that purpose.

Not all these types of administrative arrangements, curriculum modifications, and training programs are available in every school system. In fact, you will find a great deal of variation in the type of provision made for the gifted and talented from one community and state to another. Larger metropolitan areas typically make more program options available to students than do small towns or rural areas. And different program options are more often provided for students at certain levels.

PRESCHOOL AND PRIMARY LEVEL

As is true of preschool programs for the handicapped, preschool education of gifted and talented children requires participation by parents if it is to be effective. In fact, it is likely that special provisions of any kind for the gifted and talented will not be as effective as they might be without parental involvement (Bloom, 1982; Callahan and Kauffman, 1982). In most cases, parents will be the first to notice the superior abilities of the child, and they will have the responsibility for providing special instruction and obtaining help from others. Bruce (1982) suggests what parents should look for and what they can do to help a gifted child be happy and enjoy his or her abilities (see Focus).

FOCUS

GIFTED PRESCHOOLERS: TIPS FOR PARENTS AND TEACHERS

Debra Bruce, mother of a highly intelligent preschooler, describes her son Biff as an extremely active, inquisitive little boy. He learned to do nearly everything at a younger age than most children. And his precociousness seemed almost constantly to present dangers and problems.

Dealing with Biff was not always easy for his parents, and they did not immediately recognize that he was a highly gifted child. Eventually, they obtained help from psychologists, a special preschool for gifted children, and professional literature on giftedness. Biff's mother summarizes her recommendations to other parents as follows:

Most of what happens to Biff and other gifted young preschoolers is up to us, the parents. Had we ignored the symptoms, he surely would be labeled "over-active" or an "aggressive troublemaker." Yet, unlike so many undiagnosed gifted children, we feel we have a headstart in nurturing his abilities, supporting his interests, and mainly, directing and encouraging his energies in the proper channels.

To the parent of the gifted preschooler, I would recommend filling their young lives with enrichment. This includes supplementing your day with trips to museums . . . or to the neighborhood grocery warehouse, anything that can develop keener insight into the workings of the world. Keep a corner aside in the child's room with a globe, a map of the world, newspaper clippings with large pictures. Talk to your child, rhyme with him, play with him, and help him to learn to like himself and like his special ability.

Remember, no matter how bright your child is, he is still a child. Quite often, we found ourselves expecting our young son to be years older emotionally and socially when, quite the contrary, he is still only a little boy with a little boy's feelings.

Support your child; you know him best. Assist the preschool or kindergarten teacher in discovering ways to deal with his talents. Many public schools have special programs that meet one day a week for gifted students. A parent support group does wonders for you in caring and problem solving too. . . .

A gifted child is not different from other children in most ways, yet, the different problems you will encounter may seem unsurmountable if not diagnosed and your child's energy guided properly early in life. Realizing the situation at the preschool level, hopefully, can result in building positive feelings about being intelligent. Ignoring the problem, on the other hand, could result in years of frustration for both parents and child.

Source: D. F. Bruce, Is your baby a genius? *Baby Talk*, 1982, *47*, 42–45.

Programming for the preschool and primary child often involves advanced curriculum in all areas, and this often means that the child must attend a special school or class or spend a large percentage of the school week in a resource room. Children who are recognized as gifted at the preschool or primary level very often are significantly ahead of their agemates in nearly all pre-academic and academic skills. But as Robinson, Roedell, and Jackson (1979) have suggested, these children's minds do not appear to work in any qualitatively different way compared to those of average children. They are simply developmentally advanced—they have the mental capacity to do things most children cannot do until they are considerably older. So most preschool and primary programs emphasize helping the child adopt positive attitudes toward learning and using his or her special talents. They focus on teaching academic skills consistent with the child's abilities in all areas.

ELEMENTARY AND MIDDLE SCHOOL LEVEL

Enrichment and resource programs are often emphasized in the elementary and middle school grades. Sometimes, however, students at this level are offered acceleration in certain academic subjects, or special classes or schools are provided.

Renzulli (1977) has described a model of enrichment consistent with his definition of the gifted and talented. His model also addresses the issue of how education for all students should be similar to and different from education of the gifted and talented. He believes that all children should be exposed to general exploratory activities that give them opportunities to develop special interests and to group training activities that teach them to think critically and creatively. Only a relatively small number of children are capable, however, of engaging productively in a third type of enrichment activity—individual and small group investigation of real problems. A student must have above-average creativity, intelligence, and motivation to define a real-life problem and conduct a productive real-life investigation of it.

Real-life problems and investigations on which gifted and talented elementary or middle school students might work could include, for example, making a useful environmental impact study of the effects of building a factory, conducting a survey of public opinion on a politically sensitive issue, or writing a computer program to monitor water consumption in their homes. Gifted and talented youngsters have the personal resources to follow through to the successful completion of such projects, whereas most children do not.

As you might have guessed from your reading thus far, Renzulli does not believe the same children will always have the necessary characteristics to perform successfully in a resource program for the gifted and talented. That is, a given child seldom will have the intelligence, creativity, and motivation to participate in every activity offered in a good resource program. So, Renzulli and Smith (1980) described a "revolving door" plan for identifying and serving gifted and talented students. Under this plan, children are rotated into and out of the resource program, depending on their interests and performance. This plan is consistent with the belief that students are gifted or talented in terms of their ability and willingness to perform particular valued activities at a particular time.

HIGH SCHOOL AND POSTSECONDARY LEVEL

When gifted and talented students reach high school, their educational needs can be met most effectively by accelerated placement in specific academic subjects, enrollment in special schools, or early enrollment in college classes. Today, increasing interest is being shown in special high schools for the gifted and talented.

Accelerated placement, allowing a student to proceed through the curriculum in a given subject as rapidly as possible, is supported not only by research on children's achievements and attitudes, but by analysis of costs as well (Weiss and Gallagher, 1982). That is, one result of letting students pass as quickly as possible through the secondary school and college curriculum is a considerable saving of money. And the research to date suggests very clearly that students' attitudes and social relationships do not suffer from such accelerated placement.

Two of the best known programs of advanced placement are the Study of Mathematically Precocious Youth (SMPY) at the Johns Hopkins University in Baltimore (Stanley, 1979) and the Minnesota Talented Youth Mathematics Program (Keating, 1979). These programs have shown that exceptional mathematical abilities can be identified early and that students benefit by being allowed to compete with older students whose abilities in mathematics are similar to theirs. Special high schools for students with talents in specific areas, such as the North Carolina School of Science and Mathematics and Houston's High School for the Performing and Visual Arts, are recognized today as important parts of the public education system (Churchwell, Gonzalez, and Orlando, 1981). In these schools students receive a general education that is appropriate for their abilities and advanced training in the areas in which they have exceptional talent.

As gifted and talented students approach adulthood, they have increasing opportunities to put their special abilities to work. Career planning, which should be an aspect of all children's education from the elementary grades on, becomes a major concern (Hagen, 1982). In most colleges and universities, in graduate schools, and in the adult world of business, commerce, and the arts, relatively few restraints on talent are found. People are free (aside from occasional discriminatory practices and bureaucratic restrictions) to compete to the full extent that their abilities will allow. Some gifted and talented adolescents and young adults achieve remarkable status on their own initiative, with help from their parents or other mentors. Educational programs could contribute to such achievements by being more open and flexible in response to students' interests and needs. Any lock-step system, whether a policy that reading will not be taught in kindergarten or a policy that all college graduates must have earned a certain number of credit hours in biology, is likely to stifle the progress and outstanding achievement of some exceptional students.

In concluding our discussion of educational programming, we want to comment on one type of accelerated placement many people think of when they think of gifted children—grade skipping. The recent review of research by Weiss and Gallagher (1982) indicates that skipping more than one grade in elementary school may result in social adjustment problems. That is, young children apparently need social contact at school with others fairly near their chronological age. If grades are to be skipped, the best time to skip probably is between grade groupings—that is, between elementary and junior high or between junior high and high school. Accelerated placement for children before they are the usual high school age appears to be most beneficial for the child (except, perhaps, in rare cases of extremely high intelligence) when it involves only selected academic areas in which the child excels. On the other hand, early admission to college for many gifted and talented high school students is probably a very defensible advanced placement option.

TECHNOLOGICAL ADVANCES

The technological advances most likely to be of benefit to most gifted and talented students are advances in information management. Improvements in computers and communications, which allow information to be stored, manipulated, and retrieved more efficiently, are most likely to improve the education of able students. Such advances are aids for these students' minds—they help them overcome limitations and extend their abilities in the same way that prosthetic devices help the physically disabled. Computers and telecommunications will increasingly make more information available to the gifted and talented and give them additional tools to use in searching for solutions to problems. The explosive growth of microcomputer technology and the increasing availability of computers in public schools should play a large role in providing appropriate education for many gifted and talented youngsters.

Two special points should be kept in mind. First, the gifted and talented are the students most likely to contribute to future technological advances that will benefit many types of persons, including the handicapped. So providing them an education that fosters growth of their special abilities is likely to be beneficial not only to them, but to others as well. Second, the handicapped gifted and talented are likely to benefit immeasurably from the technological advances we have described in other chapters of this book. For example, technology that allows a physically disabled person to communicate or move effectively may mean the difference between recognition and neglect of special gifts and talents. Certainly, not every handicapped person possesses brilliant intelligence or remarkable creativity that goes unrecognized. But for the handicapped whose special gifts or talents go unnoticed, the waste of ability seems doubly sad; any technology that allows them to demonstrate their gifts and talents is itself a very special gift.

ANSWERS TO FREQUENTLY ASKED QUESTIONS
GIFTEDNESS

1. Intelligence is determined by a combination of genetic and environmental factors. Unquestionably, the genetic influence on intelligence is very substantial. Highly intelligent parents are more likely than parents of average or lower intelligence to have a gifted child. But genetic factors affect only the *probability* that a given child will have low, average, or high intelligence; they do not guarantee it. Your friends' children are likely to be highly intelligent, but it is possible they will not be. Remember too that the environment your friends provide, regardless of biological inheritance, will be important in determining how intelligent their children become.

2. Teachers of the gifted and talented should be role models for their students. If your friend has not been a good student, he is very unlikely to be a good teacher of gifted and talented kids for one of two reasons: Either he does not have the ability to achieve at a high level, or he has not learned the study skills and developed the self-motivation required to be a successful student. Regardless of which is the reason for his poor performance as a student, we recommend that he consider other career options. Incidentally, he may be a bright person even though he does not appear to be—he may be an underachiever. Successful teachers of the gifted and talented need to be very bright themselves, but they must also be self-motivated high achievers with a high level of energy and commitment to teaching.

3. We recommend they stick to their guns about the enrichment program and, in addition, try to work out a compromise with the teachers in which the boy attends a seventh-grade class or two in his best academic areas, if he is really achieving at a seventh-grade level. When an elementary age child skips more than one grade, social adjustment problems sometimes occur. At the same time, gifted children are often better off when they can compete with others whose academic abilities match their own, even if the other children are quite a bit older. It seems to us that a combination of enrichment activities and advanced placement in one or two academic subjects might be a good plan. That way he could maintain social contact with other kids his age, participate with them in many school activities, and still have challenging work to do. We recommend too that your cousin talk with the school psychologist about counseling for the boy to help him deal with his obvious differences and about the best educational options for the child.

4. Don't worry. The saying is an old wives' (or husbands') tale. Although there are exceptions, most highly gifted individuals maintain their productivity over a greater span of years than those who have lesser abilities.

5. You are not the only one with this opinion. Education for all children could be improved, and we hope it will be. But we feel all children are entitled to an education that is in line with their abilities. The abilities of some children are so much higher than those of most children their age that special provisions must be made for them, even if all schools are improved. A special program is required to provide them with a reasonably challenging education and give them a chance to achieve what they can. We believe there is so much variation in children's characteristics that education cannot be improved for everyone unless special provisions are made for the education of some. This includes special education for the gifted and talented as well as for the handicapped.

SUMMARY

Because special education has been focused primarily on helping those who do not have the ability to perform well in school, one category of exceptional children, the gifted and talented, has often gotten lost in the shuffle of government priorities and programs and professional interest. But as long as special education is guided by the idea that every exceptional child is entitled to an appropriate education, the gifted and talented will always have a place in the field.

Much less money and attention are given to this group of exceptional children, in part because many people question the need for special services for them. The opposite view is that such people are a vital resource in any society—the source of much public pleasure as well as much innovation, advancement, and growth.

The category of gifted and talented differs from other kinds of exceptionality in three major ways: (1) Being gifted or talented is regarded as desirable; (2) despite the many kinds of gifts and talents, these individuals typically are considered a single category; and (3) no federal law requires free, appropriate public education for the gifted and talented.

The term gifted and talented today is defined as especially high ability or potential in one or more of several valued areas of performance. Traditionally, gifted was used to describe very high intelligence, and talented, high ability in a particular skill or art. Other terms used to describe these people are precocious (early developing), genius (extremely intelligent or creative), and creative (able to see and do things in novel or unique ways).

Defining potential is difficult, so identifying children as gifted and talented is often an arbitrary, chance procedure. One researcher has suggested three important defining characteristics: high ability, high creativity, and high commitment to a task.

Today we recognize not only that IQ tests alone are not sufficient to identify all the gifted and talented, but that giftedness and special talents may change with time and circumstances. An adequate identification system requires both testing and observation. Tests of intelligence and achievement are still an important part of the procedure, but they must be accompanied by assessments of creativity and motivation.

Using the federal definition of gifted and talented, 2 to 5 percent of the population probably could be given this label. What criteria should be used—and therefore the numbers of people who could be so classified—is the subject of some debate. Much depends on the standards and the comparison groups used.

The causes of giftedness are unclear. We do know that both heredity and environment are involved, but exactly how and to what extent these factors operate in a given case is still a mystery.

The old view of the gifted as eccentric oddballs and misfits—as "brains" connected to weak or unattractive bodies—has received a severe jolt as the results of two generations of studies have begun to show the opposite. Today we know that the gifted and talented tend to be healthy, both physically and emotionally, and often excel in more than one special area. Since the 1950s, we have also come to realize that those who show great creativity may not necessarily score extremely high on IQ tests. In addition, it is becoming clear that the gifted and talented are not always recognized if they possess certain other characteristics—if they are female, underachieving, culturally different, or handicapped.

Gifts and talents can also sometimes be a burden and a stigma: There is the constant pressure to perform, and there is also the envy of others, which can make personal relationships and peer acceptance difficult.

In the United States, educational programming for the gifted is sometimes subject to attack on the ground that it fosters destructive elitism, but it is clear that these children require something other than the usual education program if they are to realize their potential to the same degree as average learners. They also require teachers who have a high degree of commitment and who can serve as role models and withstand a good deal of stress.

Programs for the gifted fall into three major categories: training in thinking skills, modification of curriculum content, and modification of the learning environment. All have been tried somewhere at every level from preschool to high school. Administrative plans for curriculum modification include enrichment in the classroom, consultant teachers, resource room programs, community mentor programs, independent study programs, special classes, and special schools. There is a great deal of variation in the provisions made for the gifted and talented from one community and state to another.

Like preschool programs for the handicapped, preschool education of the gifted and talented requires parent participation. Primary school programming often involves advanced curriculum in all areas. Enrichment and resource programs are often emphasized, and acceleration is also used. At the high school level, needs can often be met most effectively by accelerated placement in specific subjects, enrollment in special schools, or early enrollment in college classes.

The technological advances most likely to benefit the gifted and talented are those in information management, which are aids for these students' minds just as prosthetic devices are aids for physically disabled students' bodies. Technological advances, especially those in computer technology, will give the gifted and talented more tools to use in solving problems and generating the new ideas our society needs.

REFERENCES

BAER, D.M., ROWBURY, T.G., & GOETZ, E.M. Behavioral traps in the preschool: A proposal for research. In A.D. Pick (Ed.). *Minnesota symposia on child psychology* (Vol. 10). Minneapolis: University of Minnesota Press, 1976.

BAER, N.A. Programs for the gifted: A present or a paradox? *Phi Delta Kappan*, 1980, *61*, 621–623.

BLOOM, B.S. The role of gifts and markers in the development of talent. *Exceptional Children*, 1982, *48*, 510–522.

BLOOM, B.S., & SOSNIAK, L.A. Talent development vs. schooling. *Educational Leadership*, 1981, *39*, 86–94.

BOUCHARD, T.J., & MCGUE, M. Familial studies of intelligence: A review. *Science*, 1981, *212*, 1055–1059.

BRIGHAM, R.A., GRAUBARD, P.S., & STANS, A. Analysis of the effects of sequential reinforcement contingencies on aspects of composition. *Journal of Applied Behavior Analysis*, 1972, *5*, 421–429.

BRUCE, D.F. Is your baby a genius? *Baby Talk*, 1982, *47*, 42–45.

CALLAHAN, C.M. Superior abilities. In J.M. Kauffman & D.P. Hallahan (Eds.). *Handbook of special education*. Englewood Cliffs, N.J.: Prentice-Hall, 1981.

CALLAHAN, C.M. Myth: There must be "winners" and "losers" in identification and programming! *Gifted Child Quarterly*, 1982, *26*, 17–19.

CALLAHAN, C.M., & KAUFFMAN, J.M. Involving gifted children's parents: Federal law is silent, but its assumptions apply. *Exceptional Education Quarterly*, 1982, *3*, 50–55.

CHURCHWELL, B., GONZALEZ, C., & ORLANDO, J.E. The High School for Performing and Visual Arts: Where arts and academics flourish. *Today's Education*, 1981, *70*, 23–24.

DELISLE, J. The non-productive gifted child: A contradiction of terms? *Roeper Review*, 1981, *3*, 20–22.

DELISLE, J. The gifted underachiever: Learning to underachieve. *Roeper Review*, 1982, *4*, 16–18.

DETTMER, P. Preventing burnout in teachers of the gifted. *Gifted/Creative/Talented*, 1982, January–February, 37–41.

FISCH, R.O., BILEK, M.K., HORROBIN, J.M., & CHANG, P. Children with superior intelligence at 7 years of age. *American Journal of Diseases of Children*, 1976, *130*, 481–487.

FREEMAN, J. The intellectually gifted. In K.I. Abroms & J.W. Bennett (Eds.). *Genetics and exceptional children*. San Francisco: Jossey-Bass, 1981.

GALLAGHER, J.J. *Research summary on gifted child education*. Springfield: Illinois State Department of Education, 1966.

GALLAGER, J.J. *Teaching the gifted child* (2nd ed.). Boston: Allyn and Bacon, 1975.

GALLAGHER, J.J., & WEISS, P. *The education of gifted and talented students. A history and prospectus*. Washington, D.C.: Council for Basic Education, 1979.

GETZELS, J.W., & JACKSON, P.W. The meaning of "giftedness"—An examination of an expanding concept. *Phi Delta Kappan*, 1958, *40*, 75–77.

GOETZ, E.M., & SALMONSON, M.M. The effect of general and descriptive reinforcement on "creativity" in easel painting. In G. Semb (Ed.). *Behavior analysis and education—1972*. Lawrence: Kansas University Department of Human Development, 1972.

GUILFORD, J.P. Three faces of intellect. *American Psychologist*, 1959, *14*, 469–479.

GUILFORD, J.P. Varieties of creative giftedness, their measurement and development. *Gifted Child Quarterly*, 1975, *19*, 107–121.

HAGEN, J.C. Career education for the gifted and talented: An analysis of issues and programs. *Exceptional Education Quarterly*, 1982, *3*, 48–57.

HOLLINGWORH, L.S. *Children above 180 IQ, Stanford-Binet: Origin and development*. Yonkers-on-Hudson, N.Y.: World, 1942.

KEATING, D.P. Secondary school programs. In A.H. Passow (Ed.). *The 78th yearbook of the National Society for the Study of Education, Part 1. The gifted and talented*. Chicago: University of Chicago Press, 1979.

KHATENA, J. *Educational psychology of the gifted*. New York: Wiley, 1982.

LINDSEY, M. *Training teachers of the gifted and talented*. New York: Teachers College Press, 1980.

LOMBROSO, C. *The man of genius* (2nd. ed.). New York: Walter Scott, 1905.

LYON, H.C. Our most neglected natural resource. *Today's Education*, 1981, *70*, 15–20.

MAKER, C.J. *Providing programs for the gifted handicapped*. Reston, Va.: Council for Exceptional Children, 1977.

MITCHELL, B.M. An update on the state of gifted/talented education in the U.S. *Phi Delta Kappan*, 1982, *63*, 357–358.

MYERS, D.G., & RIDL, J. Aren't all children gifted? *Today's Education*, 1981, *70*, 30–33.

PETROSKO, J.M. Measuring creativity in elementary school: The current state of the art. *Journal of Creative Behavior*, 1978, *12*, 109–119.

PORTER, R.M. The gifted handicapped: a status report. *Roeper Review*, 1982, *4*, 24–25.

RENZULLI, J.S. *The enrichment triad model: A guide for developing defensible programs for the gifted and talented*. Wethersfield, Conn.: Creative Learning Press, 1977.

RENZULLI, J.S. Dear Mr. and Mrs. Copernicus: We regret to inform you. . . . *Gifted Child Quarterly*, 1982, *26*, 11–14.

RENZULLI, J.S., HARTMAN, R.K., & CALLAHAN, C.M. Scale for rating the behavioral characteristics of superior students. In W.B. Barbe & J.S. Renzulli (Eds.). *Psychology and education of the gifted* (2nd ed.). New York: Irvington, 1975.

RENZULLI, J.S., & SMITH, L.H. Revolving door: A truer turn for the gifted. *Learning*, 1980, *9*, 91–93.

ROBINSON, H.B., ROEDELL, W.C., & JACKSON, N.E. Early identification and intervention. In A.H. Passow (Ed.). *The 78th yearbook of the National Society for the Study of Education, Part 1. The gifted and talented*. Chicago: University of Chicago Press, 1979.

SANBORN, K. *The vanity and insanity of genius*. New York: George J. Coombes, 1885.

SCARR-SALAPATEK, S. Genetics and the development of intelligence. In F.D. Horowitz (Ed.). *Review of child development research* (Vol. 4). Chicago: University of Chicago Press, 1975.

SCHWARTZ, L.L. Advocacy for the neglected gifted: Females. *Gifted Child Quarterly*, 1980, *24*, 113–117.

SISK, D.A. Educational planning for the gifted and talented. In J.M. Kauffman & D.P. Hallahan (Eds.). *Handbook of special education*. Englewood Cliffs, N.J.: Prentice-Hall, 1981.

STANLEY, J.C. The study and facilitation of talent for mathematics. In A.H. Passow (Ed.). *The 78th yearbook of the National Society for the Study of Education, Part 1. The gifted and talented*. Chicago: University of Chicago Press, 1979.

TERMAN, L.M. *Genetic studies of genius, Vol. I: Mental and physical traits of a thousand gifted children* (2nd ed.). Stanford, Calif.: Stanford University Press, 1926.

TERMAN, L.M., & ODEN, M.H. *Genetic studies of genius, Vol. V: The gifted group at midlife*. Stanford, Calif.: Stanford University Press, 1959.

TIDWELL, R. A psycho-educational profile of 1,593 gifted high school students. *Gifted Child Quarterly*, 1980, *24*, 63–68.

TORRANCE, E.P. *Guiding creative talent*. Englewood Cliffs, N.J.: Prentice-Hall, 1962.

TORRANCE, E.P. *Torrance tests of creative thinking: Norms—technical manual*. Princeton, N.J.: Personnel Press, 1966.

TORRANCE, E.P., & WU, T. A comparative longitudinal study of the adult creative achievements of elementary school children identified as high intelligent and as highly creative. *The Creative Child and Adult Quarterly*, 1981, *6*, 71–76.

TREFFINGER, D.J. Demythologizing gifted education: An editorial essay. *Gifted Child Quarterly*, 1982, *26*, 3–8.

TREFFINGER, D.J., RENZULLI, J.S., & FELDHUSEN, J.F. Problems in the assessment of creative thinking. In W.B. Barbe & J.S. Renzulli (Eds.). *Psychology and education of the gifted* (2nd ed.). New York: Irvington, 1975.

WEISS, P., & GALLAGHER, J.J. *Report on education of gifted* (Vol. II). Chapel Hill, N.C.: Frank Porter Graham Child Development Center, 1982.

WHITMORE, J.R. *Giftedness, conflict, and underachievement*. Boston: Allyn and Bacon, 1980.

PARENTS
AND
FAMILIES
10

1. My 8-month-old daughter is not responding the way my two older children did at her age. She still is not able to hold her head up steadily for very long and she has made no beginning attempts to sit up or to crawl. I just know something is wrong, and yet my pediatrician keeps telling me that children develop at very different rates and for us to give her more time. I don't want to keep waiting because with each passing month I worry that she is missing some kind of help. What should I do?

2. My 11-year-old niece Shari is physically handicapped and must walk with crutches. She has four brothers who are the rough and tumble type—the whole family, in fact, is very active and athletic. What concerns me is that my sister includes Shari in all the family adventures and never seems to make allowances for the fact that she is handicapped. Last year, Shari broke her arm on a camping trip with her father. I worry that she'll encounter serious injury unless her family slows down a bit and takes into account her disability.

3. I have an 8-year-old boy with cerebral palsy in my class. Andrew's parents seem to care about him, but lately when I asked them to follow up in the evenings with exercises for better fine motor control, they seemed to balk. Later, when I questioned why they wouldn't do what I asked, they got very defensive and angry, telling me that they have four children and very little time. What can I do to get them to care more about helping their child?

4. My 13-month-old son, Jeffrey, is autistic. He is a beautiful child, but he hardly responds to me at all. When I hold him, he tenses his body and doesn't relax until I put him down. He seems to like my voice, but does not look directly at me when I speak. I feel horribly guilty, because some days I feel such a mixture of feelings about Jeffrey and the way he is—anger, rejection, loneliness, fear, depression. Recently, I have avoided taking him outside because of other people's cruel stares and questions. I am all mixed up and I hate myself. Some days I'm not even sure I love my son the way a mother should. What is wrong with me?

5. My son's teacher has called me to say I must attend the next IEP meeting. She says the law says I must be present, or he won't get into the program he needs. It's hard for me to get off work and, besides, I'm no expert on what he needs—isn't that the educators' job? If I go, I won't understand what they're saying, and I don't feel that I would have anything to say. Can't I tell his teacher to get off my back?

In the first nine chapters of this text, we've attempted to present you with factual information pertaining to each of the areas of exceptionality. We've been able to present what we know today about the definition, prevalence, causes, assessment, characteristics, and educational methods for each of the areas of special education. At the same time, however, we hope you have an appreciation for just how much still remains unknown about exceptional individuals. We will feel good about our ability to communicate in this text if at this point you have the slightly uneasy feeling that you have more questions than answers about exceptionality. By now, we hope you consider the education of exceptional individuals an extremely complex business.

An understanding of the complex nature of exceptionality should also prepare you for the topic of this chapter—parents and families. To grasp the major concepts surrounding families of the disabled, we must have some appreciation of the intricacies of human interaction. There are no more "human" interactions than those among family members. Think of your own family as you were growing up. Think of the dynamics of interaction among you and your brother(s) and sister(s) and parent(s). These interactions were no doubt carried out within the context of a full range of human emotions. Now, add to this mixture of human interaction a dose of handicaps. Consider how much more complex living in your family would have been if you had had a mentally retarded or autistic brother or sister.

One of the primary reasons why the dynamics within a family with a handicapped child can be so complex is due to society's reaction to exceptional individuals. All families, including those with a handicapped member, operate within the context of a larger society. And society, at times, can be heartless. The following quote from *Geri* (Jewell, with Weiner), is instructive. Written by the actress Geri Jewell, who has cerebral palsy, the book gives us a glimpse of how one handicapped child dealt with the cruel blows of society and the effects of these on herself and her mother. The following event took place shortly after Geri and her family moved to a new neighborhood:

> When we got to the foot of the walk, Karen grabbed my hand to shake it. For a second, she held it too tightly. Really tightly. *Wait a minute.* "Ouch."
>
> "Sorry," she said and that's when I saw The Eyes. Most people get these Eyes when they find themselves around a handicapped person; the Eyes which dart to take a look at you and then dart away so as not to get caught. Sometimes I can feel them when mom takes me shopping. I can feel the heat of people's stares but when I swivel to return the glimpses, the Eyes have hopped elsewhere leaving no trace.
>
> I should have been warned by Karen's Eyes but many forces were at work on me that day. I knew I'd be needing friends, for one thing, and this was the best offer I'd had all day. And it did seem to be a whole new beginning for me—what a great time, I thought, to give people the benefit of the doubt. My thoughts were interrupted when Karen spotted my Radio Flyer.
>
> "Can we play with your wagon?" Karen asked. "I've got a great game we can play."
>
> "Yeah, tell her," Tracy urged.
>
> "Yeah, tell me," I said over and over, excitedly.
>
> "OK, OK. The game is called Tourists. You know what a tourist is, Geri?"
>
> I didn't.
>
> "They're people from all over the country who come around here in buses and stare at

things. We get a lot of them around here because of Disneyland. Have you ever played Tourists before?"

I hadn't.

"OK, then," Karen said, relishing the spotlight. "Here's how you play. Geri, you'll be leader. You like being the leader, don't you?"

My head was nodding.

"You'll be our guide. Tracy and I will be the tourists. Quick, Tracy, get in, the tour bus is leaving!!!"

That's when they both jumped into my wagon and held out the handle to me. "You just pull us along and point to all the tourist attractions," Tracy said, giggling.

I pulled them up the street, chattering away, making up things about the neighborhood as I went along. I was really good at this. While Karen and Tracy laughed themselves silly in the wagon, I pointed out the mystical home of the Queen of Orange County who lived with one hundred servants. I dragged them past the home where Pinocchio was carved by the gentle woodcarver Gepetto. They already knew that story. I made up stories about the cars going by, on their way to glamourous parties with lots of sequined evening gowns and handsome movie actors. To me it was all real and it made me feel good to hear Tracy and Karen laugh.

Things went along great until we passed by one house with some older kids sprawled out on a lawn smoking cigarettes. They started to yell things.

"Hey Tracy, what took you so long to get the crip's wagon? We've been waiting here forever," one of them shouted.

My blood turned to ice as I realized that I had been ambushed. Then Tracy looked at me with the meanest Eyes I'd ever seen. "She's such a retard," Tracy said. "It took us forever for her to figure out how to pull us." Then she started to mock me, twisting her face and holding her hands together like a monkey.

"Hey, don't you girls know you can *catch* what she's got?" At the sound of that, Tracy and Karen both leaped out of the wagon and everybody started screaming and running in circles around me.

"Why don't you run home, you retard," one of them yelled.

"You know she can't run with that wagon," someone else said.

"Well, why don't we just *take* the wagon?"

Apparently that seemed like a glorious idea to them and they all gathered around me and dozens of their fingers grabbed mine trying to pry my hands from the wagon's handle. Little do most people know of the strength in the wrists of most of us with CP. They couldn't get these strong fingers off the handle. Even worse, they couldn't make me cry, either. That really got to them. They tried calling me every name in the book. They tried "cripple" and "gimp" and "freak" and "retard" the old reliable. None of the names worked; I still wouldn't cry. I knew I would later because most of the names stung but right now I wouldn't give them the satisfaction.

Then things got rough. All I remember is hitting the pavement. Suddenly, everything got darker, the taunting voices faded away. . .

When I came to, everyone had disappeared. And they hadn't left empty-handed. Not only did they take my wagon, but they also took my shoes. My shoes! Maybe they thought I couldn't walk without them, like the shoes were orthopedic or something.

It was the longest walk back—those two blocks to my new house. Even though I really hadn't traveled far, every pigeon-toed step seemed to take an hour. For the first time in my life, the full weight of having cerebral palsy had landed squarely on my shoulders. I was never going to be normal, I knew that now. I was never going to be accepted. People just don't like you if you're different, that's all.

Until that day I had never really felt all that different. For years, all of my parents' friends kept saying (at least to my face) how adorable I was. Heck, I'd even been a poster child a few times. Strangers remarked how cute I was; how people had fawned over me then!

And now all of my accomplishments suddenly amounted to zero. I realized for the first time that I was just what these kids said I was. A cripple, someone to take advantage of. Someone to hate and be afraid of. Nobody would ever know what I was really like on the inside because on the outside I was scary and ugly and different. I could hardly make it the last block—I was so loaded down with this terrible weight. If I could have killed myself right then and there, I would have. I couldn't stop crying. The tears filled my eyes and as I walked, stumbled really, along these strange streets, these streets filled with this new painful truth, I could hardly see where I was going. And what did I do to deserve all this, I thought. All I did was be born. Why did God make people like me, anyway?

I must have looked unbelievably awful by the time I got home because when my folks saw me, they went into hysterics. "My God," my mother screamed in a pitch I can still hear in my memory. "What happened to you?"

"They took my wagon, mommy."

Dad looked totally outraged; Mother was horrified. Worst of all, I could sense in both of them a great deal of disappointment. This new neighborhood, so full of promise only this morning, had let them down already. I had let them down too. Up until now, maybe they still harbored a remote hope that somehow I might still make it as a normal child. Standing before them now, however, was living proof that things were going to be even rougher than they had counted on. The tears began to stream down Mom's cheeks; she covered her face as she cried. . .

"Promise me one thing, Geri," she said that night as she put the stinging mercurachrome on my left ear, gave me a hot bath and tucked me into bed. "Promise me that no matter how bad things get, don't ever lose yourself to it. There's no point in letting other people decide who you will be. You will meet more people like you did today. You'll meet people who will be even more cruel, without even meaning to be, just because they don't know what they're doing. . ."

She was determined to minimalize the damage and I knew she meant well but right then I needed something more than just her comforting words. I needed to know where in myself I would get the resolve to handle shocks like the one I got today. The fact that I didn't cry proved I had the goods but a shiver went up my spine anyway.

"Geri, stop daydreaming and listen to me." Geez, she must have been thinking, where *is* this girl's head most of the time? "I'm not going to leave this bedroom tonight until you promise."

"Promise what?" I had been deep in my own thoughts.

"Promise you'll keep your spirits up. OK? Do you promise? Will you shake with me on it?" She put out her hand.

I looked up at my mother's face, so in need of encouragement. A tear dropped from her face onto the blanket covering my chest. All I wanted to do was make her feel better about having me. I wanted to make things right again. I began to remove myself from her a little; I could feel myself moving away from this pain to a place where my heart could perch, relaxed. When she asked me to shake with her, I gathered all the strength and answered her: "You know me, mom, I'll always shake with you." And then I grinned a grin as big as our doctor bills. "Shake, mom, get it?"

At that moment, the sunshine broke through in my mother's eyes. The dark cloud that seemed to hover over us evaporated. Everything changed in an instant. She started to laugh at my joke, her face eased, her worry lines loosened. Suddenly all of the crummy parts of this lousy first day in this scary new neighborhood dissolved. We sat and laughed with each other until it hurt our stomachs, the ripples of laughter forming a whirlpool that sent our cares down the drain. And her laughter made me feel glorious. Powerful. Invulnerable.

And it was right there that night that I decided if I couldn't overcome cerebral palsy, I could at least laugh it out of the ring. I would make it. I would deserve respect.

A lot of things have happened to me before and since this incident but I've always said that my life really began that day in that empty house on that cruel street when I chased my mother's tears away with a joke. (From *Geri* by Geri Jewell with Stewart Weiner. Copyright © 1984. By permission of William Morrow & Company and Ballantine Books.)

FAMILY INTERACTION AND THE HANDICAPPED CHILD

CHANGING ATTITUDES

Today's knowledgeable special educator is aware of the importance of considering the family in dealing with exceptional individuals. We now recognize that the family of the exceptional individual, especially the parents, can help us in our educational efforts. To ignore the handicapped individual's family is not only shortsighted, but can also lessen the effectiveness of our own teaching efforts.

In the past, we have often looked to the parents as a cause of some of the child's problems or as a place to lay blame when our intervention didn't go well. Today we are less willing to point to parents as the primary cause of their children's problems. Instead, we acknowledge that the family can have a positive or a negative influence on the development and adjustment of the disabled child.

Why has the field of special education begun to recognize the potentially positive input by the family in the educational process? In many ways, the special education profession has been convinced (or some would say, "forced") to consider the family by factors external to the field itself. At least three factors have contributed to the change in attitude toward parents:

1. Parents themselves have become more and more active in advocating services for their children in an organized and effective way. In the process, they have also frequently argued that they themselves should be given a voice in how their children are educated.
2. Some research has demonstrated that intervention programs which include the parent as an active participant are more successful than those that do not (Bronfenbrenner, 1974).
3. Federal law, PL 94-142, stipulates that an attempt must be made to involve parents in the educational process. There are specific provisions in the law to ensure the parent's rights to information and participation in decisions regarding their child. (We'll say more about this later.)

BABY POWER

Psychologists and educators, traditionally, have been preoccupied with the idea that the infant and young child are shaped by their parents and other aspects of their environment. The hypothesis that infants or children themselves could exert the same influence on their parents was for many years largely ignored. In the 1970s, however, Bell introduced us to the notion that the direction of influence is a two-way street (Bell, 1971; Bell and Harper, 1977). Sometimes, the parent changes the behavior of the infant or child;

sometimes, the reverse is true. Observe a young infant and his or her parents objectively and you'll wonder why it took so long for psychologists to discover that the behavior of a parent is often shaped by the behavior of the child. Note how the parent responds to the cries of the child. Note too how quickly a smile from the baby can bring loving caresses from the parent.

The concept that children are frequently responsible for how parents respond to them is important to keep in mind when considering the interaction of families with a handicapped child. If normal infants can exert such influence on their parents, it's a cinch that this will often be true for handicapped infants. Handicapped infants are frequently characterized by extremes of behavior, and these extremes can directly influence how the parents respond. Parents of handicapped infants often tell of how their children have difficult temperaments. They may be difficult to console, cry for long periods of time, and go for months without sleeping through the night. Have you ever tried to comfort a screaming infant in all the loving ways you could think of—and not been successful? Even a few moments of such an experience is extremely unnerving; imagine hours every evening spent in this manner! Also, ask any parent about the importance of the characteristic of sleeping through the night, and you'll get a feeling for how stressful life with some handicapped infants can be.

At the other extreme, many parents report that their exceptional infants are unre-

If you've been around infants much, you know how good they can make you feel when they smile and gurgle at you. Hans Namuth, Photo Researchers, Inc.

sponsive. If you've been around infants much, you know how good they can make you feel when they smile and gurgle at you. The more they bubble, the more you want to cuddle them, tickle them, pop your lips at them, and do all of those other behaviors that would look absurd in any other context. We take joy in being able to bring pleasure to babies. We act silly *because* of them. In short, we are reinforced by these little creatures. Handicapped infants, however, are not always so reinforcing. The blind baby, the deaf baby, the retarded baby, the autistic baby may be delayed in the development of such delightful behaviors as smiling, cooing, or looking into the parent's eyes. Parents of such children will often admit to the difficulties they had in building strong emotional attachments to their infants. This does not mean the parents were cold and rejecting. It is much more likely that the parents started out as all parents do, but due to their infant's lack of responsiveness, they began to develop feelings of rejection and frustration. Emotional attachments between parents and unresponsive children are not impossible, but they do sometimes require a great deal of patience on the part of parents.

Today's special educators recognize the potential power even very young infants can have in the dynamics of family life. They are alert to the idea that how handicapped children develop is influenced by how their families act towards them. They know, however, that how their families act toward them can be determined, in large measure, by the behavior of the children themselves.

FEELINGS

When you're talking about the impact an exceptional child has on the family, you're talking for the most part about *feelings*—the feelings of the parents toward the child and toward society's reactions to the child, the feelings of the child's brothers and sisters toward the child and society, and the feelings of the handicapped child. When you're talking about feelings, of course, you're dealing in the realm of subjectivity. Psychologists are notoriously good at describing people's emotions, but poor at understanding them. The subjective and complex nature of the familial feelings aroused by exceptional children make our job of comprehending their nature extremely difficult. There is an important point we should keep in mind, however: Our difficulty in understanding these feelings is nothing in comparison with the problems faced by the handicapped children and their families in coming to grips with these emotions.

FEELINGS OF PARENTS

In considering how parents interact with their exceptional child, it helps to keep in mind that parents' initial reactions to having a handicapped child can be, and often are, very different from the feelings they will experience later on. One of the initial reactions, for example, is a change of expectations about many aspects of the child's life (see Focus). So we will discuss these two time periods separately. Keep in mind, however, that the line between early and later reactions is not a sharp one. And there are no hard and fast rules regarding when an individual parent will leave behind the earlier feelings and experience the later set of reactions.

SO WHAT DID YOU EXPECT? SUPERBABY?

FOCUS

So what did you expect? Superbaby? Of course you did. Every mom and dad dream that their forthcoming child will be a superbaby. Remember those secret thoughts? "Maybe our child will be . . .

a president
or a prime minister
a famous scientist
an all-star athlete
a celebrated musician
a 'mother-of-the-year'
a brilliant author
a sensitive artist
or a saint."

Whatever you fantasied about your unborn child probably had something to do with the person you wanted to be—but never could. And the closest you came to facing your secret expectations showed up in statements such as, "I only hope it's healthy."

Everybody quietly hopes for a superbaby, but nobody gets one.

Many times those who actually become great leaders, scientists, or artists do so out of a personal need to compensate for deficiencies and defects in their lives. And their success is often an utter surprise to their parents—mothers and fathers who felt that *this one* was too sickly, nervous, loud, or strange.

Source: Perske, R. and Perske, M. *Hope for the Families: New Directions for Parents of Persons with Retardation or Other Disabilities*. Nashville: Abingdon Press, 1981. Illustrated by Martha Perske. Reprinted with permission.

INITIAL FEELINGS. What little research that has been done on the subject suggests that some parents tend to go through a series of stages after learning that they have a handicapped child (Turnbull and Blacher-Dixon, 1980). Different stages have been proposed by different authorities. For the most part, however, the different proposed sequences are strikingly similar. A representative set of stages based on interviews of parents of malformed infants includes shock and disruption, denial, sadness, anxiety and fear, anger, and finally adaptation (Drotar, Baskiewicz, Irvin, Kennell, and Klaus, 1975).

But we shouldn't think in terms of all parents marching through such stages in lockstep fashion. As professionals, it is better for us to think of such emotions as shock, denial, anger, and so forth as reactions parents may or may not experience and may or may not experience in sequential fashion.

One of the strongest arguments against a rigid stage model comes from the fact that *parents are often the first to suspect that their child has a problem*. To be sure, there are parents who engage in denial, who go from physician to physician seeking a more favorable diagnosis. Talk to a group of parents of handicapped children, however, and you'll be astounded at how often it's the other way around—the parents had to go from doctor to doctor before they could convince someone there was something wrong with their child. Ackerley (1978), the mother of an autistic son, describes her experiences along these lines:

> We don't begin in anger. We start out the way all parents of all children do: with respect, reverence really, for the professional and his skills. The pediatrician, the teacher, the writer of books and articles on child development, they are the sources of wisdom from which we must draw in order to be good parents. We believe, we consult, we do as we are told, and all goes well unless . . . one of our kids has a handicap.
>
> We parents are almost always the first to notice that something is amiss, and one of our early consolations is often our pediatrician's assurance that "it's nothing—he'll outgrow it." That, of course, is exactly what we want to hear because it corresponds perfectly to the dwindling hope in our hearts, so we defer to the expert and our child loses another year. Finally, the time does come when not even the most conservative professional can deny the existence of a problem. The difficulty now is to define it and plan accordingly. With luck, our pediatrician refers us to an appropriate specialist and we are (or should be) on our way.
>
> We transfer our trust to the new god and wait expectantly for the oracle to speak. Instead of the strong, authoritative voice of wisdom, we more often hear an evasive stammer: "Can't give you a definite diagnosis . . . uh, mumble, mumble . . . virtually untestable . . . let us see him . . . cough, cough . . . again in a year." Ironically, when the oracle is loud and clear, it is often wrong: "Seriously emotionally disturbed; it's a severe withdrawal reaction to maternal ambivalence." The parents have just been treated to their first dose of professional puffery, and it is very bitter medicine, all the more so for being almost totally ineffective.
>
> Its one potentially redeeming feature may be realized if the parents react with sufficient anger to take charge, to assert their right to be their child's "case manager." Unfortunately, this is not likely to happen at such an early stage; it takes more than one false god to make us give up religion entirely. And when (or if) we do manage to assert ourselves, our behavior is viewed by professionals as the final stage in our own pathology; any of us who may still be practicing religion are immediately excommunicated. (Ackerly, 1978, p. 40)

Ackerly's feelings are representative of those of many parents. And her frustrations are not unique to the particular exceptionality of her son. Parents of the retarded, from mild to profound, parents of the cerebral palsied, from mild to profound, and so forth, will tell you similar stories.

Parents' first encounters with professionals can color their feelings about their handicapped child for some time. Whether it be a teacher telling Mr. and Mrs. Jones he or she suspects that their 8-year-old son David has a learning disability, or whether it be a doctor confirming the suspicions of Mr. and Mrs. Campbell that their 4-month-old daughter has cerebral palsy, how the professional deals with the parents at this sensitive time can be critical. From the accounts of numerous parents about the insensitivity of some professionals (Paul and Beckman-Bell, 1981; Turnbull and Turnbull, 1978), it's no wonder parents have difficulties dealing with their feelings toward their handicapped child.

Even though we can't be sure what emotions each parent of a handicapped child will feel, and even though we can't be sure that he or she will experience them in stages, numerous parental accounts document the existence of a number of relatively common reactions. Featherstone (1980), herself the mother of a blind, hydrocephalic, retarded boy with cerebral palsy and seizures, has written a highly informative book that discusses the most commonly reported parental feelings—fear, anger, loneliness, and guilt and self-doubt. We will briefly discuss two of these—loneliness, and guilt and self-doubt.

LONELINESS. Having a handicapped child sets you apart from the rest of society. According to Featherstone (1980), loneliness is the most pervasive emotion experienced by parents of the handicapped. She describes three different types of loneliness:

> Some feel shut out by the physical limitations that the disability imposes on the family activity. Others suffer most deeply from a personal and internal sense of their own family's uniqueness: they feel most bleakly alone when they glimpse Madison Avenue's image of the grinning, healthy "typical American family" in a commercial for life insurance. A third group are wounded by the lack of understanding they encounter in the wider world—or even among family and friends. (From *A Difference in the Family: Life with a Disabled Child* by Helen Featherstone. © 1980, by Basic Books, Inc. Publishers. p. 52. By permission of the publisher.)

GUILT AND SELF-DOUBT. Guilt is another common reaction of parents, especially mothers, of the handicapped. Parents often wrestle with the terrifying theme that they are in some way responsible for their child's problems even when there is no rational basis for such thoughts. It can seem completely illogical to the parent of normal children that guilt should be so common, but there's no doubt that many parents of exceptional children experience it. One factor that probably contributes to the prevalence of feelings of responsibility is our general lack of knowledge concerning the causes of disability. In your reading of the first nine chapters, you've probably been struck by how frequently we're unable to specify a particular cause for a child's disabilities. This context of uncertainty is fertile ground for guilt. Featherstone describes the situation well:

> Our children are wondrous achievements. Their bodies grow inside ours. If their defects originated *in utero*, we blame our inadequate bodies or inadequate caution. If, like Mrs. Park, we accept credit for our children's physical beauty (and most of us do, in our hearts), then inevitably we assume responsibility for their physical defects.
>
> The world makes much of the pregnant woman. People open doors for her, carry her heavy parcels, offer footstools and unsolicited advice. All this attention seems somehow posited on the idea that she is creating something miraculously fine. When the baby arrives imperfect, the mother feels she has failed not only herself, and her husband but the rest of the world as well.

Most women take great joy in their pregnancy. Featherstone (1980) notes, however, that if the baby is handicapped, the attention paid the expectant mother may contribute to her feelings of guilt! ERIKA, Photo Researchers, Inc.

Soon this diffuse sense of inadequacy sharpens. Nearly every mother fastens on some aspect of her own behavior and blames the tragedy on that. (pp. 73–74)

Besides the feelings of guilt about the cause of their child's condition, parents often have serious doubts about their own ability to provide for the child in the best possible way. They feel vulnerable to the criticism of others. They don't want to "look bad." As Featherstone again relates:

The exceptional family stands in a strange, and at times rather sad, relationship to outside opinion. Guilty, unsure, unprepared, and lonely, both parents and children long for understanding, reassurance, and approval. In the war against inner demons, they turn to others. I remember my struggles during Jody's earliest years. We had to decide whether to keep our difficult baby at home or to look around for a good residential school. Many things played into this momentous decision, but I remember, quite uncomfortably, that one factor was the opinion of other people. I was afraid that the world would judge me a rejecting, inadequate mother if I let Jody live somewhere else. If there was one person left in all the world who opposed placement, I did not want to do it. I paid no attention to a phalanx of friends and relatives advising institutional care; I figured I was doing more, not less, than they advised.

The whole situation recalled a problem that had troubled me as a child: the problem of the hero. Most of us, I reasoned, are neither heroes nor cowards, and no one judges us in these terms. We are ordinary people. Yet suppose I, an ordinary person, am walking alone beside an icy, isolated river, and see someone drowning. I have two options: I can jump in and try to save him (risking death myself), or I can agonize on the shore. In the first case I am a hero; in the second, a coward. There is no way I can remain what I was before—an ordinary person. As the mother of a profoundly retarded child, I felt I was in the same position: I had to look like a hero or a coward, even though actually I was still an ordinary person. (pp. 83–84)

LATER FEELINGS. As time passes, parents of handicapped children undergo two changes with regard to their feelings:

1. The parents' feelings become more "normalized" in the sense that they focus on things that are more similar to what parents of normal children have concerns about. Their feelings revolve around everyday occurrences related to such things as physical care and school experiences.
2. Many of their frustrations are because of society's reaction to them and their child. More and more, the object of their feelings becomes society. They become very sensitive to how they and their child are treated by others in the community.

With regard to the first point, it is easy for the professional to overlook how physically and emotionally taxing life with a handicapped child can be. The physical care alone can be a great burden, depending on the severity of the child's disability. Imagine for a moment, having to feed your 6-year-old all his meals, having to carry your 4-year-old because she can still only crawl, having to keep a watchful eye on your hyperactive and aggressive son when you go shopping for fear he will destroy everything in sight. Morton (1978), the mother of five daughters, one of whom is profoundly retarded, says it well:

> There is expectation by others that we should live "normally," as if, in fact, there were nothing unnormal about our lives. Who—besides another parent of a handicapped child— understands the extraordinary effort it takes to hang onto friends, respond to family, attend back-to-school nights, take children to dentists, entertain for husbands, shop for groceries, do the housework, take the car to be fixed, drop one child off to play with a friend, pick up another after a piano lesson, or, heaven forbid, hold down a job while attending to the needs of a child who is disabled and needs extraordinary care?
>
> It is not a one-time demand. We all know mothers whose children are recuperating from illnesses or other temporary catastrophes. Those mothers get reprieve from life's daily expectations. Husbands will shop for groceries, a friend can drive in the car pool that week, the dentist appointment can be postponed, the piano lesson cancelled, back-to-school night skipped. But there is nothing temporary about the catastrophic demands on time and energy made by a retarded child, and one cannot expect friends and family to respond endlessly to a crisis which is chronic. Each day presents us with the challenge of figuring out how to do everything that would be done if we didn't have a handicapped child, while managing the handicapped child who we clearly do have. (pp. 143–44).

How parents of the handicapped feel about society's response to them and their child can be very complex. Parents are often distraught because of the way they and their exceptional child are treated by others. But though parents of the handicapped may feel resentment and hatred toward some people, the experience of having a handicapped child also tends to make them more sensitive to the plight of others. Talk with parents of the handicapped, and you'll find they often experience a change in their value systems. They become more tolerant and compassionate toward individuals who undergo misfortune of one kind or another. As Helsel (1978), the mother of a cerebral-palsied and retarded son, recounts:

> By the time Robin was born, my life style and career plans were fairly well set. I had completed my Ph.D. in genetics and was playing out the role of faculty wife and mother. Vaguely, at some undetermined point in the future, I planned to return to the university and continue my research on chromosome mapping. To be honest and blunt, I was smug, self-centered, and an intellectual snob. Robin's birth and the problems attendant to trying

to find services and adequate care for him abruptly changed the pattern of my life, my attitudes, and my plans for the future. Suddenly I was thrust into a totally different world with people from all levels of society. We had common problems and our children had common service needs. Through working together, we learned to know and appreciate people for what they were and not for their professional, financial or social status. My attitudes changed not only toward people with handicapped children but toward all people with problems. Now I knew what it meant to be stared at, shunned, avoided. People became embarrassed when we brought Robin out in public or when we explained his condition—especially when they learned that he wasn't going to grow out of it or recover from it. (p. 98)

FEELINGS OF BROTHERS AND SISTERS

Although there is a relatively large body of literature concerning parental feelings, much less has been written about siblings of the handicapped. What has been written about them, however, indicates that they can, and frequently do, experience the same emotions—fear, anger, guilt, and so forth—that parents do. Siblings, however, are at a disadvantage in two ways in dealing with these emotions. First, they are less mature and do not have a large group of adults (doctors, teachers, other parents) on whom they can rely for information about their handicapped brother or sister (Featherstone, 1980). Second, they often don't feel comfortable in asking their parents the questions that might nag them—whether they will "catch" what their brother Sam has; whether they will be called on to take care of Sara after their parents die; whether they were in some way responsible for Bill's handicap.

Although some feelings about their sibling's handicap may not appear for many years, a substantial number of accounts indicate that normal siblings are aware at an amazingly early age that their brother or sister is different in some way. Jewell (in press) recounts, for example, how her sister would make allowances for her handicap of cerebral palsy by playing a special version of "dolls" with her, a version in which all the dolls had handicaps.

As the exceptional child and his or her sibling(s) grow older, the latter often become more and more concerned about how society views them and their handicapped brother or sister. They are frequently torn by society's negative view and their own love for their brother or sister. Some excellent children's books show this complexity of emotion (see Focus).

FOCUS

HE'S MY BROTHER

There are now many children's books that deal with the subject of exceptional children. The following excerpts from Joe Lasker's *He's My Brother* deal specifically with the feelings a brother or sister of a handicapped child often has.

Jamie's my brother.
He doesn't have many friends.
Little kids play with him.
Sometimes a big kid plays when no one else is around.
Jamie gets teased.
He doesn't know how to answer back.

It took Jamie a long time

to learn to tie his shoelaces.

When he tries, he gets in trouble, and comes home.
Becka is our sister.
She likes Jamie.
She bakes brownies for him.
When kids on the block choose up teams, they choose Jamie last.
It took Jamie a long time to learn to tie his shoelaces.
He still has trouble hanging up his clothes.
I guess I have, too.
School is easy for me.
But hard for Jamie.
Jamie gets mixed up at school.
Especially when it gets noisy.
When it's time for a test, Jamie thinks he knows the answers.
Then everything goes wrong.
Sometimes the kids make fun of Jamie.
They take his cookies or spill his milk.
Sometimes I get mad at him because he is so slow.
Then I feel sorry and play a game of checkers with him.
But there are things Jamie likes a lot.
He loves babies.
He loves animals . . .
He never hurts them.
One day Jamie said, ''Wouldn't it be nice if we could be friends with all the animals in the world?''
I wish I'd thought of that! . . .
Mom helps Jamie with his schoolwork.
Dad reads to Jamie.
I make up stories for Jamie.
Stories to tell him we love him.
He laughs.
He's my brother.

Source: J. Lasker, *He's my brother*. Chicago: Whitman, 1974. Reprinted with permission.

These concerns, of course, parallel normal child development. We can all recall how important it was to fit in with the "right crowd" in high school. As Featherstone notes, it's important for teenagers not to be considered different by their peers, but at the same time to be considered special, with all the attention that goes with being special, within the confines of their own family. Unfortunately, the brother or sister of a disabled child often comes up on the short end of the stick in both departments. Having a handicapped sibling can set you up as different from your peers. At the same time, the handicapped sibling, usually for legitimate reasons, draws most of the special attention and energy from the parents. The following account, by the sister of a cerebral palsied, mentally retarded brother, provides us with a representative example of the embarrassment experienced by some siblings:

> I cannot pinpoint exactly the time or the circumstance when I first became aware of Robin's handicaps. Several incidents come to mind, all of which occurred around the time I was eleven years old. One involved a trip to the shoe store where Robin was to be fitted for orthopedic shoes; another, a trip to the town near our country home for dinner at the YMCA. On both of these occasions, I can remember being acutely embarrassed by the ill-conceived stares our family received as we entered pushing Robin in his wheelchair. I was certain that everyone was looking at my brother with his obvious handicap and then wondering what was wrong with the rest of us. As a result of the feelings aroused in me by these occurrences, I began to refuse to go out to dinner or shopping with my family and took precautions to avoid being seen on the street or in the yard with Robin.
>
> These avoidance procedures on my part were not taken without an accompanying sense of guilt. I knew that it was wrong for me to be ashamed of my brother. I loved Robin dearly and realized that the opinions (real or imagined) of others should have had no bearing on my relationship with him. . . .

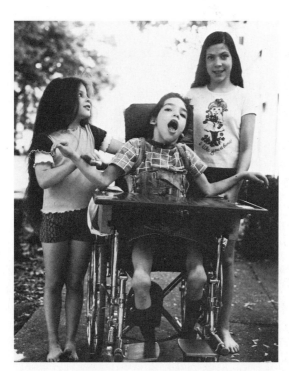

Reactions and feelings of the handicapped child's siblings should not be ignored. They are as important as those of parents in determining the total adjustment of the family.
Arthur Glauberman, Photo Researchers, Inc.

Following my period of avoidance, I entered a phase of false pretenses. I forced myself to appear in public with him—but only if I felt I looked my very best (freshly washed hair, make-up, a snazzy outfit, etc.). My specious reasoning was that if people were going to stare, they weren't going to find anything wrong with me. Also, though I am reluctant to admit such a selfish thought, I suppose I wanted to encourage people to think along the lines of "Oh, dear, look at that sweet young girl pushing her poor crippled brother around. What a wonderful child she must be." This period extended into my college years, at which time several events occurred that led to an abrupt change of attitude on my part.

Robin has periodically undergone hospitalization following seizure episodes which left him in a comatose state. . . . Because I was too young at the times of his early hospitalization to visit Robin, these episodes did not really have too much impact on me. Robin always came home after a few days, perhaps a bit less alert, a bit less his enthusiastic self; and our family life resumed its usual course. One day when I was a freshman in college, I drove out to my parents' house for a visit. I went into Robin's room to say hello only to find it once again empty and to hear my mother tell me that Robin was in a coma at the hospital. I remember the shock of the news and my sense of urgency to see my brother. I recall the agonizingly slow drive to the hospital, the walk down the long, forbidding corridor to his room. There my brother lay in bed, connected to all sorts of tubes and looking quite pale and helpless. My heart went out to him. I rushed over to the bed and picked up one of his hands. I felt that if I could only get him to give me some sign of recognition, he would recover. I stood by that bed and called "Bucky"—our pet name for him—over and over, praying that he would hear me and respond. After a seemingly interminable period of time, he finally did open his eyes and weakly squeezed my hand. I felt I had been given the best gift in the world. It really hit me hard then how much I did love Robin and how very precious he was to me just the way he was. (Helsel, 1978, pp. 110–112)

As is the case with parental reactions, the responses of siblings to their disabled brother or sister needn't always be negative. Research done on the subject indicates a wide range of reactions—some positive, some negative—on the part of siblings (Grossman, 1972; Simeonsson and McHale, 1981). Why some individuals respond negatively to having a handicapped sibling, while others do not, is not completely understood. Some of the factors Simeonsson and McHale (1981) have identified as being associated with better adjustment are these:

1. *Family size*. The larger the family the better.
2. *Sibling order relative to handicapped child*. Older siblings, except older girls (who often end up bearing much of the burden for care of the handicapped child) fare better.
3. *Level of handicap*. The less severe the handicap the better.
4. *Type of handicap*. The more "visible" and clearly defined the handicap, the better.
5. *Parental attitudes*. Good parental attitudes toward the disabled child foster good sibling attitudes.

FEELINGS OF THE EXCEPTIONAL INDIVIDUALS THEMSELVES

It shouldn't be forgotten, of course, that exceptional individuals also have feelings about their handicaps and about their parents and siblings. These emotions, in interaction with the reactions of parents and siblings, are the ingredients that make up the mix known as "family interaction" or "family dynamics."

BEING EXCEPTIONAL HURTS. It is often easy for us to overlook the heartache that having a handicap can bring to disabled individuals themselves. With the best of intentions, we so much want everything to be all right for the exceptional child that we often don't admit just how difficult it can be to live with a disability. The popular media has contributed to this one-sided view. Television, for example, has provided much-needed and long overdue exposure to handicapped people. Note how often handicapped individuals are shown performing remarkable feats on such shows as "Real People." Unfortunately, such depictions may give the public the distorted perception that handicaps are easily overcome and rarely take a psychological toll. Geri Jewell presents a more realistic assessment of the situation. Even though she has outstanding achievements in the field of acting and has made a successful adjustment to her cerebral palsy, it has left its emotional scars:

> Cerebral Palsy. If I had to pick the two ugliest words in the English language, it would have to be those two. I hate the disability; I hate the very idea of it, and I wish it had never been invented.
>
> You watch the telethons and you see all of us achievers and we're all smiles and we don't want your pity and we use all of the PR lingo to sugarcoat our feelings to the outside world. But cerebral palsy is something you can never make peace with—it sticks in your throat and gives you skin as thick as a rhino's, making you impervious to insults. And it hurts. Let's get that out of the way right away. CP hurts.
>
> Sometimes, in fact, it hurts so much you have to move beyond tears to laughter. Which is the story of my life. (Jewell, with Weiner)

EXCEPTIONAL CHILDREN ARE CHILDREN FIRST. Family members are much less apt than the general public to forget the child's disability. In fact, in some ways they may be all too aware. Parents, for instance, may go overboard in their attempt to help their exceptional children. Sondra Diamond, a psychologist who is also severely disabled by cerebral palsy, has been a determined advocate for the notion that parents need to keep in mind that exceptional children are children first and exceptional children second:

> Something happens in a parent when relating to his disabled child; he forgets that they're a kid first. I used to think about that a lot when I was a kid. I would be off in a euphoric state, drawing or coloring or cutting out paper dolls, and as often as not the activity would be turned into an occupational therapy session. "You're not holding the scissors right," "Sit up straight so your curvature doesn't get worse." That era was ended when I finally let loose a long and exhaustive tirade. "I'm just a kid! You can't therapize me all the time! I get enough therapy in school every day! I don't think about my handicap all the time like you do!" (Diamond, 1981, p. 30)*

NEED FOR INDEPENDENCE. Each exceptional child's needs are different, of course, but one need that many experience is the desire to be allowed to function independently. A particularly stressful time for parents and exceptional children can be adolescence, when the teenager strives to break some of the bonds that have tied him or her to the family. This need for independence is a healthy, normal behavior.

* Adapted from "Growing up with parents of a handicapped child: a handicapped person's perspective" by Sondra Diamond in UNDERSTANDING AND WORKING WITH PARENTS OF CHILDREN WITH SPECIAL NEEDS, James L. Paul, ed. Copyright © 1981 by Holt, Rinehart and Winston. Reprinted by permission of Holt, Rinehart and Winston, CBS College Publishing.

We've all gone through it. What makes it so difficult for many families of the disabled is that the exceptional child, because of his or her disability, has often by necessity been more protected by parents. Diamond (1981) recounts her own experiences along these lines:

> I remember the first time I wanted to travel alone, I had just turned sixteen. Some friends had invited me to stay with them in Baltimore. I sat down and discussed this with my parents. I said that I wanted to go by train, and that my friends would meet me in Baltimore at the train station. My parents were frightened and said so openly. They expressed their fears of my physical safety, of the fact that I couldn't help myself in case of an emergency, of possible physical attack by a strange man. We talked and argued and cried for hours. The decision was that I was to go. . . . I'll never forget that day. My mother did not go to the train station with my father and me. She said she could give her permission for this to happen, but she couldn't watch it. My father settled me in a train seat and stood on the platform waving goodbye. I was trying not to cry and so was he. Blinking back tears, I waved goodbye to my father from the train window. He was also vigorously waving goodbye with one hand—for his other was resting on the arm of my wheelchair. The train began pulling out of the station and a panic gripped me. "My God! He still has my wheelchair." I had to forget how badly I was feeling about my first unescorted trip away from home. I yelled to a conductor who was passing my seat, "Stop this train!" By this time we were a few blocks out of the station. What a ridiculous scene this must have appeared, this wriggly, little kid (I always looked young for my age) screaming at the top of my lungs to stop the train. Thank goodness the conductor had seen my father carry me onto the train, making him realize the seriousness of my plea. He pulled the emergency cord and stopped the train. The words stuck in my throat as I looked up at this towering man. What a big question this little kid was about to ask, "Would you please back up the train so that I can get my wheelchair?" As the train backed up to the platform, there was my poor father still standing there waving goodbye with one hand and holding my wheelchair with the other, unaware of anything but his departing daughter. He was shocked out of his numb pose only when the conductor jumped off the train and wrenched the chair from his hand. (pp. 41–42)

NEED FOR A ROLE IN THE FAMILY. At the same time as exceptional children ultimately need to gain as much independence as possible from their family, they also need to feel like part of the family. They require a responsible role within the family,

If at all possible, exceptional children should be expected to assume normal responsibilities within the family. Bruce Roberts, Photo Researchers, Inc.

and they want to be treated like other children in this regard. Parents sometimes don't realize, for example, that handicapped children should, if possible, be given household chores to do. Diamond notes that certain adaptations might need to be made, such as taping a dish towel to the hands of a cerebral palsied child so that it won't drop on the floor. The other major adjustment parents may need to make is in their expectations regarding how long it will take for the chores to be completed. Patience is just a necessity.

NEED TO FIT IN. Read an account of almost any exceptional individual's life, and it will contain comments about how important it was to fit in as much as possible with his or her peers. It is often difficult for parents to recognize that their exceptional children, especially when they are adolescents, often desire the same active social life that their normal peers have. Geri Jewell, a witty and outgoing teenager, was restricted by her cerebral palsy from normal dating activities. The following passage from her autobiography shows, however, that although she certainly felt the pain at the time, she is now able to talk about it in a humorous vein.

> Certainly I had none of the social life I dreamed of. Even though the kids had warmed up to me eventually—I kept working at it—it still didn't translate into any kind of social interaction, not even a date. In fact, the only date I went on during my high school years was the time I went out with good old Steve Hughes.
>
> He had gotten his driver's license and we decided to go to the drive-in movie. We were both expecting that we'd make out and neck like everybody else but nothing seemed to happen. Just the act of holding hands created problems for us. He was on the left side of me and his right arm was spastic so we couldn't do that very well.
>
> About ten minutes before the dumb movie ended, as we both sat there in frustration and repressed rage, I told Steve to start the car. I wanted to leave before everybody else did so we wouldn't end up in a collision. Steve was agreeable.
>
> In a panic, however, he put the car into forward instead of reverse and the car lurched up onto the cement bumper and stalled there, blocking the view of the other cars behind us. Since he had forgotten to take the speaker out of the window, as he drove away, he ripped it right off the pole. It cracked the window and hung there.
>
> Excited by the confusion, Steve turned his headlights on to see what he was doing, a very big mistake at a drive-in, and then horns were blowing from all directions. Headlights were flashing off and on and people were screaming. I did the only honorable thing I could do, faced with this much embarrassment. I hid on the floor.
>
> Steve looked down at me crouched on the floor and he started to yell at me. "Damn it Geri, you'd better sit up. People are going to think I came here all by myself." He handed me the speaker and told me to hide it under the seat.
>
> I poked my head up and looked around. We were driving out of the exit now and things had calmed down. In order to change the subject I asked if he wanted to go to McDonald's. Steve was ready for the golden arches.
>
> Unfortunately when we got there, Steve, still a little shaken, ended up locking his keys into the car and had to get a hanger from the manager to open the latch. He put the food on the hood of the car and struggled to get the window open. Because the window was already partially open, it was fairly easy.
>
> We then both sat in the front seat and laughed. What else could we do? "Come on, Geri, let's go home," he said and drove away. Big Macs, french fries and vanilla milkshakes landed on the windshield as we tore off.
>
> I laughed so hard I soaked the seats of his mother's car. Yup, I had a great social life in high school, no doubt about it. (Jewell, with Weiner)

THE EXCEPTIONAL CHILD AND THE STABILITY
OF THE FAMILY

Given the fact that any family can be a boiling pot of human emotions, what is the ultimate outcome for families of the handicapped? Are exceptional children mistreated? Do the parents always end up in divorce court? Do the parents all end up on Valium? Actually, there is no typical reaction. The effect on the stability of the family varies widely. Some studies have shown a greater incidence of family breakdown, but others have found no such effect (Simeonsson and Simeonsson, 1981; Stanhope and Bell, 1981). It is indeed remarkable that *for most families, the ultimate impact of having an exceptional child is minimal.*

In fact, many parents have reported that the crisis of having an exceptional child actually brought them closer together. Perske's (1981) advice to parents is interesting in this regard:

> Face a hard fact: All of life involves dying to some things and rising toward others. Many might attribute the fact that their lives are satisfying and productive to the gracious way they let themselves die to some things and come alive to others. When something in life delivers a flattening blow, they possess the audacity and the resilience to get up and come even more alive than before.
>
> The "coming alive" of many families of children with handicaps is beautiful to behold. They have expanded and enriched . . .
>
> their knowledge
>
> their tenderness
>
> their faith
>
> their ability to relate to others

Many parents have reported that the crisis of having an exceptional child actually brought their family closer together. Ray Solomon, Monkmeyer.

their sense of social justice

their family interactions.

Somehow they found untapped energies they never knew they possessed, and they became people they never dreamed they could become. . . . (pp. 14–15)

You shouldn't come away from reading this chapter, however, with the impression that tension never arises, even within the most well-adjusted families of the handicapped. There are many sources of stress in families with normal children. The addition of a handicapped child to the mix vastly increases the potential number of points of contention between spouses: Are we going to let Billy ride the special bus even though he's only 2 years old, or is Billy's father going to drive him to school? Are we going to have more children or not? Are we being too restrictive about our blind infant's exploration of the house? Are we going to encourage manual sign language or not with Kevin?

Nevertheless, most families do survive a disabled child and come away relatively unscathed. And some even seem to benefit in some ways from the experience. Unfortunately, no one yet has the answer to why some families respond favorably and others do not.

PARENT INVOLVEMENT IN TREATMENT AND EDUCATION

Today's parents of an exceptional child have more opportunity than ever before to be involved in the education of their child. Public Law 94-142 has ensured that they can have a say in many aspects of their child's education. The law specifically states that its purpose is to protect the rights of handicapped children *and* their parents. Among the many rights and protections provided parents by the law are these: The school must obtain the parents' consent prior to evaluation for eligibility for special education services, before implementation of the child's IEP (individual educational plan), and before any change in the placement is made. In addition, parents have the right to take part in the actual writing of their child's IEP.

Because parents have the opportunity to participate, of course, doesn't mean that they will. In fact, available evidence indicates that very few parents have thus far taken advantage of the law. For example, few parents have participated actively in the development of the IEP (Lynch and Stein, 1982; McKinney and Hocutt, 1982). There are many reasons why this may be so. Some authorities have claimed that school systems are complying with the law in principle but are not making the necessary extra effort to ensure that parents understand their rights fully. Still others believe that parents themselves don't want to take a more active part in the education of their children.

At first glance, this seems like a negligent attitude. Turnbull and Turnbull (1982), however, make a strong case for the idea that we shouldn't assume involvement is for everybody. They believe parents should be allowed to choose how much participation they want without feeling pressured into involvement. They point out, for example, that many parents think it's not up to them to educate their exceptional children, that it's inappropriate to assume they have the same expertise as professionals trained to work with these children on educational tasks. In addition, Turnbull and Turnbull raise the controversial point about whether parents' needs should always take second

PARENTS
AND
FAMILIES

329

place to the child's needs. For example, they question whether it is best, for the family as a whole, to consider only the needs of the child with regard to the issue of institutionalization. For some parents, institutionalization of their child greatly reduces their own stress.

The questions raised by the Turnbulls are interesting and not easily resolved. No matter how you feel about these issues, the fact remains that, even though more parents of exceptional children are getting involved in their child's education, the majority still prefer limited involvement (Winton, 1980; Winton and Turnbull, 1981). For those who do wish to participate, there are many different types of programs. Many of the programs we're about to describe were established on an experimental basis by researchers interested in studying parent-child interactions. Parents who want such programs for their children will need to lobby with their local school systems. As Perske (1981) states, parents can exert a tremendous amount of power when they organize:

> And so, gentle parent, ordinary citizen, keep your kind manner. At the same time, however, remember that you can generate an awesome power, a force that can help your son or daughter with a handicap be accepted, helped, and treated as the rest of this continent's citizens are treated. That is *"kind"* power. For only the strong can be truly kind—the others fake it out of fright.

> Powerlessness is a horrible state. It is like standing at the bottom of a well and trying to climb out on a trick ladder—everytime one puts a foot on a rung, it slips down. Do not let anyone render you powerless in that way.

> A standard statement in a powerful corporation where I once worked was Power Creates Its Own Opportunities. And it certainly does. In thousands of different ways, power can be used to gain more power.

> Power is used to move Amtrak's train 61 from Montreal to Washington, or Air Canada's flight 823 from New York to Vancouver. And power can be used to move people, too.

> Use the power you generate as honestly and as fairly as you can. You may not feel the need to generate it for your own sake, but you do need to generate it for the sake of your son or daughter with a handicap. (p. 86)

PARENT INTERVENTION PROGRAMS

Parent intervention programs can be classified in at least two ways—according to the general approach they take to working on parent-child interaction, and according to the type of delivery system.

INTERACTION APPROACHES. Lillie (1981) states that parent programs can be grouped under one or a combination of three general models: (a) a behavior-modification, (b) a psychological insight, and (c) an experiential model. Which one is used with a particular family depends on a number of factors, including the type of exceptionality and the level of its severity. For the most part, the behavioral approach is used with more severe problems.

BEHAVIOR MODIFICATION MODEL. The behavioral approach is highly structured. Parents are taught the basic principles of reinforcement and punishment, and then taught to use these behavioral principles with their child at home. They are also usually taught how to observe, record, and chart their child's behavior so they can tell how much progress he or she is making.

Parent programs using behavior modification have been used with a wide variety of exceptionalities, ranging from mild to severe levels of severity. The Portage Project in Portage, Wisconsin, is an example of a parent program that uses a behavioral approach (Shearer and Shearer, 1972). This project, serving rural families of multiply handicapped children under the age of 6, uses teachers who visit the homes once a week. The home teacher shows the parents exactly what it is they are to work on for the week. The parents work with the child on such things as language, cognition, and socialization, and chart his or her progress.

PSYCHOLOGICAL INSIGHT MODEL. According to Lillie (1981), this approach emphasizes arriving at an understanding of why children behave the way they do. It is heavily psychoanalytic in orientation. Conflict situations between parents and their children often serve as discussion points for understanding the reasons for the child's behavior.

Parent programs using the psychological insight model usually focus on mildly handicapped youngsters with behavioral problems. One of the most popular of these programs is PET (Parent Effectiveness Training) (Gordon, 1970). Many PET techniques have become so popular that they have entered the vocabulary of parents who have not even received the training. Lillie (1981) notes, for example, how often it is that we hear parents saying such things as " 'You're really angry at Johnny for taking your tricycle'; or 'I hear you saying that you think that I have been unfair to you' " (p. 104).

EXPERIENTIAL MODEL. This approach stresses getting parents to provide as many enrichment experiences as possible. It is a developmental orientation: The parent attempts to lead the child through the sequence of normal child development. The experiential model is most often used with families who have children with mild to moderate learning problems.

FOCUS

CONSUMER'S GUIDE TO THE EVALUATION OF PARENT INVOLVEMENT PROGRAMS

	Yes	No
1. Is there a formal procedure used by the program to determine parent and family needs?	_____	_____
2. Are the needs of parents arrived at by mutual agreement of program staff and parents?	_____	_____
3. Are parents and family seen by the program staff as recipients of services rather than as a conduit through which to provide services to handicapped children?	_____	_____
4. Are the services the program provides based on a clear model or theory?	_____	_____
5. Is there evidence that the program has a good understanding of the resources available in the community?	_____	_____
6. Does the staff have time to discuss various aspects of the services with the parents?	_____	_____

7. Is the program staff interested in parents' comments and feedback about the program services? _____ _____

8. Are parents involved in the decision-making process— in setting goals and objectives? _____ _____

9. Is information routinely provided to parents, such as a regular newsletter or report, or through regularly scheduled parent conferences? _____ _____

10. Do parents have opportunities to talk together and share information and feelings? _____ _____

11. Is there a clear written statement of the services available to parents? _____ _____

12. Does the program provide learning opportunities for parents in topic areas of child development, training in the home, and special needs for their children? _____ _____

13. Are parents provided ample opportunity to participate as contributors to the program: as program aides, materials developers, helping with transportation, and so on? _____ _____

14. Is the program interested in helping the parents as individuals, as opposed to helping them as the parents of handicapped children? _____ _____

15. Do parents receive individual attention as opposed to interaction with the program only as a member of a group? _____ _____

16. Do the interactions between staff and parents indicate equality, as opposed to social distance? _____ _____

17. Are there reports available to the parents that provide information on the past performance of the program? _____ _____

18. Is the program staff open to a number of ways of working with parents in meeting their needs, as opposed to having their own agenda or interests? _____ _____

19. Does the program have adequate physical facilities (such as space, equipment, and so forth)? _____ _____

20. Does the program staff project an atmosphere of joy and happiness, as opposed to anxiety and concern? _____ _____

Adapted from "Educational and psychological strategies for working with parents" by David Lillie in UNDERSTANDING AND WORKING WITH PARENTS OF CHILDREN WITH SPECIAL NEEDS, J. L. Paul, ed. Copyright © 1981 by Holt, Rinehart and Winston. Reprinted by permission of Holt, Rinehart and Winston, CBS College Publishing.

DIFFERENT DELIVERY SYSTEMS. In addition to approach toward parent-child interaction, parent involvement programs can also be classified according to the delivery system used. Stanhope and Bell (1981) have placed parent programs along a continuum according to how much the "training" of the parent takes place in a setting that resembles the home situation. The five kinds of programs they describe are these: (a) clinic-based, (b) simulated home environment, (c) combination clinic-home, (d) school-home, and (e) home-based.

CLINIC–BASED PROGRAMS. Most early parent intervention efforts were clinic-based. In these programs, parents, sometimes along with their children, come into the clinic to receive counseling or training. Tyler and Kogan (1977), for instance, set up a program to reduce stress between mothers and their physically handicapped preschool children. Therapists videotaped mothers and their children interacting and then reviewed the

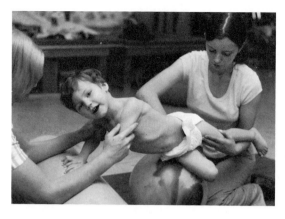

Today, professionals realize that parents themselves should be involved as much as possible in intervention programs with their children. Here, the mother of a physically handicapped child is being trained to use physical therapy exercises with her son. D. Grogan, UVA/CRC

tapes with the mothers. The mothers then practiced interacting with their children while a therapist coached them via a "bug-in-the-ear" earplug device. You can see that an advantage to clinic-based programs is that it allows a great deal of control over what goes on in the interaction between parent and child. You can also see, however, that the training takes place in an artificial environment rather than in the home or school situations where the problems are in fact occurring.

SIMULATED HOME ENVIRONMENT. In this situation the parent is also brought into the clinic, but the clinic is furnished and equipped to look just like an ordinary household. The assumption is that both parents and child will act more naturally in this kind of setting.

COMBINATION CLINIC–HOME. Compared to the two approaches above, this orientation places more stress on getting parents to use procedures with the child in the home. Patterson and his colleagues have used this approach in working with families of highly aggressive children (Patterson, 1976; Patterson, Reid, Jones, and Conger, 1975). In the clinic, they introduced parents to the principles of behavior modification, how to observe and record their child's behavior. Role-playing is a part of the clinic training. Parents are given "assignments" to work on with their child until the next clinic session, at which they bring back the data on how well the intervention has worked at home.

SCHOOL–HOME PROGRAMS. These programs are similar to the clinic-home combination except that the cooperating agency is the school and not the clinic. Such programs can take many forms, from highly structured involvement in which the teacher assigns the parent specific activities to a relatively loose form of communication between teacher and parent about the child's progress. The Focus provides a good example of the latter.

FOCUS

PARENT AND PROFESSIONALS

The following short excerpts are taken at random from a notebook that accompanies 2-year-old Lauren, who has cerebral palsy, back and forth to her special class for preschoolers. The notebook provides a convenient mode for an ongoing dialogue among her mother Lyn, her teacher Sara, her occupational therapist Joan, and her speech therapist Marti. As you can see from this representative sample, the communication is informal but very informative on a variety of items relating to Lauren.

9/7

Lyn,
    Lauren did very well — We had several criers but — She played + worked very nicely. She responds so well to instruction — that's such a plus!
    She fed herself crackers + juice + did a good job. She was very vocal + enjoyed the other children, too. She communicated ō me very well for the 1st day.
    Am pleased ō her first day
                    Sara

9/15

Sara,
    Please note that towel, toothbrush/paste & clean clothes may be removed from bag today. — WED. We witnessed an apparently significant moment in her oral communication: she'll try to say "all done" after a meal. The execution is imperfect, to say the least, but she gets an "A" for effort. Could you please reinforce this after snack? Just ask her "What do you say after you finish your snack?" Thanks.
                    Lyn

9/28

    Lauren had an esp. good day! She was jabbering a lot! Being very expressive ō her vocalness + jabbering. I know she said "yes," or an approximate thereof, several times when asked if she wanted something.

She was so cute ō the animal sounds esp. pig & horse — she was really trying to make the sounds. It was the first time we had seen such a response. Still cruising a lot! She walked ō me around the room & in the gym. She used those consonant & vowel sounds: dadada, mama ma — her jabbering was just so different & definitely progressive. I am sending her work card ō stickers home tomorrow for good working.

Several notes:

① Susie (VI) came today & evaluated Lauren. She will compile a report & be in touch with you and I. She seemed very pleased ō Lauren's performance.

② Marti (speech) will see Lauren tomorrow at 11 AM for evaluation. She'll be in touch afterwards.

③ Susie informed me about the addition to the IEP meeting on Mon. Oct 4 at 10 AM here at Westbrook.

How's the tape & cards working at home? I know you both are pleased ō her jabbering. She seems so ready to say "something" — we are very, very pleased. See you tomorrow.

Sara

9/29

Lauren was a bit fussy during O.T. today — she stopped fussing during fine motor reaching activities (peg board, block building) but wasn't too pleased with being handled on the ball. She did a great job with the peg board & readily used her left hand.

I want to bring in some different spoons next week to see if she can become more independent in scooping with a large handle spoon or a spoon that is covered.

Joan

10/1   Joan —

Although Lauren would very much approve of your idea for making her more independent during feeding, we'd rather not initiate self-feeding with an adaptive spoon at this time. Here's why:

1. When I feed Lauren or get her to grip a spoon and then guide her hand, I can slip the entire bowl of the spoon into her mouth and get her to close her lips on it. When Lauren uses a spoon without help, she turns it upside down to lick it or inserts just the tip of it into her mouth and then sucks off the food...

2. Lauren has always been encouraged to do things "normally." She never had a special cup or a "Tommy Tippee," for instance. Of course, it took a year of practice before she could drink well from a cup, and she still dribbles a little occasionally; but she's doing well now. We really prefer to give Lauren practice in using a regular spoon so that she doesn't get dependent on

an adaptive utensil. I'd like to assure you that we appreciate your communication about sessions with Lauren and ideas for her therapy. Coordinating her school, home, and CDC programs is going to be a challenge, to say the least.

Lyn

☺! Lauren walked all the way from the room to Gym + back — She also walked up + down the full length of the gym!
Several other teachers saw her and were thrilled.
She fell maybe twice!
But picked herself right up —

Sara

3/2 Lauren had a great speech session! We were playing w/ some toys and she said "I want help" as plain as day. Later she said "I want crackers" and at the end of the session, she imitated "Cindy, let's go." Super!!

Marti

HOME-BASED PROGRAMS. This approach takes the professional into the home situation. The rationale is that: (a) If intervention takes place in the home rather than the clinic or school, parents won't need to transfer what they've learned in one situation to another one; (b) the intervention can be tailored to the unique features of each home setting; and (c) the intervention allows for more involvement of all family members (Baker, 1976). An example of this kind of approach is the Portage Project, the rural-based program for families of multihandicapped children mentioned above.

COMMUNICATION BETWEEN PARENTS
AND PROFESSIONALS

No matter which approach parents participate in, the key to the success of the program is how well parents and professionals are able to work together. No matter what the philosophy or the mode of delivery of the program, it is doomed to failure if parents and professionals do not have mutual respect for one another (see Focus). Unfortunately, special education does not have a long tradition of excellent working relationships between parents and teachers (Morgan, 1982). This is not too surprising if you consider the ingredients of the situation. On the one hand, you have the parents, who may be trying to cope with the intense feelings (anger, guilt, fear) we discussed earlier; on the other hand, you have the professionals—teachers, speech therapists, physicians, psychologists, physical therapists, and so forth—who may be frustrated because they do not have all the answers to the child's problems. Nevertheless, today a great deal more attention is being given to how professionals and parents can work together better.

FOCUS

AN OPEN LETTER TO TEACHERS FROM A PARENT

I am the parent of a handicapped child who has been in seven different therapy and/or school programs in four different states in the last ten years. I have always taken an active part in my daughter's education and training. I'm taking this opportunity to share what I believe special educators should, as professionals, know and be willing to do for their students and parents. I am not claiming to speak for all "special" parents, but I have been a leader in education and parent groups, as well as being an advocate in individual cases. I am claiming to speak for all the parents I have worked with so far.

There are three basic types of parents you'll encounter. Some, obviously, will fall in between "categories" just as many of your students will cross the boundaries of their "categories." *The first category of parent is one who believes that the teacher knows everything and themselves nothing about educating their child*. (And I hope everyone knows this is rarely ever the case.) This is a parent you may never be able to persuade to come in for a meeting. Or, if you do, they may remain silent except for "Hello" and "Goodbye." Unfortunately, they think that because of your education, and most typically, their lack of it, that you don't need any help from them. They may be afraid to talk to you because they think you might tell them what they've done wrong with their child. You will also find parents in this category that, because of their lack of understanding of their child's handicapping condition and/or lack of acceptance, they are grateful for the time that the school will take the child. Some parents will look to the schools to make their child normal.

The second category is one where there is equal distribution between the teacher and parent in terms of knowledge, communication, and respect. This is, of course, the ideal situation but is seen the least. (I have only encountered it twice.) Parent/teacher cooperation is vital in working with a handicapped child because there are often two "different" children involved. The child will often exhibit one type of behavior and capabilities at home and another at school. These "different" abilities and behaviors have to be blended in order for the special student to reach his potential in society. A parent who can get his child to sit calmly at the dinner table and use utensils appropriately needs to share those abilities and how it is accomplished with the teacher that sees that same child as hyperactive in the cafeteria. One teacher had a student that consistently incorrectly identified his colors, but his academic level in other areas was much higher. After meeting with the parent and showing the work done by the child, the teacher found out that the parent is colorblind.

Many category two parents, like those in category one, still need help in understanding their child's handicap and the way he learns, but these parents will be much more eager to listen and learn. Often suggesting a pamphlet, or book on their child's problem is helpful.

But one thing to be careful of is not giving a parent more homework for them to do with their child than they can handle. Many parents have trouble playing the role of both teacher and parent and will end up not doing any of the work and feeling very guilty besides. The quickest way I've ever seen to alienate communication between parents and teachers is to have the teacher make the parents feel guilty about something they are or are not doing for their child.

Category two parents may disagree with a teacher, but are willing to listen to the teacher's explanation and work toward a solution. And the reverse of that situation should also be true. The key is respect and understanding in communication.

Category three parents believe that they, and only themselves (except one or two professionals that agree with them) know how to handle their child and what is best for him. This type of parent causes the teacher the most frustration and takes the most time. This type parent may seem to do nothing but berate and belittle the teacher. I suggest that the teacher be extremely knowledgeable about the child's history, disorder, and all current teaching methods employed. Seek administration support and other professionals in the field. Remember that the parents disapproval is often of the teaching method and not the teacher personally. If communication reaches the point where the parent will not come in for meetings, or has even taken the child out of school, a reevaluation of the parental and LEA position must be made. Often a mediator or advocate can bridge the communication gap before a due process hearing becomes necessary.

Source: Elizabeth City, North Carolina—Barbara Rhodes

DESIRABLE CHARACTERISTICS FOR PROFESSIONALS. Karnes and Teska (1980) list five characteristics of competent professionals:

> First, the professional must be able to establish rapport and generate confidence in family members. . . .
>
> Second, staff should be competent to work with every family member, including siblings, if their ages permit. . . .
>
> Third, staff must be able to provide parents with clear and accurate information. . . .
>
> Fourth, feedback on the contributions of family members to the growth of the handicapped child encourages involvement. . . .
>
> Fifth, enlisting the help of other parents strengthens the family involvement program. (pp. 96–98)

ISSUES NEEDING CLARIFICATION. Roos (1978) states that five issues need to be recognized when considering the relationship between parents and professionals. These issues are related to values, objectives and priorities, temporal orientation, and competition. These issues need to be dealt with by professionals and parents if an effective working relationship is to be achieved.

Roos notes that it's not always accurate to assume that parents and professionals hold the same values. The welfare of the exceptional child may not always be the only concern of all the parties involved. Parents have their own set of needs, which may not always be in the best interests of the exceptional child. Some professionals may be more interested in such things as their reputations and their budgets.

Parents and professionals may also disagree on some of the objectives for the child. An example of this kind of disagreement would be if the parents are more interested in the child's developing independent living skills, whereas the teacher is more concerned

Professionals need to appreciate the time and effort required of parents, especially those with a handicapped child, in meeting the everyday needs of all family members.
Paolo Koch, Rapho/Photo Researchers, Inc.

about the child's academic progress. Another example would be if parents of a deaf child wanted their child to communicate via sign language, but the teacher wanted to use an oral approach exclusively.

The third issue noted by Roos is temporal orientation. Parents of exceptional children often learn to adopt a one-day-at-a-time attitude. Because of this, they want their children to be taught things that will help them in present-day situations. Professionals, on the other hand, are often more likely to stress long-term goals.

Roos also points out that parents and professionals may also feel in competition with one another. Sometimes pride in one's parental and professional abilities is at stake. It's only natural, to some degree, that parents and professionals should be somewhat jealous of each other's accomplishments. It's unfortunate, however, if either one lets such feelings escalate to the point where a good working relationship is impossible.

Some of the frustrations parents are likely to feel when these issues are not resolved are aptly described by Featherstone (1980). This excerpt also reminds us that professionals may not always fully appreciate the time and effort required of parents, especially those with a handicapped child:

I remember the day when the occupational therapist at Jody's school called with some suggestions from a visiting nurse. Jody has a seizure problem which is controlled with the drug Dilantin. Dilantin can cause the gums to grow over the teeth—an effect that is especially likely if the gums are irritated by either poor hygiene or erupting teeth. The nurse had noted that nearly all the preschoolers at the school suffered from this overgrowth, and recommended, innocently enough, that the children's teeth be brushed four times a day, for five minutes, with an electric toothbrush. The school suggested that they could do this once on school days, and that I should try to do it the other three to four times a day. I trotted out a valid and convenient excuse: Jody's dentist had advised against an electric toothbrush.

Although I tried to sound reasonable on the phone, this new demand appalled me. I rehearsed angry, self-justifying speeches in my head. Jody, I thought, is blind, cerebral-palsied, and retarded. We do his physical therapy daily and work with him on sounds and communication. We feed him each meal on our laps, bottle him, change him, bathe him, dry him, put him in a body cast to sleep, launder his bed linens daily, and go through a variety of routines designed to minimize his miseries and enhance his joys and his development. (All this in addition to trying to care for and enjoy our other young children and making time for each other and our careers.) Now you tell me that I should spend fifteen minutes every day on something that Jody will hate, an activity that will not help him to walk or even defecate, but one that is directed at the health of his gums. This activity is not for a finite time but forever. It is not guaranteed to help, but "it can't hurt." And it won't make the overgrowth go away but may retard it. Well, it's too much. Where is that fifteen minutes going to come from? What am I supposed to give up? Taking the kids to the park? Reading a bedtime story to my eldest? Washing the breakfast dishes? Sorting the laundry? Grading students' papers? Sleeping? Because there is no time in my life that hasn't been spoken for, and for every fifteen minute activity that is added, one has to be taken away. (pp. 77–78)

The field of special education has changed in many ways in its view and treatment of parents. Today's special educator sees parents as allies who, in varying degrees, can offer great assistance in the overall development of the exceptional child. In trying to understand the child as fully as possible, today's special educator needs to be more aware of parental feelings and of the family interaction as a whole.

Parents of exceptional children are generally more informed about their children's educational needs and abilities than ever before. Assisted by recent legislation and by parent support groups, today's parents have a greater impact on the provision of needed services for their children. Working together, today's teachers and parents can be an unbeatable team in effective education of exceptional children.

ANSWERS TO FREQUENTLY ASKED QUESTIONS
PARENTS AND FAMILIES

1. Your concerns sound quite valid. Unfortunately, in many cases, physicians do seem reluctant to confirm the existence of a handicap. Many parents of children with special needs recount situations similar to yours. From what you've described about your daughter, and given your own firsthand knowledge of the development of your other youngsters, it seems advisable that you seek another professional opinion. You are quite right that, depending on the diagnosis, she could be benefiting from early treatment and that a prolonged "wait and see" attitude could cause her to miss some needed therapy and get farther behind.

2. I'm sure Shari and her family are well aware of the inconvenient limitations of her physical disability. It sounds, however, as though they have not chosen to add on *additional* handicaps of further limiting her activities. Not "making allowances for the fact that she is handicapped" may be the best thing they can do for Shari's self-sufficiency and overall self-esteem. It is too bad she broke her arm, as it would be for any child, but accidents such as that can happen when people are exercising the greatest caution. If Shari is enjoying the activities, nothing should stop her from participating as much as her physical disability will allow.

3. First of all, they probably do care a great deal and are already helping him in countless ways every day. It is often hard for those who are not the parents of a handicapped child to realize how many hours of care and hard work are required on a no-time-off basis. It is possible that your request will require too much time from an already crowded schedule. It may also be that the parents don't see the value of the exercise you are prescribing. Perhaps you could rethink the objective of the exercise—will it achieve a goal the parents might find helpful, such as improved self-feeding? Also, rethink the time needed and remember that it must be sandwiched in between many important activities. If, after reconsidering, you still think the exercise is of great value and requires only a reasonable amount of time, you might discuss it again with the parents. This time be more sensitive to their time pressures and other demands and not so quick to judge them as noncaring or unhelpful.

4. Nothing is wrong with you. Your reactions to your child and to your situation are normal. Jeffrey's unresponsiveness makes it very hard for you to play with him in the loving ways most mothers and babies do. Naturally you feel a mixture of feelings toward him—all parents experience this mixture to some degree—but Jeffrey's problems make you feel a stronger conflict. In addition to Jeffrey himself, other people—even well-meaning ones such as grandparents—can make you feel more lonely, hurt, and depressed. One way of coping with these feelings is by reading about how other parents of handicapped children cope in books such as Helen Featherstone's *A Difference in the family: Life with a disabled child*. Later, you might be interested in joining other parents whose children have similar problems. Communication with other parents who understand your situation can make you feel much less lonely and can reassure you that your feelings aren't strange.

5. You do not *have* to attend the meeting, of course. The law was designed to ensure that you had the *right* to be notified of meetings regarding your child's placement and that you had the *right* to attend. The school personnel in many cases are willing to meet at a time convenient for you so that you don't have to take off work. It would be good if you could attend. Even if you think you have nothing to gain from such a meeting, it does provide an opportunity for you to see the people involved with your child's daily school routine. You may be able to communicate some ideas about your son's needs or interests that could be very helpful. You may not be an expert on education, but chances are good that no one knows your son as well as you do. You probably have a good sense of what would be good for him and what would not.

SUMMARY

One of the reasons why the dynamics in families with exceptional children are so complex is the added factor of society's attitudes toward exceptional individuals and handicaps. But despite the complexity and the difficulties, special educators today realize how important the family is in the success of any educational effort. They are less willing to blame the parents when interventions do not go well, to welcome the parents' active involvement in the process, and to realize the positive impact that involvement can have.

This change has happened because of several factors: Parents have become more active and organized; research has demonstrated how important active parent participation can be; and PL 94-142 stipulates that parents have a right to a voice in decisions regarding their child.

Furthermore, psychologists and educators have come to realize that infants affect their parents as much as the parents affect them. Children are frequently responsible for how parents respond to them. All these responses and reactions have to do with subjective feelings, which makes coping and understanding difficult for the family and the child, and also for the special educator and the professional.

Parents' feelings and reactions change over time. There is the initial shock of learning they have a handicapped child, the adjustment, and the feelings of anger, guilt, loneliness, and self-doubt. Parents are often the first to suspect the child has a problem, and their initial encounters with professionals can color their feelings and their actions for a long time. In addition to dealing with their feelings and others' reactions, for parents there is the physically and emotionally draining task of everyday life with a handicapped child, with its incessant demands and no time off.

Brothers and sisters of the handicapped child frequently experience the same emotions as the parents, but have greater difficulty coping simply because they do not have access to support and resources as the parents do. Siblings, like parents, have a wide range of reactions, from positive to negative, to the situation.

The feelings of the handicapped themselves are a vital factor in family dynamics. Exceptional children are children first. They have the same needs and feelings as other children, but they have some special concerns. Perhaps more than other children they have a great need to function independently, yet of necessity must be more protected by their parents. They also need a responsible role in the family, and want to be treated like other children in this way. And they want to fit in with their peers.

Despite the problems and the emotional turmoil, for most families the ultimate impact of having an exceptional child is minimal. These families do experience great stress, but they also learn to cope, sometimes better than other families. Many have reported that they have actually been drawn closer together and have become a stronger unit than they might have been otherwise.

Parental involvement in treatment and education today is far different from what it was in the past: Parents now can participate to whatever extent they choose. For some this means active, daily interaction with teachers and therapists; for others, it means a more limited involvement. Parents today are also organized; many support groups lobby with local school systems and governments on behalf of their children.

Parent intervention programs can be categorized by type of approach to the parent-child interaction and by type of delivery system. Interaction approaches can be based on behavior modification techniques, psychological insight models, and experiential models. Delivery systems are of five kinds: clinic-based, simulated home environment, combination clinic-home, school-home, and home-based.

No matter what the approach or the delivery system, the key to the success of the process is how well parents and professionals are able to work together. Today this aspect of intervention is being given greater attention than ever before. Special educators now see parents as allies who, in varying degrees, can offer great assistance in helping the exceptional child develop his or her potential to the fullest.

REFERENCES

ACKERLEY, M.S. False gods and angry prophets. In A.P.Turnbull & H.R. Turnbull (Eds.). *Parents speak out: Views from the other side of the two-way mirror*. Columbus, Ohio: Charles E. Merrill, 1978.

BAKER, B.L. Parent involvement in programming for developmentally disabled children. In L.L. Lloyd (Ed.). *Communication assessment and intervention strategies*. Baltimore: University Park Press, 1976.

BELL, R.Q. Stimulus control of parent or caretaker behavior by offspring. *Developmental Psychology*, 1971, *4*, 63–72.

BELL, R.Q., & HARPER, L.V. *Child effects on adults*. Hillsdale, N.J.: Lawrence Erlbaum Associates, 1977.

BRONFENBRENNER, U. *Is early intervention effective? A report on longitudinal evaluation of preschool programs*. Vol II. Washington, D.C.: Dept. of Health, Education, and Welfare Publication No. 74–75,1974.

DIAMOND, S. Growing up with parents of a handicapped child: A handicapped person's perspective. In J.L. Paul (Ed.). *Understanding and working with parents of children with special needs*. New York: Holt, Rinehart and Winston, 1981.

DROTAR, D., BASKIEWICZ, A., IRWIN, N., KENNELL, J., & KLAUS, M. The adaptation of parents to the birth of an infant with a congenital malformation: A hypothetical model. *Pediatrics*, 1975, *56*, 710–717.

FEATHERSTONE, H. *A difference in the family: Life with a disabled child*. New York: Basic Books, 1980.

GORDON, T. *Parent effectiveness training*. New York: Peter H. Wyden, 1970.

GROSSMAN, F.K. *Brothers and sisters of retarded children: An exploratory study*. Syracuse, N.Y.: Syracuse University Press, 1972.

HELSEL, E. The Helsel's story of Robin. In A.P. Turnbull & H.R. Turnbull (Eds.). *Parents speak out: Views from the other side of the two-way mirror*. Columbus, Ohio: Charles E. Merrill, 1978.

JEWELL, G. (with Weiner, S.). *Geri*. New York: William Morrow and Ballantine Books, 1984.

KARNES, M.B., & TESKA, J.A. Toward successful parent involvement in programs for handicapped children. In J.J. Gallagher (Ed.). *New directions for exceptional children: Parents and families of handicapped children*. San Francisco: Jossey Bass, 1980.

LILLIE, D. Educational and psychological strategies for working with parents. In J.L. Paul (Ed.). *Understanding and working with parents of children with special needs*. New York: Holt, Rinehart and Winston, 1981.

LYNCH, E.W., & STEIN, R. Perspectives on parent participation in special education. *Exceptional Education Quarterly*, 1982, *3*, 56–63.

MCKINNEY, J.D., & HOCUTT, A.M. Public school involvement of parents of learning disabled children and average achievers. *Exceptional Education Quarterly*, 1982, *3*, 64–73.

MORGAN, D.P. Parent participation in the IEP process: Does it enhance appropriate education? *Exceptional Education Quarterly*, 1982, *3*, 33–40.

MORTON, K. Identifying the enemy—A parent's complaint. In A.P. Turnbull, & H.R. Turnbull (Eds.). *Parents speak out: Views from the other side of the two-way mirror*. Columbus, Ohio: Charles E. Merrill, 1978.

PATTERSON, G.R. The aggressive child: Victim and architect of a coercive system. In E.J. Mash, L.A. Hammerlynck, & L.C. Handy (Eds.). *Behavior modification and families*. New York: Brunner/Mazel, 1976.

PATTERSON, G.R., REID, J.B., JONES, R.R., & CONGER, R.E. *A social learning approach to family intervention (Vol. 1)*: Families with aggressive children. Eugene, Ore.: Castalia Publishing, 1975.

PAUL, J.L., & BECKMAN-BELL, P. Parent perspectives. In J.L. Paul (Ed.). *Understanding and working with parents of children with special needs*. New York: Holt, Rinehart, and Winston, 1981.

PERSKE, R. (Illustrated by M. Perske.) *Hope for the families: New directions for parents of persons with retardation or other disabilities*. Nashville: Abingdon, 1981.

ROOS, P. Parents of mentally retarded children—misunderstood and mistreated. In A.P. Turnbull & H.R. Turnbull (Eds.), *Parents: Views from the other side of the two-way mirror*. Columbus, Ohio: Charles E. Merrill, 1978.

SHEARER, M.S., & SHEARER, D.E. The Portage project: A model for early childhood education. *Exceptional Children*, 1972, *39*, 210–217.

SIMEONSSON, R.J., & MCHALE, S.M. Review: Research on handicapped children: Sibling relationships. *Child Care, Health and Development*, 1981, *7*, 153–171.

SIMEONSSON, R. J., & SIMEONSSON, N.E. Parenting handicapped children: Psychological aspects.

In J. L. Paul (Ed.). *Understanding and working with parents of children with special needs.* New York: Holt, Rinehart and Winston, 1981.

Stanhope, L., & Bell, R.Q. Parents and families. In J.M. Kauffman & D.P. Hallahan (Eds.). *Handbook of special education.* Englewood Cliffs, N.J.: Prentice-Hall, 1981.

Turnbull, A.P., & Blacher-Dixon, J. Preschool mainstreaming: Impact on parents. In J.J. Gallagher (Ed.). *New directions for exceptional children: Ecology of exceptional children.* San Francisco: Jossey-Bass, 1980.

Turnbull, A.P., & Turnbull, H.R. (Eds.). *Parents speak out: Views from the other side of the two-way mirror.* Columbus, Ohio: Charles E. Merrill, 1978.

Turnbull, A.P., & Turnbull, H.R. Parent involvement in the education of handicapped children: A critique. *Mental Retardation*, 1982, *20*, 115–122.

Tyler, N.B., & Kogan, K.L. Reduction of stress between mothers and their handicapped children. *American Journal of Occupational Therapy*, 1977, *31*, 151–155.

Winton, P.J. A descriptive study of parents' perspectives on preschool services: Mainstreamed and specialized. Doctoral dissertation, University of North Carolina, Chapel Hill, 1980.

Winton, P., & Turnbull, A.P. Parent involvement as viewed by parents of preschool handicapped children. *Topics in Early Childhood Special Education*, 1981, *1*, 11–19.

GLOSSARY

Adaptive behavior How well a person is able to adapt to environmental demands.

Adventitious defect Defect acquired after birth through accident or disease.

Allergy tension fatigue syndrome A condition characterized by two stages, tension and fatigue, and due to a food allergy.

American Sign Language (Ameslan) Standard system of signing used in the United States; has its own grammatical rules and is considered by many to be a true language.

Amniocentesis A medical procedure in which a needle is inserted into the anmiotic sac of a pregnant woman and a small amount of fluid is withdrawn for testing for certain abnormal conditions.

Anorexia nervosa Eating disorder common in adolescent girls and characterized by a pattern of self-starvation and binge eating that eventually results in malnutrition and sometimes death.

Aphasia Complete loss of language or drastically disordered language.

Aqueous humor A watery fluid between the lens and cornea.

Arthritis A painful condition of the muscles and/or joints, often involving inflammation.

Articulation disorders Disorders in the way speech sound is made; range from relatively mild defects to severe handicaps.

Astigmatism Blurred vision caused by irregularities of the cornea or lens.

Audiologist A person trained in the measurement and remediation of hearing impairments.

Audiometer Machine that produces tones of known pitch and loudness; used to test hearing.

Auricle The fleshy, visible part of the outer ear.

Autism A severe developmental disability manifested in a variety of behaviors and problems, usually including withdrawal, self-stimulation, and cognitive and language deficits.

Autocuer A portable minicomputer that mechanically "hears" words spoken to a deaf person and projects symbols onto the lens area of eyeglasses.

Behavior modification The use of reinforcement and/ or punishment to increase or decrease behaviors.

Behavioral assessment The observation and recording of specific behaviors on a continuous (usually daily) basis.

Behind-the-ear hearing aid Small device worn behind the ear; used by the largest percentage of hearing-impaired persons.

Bimodalism *See* Total communication approach.

Body aid A hearing aid for those with profound loss or inability to manipulate tiny controls; made up of a receiver in the ear attached by a cord to a box worn on the chest.

Braille A complex system of raised dots representing different letters and symbols; enables the visually impaired to read with their fingertips.

Cataracts A clouding of the lens of the eye causing a distortion of light rays onto the retina.

Cerebral palsy Damage to the brain before, during, or shortly after birth that impairs the ability to control the muscles; sometimes accompanied by other handicaps.

Chronological age Age in years.

Closed captioning TV program captions visible only on sets equipped with a decoder.

Cluttering Excessively fast and garbled speech characterized by omitted and substituted sounds.

Cochlea Component of the inner ear that receives vibrations and converts them into electrical impulses that are sent to the brain for decoding.

Cognitive behavior modification (CBM) A variety of methods that emphasize teaching the individual to control his or her own thought processes through behavioral techniques.

Coloboma A degenerative disease in which parts of the retina are incompletely formed.

Communication A broad term covering verbal and nonverbal ways of exchanging information.

Communication board A board that contains on it such things as the alphabet, frequently used words, pictures, and so forth. It allows speechless individuals to communicate by pointing to different items on it. Some of the more sophisticated devices are used by pushing buttons that light up the items.

Community residential facility (CRF) A place, usually a group home, in an urban or residential neighborhood where from about three to ten retarded adults live under the supervision of houseparents.

Compressed speech device An electronic filtering machine that shortens the duration of taped speech while maintaining its intellegibility.

Conductive losses Hearing losses due to a problem in sound moving along the conductive pathway of the outer ear.

Congenital defect   Physical defect with which a person is born; may be caused by genetic factors or by accidents or injuries during fetal development.

Consultant teacher   Teacher who gives advice on special methods, equipment, and materials to the regular teacher.

Convergent production   A mental operation in which a person must arrive at one best or correct answer.

Cornea   The transparent covering over the eye that refracts incoming light rays.

Creativity   The ability to see and do things in ways most people do not, to come up with novel ideas that are useful or stimulating to others in a productive way.

Crisis-helping teachers   Teachers who are especially well equipped to provide assistance at a time of child or child-teacher crisis; function in schools like resource teachers and work with children, parents, and teachers.

Criterion-referenced test   A test that measures whether or not an individual scores above or below a preset criterion.

Cued speech   A variation of the total communication approach in which hand shapes represent specific sounds at the same time that spoken words are produced.

Cultural-familial retardation   Mild retardation with no evidence of brain pathology in someone from an economically disadvantaged background.

Deaf   Those who have the greatest hearing loss and whose development of speech and language is visually based.

Decibel (dB)   Unit for the measurement of intensity or loudness of sound.

Deinstitutionalization   Movement to move the handicapped from large institutions to smaller community homes.

Diabetic retinopathy   A condition resulting from loss of blood supply to the retina due to diabetes.

Dimensional classification   A system of categorizing the major types of behavior disorders a child is likely to develop based on four dimensions.

Direct selection   Technique for providing input to communication devices; requires that user point directly to elements of the message.

Distortions   Articulation problems that include both close and remote approximations of what a sound should be.

Divergent production   A mental operation in which a person suggests many possible answers to a question or problem.

Down's syndrome   A form of moderate or severe retardation caused by a chromosomal abnormality and easily

identifiable because of distinctive physical characteristics.

Dysarthria   Lack of muscle control due to neurological damage (as in the case of cerebral palsy).

Dysphasia   Partial loss or disruption in language.

Ear canal   The passageway in the middle ear that contains protective hairs and a substance we call earwax.

Eardrum   A membrane stretched across the opening of the ear canal in the middle ear.

Echolalia   A robotlike repeating of exactly what is heard; common among autistic children.

Ecological approaches   Programs for the emotionally disturbed that include a broad-based attack on the interaction of the child with all aspects of his or her environment.

Electroencephalogram (EEG)   A measure of the electrical activity of the brain through electrodes attached to the skull.

Encoding   A technique for providing input to communication devices in which codes represent elements of the message to be entered in the device.

Engineered classroom   A classroom environment "engineered" to decrease behaviors interfering with learning and increase behaviors needed in learning; developed by Hewett in the 1960s.

Epilepsy   Condition in which the person has recurrent seizures but between the seizures is perfectly normal.

Eustachian tubes   Canals connecting the middle ear and the throat.

Exceptional children   Children whose characteristics are so different from most children's that the usual educational programs of the public schools are not appropriate for them.

Executive control processes   Strategies an individual can use to help himself or herself do better on a variety of tasks involving concept learning, memory, attention, and language.

Eyeglass hearing aid   Hearing aid contained in eyeglasses; various models are available.

Farsightedness (hyperopia)   Difficulty in seeing things at near distances; usually results when eyeball is too short, causing light rays to focus behind rather than on the retina.

Fetal alcohol syndrome (FAS)   Term used to describe the condition of impaired offspring of mothers who drink heavily during pregnancy.

Fingerspelling   A complement to sign language; words not represented by a specific gesture in Ameslan are spelled out letter by letter.

Fluency disorder Interruptions in the flow of speech so frequent or so obvious that they draw attention to the speaker or seriously hamper the understanding of what is being said.

Functional academics Academics taught in order to help the student function in everyday life; practical skills rather than readiness for more academic learning.

Genius Extremely high intelligence (IQ 180 or higher) or someone who is highly innovative or creative.

Gifted Traditionally, persons who possess high intelligence; those who score 130 or above on IQ tests.

Gifted and talented Term used today to cover especially high ability or potential in one or more of several valued areas of performance.

Glaucoma A condition in which excessive pressure exists within the eye, leading to damage to the retina and optic nerve.

Grand mal seizures Seizures in which the person loses consciousness and goes through a period of involuntary movements; may be accompanied by loss of bowel or bladder control, drooling, unusual noises, and other effects.

Handicapped Having a physical, intellectual, sensory, emotional, or language impairment, which results in a person being at a significant disadvantage when compared to those who do not have such a disability.

Hard of hearing Those with lesser hearing loss who develop basic communication skills through the auditory channel, generally with the use of a hearing aid.

Hertz (Hz) Unit for the measurement of frequency of sound; indicates highness or lowness of sound.

Homebound instruction Education at home or in a hospital for children who are confined due to illness, physical injury, or other problems.

Hoover cane (long cane) A mobility aid for the visually impaired; enables its carrier to detect obstacles and changes in the terrain.

Humanistic approaches Programs for the emotionally disturbed in which the emphasis is on an open atmosphere in which children are free to choose learning directions and to participate in setting up their own individualized study programs.

Incus Anvil-shaped bone; one of the three interconnected bones in the middle ear that carry vibrations to the inner ear.

Informal reading inventory (IRI) A teacher-designed assessment tool consisting of a series of progressively more difficult paragraphs.

Internal and external locus of control Control exercised by the self (internal) or control from outside sources (external); personality characteristic.

In-the-ear hearing aid Least conspicuous hearing aid, and model showing the most constant increase in sales as technology improves.

Iris The colored membrane in the front of the eye which expands and contracts around the pupil to regulate the amount of light passing through.

Itinerant teacher Teacher who visits children and teachers in different schools and gives special instruction to the child and advice to the teacher.

Jaeger chart A desk chart consisting of lines of type that progressively diminish in size; central visual acuity for near distances—which is necessary for reading—is determined by the number of lines read correctly at a given number of inches from the chart.

Kurzweil Reading Machine A computerized reading device for the visually impaired; converts print into electronic speech.

Language A symbolic code for communicating thoughts.

Language disorders Handicapping deviances in the communication code or system, such as an apparent absence of verbal and/or receptive language.

Laser cane An electronic mobility aid for the visually impaired; emits infrared light beams that reflect off objects in the environment and are then converted into sound.

Learning disabilities Term used today to describe exceptional children who, while of normal or near normal intelligence, display a wide variety of learning problems.

Least restrictive environment Placing the handicapped child in as normal an environment as is consistent with an appropriate education, according to PL 94-142.

Lens A curved, transparent part of the eye that focuses incoming light rays onto the retina.

Life space interview A method for dealing with emotional crises that has two broad goals: emotional first aid for immediate intervention, and clinical exploration of life events to help the child in the future.

Mainstreaming Placing handicapped and nonhandicapped children together for education.

Malleus Hammer-shaped bone; one of three interconnected bones in the middle ear that carry vibrations to the inner ear.

Manual communication System of communication that uses sign language and fingerspelling.

Meningitis An infection of the covering of the brain that can result in mental retardation in children.

Mental age On IQ tests, performing as well as the average child of a certain age; different from chronological age.

Mental retardation Significantly subaverage general intellectual functioning resulting in or associated with impairments in adaptive behavior and manifested during the developmental period.

Metacognition The ability to use study skills and to be aware of what strategies are available for problem solving.

Metacognitive deficits Difficulties in the ability to use study skills and to know what strategies are available for problem solving.

Microcephalus Condition characterized by a small head with a sloping forehead; may result from infection.

Minimal brain dysfunction Condition in which it is assumed that the brain does not work correctly; term sometimes used to describe learning disabilities.

Mixed dominance An inconsistent preference for the left or right sides of the body.

Mobility The ability of an individual to move about independently.

Moro reflex A whole-body startle response to loud sounds in the first few weeks of life.

Motivation A person's tendency to perform a task or accomplish a goal.

Multisensory programs Approaches that focus directly on academic materials and involve a multitude of senses in teaching and learning.

Muscular dystrophy A hereditary disease characterized by progressive weakness caused by wasting away of muscle fibers.

Myelomeningocele Tumorlike sac on the back into which the spinal cord or a part of it protrudes from the opening in the spine; type of spina bifida.

Nearsightedness (myopia) Difficulty seeing things at far distances; usually results when the eyeball is too long, causing light rays to focus in front of rather than on the retina.

Neurological impairments Damage to or dysfunction of the brain, spinal cord, or nerves that supply muscles and other organs.

Normal distribution A continuum of scores that vary from the average score by predictable amounts.

Normalization Making the handicapped child's life, including his or her education, as much like that of the nonhandicapped as possible.

Norm-referenced test A test administered to a large group so that any one individual's score can be compared to the average, or norm.

Nystagmus A condition in which involuntary rapid movements of the eye occur.

Omissions and substitutions Relatively minor articulation errors sometimes called babytalk or lisping that are distracting but do not necessarily make speech unintelligible.

Open captioning TV captions that can be seen on all sets; used with selected programs since the 1970s.

Ophthalmologist A physician trained to diagnose and treat eye disease.

Optacon An electronic reading device for the visually impaired; converts print into vibrating letters that can be read with the fingertips.

Optic nerve A bundle of nerves that carries electrical impulses from the retina to the brain.

Oral communication System of communication that emphasizes auditory training, speechreading, and speech.

Orienting responses Reflexive behaviors that indicate a child is hearing—eye movements toward the sound, head turning, and a overall quieting of the body when a sound occurs.

Otitis media An infection of the middle ear involving the Eustachian tube.

Oval window The structure that connects the middle and inner ear.

Paperless Braille recorder An electronic reading device for the visually impaired; encodes Braille onto tape and provides a Braille printout.

Parallel talk Verbalizing simple phrases that describe things from a child's perspective.

Paraplegia Paralysis or weakness of both legs.

Perkins Brailler A six-keyed typing machine that enables the visually impaired to write Braille.

Petit mal seizures (absence seizures) Brief seizures manifested by a clouding or lapse in consciousness in which afflicted individuals suddenly stop whatever they are doing for a short time and then resume the activity.

Phenylketonuria (PKU) An inherited condition involving the inability to convert phenylalanine, a common food substance, within the body, resulting in a buildup of the substance and abnormal brain development.

Physically disabled Children and youth who have a physical impairment (other than a visual or hearing impairment) that interferes with school attendance or learning to such an extent that special services are required.

Pitch   Frequencies (high or low) of sound tones; measured in Hertz (Hz).

Play audiometry   A technique for testing hearing within a game situation; frequently used with young children.

Postlingual deafness   Hearing loss that occurs after the person has acquired language and learned to speak.

Precocious   Developing or maturing very early.

Prelingual deafness   Deafness that is present at birth or occurs soon after, before the development of spoken language to any substantial degree.

Prevalence   The number or percent of the population that has a handicap.

Process test   A test that attempts to measure underlying processes of learning such as visual and auditory perception, visual and auditory memory, and eye-hand coordination.

Process training   An attempt to train psychological processes (such as visual and auditory perception) that are assumed to underlie the ability to achieve in academic subjects.

Projective techniques   An assessment technique for emotional adjustment in which the subject is given ambiguous stimuli in the hope that he or she will respond with material about inner conflicts or problems.

Psychoeducational methods   Educational methods for the emotionally disturbed based on psychoanalytic concepts and employing various forms of psychotherapy to uncover unconscious internal problems.

Pupil   The opening in the center of the iris through which refracted light rays pass into the eye.

Pure-tone audiometry   Test to determine an individual's exact threshold for hearing pitch and loudness of various sounds.

Related services   Services necessary in order for a handicapped child to benefit from special education—transportation, physical and occupational therapy, psychological and counseling services, recreation, diagnostic medical services.

Resource teacher   Teacher who provides instruction in specific subjects from a half-hour each week to several hours each day in a special resource room.

Retina   The back portion of the eye containing nerve fibers connected to the optic nerve.

Retinitis pigmentosa   A hereditary disease resulting in deterioration of the retina.

Retrolental fibroplasia (RLF)   A condition characterized by damage to the retina as a result of a high concentration of oxygen administered at birth.

Rochester method   A variation of the total communication approach that uses spoken and fingerspelled language simultaneously.

Rubella (German measles)   Infectious disease that can result in severe abnormalities (blindness, deafness, speech defects, mental retardation) in the fetus if contracted by the mother during the first three months of pregnancy.

Scanning   Input technique for communication devices that requires a minimal amount of physical control.

Seizure   Abnormal discharge of electricity by nerve cells in a part of the brain that sends the person into a convulsion in which muscles twitch and jerk uncontrollably.

Self-contained classes   Special classes in which an exceptional child spends most or all of the school day with a small group of other exceptional children and a specially trained teacher.

Self-monitoring   Self-evaluation of one's own behavior and keeping a record of that evaluation.

Self talk   Verbalizing aloud what one is doing or feeling for the benefit of a child's language development.

Sensorineural impairments   Hearing impairments in the inner ear that frequently result in profound hearing loss and are the most difficult to correct or improve.

Slate and stylus   A portable writing aid for the visually impaired; Braille cells are formed by pressing the stylus through openings in the slate.

Snellen chart   A wall chart consisting of rows of letters that progressively diminish in size; central visual acuity for far distances is determined by the number of rows read correctly at a given number of feet from the chart.

Sonic glasses   An electronic mobility aid for the visually impaired; emit high-frequency sound waves that reflect off objects in the environment and are then converted into audible sound.

Sonicguide   An electronic mobility aid worn on the head by visually impaired infants; emits high-frequency sound waves that reflect off objects in the environment and are then converted into audible sound.

Spasticity   Involuntary contraction and tight, jerky motion when a person tries to use the muscles; most common effect of cerebral palsy.

Special education   Specially designed instruction intended to meet the particular needs of exceptional children; may require special teaching procedures, materials, equipment, and/or facilities.

Speech   The vocal production of language.

Speech audiometry   Testing designed to measure a person's detection and understanding of speech.

Speech disorders   Problems in the intelligible production of language composed of specific characteristics or behaviors that hamper vocal production.

Speech synthesizers Communication aids that produce electronic sounds which resemble human speech.

Spina bifida Condition in which bones of the spine do not close completely at the midline of the body during fetal development.

Stereotypic behaviors Any of a variety of behaviors (eye rubbing, hand flapping, for example) that are engaged in repetitively over a short period of time.

Stimulus reduction An attempt to keep the hyperactive and distractible child away from irrelevant stimulation or events that interfere with learning.

Stapes Stirrup-shaped bone; one of three interconnected bones in the middle ear that carry vibrations to the inner ear.

Strabismus A condition in which the eye ("lazy eye") or eyes are directed inward or outward.

Structured method Program for dealing with hyperactive and inattentive children that is heavily teacher-directed and organized.

Stuttering Difficulty in producing certain sounds or sound combinations in a smooth, fluent manner.

Superphone New device that enables a deaf person to communicate with anyone who has a pushbutton phone. The device changes the keyboard message typed by the deaf person into an electronic voice; the hearing person may then type a response on the phone keys that will appear on the deaf person's teletypewriter.

Sweep test Common screening instrument that uses a portable audiometer to present tones in a certain range.

Talented Traditionally, high ability in a particular skill or art.

Task analysis Breaking down more complex activities into their component skills so that these skills can be improved.

Tay-Sachs disease An inherited condition that can appear when both mother and father are carriers; it results in brain damage and eventual death.

Teletext System for presenting information on a standard television screen which the viewer can see whenever he or she wishes; requires a decoder and keypad for retrieving information.

Token economy A behavioral method widely used with disturbed elementary school children; consists of a system of earning tangible rewards ("tokens") for performing certain behaviors.

Total communication approach (bimodalism) A combination approach that uses speech, speechreading, amplification, and the manual sign system (usually Ameslan).

TTY A teletypewriter connected to a telephone by a special adapter; allows communication between the hearing and the hearing impaired over the telephone.

Underachievement Failure to achieve at a level consistent with one's ability.

Vestibular mechanism Component of the inner ear that registers changes in balance and body movements.

Visual perception problems Problems in vision, such as reversals of letters and figure-ground difficulties, that are not caused by physical problems.

Vitreous humor A transparent jellylike substance that fills the eyeball between the retina and the lens.

Work-study programs A type of secondary school programming for mildly retarded students to prepare them to find and hold a job by combining actual work experience with regular schoolwork.

NAME INDEX

SUBJECT INDEX